The
Psychotic Core

The
Psychotic Core

Michael Eigen, Ph.D.

Jason Aronson Inc.

Northvale, New Jersey
London

To my Wife and Parents

First softcover edition 1993

Copyright © 1986 by Michael Eigen, Ph.D.

Library of Congress Cataloging-in-Publication Data

Eigen. Michael
  The psychotic core.

  Bibliography: p. 371
  Includes index.
  1. Psychoses.   2. Self.   3. Psychotherapy.
I. Title. [DNLM: 1. Ego.   2. Psychotic Disorders.
WM 200 E34p]
RC512.E36   1986   616.89   85-3956
ISBN 0-87668-895-4 / hardcover
ISBN 0-87668-153-4 / softcover

Manufactured in the United States of America. Jason Aronson Inc. offers books and cassettes. For information and catalog write to Jason Aronson Inc., 230 Livingston Street, Northvale, New Jersey 07647.

CONTENTS

PREFACE

Understanding the psychodynamics of madness is essential to the therapy of most patients, including those who are not diagnosed as mad in the literal sense. Overtly psychotic individuals make up a relatively small proportion of both the general and patient populations, but psychotic attitudes and stages can be components of a broad range of emotional states and mental disorders. The borderline and narcissistic personalities are but two examples of disorders of the self that necessitate the therapist's awareness of the mad dimension of life.

This volume draws on Freud, Jung, recent object relation and self psychologies, and, particularly, the work of Winnicott, Bion, and Elkin. My aim is to describe and critique the basic ideas on the dynamics of psychoses, and contribute a working orientation that does madness justice. The view that a basic madness marks human affairs cannot easily be discarded.

Such a study inevitably becomes an exploration of the self. An area of special concern is the fate of our cogenerative sense of self and other in hallucinations, states of mindlessness, expansion–contraction of boundaries, hate-dominated structures, and epistemological complexities. Similarly, core shapes and patterns that our sense of mental and physical self assumes in psychosis are delineated. I trace our double sense of self–other and mental-physical self through what I call the "kernel of psychosis."

Freud's delineation of narcissism was inspired by his fascination with psychotic states and with the ways that megalomania runs through human life. Religious thinkers had long associated grandiosity with madness and evil, but Freud studied the phenomenon of self-inflation with new, breathtaking specificity. Investigation of the excruciating sensitivity to slights and the fragility, vulnerability, and tenacity of narcissistic character disorders throws light on psychosis, and vice versa. To an important extent, the quality of therapeutic work with narcissism depends on one's view of psychotic processes. Later investigators, such as Kohut and Winnicott, emphasized that grandiosity and idealization are normal aspects of developmental processes. But what kind of being raises wounds to an infinite power? What sort of person incessantly overestimates and underestimates himself as part of a lifelong drama?

Winnicott summarized the depth of what is at stake in his belief that neurosis often masks psychosis. He noted that therapy may go on for years with apparently good results. The patient may feel better in many ways and have a more successful life. Yet often underneath such gains, a nagging feeling that something is wrong cannot be dispelled. The individual may succeed in securing better defenses and raising self-esteem, but still be haunted by the sense that life is a lie. For Winnicott, madness is associated with the sense of falsity in one's existence. Therapist and patient may sidestep basic agonies that undercut the sense of mastery. Neither may wish to acknowledge how subtle or thoroughgoing inner human deformity may be. In such instances, feeling alive and real may require facing psychotic anxieties.

Bion's work, like Winnicott's, focuses on the sense of catastrophe that underlies psychotic experience. Even the term *annihilation anxiety* does not do justice to the nameless dread that pervades psychosis. The very namelessness of the dreaded catastrophe stamps experience with an unknown and perhaps unknowable factor. How one relates to what continues to be beyond one's reach may mark the difference between madness and sanity.

In the consulting room, one can try to be absolutely honest, come what may. The usual injunctions against the destructive effects of full self-expression are lifted. Here madness can surface and be worked with. The mad individual may be startled to find that communication—and communication of the most subtle kinds—is possible. One can speak the lie one lives. One can glimpse the horrific depths of self-deception and the impossibility of cure. Yet somehow one can get better; richer, more tolerant, more able. One finds a way of moving toward one's center. One finds a way of moving beyond oneself.

In the chapters that follow, we will see in psychotic individuals holocaustal rages, insidious self-poisoning, ghastly vacuousness, the abuse of cleverness, a poignant inability to keep pace with one's heightened sensitivity, the giving of oneself over to spirits and things, crippling shyness, hellish torment and self-deadening, the loss and rebirth of the self in fantastically rich and impoverished scenarios, and more. My hope is that this book will help us to relax our gaze. The horrific has its own beauty, its own ecstasy, and we ought not walk around it as if it were not there, no more than we should become one with it.

This book is a bearing witness, a probing. Its value lies in whether it helps us become a little less afraid of ourselves in ways that are not destructive, enriching the quality of our experiencing capacity.

ACKNOWLEDGMENTS

The immediate catalyst for this work was the seminar on psychosis I gave over the last several years in the Institute of the National Psychological Association for Psychoanalysis. I am grateful to the NPAP and its students for this stimulus. However, my work with psychosis has a long history.

I was privileged to work with autistic and schizophrenic children at the Reece School in Manhattan and Blueberry in Brooklyn during the 1960s. I immediately felt at home with them, as if a mask had been torn away. I was given a chance to meet myself in a way that has remained decisive. I am especially grateful to Mira Rothenberg for not only tolerating but also finding therapeutic meaning in my sometimes bizarre groping to make useful contact with my charges. In the 1960s I also began my long tenure as a therapist at New Hope Guild, a private psychiatric clinic in Brooklyn and Manhattan. I am grateful for the clinical atmosphere, dedication, and openness I found there. I am not the type who does well in authoritarian settings, and Dr. Sherman Shachter, New Hope Guild's director, provided a tone and mood that allowed me steeping time, seasoning, and real apprenticeship. Dr. Richard Mulliken, who directed New Hope Guild's training program when I started, could be counted on for support and discernment.

My work in personality theory and phenomenology at the New School for Social Research, particularly with Drs. Aaron Gurwitsch, Mary Henle, and Bernard Weitzman, was salutory and enriching. I had long been interested in the relationships between gestalt psychology, phenomenology, and the depth psychologies and was lucky to find teachers who were masters in these areas.

My thanks go to Dr. Thomas Smith, Mrs. Marie Coleman Nelson, Dr. Robert Stolorow, and Mr. David Hoffman for encouragement and advice during the early phases of writing this book, and to

Dr. James S. Grotstein for his critique and support as the book neared publication. Dr. Nathan Schwartz-Salant has been a friend, support, and stimulus throughout. Dr. Henry Elkin played a special role in stimulating certain lines of thought in these pages: I have been reading his work and speaking with him since 1957.

We all stand on the shoulders of the giants Freud and Jung. Other special giants for me include Winnicott and Bion and many of the workers connected with them. I doubt that these pages could have been possible without the early writings of H. Searles and R. D. Laing, although they are scarcely mentioned. Current schools of "body work" (A. Lowen, S. Keleman) run silently through these pages. The list of other influences is too great to enumerate here. I have made my own use of what I have learned and assume the responsibility connected with putting words on paper.

I wish to thank the editors at Jason Aronson Inc. for their help in bringing this book to publication. They include Ms. Melinda Wirkus, Ms. Carol Miller, Ms. Barbara Sonnenschein, and Ms. Lori Williams. I am grateful for the enthusiastic response and guidance of Dr. Aronson and Ms. Joan Langs.

Above all I am grateful to my patients, who have endured our work together and who, with me, have undergone an education in what is possible, an education very much in progress. My wife, Betty, contributes an inner vision which complements my own. Our learning comes from, in Freud's phrase, "a common source."

I have drawn material from some of my earlier papers and wish to acknowledge and thank my publishers:

(1974). On pre-oedipal castration anxiety. *International Review of Psycho-Analysis* 1:489–498.

(1977). On working with "unwanted" patients. *International Journal of Psycho-Analysis* 5:109–121.

(1980). On the significance of the face. *Psychoanalytic Review* 67:427–441.

(1980). Instinctual fantasy and ideal images. *Contemporary Psychoanalysis* 16:119–137.

(1981). The area of faith in Winnicott, Lacan and Bion. *International Journal of Psycho-Analysis* 62:413–433.

(1981). Guntrip's analysis with Winnicott. *Contemporary Psychoanalysis* 17:103–117.

(1981). Comments on snake symbolism and mind-body relations. *American Journal of Psychoanalysis* 41:73–79.

(1981). Breaking the frame: stopping the world. *Modern Psychoanalysis* 6:89–100.

(1982). Creativity, instinctual fantasy and ideal images. *Psychoanalytic Review* 69:317–339.

(1983). Dual union or undifferentiation? A critique of Marion Milner's sense of psychic creativeness. *International Review of Psycho-Analysis.* 10:415–428.

(1984). On demonized aspects of the self. In *Evil: Self and Culture*, eds. M. C. Nelson and M. Eigen. New York: Human Sciences Press.

(1985). Toward Bion's starting point. *International Journal of Psycho-Analysis* 68:321–330.

(1986). Aspects of mindlessness-selflessness: a common madness. *The Psychotherapy Patient* 2:75–81. Also in *Psychotherapy and the Selfless Patient*, ed. J. Travers, pp. 75–81. New York: Haworth Press.

The author gratefully acknowledges permission to reprint portions of the following:

American Psychiatric Association (1980). *Diagnostic and Statistical Manual of Mental Disorders*. Washington, D.C.: American Psychiatric Association, p. 186.

M. Balint (1968). *The Basic Fault*. London: Tavistock, p. 24.

W. R. Bion (1962). *Learning from Experience*. London: Heinemann; New York: Jason Aronson, 1977, p. 9.

W. R. Bion (1963). *Elements in Psycho-Analysis*. London: Heinemann; New York: Jason Aronson, 1977, p. 23.

W. R. Bion (1965). *Transformations*. London: Heinemann; New York: Jason Aronson, 1977, p. 115.

W. R. Bion (1970). *Attention and Interpretation*. London: Tavistock; New York: Jason Aronson, 1977, pp. 10, 35-36.

Blake: Complete Writings. Ed. G. Keynes. London: Oxford University Press, 1976. William Blake's *Milton*, 28.62-29.3.

E. G. Boring (1957). *A History of Experimental Psychology*, 2nd edition. Englewood Cliffs, N.J.: Prentice-Hall. © 1950, renewed 1978, pp. 278-279. Reprinted by permission of Prentice-Hall, Inc., Englewood Cliffs, N.J.

S. Freud (1900). *The Interpretation of Dreams*. Translated by James Strachey. Third printing, 1958. Published in the United States by Basic Books, Inc., by arrangement with George Allen & Unwin Ltd. and The Hogarth Press Ltd.

S. Freud (1914). On narcissism. In *The Collected Papers*, Vol. 4, by Sigmund Freud, authorized translation under the supervision of Joan Riviere. Published by Basic Books, Inc., by arrangement with The Hogarth Press Ltd. and The Institute of Psycho-Analysis, London. Reprinted by permission. Thanks to Sigmund Freud Copyrights Ltd., The Institute of Psycho-Analysis and The Hogarth Press for permission to quote from *The Standard Edition of the Complete Psychological Works of Sigmund Freud* translated and edited by James Strachey.

S. Freud (1937). Constructions in analysis. In *The Collected Papers*, Vol. 5, by Sigmund Freud, edited and translated by James Strachey. Published by Basic Books, Inc., by arrangement with The Hogarth Press Ltd. and The Institute of Psycho-Analysis, London. Reprinted by permission. Thanks to Sigmund Freud Copyrights Ltd., The Institute of Psycho-Analysis and The Hogarth Press for permission to quote from *The Standard Edition of the Complete Psychological Works of Sigmund Freud* translated and edited by James Strachey.

S. Freud (1940). *An Outline of Psycho-Analysis*. Translated and edited by James Strachey. Used by permission of W. W. Norton & Company, Inc. Copyright 1949 by W. W. Norton & Company, Inc. Copyright © 1969 by The Institute of Psycho-Analysis and Alix Strachey. Thanks to Sigmund Freud Copyrights Ltd., The Institute of Psycho-Analysis and The Hogarth Press for permission to quote from *The Standard Edition of the Complete Psychological Works of Sigmund Freud* translated and edited by James Strachey.

J. Laplanche and J.-B. Pontalis (1973). *The Language of Psycho-Analysis*. Trans. D. Nicholson Smith. New York: Norton, pp. 312-314. An English translation of a passage by C. Laurin (1964) from Phallus et sexualité feminine, *La Psychoanalyse* 7:15.

R. C. Lewontin (1983). The corpse in the elevator. *The New York Review of Books* 29:37.

J. W. Perry (1974). *The Far Side of Madness*. Englewood Cliffs, N.J.: Prentice-Hall, p. 94.

J. W. Perry (1976). *The Roots of Renewal in Myth and Symbols*. San Francisco: Jossey-Bass, p. 195.

M.-L. von Franz (1975). *Creation Myths*. New York: Spring Publications.

D. W. Winnicott (1967). The location of cultural experience. *International Journal of Psycho-Analysis* 48:368-372.

D. W. Winnicott (1969). The use of an object and relating through identifications. *International Journal of Psycho-Analysis* 50:711-716.

D. W. Winnicott (1971). Playing, creative activity and the search for the self. *Playing and Reality*. New York: Basic Books, pp. 54-55.

CHAPTER ONE

The Core of Psychosis

IF IT IS DEBATABLE whether or not there is a psychotic kernel in every person, it can at least be said that psychosis is one of the phenomena of human life that take us to the edge of what it is possible to experience. It both challenges and freezes the presuppositions that make personality possible. In psychosis, what we ordinarily take as material may be treated as if it were immaterial, and vice versa. Space and time become bizarre and poisonous playthings, or vacuous. An ecstatic spasm of color may shoot across a dangerous wasteland and for the moment save and uplift the subject's sense of self and other. In another moment, self and other fragment, collapse, spill into, menace, and deplete each other, and possibly vanish altogether.

It is in the psychoses that one encounters the most extreme rigidities and fluctuations of symptoms. In a short period of sometimes moments, an individual may seem to run through the whole gamut of clinical possibilities. It is as if his psyche has become a speeded-up movie, racing madly through a sequence of mental deformities, unable to choose and settle on the one that best suits it. Perhaps if he tries them all, he will finally find some combination he can live in, or, more likely, be able to breathe forever the freedom of limitlessness.

Yet the psychotic individual also experiences himself as desperately trapped. His fixity and fluidity mimic the continuity and change that characterize personal identity. The dualities that make up human experience are separated and exaggerated in psychosis. At times, it seems that the psychotic person dissolves his mind in order to rebuild himself from its elements. Or he may seem to need to search grimly through its debris, leaving nothing out, as if he were looking for something essential, but still unknown. He cannot rest until he sees everything. Yet everything dissolves and starts over without any sense of experience building on itself. The individual stares at himself through a kaleidoscope, but does not evolve. The flux itself becomes fixed and imprisons him.

It is often a relief when the individual drifts into a stable state, even if it turns out to be one from which he may never return. Things at last slow down, or one becomes used to the turns of the revolving door. To an observer, and sometimes to the individual himself, this may seem like the burn-out of a great volcano. But even when a person is chronically somnambulistic, deep rumblings are heard periodically, and one may momentarily glimpse fire and water. Thus we may also ask, if psychosis is a way of organizing experience, what happens when this last way breaks down?

In psychosis, as in creativity, ordering and disordering processes are interwoven. Rigidity and chaos alternate, and boundaries are distorted or dissolve. No wonder that it took so long to discover that a basic order informs psychosis.

A Basic Order

Whatever the drawback of classifications, they have made it possible to begin to think systematically about clusters of symptoms and behavior that seem to go together. Investigators may disagree as to which schematic grouping works best, but what is important is that the serious student of the subject can recognize the patterns another talks about. A common ground often makes possible meaningful disagreements.

At the end of the last century, an orderly classification of the various types of psychoses was made. Kraepelin[1] grouped several

1. Kraepelin's *Psychiatrie: Ein Lehrbuch für Studierende und Aerzte* is usually cited as the reference work for Kraepelin's initial contribution. (See Stone, *Borderline Syn-*

mental conditions under the heading of dementia praecox, but in 1911, Bleuler[2] reworked Kraepelin's subdivisions in terms of primary symptoms and splitting processes. In light of the severe splitting processes, he changed the name of this grouping to schizophrenia (literally, split or cut mind), a name in the mental sphere as dreaded as cancer in the physical. Classifications have perhaps become more sophisticated, but these early attempts to organize mental illness into discernible and useable networks can easily be read today.[3]

Many of the dangers of such classifications are now obvious. They establish stereotypical sets that persevere for decades (or longer) and may delay the investigation of the subtle processes that underlie genuine similarities and differences. Certain schizophrenic defenses mask a depressive illness and vice versa. A neurosis may mask a hidden psychosis. An initially mild symptom pattern may give way to an intractable, malignant one, whereas a seemingly florid madness will respond to careful therapeutic work. If one aims to cure a psychosis, one must be ready to run the gamut of all possible psychoses as therapy unfolds. In the consultation room, as in life, no *a priori* picture is invulnerable.

And yet the very fact that one can and will be wrong indicates that there is something to be wrong about. We make educated guesses from moment to moment. Investigators from different and even the same schools disagree. One disagrees with oneself. Yet there is a sense of basic order if one can only find it, and we each fight for the truths we believe we glimpse. Our maps do not simply capture or impose order; they also express aspects of our encounter with an order we help mediate.

---

dromes, pp. 211, 516; McGhie, *Pathology of Attention*. See also Kraepelin, *Clinical Psychiatry*, pp. xvii, 1–29; idem, *Dementia Praecox and Paraphrenia*, pp. 1–3.)
2. Bleuler, *Dementia Praecox*, pp. 3–12. Schizophrenia literally means split or cut mind. Freud thought it too general a term and tried to discover dynamics that characterized specific types of splits.
3. Stone, *Borderline Syndromes*, Part 3. Stone evaluates recent methods of diagnosing the psychoses and provides a sense of the basic structure of evaluation techniques.

For the most part, Freud used the classifications he found ready made and appreciated the heroic work of others who made his own work possible. A fundamental obsession of his throughout his life's work, especially at its outset, was how individuals choose the internal defenses that account for the external patterns of symptoms we observe. His emphasis was on the inside, the invisible depth dimension, but taxonomy was a stimulus and an anchor. Thus, he wrote about the psychic life of individuals one might "classify" as hysteric, depressive, paranoid, or schizophrenic. He did not try to change the hard-won nosologies that facilitated communication and exploration, but rather opened these "boxes" to see what made them what they were. To be sure, Freud's particular concept of obsessional neurosis changed the meaning of this syndrome, so much so that we would not be wrong to say that psychoanalysis invented (discovered) the way we see obsessional behavior today. He also tried to redesignate Kraepelin's dementia praecox and Bleuler's schizophrenia as *paraphrenia*,[4] but his attempts failed. Generally, Freud worked with conventional psychopathological categories.

The ordering of certain psychopathologies stimulated much of Freud's thinking. He was particularly fascinated by the amount of fluidity between categories that could coexist with a basic descriptive stability. He attempted to do justice to the continuum he felt existed between the normal and the pathological and among the various types of psychopathologies. Such concepts as fixation and regression express his view of a fluid or mobile energy, which can take on different forms. It was a momentous breakthrough to link psychical energy with ontogenetic development. According to his concept, this energy assumes typical forms, according to the current phase of development. At the same time, congenital predisposition and environmental factors (e.g., extent and quality of trauma) influence which aspects of developmental phases become dominant or fail to appear.

According to Freud, all aspects of development contribute to how the individual organizes meaning and is affected by meaning. In the

4. Freud, "Psycho-analytic Notes on an Autobiographical Account of a Case of Paranoia," p. 75.

end, Freud is less concerned with the exactitude of developmental ordering than with how a variety of developmental factors are typically organized. Given a life history, there is no *a priori* schema to understand adequately the ways in which an individual makes use of the developmental spectrum. This explains Freud's flexibility in his use of the developmental sequences he helped discover (the oral, anal, phallic, and genital phases and their subphases). Freud used his developmental schema as a kind of musical scale, a resource that changes in value according to context. It is always an open question as to just what meaning or use individuals may make of their developmental possibilities.

The Centrality of Psychosis in Psychodynamics

Later in this chapter, I will outline my approach to the vast chasms and subtleties of psychotic experience. And throughout this book we will study, in detail, the key ordering–disordering processes of the psychotic self. Before reaching that point, however, several preliminary issues must be discussed; the first is the centrality of psychosis in the depth psychologies and, by implication, in the makeup of humankind.

Psychosis has been the Cinderella of psychoanalysis. Freud spent most of his efforts formulating the structures and psychodynamics that distinguish the psychoneuroses, and insisted that psychoanalysis was not equipped to deal with the psychoses. Yet some of the most important psychoanalytic advances (e.g., the work with narcissism) were made in attempts to understand psychosis. Freud's theory would not be what it is, if it were not implicitly based on a phenomenology of psychosis. An awareness of psychotic experience played a significant role in the foundation and growth of psychoanalytic theory. Let us briefly review some aspects of Freud's thought in order to convey just how central a subject psychosis is to his understanding of psychic life. The importance of this centrality cannot be overemphasized.

Freud's depiction of primary process owes much to his fascination with psychotic thinking. For example, the fusion and dispersal of meaning characteristic of the associative spread, yet fixed preoccupation, of psychosis influenced the development of Freud's concepts of condensation and displacement. Similarly, his depiction of the unconscious as timeless, without contradiction and possessing an internal, not external, reality, is steeped in the phenomenology of psychosis. His later descriptions of the id draw on affectively cataclysmic aspects of psychosis (volcanic upheaval, the seething caldron). For Freud, libido itself had not only a plasticity and fluidity, but also a relentless drivenness that, if unchecked and rerouted, would amount to madness. Thus, Freud was able to describe an aspect of the infantile mind as out of contact with the outside world and given to hallucinatory, wish-fulfilling operations. A radical disregard for usual boundaries, which is so characteristic of psychosis, runs through Freud's descriptions of unconscious processes. It is as if Freud is saying that the human psyche is rooted in the same type of world the psychotic lives in, that, in some sense, psychotic experience has a certain primacy. From this vantage point, neurotic defenses arise, in part, to master or restructure a basic psychotic propensity. A basic madness thus informs human life, and sanity (including neurotic sanity) is a positive and, possibly, a heroic achievement.

Freud emphasized his position when he informally spoke of psychosis as an irruption of the unconscious and a weakening of the ego's ties with reality. For Freud, psychosis represents a more extreme, fundamental dominance of the pleasure principle, primary process thinking, and the id than neurosis represents. If repression (the cornerstone of psychoanalysis) has difficulty maintaining itself in neurosis, it is still more defective and more fragile in psychosis, to the point of seeming to disappear entirely.

To be sure, Freud, formally, in his explicit theoretical statements, saw neurosis as opposing perversion.[5] In his official doctrine, neurotic defenses structured the psyche's polymorphous perverse dispo-

5. Freud, "Three Essays on the Theory of Sexuality," pp. 50, 165, 170–172, 231.

sition, and, especially, contrasexual tendencies. But his image of the deepest psychic events uses psychotic phenomena as its model. For example, he depicted dream life as a psychosis that occurs for every individual each night. To take only one of his references, virtually at random:

> A dream, then, is a psychosis, with all the absurdities, delusions and illusions of a psychosis. A psychosis of short duration, no doubt, harmless, even entrusted with a useful function, introduced with the subject's consent and terminated by an act of his will. None the less it is a psychosis, and we learn from it that even so deep-going an alteration of mental life as this can be undone and can give place to normal function. Is it too bold, then, to hope that it must also be possible to submit the dreaded spontaneous illnesses of mental life to our influence and bring about their cure?[6]

This affirmation of hope came near the end of Freud's life. The dream remained, to the end, "the royal road to the unconscious," and his association of dreams with psychosis runs through his entire *oeuvre*. This strong association again suggests that the phenomenology of psychosis played a fundamental role in Freud's depiction of the unconscious.

As Freud developed his views on narcissism, he wrote that psychosis might be the key to the understanding of the human ego. "Just as the transference neuroses have enabled us to trace the libidinal instinctual neuroses, so dementia praecox and paranoia will give us insight into the psychology of the ego."[7] He developed his theory of narcissism, in part, as a response to the phenomena of psychosis as he understood them.

> A pressing motive for occupying ourselves with the conception of a primary and normal narcissism arose when the attempt was made to subsume what we know of dementia praecox (Kraepelin) or schizophrenia (Bleuler) under the hypothesis of libido theory. . . . Let me insist that I am not proposing here to explain or penetrate further into the problem

6. Freud, "An Outline of Psycho-Analysis," p. 172.
7. Freud, "On Narcissism," p. 82.

of schizophrenia, but that I am merely putting together what has already been said elsewhere, in order to justify the introduction of the concept of narcissism.[8]

He postulated an "original libidinal cathexis of the ego" (a "primary narcissism," which unified earlier and diffuse autoerotic impulses) as a frame of reference in which to situate what he called the two principal characteristics of psychosis: megalomania and "the diversion of interest from the external world, from people and things." Psychosis makes markedly explicit a megalomanic dimension that runs through human life.

> Thus we form the idea of there being an original libidinal cathexis of the ego, from which some is later given off to objects, but which fundamentally persists and is related to object-cathexes much as the body of an amoeba is related to the pseudopodia which it puts out.[9]

Freud emphasized self-inflation along with idolatry. He was struck by the ego's ability to lose itself in objects. In various forms of identification, the ego could become like its object—placing itself in an object or taking the object into itself. He traced ways in which the distance between ego and object seemed to close up in ordinary life and how it formed the basis for mystical or "oceanic" experience.[10]

8. Ibid., pp. 74–75. Freud also justified his concept of narcissism by calling attention to its existence in perversion, homosexuality, children, primitives, romantic love, and group psychology. Our concern is the centrality of his emphasis on psychosis.
9. Ibid., p. 75. I am not arguing for the correctness of Freud's views on narcissism, but rather am emphasizing the centrality of the phenomenology of psychosis to Freud's psychoanalytic theory—in particular, in his polar concepts of id and ego, as well as in his formulation of primary process thinking and of the unconscious generally (see pp. 5–11, this volume).
10. Freud understood "oceanic feeling," a term he borrowed from Romain Rolland, as a remnant of the nursing situation and the infant's failure to distinguish its ego from the breast (Freud, "Civilization and its Discontents," pp. 64–67). In contrast with Rolland, Freud claimed he did not know these experiences firsthand. I believe Freud was correct in viewing Rolland's "oceanic feeling" in terms of mother-baby fusion. But to describe all mystical experience as being "oceanic" is

In his later studies of the psychology of the ego, he often used psychosis as a model or metaphor. For example, he called falling in love a kind of psychosis because it was accompanied by a loss of boundaries and the idealization, or overvaluation, of the object. He pointed out how, even in love, perhaps especially in love, idolatry is always self-idolatry (megalomania) at bottom. Or, again, he saw psychotic dynamics at work in the psychology of power, for example, the loss of self that occurs in following a leader and the leader's grandiose assertion of omnipotence. He wrote about hypnosis, love, and the army and church as common vehicles for a kind of dependency that obliterates the boundaries of self. Freud likened this loss of self to madness and saw it at work in neurosis and culture.[11] This link between megalomania and dependency is one we will return to.

Freud, too, emphasized the ego's loyalty to everyday, perceptual reality. Psychotic productions contain "a fragment of historical truth."

> . . . there is not only *method* in madness, as the poet has already perceived, but also a fragment of *historical truth*; and it is plausible to suppose that the compulsive belief attaching to delusions derives its strength precisely from infantile sources of this kind. . . . The vain effort would be abandoned of convincing the patient of the error of his delusion and of its contradiction of reality; and, on the contrary, the recognition of its kernel of truth would afford common ground upon which the therapeutic work could develop. That work would consist in liberating the fragment of historical truth from its distortions and its attachments to the actual present day and in leading it back to the point in the past to which it belongs. The transposing of material from a forgotten past on to the present or on to an expectation of the future is indeed a habitual occurrence in neurotics no less than in psychotics. Often enough, when a neurotic is led by an anxiety-state to expect the occurrence of some terrible event, he is in fact merely under the influence of a repressed memory (which is seeking to enter consciousness but cannot become

---

misleading and has led several generations of psychoanalysts to foreclose other possibilities (Eigen, "The Area of Faith in Winnicott, Lacan, and Bion," pp. 413–433; idem, "Dual Union or Undifferentiation," pp. 415–428).

11. Freud, "Group Psychology and the Analysis of the Ego," pp. 69–143.

conscious) that something which was at that time terrifying did really happen. I believe that we should gain a great deal of valuable knowledge from work of this kind upon psychotics even if it led to no therapeutic success.[12]

The intensity of belief attached to delusions indicates that the individual is trying to hold fast to a terrifyingly important dimension of his own story. The ego is rooted in common sense, as well as in madness, and tenaciously holds onto the former. Even in the pits of psychotic turmoil, it maintains an area of lucidity. Freud writes,

> The problem of psychoses would be simple and perspicuous if the ego's detachment from reality could be carried through completely. But that seems to happen only rarely or perhaps never. Even in a state so far removed from the reality of the external world as one of hallucinatory confusion, one learns from patients after their recovery that at the time in some corner of their mind (as they put it) there was a normal person hidden, who, like a detached spectator, watched the hubbub of illusion go past him.[13]

Thus, for Freud, a kind of madness of the ego marks its foundation and evolution. At the same time, this madness is balanced by, and stimulates and competes with, the ego's tie to "the real world." Madness is both innate and a form of adaptation. It is a desperate response to emotional pain and the stress of life. But it is also part of the way we are innately structured, and it has a developmental timetable of its own. In sum, the ego is sane and mad. In his letters to Jung, Freud called the ego a clown,[14] but it is a dangerous and precious clown, attached to truth, compromise, and delusion. Its polarities may support one another or tear a soul to pieces; they usually do both.

12. Freud, "Constructions in Analysis," pp. 267–268.
13. Freud, "An Outline of Psycho-Analysis," pp. 201–202.
14. In the following passage Freud writes about Adler: "I would never have expected a psychoanalyst to be so taken in by the ego. In reality the ego is like a clown in the circus, who is always putting in his oar to make the audience think that whatever happens is his doing" (Freud and Jung, *Letters*, p. 400).

In simple human terms, Freud made sanity–madness the basic polarity of human discourse. As we will see in Chapter 2, this represents a major reinterpretation of the traditional appearance–reality duality, as well as a reworking of the meaning of sin. Freud was well aware, too, how mad sanity can be, and vice versa, thus carrying forward a radical questioning of the human condition. His formulations explode on impact. They are contradictory and cannot easily be worked into a coherent whole. Alive with fertile frictions, they attempt to meet the human psyche at its point of origin. The further Freud goes, the more problematic the nature of madness and sanity becomes.

Psychotic Dynamics

Jung once said that a great psychologist is someone who must spend his life in a mental hospital, the only question being whether as a doctor or a patient. Like Freud, he stressed the importance of the doctor as patient. In his view, the depth psychologist often must come precariously close to madness. Many analysts might think this an over- or mis-statement. Yet Jung calls attention to an intimacy between psychoanalysis and madness that must be addressed.

The central concepts of psychoanalysis are rooted in the objective problems of science, but they also grow out of a psychosis-tinged matrix in the individual. Freud credited Fechner with stimulating his reformulation of the law of psychic energy in psychic terms, a gambit that made the formal structure of psychoanalysis possible. Following examples from Herbart and Fechner, Freud used physics (the laws of conservation) as a basis for a theory of mental energy. Fechner believed mental and physical energy varied in relation to each other and that his method of psychophysics was an exact science which could chart the dependency between body and mind in terms of functional relations.[15] Whereas Fechner saw consciousness in all

15. See Boring's *History of Experimental Psychology*, pp. 284–295.

things, Freud was more interested in developing a concept of the unconscious that might make sense out of the discontinuities of consciousness. However, Freud appreciated the depth of Fechner's intent and credited him with an intuition into the "other space" Freud charted.

Fechner's major work, including his discovery or invention of psychophysics, grew out of a psychotic period:

Fechner . . . had overworked. He had developed, as James diagnosed the disease, a "habit neurosis." He had also injured his eyes in the research on afterimages by gazing at the sun through colored glasses. He was prostrated, and resigned, in 1839, his chair of physics. He suffered great pain and for three years cut himself off from everyone. This event seemed like a sudden and incomprehensible ending to a career so vividly begun. Then Fechner unexpectedly began to recover, and, since his malady was so little understood, his recovery appeared miraculous. This period is spoken of as the "crisis" in Fechner's life, and had a profound effect upon his thought and afterlife.

The primary result was a deepening of Fechner's religious consciousness and his interest in the problem of the soul. Thus Fechner, quite naturally for a man with such an intense intellectual life, turned to philosophy. . . . His forties were, of course, a sterile decade as regards writing. . . . The first book that showed Fechner's new tendency was *Nanna oder das Seelenleben der Pflanzen*, published in 1848 (Nanna was the Norse goddess of flowers). For Fechner, in the materialistic age of science, to argue for the mental life of plants, even before Darwin had made the mental life of animals a crucial issue, was for him to court scientific unpopularity, but Fechner now felt himself possessed of a philosophic mission and he could not keep silence. He was troubled by materialism. . . . His philosophical solution of the spiritual problem lay in his affirmation of the identity of mind and matter and in his assurance that the entire universe can be regarded as readily from the point of view of consciousness, a view that he later called the *Tagesansicht*, as it can be viewed as inert matter, the *Nachtansicht*. . . .

Three years later (1851) a more important work of Fechner's appeared: *Zend-Avesta, oder über die Dinge des Himmels und des Jenseits.* Oddly enough this book contains Fechner's program of psychophysics and thus bears an ancestral relation to experimental psychology. . . . Fechner's general interest was that the book should be a new gospel. The title means practically "a revelation of the word." Consciousness,

Fechner argued, is in all and through all. The earth, "our mother," is a being like ourselves but very much more perfect than ourselves. The soul does not die, nor can it be exorcised by the priests of materialism when all being is conscious. Fechner's argument was not rational, but was intensely persuasive and developed his theme by way of plausible analogies, which, but for their seriousness, resemble somewhat the method of Dr. Mises' satire, *Vergleichende Anatomie der Engel* (1825), where Fechner argued that the angels, as the most perfect beings, must be spherical, since the sphere is the most perfect form. Now, however, Fechner was in dead earnest.[16]

Fechner's illness apparently catapulted him to a religious reconstitution of his life that culminated in a vision of cosmic unity.

Freud's first major breakthroughs came while he was corresponding with the psychotic Fliess.[17] Of all his friends and colleagues, he chose Fliess to share his intellectual adventure. He felt Fliess was in touch with and could understand the psychic depths he was drawn to, the dimension Fechner called "the other space." Freud wrote to Fliess: "The only sensible thing on the subject [of dreams] was said by old Fechner in his sublime simplicity: that the psychical territory on which the dream process is played out is a different one. It has been left to me to draw the first crude map of it."[18] In *The Interpretation of Dreams* he added:

No one has emphasized more sharply the essential difference between dreaming and waking life or drawn more far-reaching conclusions from it than G. T. Fechner in a passage in his *Elemente der Psychophysik* (1889,

16. Ibid., pp. 278-79. "Dr. Mises" was a pseudonym Fechner used for some of his literary and mystical writings.
17. Dr. Robert Fliess, W. Fliess's son and a gifted psychoanalyst, believed psychotic actions on the part of parents to be more common than realized. He indicated that he himself was a victim of his father's psychosis and that psychoanalysts themselves tend to resist perceptions of a mad reality: "the average analyst . . . remains ignorant of his own psychotic parent, should he have one, and hence is not equipped for patients who confront him with fragments that are replicas of his own history" (Fliess, *Erogeneity and Libido*, pp. xvii–xviii; idem, *Symbol, Dream and Psychosis*, Chapter 3).
18. Freud, *Origins of Psycho-Analysis*, pp. 244-245.

2, 520–1). In his opinion, "neither the mere lowering of conscious mental life below the main threshold," nor the withdrawal of attention from the influences of the external world, are enough to explain the characteristics of dream-life as contrasted with waking life. He suspects, rather, that *the scene of action of dreams is different from that of waking ideational life.* "If the action of psychophysical activity were the same in sleeping and waking, dreams could, in my view, only be a prolongation at a lower degree of intensity of waking ideational life and, moreover, would necessarily be of the same material and form. But the facts are quite otherwise."[19]

Fechner knew from his own experience the link between the place of dreams and the vision that cures or destroys. The meaning of Freud's fertile transference to Fliess, a man with an underlying psychosis, has been studied but not fully worked out.

Roustang[20] pointed out, in some detail, that there is much in the impetus and development of the psychoanalytic movement that reflects psychotic dynamics. The recent interest in the influence of Sabina Spielrein (a one-time psychotic patient of Jung who became a psychoanalyst) on both Jung and Freud shows the growth of awareness of just how important contact with the psychotic depths was in understanding neuroses.[21]

In a similar vein, it is difficult to overestimate the importance of Jung's impact on Freud. In a sense, Jung's influence is one of the best-kept secrets of psychoanalysis. Jung's psychiatric career began with and developed through working with psychosis, particularly its religious or mythic aspect. Freud saw in Jung a medium for applying his theory to psychosis and it was precisely around the issue of how psychotic mentation was to be understood that their differences (personal and theoretical) arose. In spite of the fact that Freud insisted his theory was meant for neurosis, he jumped at the chance to extend it to psychosis. This preoccupation never left him and determined the direction of his work.

19. Freud, "Interpretation of Dreams," p. 48.
20. Roustang, *Dire Mastery*, pp. 132–156; idem, *Psychoanalysis Never Lets Go*, pp. 33–35, 93–116, 142–149.
21. Carotenuto, *Secret Symmetry*, pp. 131–214.

His contact and break with Jung stimulated his first important writings on religion and psychosis,[22] and he continued his debate with Jung to the end. Freud was forced to develop his ego theory (dissociation, narcissism) to match Jung's theory of self.[23] Two of his best case histories (Schreber; the Wolf Man) were written with Jung in mind. And Freud proceeded to write more books on religion (in Freud's view, a universal psychosis) than on any other single cultural phenomenon.[24]

Whatever the popular belief, the basic structure of Freud's and Jung's thought is simliar. They both adopted a quasi-Kantian epistemology in which the unconscious is as unknowable a psychic reality as the material universe. And for both, in Freud's phrase, the unconscious is the "true psychical reality." What is most basic in our natures remains unknowable. We live by hints and clues and develop convictions (although, at times, Jung felt he "knew," and perhaps Freud did also). As we will later see, our relationship to the unknown or unknowable plays a crucial role in the psychology of psychosis.

Both Freud and Jung take psychotic productions to be inherently meaningful. Both relate hallucinatory imagery to innate fantasy systems that become caught in abortive developmental processes. Both find in hallucinatory activity messages about the state of the self, the nature of the injury to the self, and requirements for its evolution. Their vision is at once historical and ahistorical (the unconscious is "timeless"). Both take megalomania to be a pivotal point in their study of psychosis, and for an understanding of human life. Both admire and quote Heraclitus on the tension of opposites. Both sys-

---

22. For example, Freud's Schreber case and "Totem and Taboo" partly gained impetus from the growing break between Freud and Jung. It was as if Freud were trying to convince Jung (and himself?) that Eros, infantile sexuality, and Oedipus were enough to account for Jung's principal territory, psychosis and religion.

23. Freud says as much in the opening of his essay, "On Narcissism," pp. 74, 79–81.

24. One could justifiably argue that "Totem and Taboo," "Future of an Illusion," and "Moses and Monotheism" were, to an extent, part of Freud's long inner debate with Jung.

tems move via polarities. Each works and does not work in clinical practice. The phenomenon of psychosis brings each viewpoint to its breaking point and requires us to expand the way we speak about self or ego.

To be sure, there are basic differences between Freud and Jung. Freud repeatedly used religion as one of his greatest clues and case histories. In deciphering religion, he was decoding psychosis and the infantile psyche (for Freud, the two were related). God was not dead for Freud, but rather very much alive as a patient. Jung also believed that in studying mythology he was elucidating the depths of psychosis in human life. He showed just how universal and pervasive psychotic processes really are. However, for Jung, religion was also more than a literary metaphor or an area of research. It had to do with the core of his identity, with who he was and how he lived, and with his relationship to the cosmos. Jung's relationship to the collective unconscious was a sacred trust. His view of the roots and meaning of psychotic imagery led him away from Freud's view of hallucination as a drive-dominated perception, and he saw the religious aspect of psychotic symbolism as having roots deeper than the libido, and worth of its own. His attempt to come to grips with the religious dimension of psychosis led to his insistence that the energy involved in psychopathology was not primarily erotic; this helped him develop his later work (e.g., his use of alchemic imagery to organize the religious journey).

It is hard to imagine work with psychosis today without Jung's contribution. Although many aspects of both his and Freud's depiction of psychosis will be explored in more depth in Chapter 2, some introductory remarks are in order here. It was years before the mother–infant relationship became a primary focus in psychoanalysis, and Jung anticipated this development, although his emphasis was on the archetypal rather than the personal mother (we will come back to this in Chapter 2).

The notion of doctor as person owes much to Jung. The nature of psychotic upheaval forced him to realize that the therapy situation was one in which the therapist, as well as the patient, may be called on to undergo profound development. He used the idea of chemical interaction to describe how thoroughly patient and therapist interact with each other. Was his implicit model mother–baby interplay? To be sure, his attitude as scientist helped him through many treacherous situations, but, as he put it, he was "in the soup," too. There were times when he had to rely on the patient's curative interventions as well as his own.

Jung's explicit focus on aspects of the self, particularly in the form of personifications, contributed to existential psychology, psychodrama, and gestalt therapy. It anticipated the rise of self-psychology in psychoanalysis. Jungian openness to the use of expressive modalities in active imagination also helped pave the way for the development of art, dance, and music therapies, which are fast becoming an important part of a hospital stay.

Although both Freud and Jung exploited psychosis in their theoretical formulations, they were cautious about the outcome of actual therapy. Jung had great success with certain schizophrenic individuals, particularly in the first part of his career, but these were individuals who could enter into a meaningful relationship with him. He seemed to speak to these persons' souls, to the very heart of their existence. Some of them remained attached to him for life and made their own contributions to Jungian psychology. He expressed sober reserve about those who remained sealed off and inaccessible. Toward the end of his life, he remarked that he thought he could cure the more difficult cases, but no longer had the strength for it; he seemed to think it could be done.[25]

Freud's attitude toward psychosis also was ambivalent. He did not like to treat psychotic individuals and felt that the latter did not possess enough interest in "objects" (others)[26] to form the transfer-

25. Jung, *Memories, Dreams and Reflections*, pp. 124–145.
26. "Object" is a psychoanalytic term inherited from philosophy. Often one feels that the mechanistic terms Freud took from physics and epistemology do not fit the psychic reality he discovered. Ricoeur states that Freud's terms point to a genuine aspect of psychic reality and give something machinelike in human nature its due. Ricoeur argues that Freud's emphasis on psychic mechanisms and the play of meaning rings true to the complexities of the human predicament, where one is

ence required for psychoanalysis. Yet he did not say psychosis was untreatable. In his ironic fashion, he even suspected that the therapy of psychosis might make substantial progress in America, but not with "pure" psychoanalysis.[27] Perhaps he thought Americans were mad and would prove to be freer during therapeutic invention. Freud kept open the possibility of the reversibility of the most severe psychotic conditions, as mentioned earlier. Both Freud and Jung remained psychological visionaries, but with a strong grasp of clinical realities. Their love affair with the human psyche and the multiple dimensions it lives through uplifted their work and lives and still inspires us.

Both Freud and Jung stressed not only the difficulty, but also the demandingness of work with psychosis. All dedicated workers with psychosis have agreed. A psychotic individual often oscillates between being withdrawn and cut-off and desperately clinging and demanding. The need for others can be all-consuming or apparently nonexistent. Many see in the psychotic an infant demanding a perfect mother, or perfect fusion and control. Some see a spoiled mystic riveted to a warped or aborted relationship with God. When a subject seems "objectless," close scrutiny often shows a tenacious hold on psychotic objects (hallucinatory or delusional versions of objects). If the worker finds his way within the patient's force field, he becomes the target of obscurely fierce pressures. Body ego dispersal and mental control often go together, so that the patient is falling apart, yet hard as steel.

Therapy may bring out much in the analyst that he would rather stay quiescent. Therapy with psychosis must be a messy and harrowing business, one that plays havoc with the assumptive grounds of communication. No wonder Freud experienced psychosis as an

---

caught between force and freedom. Freud's work encompasses the tension between the personal and the impersonal. Nevertheless, Ricoeur feels that Freud's method is one of contraction, a therapy of suspicion that emphasizes self-deception. He suggests that religious faith involves the more positive impulse toward the fullness of grace (Ricoeur, *Freud and Philosophy*, pp. 341–551).

27. For example, see Brody, "Freud's Attitude Toward the United States," pp. 93–103.

assault on the rules of psychoanalysis, perhaps the latter's truest test and limit (one may also ask to what extent the rules of psychoanalysis came into existence as a conducting medium and insulation for psychotic aspects of the self organized in neurotic transferences). It is still an open question how best to meet a psychotic transference or to effect the cohesion of the scattered debris of a broken self through the formation of such an intense relationship. We have only begun to tap the meaning and possibilities of the psychology of demand. A clinical encounter with psychotic demand always touches some psychic nerve or limit, yet it is precisely where demand converges with an impasse point that psychic evolution for all concerned may occur.

Madness and Creativity

For Freud, the dominance or breakthrough of deep unconscious processes was associated not only with madness, but also with creativity. In his formal theory, creativity requires sublimation, a restructuring of primitive drives in the light of higher aims. But Freud spoke informally of the "creativity of the unconscious." In his letters to Fliess, Freud time and again wrote that he threw himself on the mercy of the unconscious and drifted along vaguely in tune with the spontaneous movement of his work.[28] This Janus-like vision of the unconscious as linked with madness and creativity is part of Freud's heritage from the Romantic tradition. The Romantics often idealized madness or, at least, were fascinated by it. It was linked with powers beyond the ordinary. The madman knows things— terrible truths—inaccessible to ordinary consciousness. The history of nineteenth-century literature is filled with the early deaths of poets who lived on the edge of madness or who, in some way, viewed madness as a privileged mode of cognition.[29]

28. Freud, *Origins of Psycho-Analysis*, pp. 236, 258, 311–312. Such references in his work are numerous.
29. For example, Rimbaud wrote to George Izambaud: "Now I am going in for

Today, in psychotherapy, an individual coming out of a psychotic episode may express both relief and regret. "Thank God I'm better, but I don't want to lose everything I saw there," said one patient. "I thought it would never end and now I'm afraid nothing will ever be so total again," remarked another. For these people, psychosis was intense and all-consuming. I have heard individuals who have gone through a war or faced death speak this way. A Hungarian freedom fighter once told me, "That was the high point of my life. Everything was alive. I rose beyond myself—I was myself fully." This latter may be a far cry from a psychotic episode, yet war and madness are scarcely unrelated.

Three of the most sensitive and knowledgeable writers about psychosis—Bettelheim, Arieti, and Milner—have reported such a sense of loss, either on the patient's or their own part, as the patient gets better.[30] In particular, these authors have described cases in which the patient's artwork has been important. However, as the individual improves, his interest in, or the force of his art, wanes. Such a phenomenon appears to confirm the poet Rilke's fear that if his devils were tampered with by psychoanalysis, his angels also would be endangered. How or if creativity and cure can go together is an issue we will return to again and again.[31]

Of course, not all afflicted persons appreciate or benefit from their

---

debauch. Why? I want to be a poet, and I am working to make myself a *visionary* . . . To arrive at the unknown through the disordering of *all the senses*" (Rimbaud, "Letter to George Izambaud," p. xxvii).

"The poet makes himself a *visionary* through a long, prodigious and rational disordering of *all* the senses. Every form of love, of suffering, or madness; he searches himself, he consumes all the poisons in him, keeping only their quintessences. Ineffable torture in which he . . . arrives at the unknown!" (Idem, "Letter to Paul Demeny," p. xxx–xxxi.)

30. Bettelheim, *Paul and Mary*, pp. 218–219; Arieti, "Cognition in Psychoanalysis" (lecture given at the American Professional Seminar Center, Columbia University, May 26, 1979); Milner, *Hands of the Living God*, pp. 386–412.

31. Rank concluded that art was a parasite on life and that one must choose whether to devote one's creativity to personal relationships or to art (Rank, *Art and Artist*, pp. 425–431). See the discussion of this issue in Eigen, "Dual Union or Undifferentiation," pp. 415–428.

psychosis. Some are permanently broken. Others may not even realize they are ill, but drift dully along at a low level of existence that barely approaches human. Many carry their illness like a stranger, or a burden they do not really feel is part of themselves. They find ways to take it into account and control it with medication, cognizant of the possibility of periodic relapses. The intensity and all-consuming quality of psychotic experience seems to have passed them by; it has never taken on meaning, except as a curse. The therapeutic task is to help the individual take his illness seriously and turn it into a challenge. It is a task that may not meet with success. Not everyone has the resources to come to grips with psychic reality and "experience his experience."[32] Much preliminary work is usually necessary before the real struggle can begin. However, a psychotic individual should have the right to discover whether or not his illness can become a true journey of the self. Even partial success leads to a quality of experiencing one might have missed if one simply tried to control, get rid of, or otherwise short-circuit what one is up against. I do not want to idealize the horror and waste of mental illness, but I do wish to stress that it *may* open up a psychic dimension of decisive significance.

The Primacy of Experience

Jung wrote that psychology is a subjective confession[33]; every mental act has its own perspective. If science tries to account for consciousness, it can only do so through consciousness. This is a circle we must live with. It is part and parcel of the nature of consciousness (as it has evolved) to explore and move beyond itself. Consciousness is both subject and object to itself, yet it needs to transcend itself as well.

32. See Bion, *Learning from Experience*, pp. 18, 62, 73, 82–99. What makes experiencing experience possible is a theme of Bion's book.
33. For example, Jung, *Memories, Dreams and Reflections*, pp. 200–222; see also Stolorow and Atwood, *Faces in a Cloud*, pp. 15–44, 47–107, 173–203.

Both physical and experiential processes open endless horizons, and it is unlikely that our knowledge of either will ever be exhausted. Professor Lewontin, a contemporary biologist, writes,

> a study of all or any significant part of the interconnections and coupled oscillations of our millions of brain cells seems a task that would consume the three billion years left before the sun becomes a red giant and fries all life. We must face the possibility that we will *never* understand the organization of the central nervous system at any but the most superficial level.[34]

Poetry and religion are as hard pressed to express and explore the depths of human experience as science. The very elusiveness of so much of what we experience keeps us wondering who and what we are as well as where we are. The poet and mystic use language evocatively, although precision and rigor are necessary for evocation to succeed. It may be that the depth psychologist must also develop his own style of evocation. Perhaps Freud and Jung do just that: Freud speaks of the unconscious both as a hypothetical construct and as "the true psychical reality." It was his convincing evocation of the latter that lent the former its force and made it possible for these two levels of discourse each to make fertile the other. The psychologist is obligated to think as clearly as possible, but it is, finally, thinking rooted in a specific sensibility. A certain tension between clarity and evocation must be maintained.

It is becoming more common today to think that brain and experience are not simply two terms split off from or reducible to one another, but rather that they may be viewed as entering into a mutually constitutive relationship. Each sets requirements that dictate the structural possibilities of the other. Our understanding of the mutual influence of brain and experience is in its infancy.

Different approaches to psychosis have emphasized possible physical and psychological factors. The "nativists" look for a genetic, neurological, or chemical basis; the "empiricists" stress environmen-

---

34. Lewontin, "Liberation of Biology," p. 37.

tal influences. Jung believed a toxic chemical was at work in schizophrenia, although he kept open the possibility of person-to-person
therapeutic help. The current tendency is to conclude discussions of
nature versus nurture by noting that both are probably involved,
with more or less emphasis of one or the other factor in a given case.

THE NATURE-NURTURE CONTROVERSY

Much controversy besets claims that psychosis is inherited or
produced by environmental influences. Schizophrenic individuals
tend to have overactive dopamine systems and to lack an enzyme to
break down and eliminate the by-products of stress. They may also
possess irregular brain patterns and abnormal neural transmission.
Most discussions which favor a genetic or neurochemical explanation
note that the specific mechanisms operative in schizophrenia remain
unknown, although there are promising leads for future research. In
one form or another, this type of report has been made for nearly a
century. A difference today is better control of mental illness
through chemical means and a greater specificity of research.

Environmentalists believe that "nativist" claims are confounded
by other variables. Studies show how alterations in the environment
(e.g., stress level, quality of affectional ties) affect body chemistry.
Opportunity for exploration and adequate perceptual and cognitive
stimulation are important to proper development. Psychotherapy
can alter one's susceptibility to physical illness; for example, it can
affect the way one deals with stress. Thus, the way we relate to
ourselves profoundly affects our bodily being, and vice versa.

Deutsch[35] has recently summarized many of the difficulties involved in disentangling genetic from environmental variables. Her
study suggests that separation from parents among certain children
may increase the risk of psychosis.

The third edition of the *Diagnostic and Statistical Manual of Mental
Disorders* gives the following summary with regard to schizophrenia:

35. Deutsch, "Early Parental Separation in Children," pp. 19–22, 201–233.

All investigators have found a higher prevalence of the disorder among family members. This includes studies in which the adopted offspring of individuals with Schizophrenia have been reared by parents who do not have Schizophrenia. Twin studies consistently show a higher concordance rate of Schizophrenia for monozygotic than dizygotic twins, and dizygotic twins have the same concordance rate as siblings who are not twins. However, being a monozygotic twin does not in itself predispose to the development of Schizophrenia. Although genetic factors have been proven to be involved in the development of the illness, the existence of a substantial discordance rate, even in monozygotic twins, indicates the importance of nongenetic factors.[36]

NATURE AND NURTURE IN RELATION TO FREUD'S THEORIES

Although Freud did not deny a possible physical basis for mental illness, he noted that a physicalistic bias could obscure ignorance and act as a resistance to discovering dynamic psychological events. He finally concluded that no amount of physical or biological knowledge could replace the study of experience for its own sake. Experiential knowledge would always be necessary.[37] His own theory is a highly sophisticated blend of nature–nurture, much on the model of modern embryology. He envisioned basic psychic structures that develop according to an innate timetable but that require specific environmental conditions to unfold ("maturational processes and the facilitating environment," in Winnicott's fine phrase[38]).

In the course of his development, Freud oscillated between innatist and environmentalist positions. Early in his career, he believed that neurosis was generally caused by actual sexual traumas in early childhood. Then he realized that the villain was the innately programmed fantasy life with which the patient structured his world. Although many psychoanalysts feel that this second was Freud's

36. American Psychiatric Association, *Diagnostic and Statistical Manual of Mental Disorders*, 3rd ed., p. 186.
37. Freud, "Outline of Psycho-Analysis," pp. 144, 157–159.
38. Winnicott, *Maturational Processes and the Facilitating Environment*, pp. 83–92, 230–248.

more considered and official position, in fact he never stopped writing about actual trauma, and the complex structure of his theory includes both. The most extreme interplay *and* polarity between external reality and fantasy characterizes Freud's work.

Thus, there is room in Freud's work for the various nativist and empiricist positions that splinter the depth psychologies. Melanie Klein is a nativist who emphasizes the unfolding of unconscious fantasy structures. Hartmann emphasizes native ego functions and the "average expectable environment." When he speaks about id, his emphasis is less on fantasy than on a raw energic force. Kohut and Winnicott emphasize the quality of parenting, although both recognize that innate developmental timetables exist. All make important contributions to our picture of psychosis.[39] The human mind swings between perspectives, acknowledging the kernel of truth in each.

The Politics of Inner Space

The mental health field has been and is beset by wars and fragmentation. Depth psychologists have formed dozens of rival ideological groups, each with splinter groups, but it may be that ideological and economic struggles in the rest of the scientific community are no less virulent: The clash between different interpretations of data goes on in every branch of human effort. There are even fights to establish what qualifies as data. Perhaps social scientists are particularly verbal about the clashes within their professions because it is part of their work to understand the dynamics of such occurrences. Psychology is its own patient, and the trend to psychoanalyze psychoanalysis is intrinsic to Freud's and Jung's belief that one's own analysis is

39. Klein, "Some Theoretical Conclusions Regarding the Emotional Life of the Infant," pp. 198–236; idem, "Notes on Some Schizoid Mechanisms," pp. 292–320; Hartmann, "Contribution to the Metapsychology of Schizophrenia," pp. 177–198; Kohut, *Analysis of the Self*, pp. 1–22, 214–215, 255–257; Winnicott, *Collected Papers*, pp. 243–254, 300–305; idem, *Maturational Processes and the Facilitating Environment*, pp. 83–92, 230–248.

central to training and practice. The mental health profession also has a closer, more intimate contact with the population at large than have students in other disciplines. What a psychologist says or writes is often addressed to potential patients and tends to affect others at that level. Therapeutic discourse, finally, is soul to soul.

Few therapists would disagree that work with psychosis often calls for a combination of approaches. In good hospitals, one is likely to find a team approach with all the difficulties and conflicts this involves. Psychotherapy, medication, art therapy, and family counseling may play some part in the patient's treatment. Nevertheless, many good professionals are tolerant of, without being too affected by, each other. There is no doubt that such tolerance can be useful and, perhaps, can pave the way for closer contact. But it is not dialogue. Interaction in the depths is more the exception than the rule. Real contact may be upsetting, and often requires moments of self-doubt and the temptation to convert to the other's viewpoint. If one takes a risk and lets go of one's habitual self, stretching through mutual impact, paradoxically, one's own position often becomes enriched.

In point of fact, real dialogue between workers has and does occur. Marion Milner, whose account of a 20-year psychoanalysis of a schizophrenic woman is a classic, was deeply influenced by Jungian ideas. A group of London Jungians, headed by Michael Fordham, has long held a substantive dialogue with psychoanalysts who are interested in the emergence of the self in infancy, particularly at levels relevant for a more vital understanding of psychotic processes. Among many others who may be mentioned are H. Elkin and Schwartz-Salant. The former has been engaged in an inner dialogue with Freud, Jung, the British School, W. Reich, and others. Schwartz-Salant is a New York Jungian who has found the work of Kohut, Kernberg, and others most helpful. Grotstein has been concerned with the interface between M. Klein, Bion, and Kohut. A. Green and Pontalis, each in his way, are steeped in Freud, Lacan, and Winnicott (in Green's case, Bion as well). More examples could easily be given.[40]

Cross-fertilization is a path of creativity in our time. The splintering of the field not only produces insulated groups that go their separate ways, but also mutual encounters in which shifts of direction register the quality of certain impacts. Different psychologists have different ideas of what a person is, which represent the many ways one encounters aspects of the self. More than eclecticism is involved, however. Through an understanding of genuine differences, the self is transformed, often in unpredictable ways. Through an exposure to other perspectives, a qualitatively real, if intangible, shift can occur in one's very being. The present book grew out of this dialogical ferment.

My early work was with seriously disturbed children, particularly autistic and schizophrenic ones. However, most of my practice has been with adults and a consistent part of it with ambulatory psychotic individuals. I soon discovered the importance of tuning into the psychotic dynamics of even "normal" persons. Most individuals have, at the very least, psychotic, neurotic, and realistic inner voices. The present book passes the materials of psychosis through my subjective filter system, as the latter has evolved over 25 years of therapeutic work.

During these years, I have been exposed to and influenced by many different theoretical and clinical positions. A good many voices compete in my inner space. If the texture of this work is personal, I do not believe it is less objective on that account, since objectivity is part of being a fully human individual. Differentiated gestalts evolve through a long immersion in an area of interest. The patterns I will share have been helpful, both to others and myself, but it remains to be seen whether they can be of use to the reader, and thus, the patient. This, after all, is the true test.

---

40. Milner, *Hands of the Living God*, pp. xxv–xxvii; Fordham, *Jungian Psychotherapy*, pp. 52–53; Elkin, "On Selfhood and Ego Structures in Infancy," pp. 57–76; Schwartz-Salant, *Narcissism and Character Transformation*, pp. 9–90; Grotstein, "Proposed Revision of the Concept of Primitive Mental States," pp. 479–546; Green, "The Analyst, Symbolization and Absence in the Analytic Setting," pp. 1–22; Pontalis, *Frontiers in Psychoanalysis*, pp. 7–11, 126–154.

Psychotic Experience and the
Raw Materials of Personality

To paraphrase Winnicott, behind a neurosis may be a hidden psychosis.[41] Often both patient and therapist are afraid to work with this
deeper dimension. A compromise "cure," which does not touch the
true nature of the difficulty, may be settled on. However, if patient
and therapist persevere, a mysterious dimension, in which boundaries between the self and the other are fluid, can open, and the sense
of the immaterial and the material shifts, seemingly at random.

Freud, in his depiction of perversion as the shadowy side of
neurosis, takes this deeper, more mysterious dimension for granted.
His formulation that the infant is polymorphous perverse assumes a
fluidity of erogenous potential for which bodily boundaries offer
little restraint. His notion that the body is originally an undifferentiated erotic playground involves a boundless interchangeability of
openings and surfaces. In psychosis, this fluidity of libido becomes a
terrifying, uncontrollable fluctuation in the sense of self and other.

Certain investigators[42] had been so impressed by the powerful
transformations the sense of self and other undergoes in psychosis
and depth therapy that they believed that the human infant must pass
through a phase of "normal" psychosis. In this view, the latter may
be partly outgrown, but it also is ever present and can reemerge if
provoked by life's difficulties. In subtle and undetected ways, the
underlying psychotic position colors everyday responses and may
even structure a whole life. It can take many decades for an individual (or society) to realize with what sort of madness he has blindly
lived.

However, data now indicate that it may be misleading to characterize infantile experience as psychotic.[43] The infant passes through

41. Winnicott, "The Use of an Object and Relating Through Identifications,"
p. 87.
42. Melanie Klein, Mahler, and Winnicott share this view.
43. Grotstein, "Proposed Revision of the Concept of Primitive Mental States,"
pp. 516–524.

many states in the course of a profoundly orderly, developmental unfolding. Perceptual, cognitive, and fantastical dimensions have their timetable. By contrast, the psychotic's timetable has gone awry, and broad possibilities of experience have been closed off. The psychotic undergoes dramatic fluctuations and constrictions of the sense of self and other, and what may seem to approximate the plasticity of infantile experience is a cruel caricature of it. Even in his lability, he lacks the infant's openness to grow through shifts in the quality of moment to moment interactions. A long-term rigidity, which is not characteristic of normal infancy, blocks all movement.

Perhaps it may best be said that certain raw materials that are basic for building up the sense of self and other are organized or employed by psychotic processes in typically damaging ways. Raw materials must be taken, in a broad sense, to include thoughts, affects, images, sensations, will, the sense of self–other, materiality–immateriality, and time–space. The sense of self–other and material–immaterial will be emphasized here.

Few phenomena lead to a more precise appreciation of just what is achieved in "good enough" personality functioning than the shock of what can happen when madness appears. In psychosis, the raw materials of personality, such as the sense of self–other and materiality–immateriality, undergo startling transformations or deformations. Mental processes can speed up or slow down to such an extent that being an adequately coherent person is no longer possible. The psychotic individual may be mutely rigid, explode, then turn to putty. Clarity of ideas may oscillate with gnomic utterances. Such tendencies play a role in the mood swings of ordinary life, but in psychosis, they have a menacing finality that threatens to abandon the individual forever in shifting currents of disintegration and horror. The way individuals are ripped apart by psychotic processes brings home the realization that the emergence of a viable sense of self and other must be counted as one of the most creative achievements of humankind.

That the capacity for psychosis is well nigh ubiquitous is suggested by the fear of breakdown so many individuals occasionally voice. Many such remarks take the form of jokes. Colloquial terms for insanity, such as "nuts," "bats," "loony," "off his rocker," and "dotty," lightly ridicule a feared grim reality. The seriousness of what is at stake is closer to the surface in such terms as "losing my mind," "losing my grip on reality," "going to pieces," or "going over the edge." The colorful and ominous array of metaphors for madness bear witness to the fear and tacit acknowledgment of serious psychic damage in human awareness.

Madness occurs in all times and places. Although its content varies, its basic forms are few. In Western nosology, the basic forms may be summarized under the broad headings of schizophrenia and depression, the so-called affective disorders and thought disorders. Although these categories are too simple, as well as culture bound, they touch on patterns found everywhere. My own interest is less in the classification than in the examination of processes, although the two may be related. The question shifts from what characteristics are typical of various psychoses to what invariants characterize psychotic processes.

I emphasize six principal elements of psychosis or six basic ways psychotic processes organize the raw materials of personality. My suggestions are inevitably incomplete. For example, whereas my emphasis on materiality–immateriality seems to be a part of psychotic phenomenology from time immemorial, questions might be asked as to when the sense of self arose in human history. That is, was madness always a disease of the self?[44] Again, could I not have selected different elements or organizing processes? My working justification is that I selected those dimensions I absolutely could not do without in clinical encounter. More dimensions might be added, but no fewer would do. The problem areas "chosen" were those forced on me in working with deep areas of personal growth. They represent the kernel of psychosis as I have come to know it.

Maps of psychic life are suspect. Yet without speaking, the mute-

---

44. Jaynes portrays the organization of early culture in terms of what we would call psychotic experience. He hypothesizes that the recent emergence of individuated consciousness is the end result of a long psychotic-like period characterizing the predawn and dawn of human history (*Origin of Consciousness*, pp. 48–144, 404–446).

ness of life would collapse in on itself. My style presupposes a taste for subjectivity. Yet my aim is to explore damaging processes that are generally significant. In so doing, I will probe what self and other can mean and the limits of the psychically possible. We must allow ourselves simultaneously to enter, yet maintain distance from, the phenomena we encounter. A certain slippage between one level of discourse and another must be tolerated. Descriptions of psychotic experience, structures, and dynamic operations slide into each other. This is necessary for ease of exposition, and at this point of research, it would be pretentious to be too explicit. If the result is a kind of map of the kernel of psychosis, we know the map is not the thing itself. The realities pointed out have the ability not only to lay waste but also to rebuild. And yet in psychic life, a map *is* inescapably a part of the reality it expresses. The results must be judged by their helpfulness in the consulting room, or whatever shifts may occur in the capacity to experience of an individual reader.

The Kernel of Psychosis

Six basic ways psychotic processes organize raw materials of personality will be explored (Chapters 2 through 6), followed by two detailed case studies, Freud's Schreber case and one of my own (Chapter 7). Chapter 8 further amplifies my concern with the structure and psychodynamics of the core of psychosis.

The six problem areas to be explored are previewed below.

HALLUCINATION

There is a sense in which the capacity to hallucinate is universal. Freud noted that we all do so in our dreams. Since the types of thought processes that create dreams also go on while we are awake, there is reason to believe that the way we construe our world has hallucinatory aspects. The ability to produce a hallucinatory state seems part and parcel of our ability to produce images and words.

Not every psychosis is characterized by hallucinations. But the fact that hallucinations frequently appear in psychosis, or exist at all, affects our very sense of what it means to be a human being. We have a fear of or joke about seeing and hearing things, but that this possibility really does exist leads to a dread in the margin of our awareness. That we respond so easily to such "jokes" suggests a hidden kinship with what the madman undergoes in a more overt, total way.

MINDLESSNESS

Among our earliest defenses is our ability to go blank or even to become stuporous. The mind tries to anesthetize itself in the face of emotional pain. On a very primitive level, the mind responds to pain by trying to blank out the latter or, if necessary, by emptying itself out entirely. That is, the mind may try to get rid of itself in order to rid itself of pain.

In everyday life, such operations are often taken for granted. Most people do not make much of or even notice momentary lapses of mental presence nor do they link such states with hidden sources of pain. Often such states merely reflect the phasic waxing and waning of attention. However, the vernacular term *spacing out* captures something of what is meant here.

In psychosis, the mind may speed up or slow down almost to a zero point. It may try either to transcend or nullify itself. Mystics describe a type of zero point as part of a larger process of renewal. In psychosis, it more often functions as a black hole that sucks in everything in its path.

BOUNDARIES

In psychosis, the issue of where the self leaves off and the other begins is paramount. In everyday life, a certain blurring of boundaries between self and other is taken for granted. It makes communication possible. But in psychosis, the problematic nature of boundaries in human life becomes explicit in dramatic ways.

For the psychotic individual, the natural interweaving of self and other may turn into a terrifying sense of dissolution or invasion. Correlatively, the natural division between self and other may become a desperate walling-off process. It is an odd property of the human self that it can vanish and harden simultaneously.

Similarly, boundaries between aspects of the self (e.g., between and within mental ego and body ego) break down and become rigid in highly distorting ways. It is as if mental space itself undergoes a serious deformation, so that whatever appears in such "space" is affected by shifts in the deformed space.

HATE

In his case histories, Freud wrote of a wounded self whose hate is withheld and rerouted. The traumatic agent is both described and experienced in aggressive terms, viz., a "blow in the face" or a "stab in the heart."[45] Freud often writes of slights that have indirect consequences. Repressed rage may harden into a chronic attitude of hatred and deform one's character. Anger, a spontaneous part of our emotional life, can run amok.

Work with psychotic organizations has found hate to be a decisive dimension. Melanie Klein's[46] writings may be regarded as one of the most detailed phenomenologies of hate yet evolved. She elucidates ways in which hate plays a key role in organizing the infant's response to pain. Infantile hate operations lay the groundwork for an abiding sense of the badness of self and other. In psychosis, hidden hate distorts the very structure of one's world. In certain instances, it can blow one's sense of self and other to bits.

EPISTEMOLOGY

Psychology and epistemology are intimately related. If psychology studies mental processes, epistemology investigates what claims these processes make about the nature of reality or truth. Psychology

45. Breuer and Freud, "Studies on Hysteria," p. 181.
46. Klein, "Notes on Some Schizoid Mechanisms," pp. 292–320.

studies perception, whereas "epistemology is interested in the cognitive pretensions of perceptions, *i.e.*, their apparent references to external objects."[47] In the present context, one might also add internal objects.

Although psychology and epistemology retain their spheres of independence as disciplines, they overlap in crucial ways. This is vividly seen, when the issues raised by psychosis are considered. Perhaps nowhere are issues concerning how our sense of reality is structured brought home more dramatically than in psychotic states. Psychotic experience overturns our basic picture of the world. It intensifies the silent fragility inherent in the ways we constitute our experience of ourselves and others.

In everyday life, we take inner and outer space for granted. We distribute objects inside and outside us as a matter of course. For example, we place motivations inside ourselves as if we assumed that an inner mental space capable of containing internal objects existed. We contrast this inner horizon with an outer one filled with nature, people, and the events of history. In psychosis, these "containers" undergo radical deformations or seem to be entirely missing. The psychotic individual is not able to maintain the sense of mental space that allows the internal ordering processes to run smoothly.

In psychosis, the individual may see through the fiction of inner space. He may be hyper-aware that experience, as such, is invisible and immaterial, and therefore cannot be located in spatial terms. He cannot or will not make the leap to act as if mind is capable of being ordered in ordinary spatial terms. The very notion of space is in jeopardy. At the other end of the spectrum, his sense of space may be overstuffed and heavy, so that he is unable to resist it. Then, rather than rejecting a sense of inner space, he collapses into it. How a "ventilated space"[48] is maintained is a basic problem.

47. Runes, *Dictionary of Philosophy*, p. 94.
48. Green, "The Analyst, Symbolization and Absence in the Analytic Setting," p. 8.

REVERSAL

Freud suggested that the operation of reversal is so basic that it seems to antedate the development of the usual defenses. He gave, as an example, the tendency of an impulse directed toward another object to turn upon the self (and vice versa). It would appear that a double-headed arrow joins self and other. However, not only may an impulse shift directions, it may also change in valence as well, as when an impulse turns into its opposite (love–hate).

As defenses develop, they exploit the mind's capacity to reverse directions and change valence. Typical styles of reversing areas of experience develop and gradually become a part of one's character. In psychosis, the capacity to reverse spirals and hardens. Reversal tends to become a steady state, which turns any experience into what it is not. The individual, however, may so place himself on one side of a duality that the excluded opposite assumes demonic proportions. The capacity to reverse may accelerate to the point at which the individual spins himself out of existence, or decelerate until what remains of existence falls in upon itself. At the same time, this capacity helps build our sense of self and other and contributes to our creative life.

Intentions and Applications

In actuality, the six areas outlined above are interwoven. Some connections between them will be obvious, but others will need spelling out. Together they form various points of entry to the dynamic kernel of psychosis. Not every point taken up will be relevant to all forms of psychosis. I have tried to sidestep the question as to whether there is one type of psychosis or many. Practitioners who emphasize nosological issues may not be happy with what follows. I do not mean to slight the importance of diagnostics, especially when the latter concerns an understanding of dynamic patterns; diagnostics play a role in a deeper clinical search. However, my aim is to convey a sense of what one may expect when one encounters psychotic phenomena—or the psychotic dimension of life. I believe that the clinician steeped in the kinds of questions dealt with here will be better able to work with psychotic manifestations of whatever diagnostic category, or at least to entertain a greater openness to doing so.

This book is meant to add to rather than substitute for standard approaches. It is an attempt to get at psychosis from the inside, while also employing whatever outside means seem handy. I believe the liberties taken have their own sort of rigor. That different approaches may have their areas of validity and weakness ought not be viewed simply as a defect in methodology. It also reflects the richness of our subjectivity, of who we are, of our possibilities.

CHAPTER TWO

Hallucination

Hallucination and the Human

THE ABILITY TO produce and to be gripped by hallucinations is one of the most spectacular of human capacities. It decisively shapes our sense of what it means to be a human being. For many, it defines the meaning of madness. When we think of a madman we are likely to imagine someone who "sees and hears things" and by that we mean "things" that do not exist.

What is this seeing? What are these things? There is no one answer for all times and places, but there are certain invariant tendencies. Our hallucinatory capacity oscillates between the divine and the demonic. We hear God tell us things. We see devils. The archetypal background of existence tends to become a prepossessing foreground. This is so not only with regard to the transcendent, but also the immanent. A psychotic individual may become obsessed with body functions and products, inhabiting a fecalized universe and smelling or seeing feces everywhere. Then, everything that exists is in danger of being spoiled, the opposite of God seeing everything as basically good. The psychotic may also live in a pansexualized world in which all that happens is sharpened or blurred by monomanic erotic concerns. Often, erotic and excretory obsessions are organized around a contemporary god or demon drawn from the political or personal realm, a Hitler, the CIA, father, or mother. Almost anyone or anything that carries a sense of overarching power can be used to organize hallucinatory concerns.

Attitudes toward those who hear voices or see visions vary widely. Cultures have waited on and followed their messages; they have been revered as divine or shunned as outcasts. Plato admired and distrusted what he called the divine madness of poets. In Shakespeare, kings seek counsel from fools, but madness itself is reserved for royalty, the highly placed, or women. It is associated with wounded sensibility and the unendurable journey of personal consciousness. At times, simply, it is the underside or culmination of evil. Shakespeare's connection of might and madness may echo a time when ruling power and visionary capability were one.

Today we are told that madness is more prevalent among the poor and powerless, but it is not clear whether this is because madness is better masked by those with advantages. It is significant that recent depictions of madness tend to emphasize the victim's sense of helplessness, whatever his socioeconomic status. The psychotic individual is portrayed as one whose will is preempted by another's. He is incapable of making decisions, but rather must submit and obey. Animal studies show that rats break down in impossible situations over which they have no control, but in situations in which there is some modicum of control they are able to function. R. D. Laing speaks of the "politics of the family" and describes deeply rooted imbalances of power that result in madness. Lacan depicts both neurosis and madness in terms of Hegel's master–slave concept. One may learn to be more helpless or powerful, but a double sense of might and weakness seems to be a basic part of our emotional life.

Hallucinations tend to command and demand. The voice orders, and the individual must follow. God may inscribe His Ten Commandments with thunder or whisper with a still voice, but woe to Israel if she does not hear. Whatever the real difference between God ordering Abraham to kill his son and a contemporary madman hearing god's command to kill his mother, both have their share of destructiveness and force. The Bible warns us to beware of false gods and prophets and to distrust our own wayward lights, but both psychosis and morals take the form of imperatives.

One might argue that the materials that form the content of hallucinations are roughly approximated by the central concerns of Freud, Adler, and Jung (we will emphasize Freud and Jung). Freud traced unconscious fantasy systems associated with the body ego. His psychosexual stages outline some of the vicissitudes of embodiment. The developing ego is expected to coordinate its sense of reality with an awareness of its origins and master, to some extent, the unconscious forces that give it birth (God's invitation to Adam to subdue nature). Freud took some pride in showing that the ego is not master of its own house, yet is enjoined to be.

Adler emphasized dramas of power and helplessness typical of the social ego, and understood the power drive as compensating for an existential sense of inferiority all humans must endure. He tried to evoke a sense of brotherhood in face of our common situation. Jung gave expression to the religious voice within and mapped a journey of liberation that hinges on fulfilling the requirements of an unfolding self, a template or blueprint that dictates the very terms of our being. The command structure of existence was perhaps most tenaciously held onto by Jung, although it played an important and ambiguous role for Freud and Adler as well.

Although none of these pioneers gave the socioeconomic and political aspects of power their due, I do not believe that an exposition of the power dimension of hallucinatory activity can be done justice without a firm sense of what the depth psychologies make contact with. The hallucinatory dimension of power must be elucidated, together with how facts of power structure hallucination. Freud's metaphor of the psyche as iceberg still has merit, in spite of its emphasis on the cold aspect of life. It tells us that much of what we experience may be shaped by unconscious hallucinatory activity and that our hold on sanity is fragile. Today, oddly and menacingly, we are increasingly aware of just how much of our conscious mental activity is also given to producing hallucinatory scenarios, often so pervasively that we do not notice it.

Freud: Wish and History

WISH AND PAIN

Freud affirmed the ubiquity of hallucination in our mental life by imagining that the baby hallucinates the breast when it has a need for it. This is a particular case of a more general tendency to maintain a sense of well-being or completion by wish fulfillment. Freud described this as functioning in terms of the pleasure principle. The primitive ego cannot endure pain and seeks to rid itself of the latter by hallucinating pleasure.

The problem of pain is fundamental to Freud's psychology. In his early works the problem is couched in terms of the danger of neurological flooding or overstimulation, and the function of the nervous system is to regulate the excitatory level. The "constancy principle"—the fiction that the mental apparatus tries to keep itself as free from stimuli as possible—is translated into psychological terms by associating increased stimulation with "unpleasure" (pain) and stimulus reduction with pleasure (satisfaction). It is assumed that the elemental psychic wish is to move from pain to pleasure. Thus the subject's self-feeling or self-perception is crucial for guiding the direction of mental work. For example, Freud summarized,

A current . . . starting from unpleasure and aiming at pleasure, we have termed a "wish"; and we have asserted that only a wish is able to set the apparatus in motion and that the course of the excitation in it is automatically regulated by feelings of pleasure and unpleasure. The first wishing seems to have been a hallucinatory cathecting of the memory of satisfaction.[1]

Whatever the correctness of the specific mechanisms Freud developed to explain this, the thrust of the phenomenology he drew on is crucial. Freud drew attention to a fundamental tendency in human life to imagine pleasure where there is pain. His concern was far more

1. Freud, "Interpretation of Dreams," p. 598. See also ibid., pp. 565–566, and idem, "Outline of Psycho-Analysis," p. 196, among numerous other examples.

radical than the usual hedonistic utilitarian philosophy that sees the ego as seeking a practical balance of pleasure over pain. Freud said that we try to imagine ourselves satisfied when we are not, even at the most fundamental levels of our being. At an early level of development, "wishing ends in hallucinating."[2]

The same urge toward painlessness informed Freud's theory of dreams. When Freud said that a dream attempts to fulfill the ego's wish to preserve sleep, he meant that the psyche (some aspect of it) is trying to achieve a painless state. Freud suggested that in sleep we regress toward an absolute, albeit incomplete narcissism. He used the fetus as a model of this imaginary disturbance-free state and noted how the dreamer often assumes a fetal position. The dream is a psychic womb. It is meant to balance forces, so that the sleeper may go on being like a fetus. The dream is seen as a kind of pearl created around an irritant, dissolving pain by representing it.

The disturbances the dream tries to mute involve day residues and deeper unconscious drives.[3] One might call day residues unthought (latent) thoughts, things that happen to us during the day that are not dwelled on or worked through. Our deeper (repressed) wishes seize on such liminal events as entrances to dream work. The dream work fobs off potential disturbance by representing our repressed longings as fulfilled, at least partially, or, better, by trying to balance competing interests. It does this, in part, by substituting things ("thing presentations") for thoughts.[4] Another way of saying this is that in dreams thought regresses to perception. By perception here, Freud meant mental presentations of objects, "things" before they have verbal meaning. Since we see things in dreams that are not actually present, such "perceptions" are called hallucinations. Again, in Freud's formula, "wishing ends in hallucinating."

Thus, the dream work short-circuits thinking by representing thoughts as hallucinated perceptual objects. Hallucination aims at

2. Freud, "Interpretation of Dreams," pp. 565–566.
3. Ibid., pp. 165–187, 227–228, 555–564; idem, "Metapsychological Supplement," pp. 224–228; idem, "Outline of Psycho-Analysis," p. 170.
4. Freud, "Interpretation of Dreams," p. 548; idem, "Metapsychological Supplement," p. 228.

satisfaction, not thought. In a sense, dreams do not think, they *thing*. Hallucination is anti- or non- or pre-thought. Dream formation often hinges more on what materials best lend themselves to plastic representation than on the criteria thinking must follow.[5] Thinking brakes the pull toward hallucination.

The goal of Freudian dream interpretation is to fathom the latent thought and the repressed wishes it supports that appear in the dream in a hallucinatory way. The latent thought poses an affective question, since it is linked with unconscious desire. It appears in a dream precisely because it failed as a thought or did not successfully enter a thinking process. It is almost as if the dream is a punishment for thoughts that failed to think or become part of or generate a thinking matrix. In dreams, thoughts are repeated until the proper emotional thinking is achieved.

The notion that dreams provide a second chance for failed thoughts seems to contradict the idea that dreams attempt to achieve a hallucinated state of satisfaction rather than carry forward a painful thinking process. One way Freud tried to "solve" this was by postulating two kinds of thinking, primary and secondary. Primary process thinking is the type of work the mind does to achieve hallucinatory satisfaction; secondary process thinking is characterized by common sense and rational logic; thus, even achieving a state of non-thinking involves a kind of thinking. Although primary process thinking aims to establish a painless or, more positively, a blissful state, it must work to do this. An early attempt to handle stress by enacting an illusion of well-being by re-creating a memory of satisfaction as a perception, it conjures up a scene. Some exertion is needed to create or select, attend to, and believe in an image that fulfills one's desire. One must be able to search for and discriminate what is wanted from what is not and substitute one for the other, thus replacing reality with illusion. That Freud was not entirely happy with making wish fulfillment the main aim of primary process thinking is seen in his later attempt to describe psychic work before the dominance of the pleasure principle. That is, he sought an even

5. Freud, "Interpretation of Dreams," pp. 339–349.

more primitive function of dreams than wish fulfillment, a still earlier mode of response to pain than hallucinated satisfaction. We will return to this in Chapter 3.

We continue by noting differences in the way Freud thought hallucinatory processes work in dreams and psychosis. Although Freud tended to identify dreams with psychosis, he also indicated ways in which they differ,[6] in terms of depth and rigidity. In dreams, a more fluid communication between topographical levels of the psyche is maintained, particularly between unconscious and preconscious processes. Preconscious "word presentations" and unconscious "thing presentations" interact in dreams in ways that are unavailable to the schizophrenic individual. The latter tends to cut off the interactions between psychic systems and to swallow up reality and things by words. This is not the same as trying to put unconscious feelings into words, one of the vital communicative tasks of psychoanalysis. In schizophrenia, reality and unconscious depths are converted into words by way of hallucination. That is, the schizophrenic person is trapped in deformed preconscious operations that treat perceptual reality and unconscious drives as if they were words; thus, the types of reality proper to them are denied, while words are blown out of proportion. "In the beginning was the Word" has momentous import for the schizophrenic conversion of drives and things into words. It is a wish, a "beginning," reached by a series of tortuous processes, a cannibalizing of other realities by the Word.

This places the schizophrenic in a precarious, paradoxical position. On the one hand, he holds fast to the preconscious as his principal mode of defense against unconscious flooding, which leads to shallowness and rigidity. On the other hand, his emphasis on words as a mode of defense creates an illusion of psychic prescience. Since the secrets of the psyche have been turned into words (word magic) as a way of warding off their reality and impact, the words seem to become the realities they absorb, hence the mystique of great depth surrounding psychosis. As in dreams, the aim is to create a disturb-

6. Freud, "Metapsychological Supplement," pp. 229–235.

ance-free condition. Freud classified the various psychoses as to how
(or how well) they do this. He rewrote the dynamics underlying
nosological categories in terms of how the subject goes about trying
to approximate a painless state.[7]

WISH AND REALITY

Since Freud treated the phenomenon of hallucination as fundamental in mental life, a basic question for development is how the
infant discriminates what is hallucinatory from what is not.[8] For
Freud, the question of how to account for the development of our
sense of reality became the other side of how to account for madness.
Thus, both sanity and madness are problematic. Neither can be taken
for granted; both must be seen as the outcome of complex developmental processes. In a sense, Freud challenged common sense by
asking why we are sane, rather than mad. If the ego starts from a
hallucinatory position, how does it come to tell truth from self-
deception?

Freud's views on narcissism heightened the problem. His theory
of primary narcissism centered on the tension and interplay between
hallucination and perception. He envisioned the primordial constitution of the ego as a complex act (or a set of actions) in which the
diffuse autoerotic currents that precede and subtend the ego unite by
taking the ego as a first love object.[9] The ego, both subject and
object, is formed as a unitary ego by being the object of instinctual
(erotic) drives. It also plays a role in its own self-creation by attract-
ing libido, appearing to create itself (or being created) by an act of
repression. As it continues to develop, it further appropriates libidinal energy for its own purposes, and so begins its biography as hero
and lover. Its first love is and, in some sense, continues to be itself

7. A crucial sleight of hand in Freudian thinking is the informal "equating" of
minimal excitation with a state of maximal fulfillment. Aspects of this linkage in
discussions of ideal states and mindlessness are discussed in Chapters 1, 2, 3, 4, 6, 7,
8, and the Epilogue.
8. Freud, "Metapsychological Supplement," p. 231.
9. Freud, "On Narcissism," pp. 73–91.

(the original ego as a "pleasure ego" and "its own ideal"). The ego has its own non-libidinal source of energy, which Freud first called ego instincts (the ego's biography as survivor, the will to self- rather than species-preservation). Freud noted that originally these two sources of energy cannot be distinguished. For Freud, psychosis was a fixation and/or regression to primary narcissism (as reflected in megalomania) or to autoerotism (the loss or the extreme fragmentation of the ego).

In effect, Freud was saying that a primary position of the ego is what we call psychotic in adult life. There is a hallucinatory aspect to Eros, whether the ego is its object or its own ideal or has other objects. It is not made clear who the original subject can be, when Eros first loves Ego (or, rather, all psychoanalysis is about the missing subject). It is clear that, in trying to find a way to account for psychosis, Freud postulated a mad dimension at the birth of psychic life that runs through all psychic agencies (in his later formulation, id, ego, ego ideal, superego). Megalomania, falling in love, and repression all seem to have hallucinatory elements. In falling in love, the subject sees qualities in the love object that may not be present. In repression, one takes as not there the most critical psychic realities, including repression itself. This may explain Freud's remark that we may understand the positive hallucinations through negative ones. In severe cases, the self and psyche may be totally hallucinated as not there (the underside of inflation in megalomania). Repression makes a more circumscribed use of this potentially deadly capacity. That repression works partly through negative hallucination makes sense of the ego's need to know and not know what it is doing (i.e., it needs to know what to repress and not know that it represses).

Freud also insisted that the ego develops under pressure from the external world and remains loyal to perceptual reality.[10] The individual learns to tell the difference between hallucination and perception simply by testing to see if his movements can make what he sees disappear or whether what he sees remains. Of course, this simple test can only be one of a series of actions in establishing the sense of

10. Freud, "Metapsychological Supplement," pp. 231–233.

reality. The centrality of the problem is important here. Freud came to see reality-testing as one of the ego's most basic institutions, the cornerstone of personal survival. At the same time, through the ego's self-constitution via repression and idealization (of self, then other), it remains the medium of an Eros-informed hallucinatory dimension. The ego is thus a double agent, with both hallucination and reality perception assigned to it as constitutive functions.

These two functions are often inseparable. Freud called attention to the germ of historical truth hallucinations express in distorted form, so that hallucination itself may also be implicated in the ego's tie to reality.[11] Reality may assume the qualities of a positive hallucination, as when the mother appears not simply in but *as* a dream ("one can claim that all dreams are images of mother, or that the mother is a dream"[12]). Reality also may fall victim to negative hallucination, as in "disavowal," wherein a significant portion of or even the whole of reality is experienced as not there. Freud eventually portrayed disavowal as functioning toward the outside world as repression does toward the inside.[13] He wished to reserve the term repression for that aspect of the unconscious that had been the special province of psychoanalysis (Freud repeatedly said that most of the unconscious was unrepressed). Does this mean that Eros is no longer the only or principal source of hallucination, but that the ego can be understood to hallucinate independently of Eros? It is unlikely that Freud meant this, but it was never clarified (Freud's clinical examples of hallucination and disavowal as ego functions tend to maintain a tie between these defenses and erotic beliefs or hopes).

Freud's early formulations were similarly ambiguous. Is hallucination a perception of a memory of an actual satisfaction or does it contribute something of its own? Or both? Freud speaks of "the hallucinatory cathexis of perception,"[14] thus distinguishing between hallucination and perception, a distinction which makes confusion possible. If hallucination cathects perception, does this mean that it

11. Freud, "Outline of Psycho-Analysis," p. 267.
12. Pontalis, *Frontiers in Psychoanalysis*, p. 66.
13. Freud, "Outline of Psycho-Analysis," pp. 201–204.
14. Freud, "Interpretation of Dreams," p. 548.

precedes perception? Freud suggested that it does when he said later that first there is id, then ego. Do both arise together? Freud suggested this when he spoke of ego versus sexual instincts as a primary psychic duality. Hallucination requires the ego's perceptual abilities as a sustaining framework, even as that framework is menaced or undone. In this earlier formulation, Freud remarked that ego capacities and erotic currents are indistinguishable from each other early in life, although they somehow are not the same (different sources, functions, aims). And even as their differences become more apparent (conflictual tensions), they remain intertwining realities. They are co-constitutive for human life.

In the Schreber case (see Chapter 7), Freud put the pieces of the puzzle together in an unparalleled fashion.[15] Hallucinations are a kind of second or reparative phase of a psychosis. They are meant to restore the world of objects lost or destroyed earlier. In hallucinations, the object-world comes back in flagrantly distorted ways, but it does return. In the acute hallucinatory phase of mental illness, the individual is involved in momentous dramas. His hallucinatory object-world can tell the story of past wounds and wishes. In them may be read the remnants of a broken history. And at the same time, they represent partial (at times, total) fulfillments of the subject's deepest longings. They at once represent the subject's keenest pain and fulfillment. Wounded wishes find a home in hallucinations.

PERCEPTION, ILLUSION, AND HALLUCINATION

Man is a hallucinatory being striving for truth and a truth-oriented being striving for hallucinatory perfection—and the two intermingle (are one and two) in strange ways. This ancient theme appears in religion, philosophy, literature, and art. It pervades the Gothic literature that was a part of Freud's time. However, the literary emphasis was not so much the confusion between inner–outer as the crossing over of natural and supernatural forces. Similarly, the traditional

15. Freud, "Psycho-Analytic Notes on an Autobiographical Account of a Case of Paranoia," pp. 35–79.

duality in the humanities was illusion, error, or appearance, more than madness, versus truth.

A momentous shift in the history of ideas (and experience of self) was crystallized when Freud called error hallucination rather than illusion, although Descartes considered the possibility that phenomenal events were induced by the devil. Freud juxtaposed science with madness. Science also addresses the distinction between appearance and reality. It asks what must be postulated in order to account for phenomenal events. Deviation from (hypothetical) reality is treated as error or illusion. Sensory experience and perception are involved in illusion or error insofar as they do not represent things as they really are. Phenomenal reality needs to be "explained" by supposed relations that must remain unknowable. The test is how fruitful scientific fictions prove to be (fruitfulness guards us from the illusory nature of hypotheses). In Freud's reworking of this theme, science aims at reality, while perception is linked with hallucination. In Freud's last great summary work, published posthumously, he wrote: "The equation 'perception = reality' (external world) no longer holds. Errors, which can now easily arise and do so regularly in dreams, are called *hallucinations*"[16] (Freud's italics).

Freud's explicit equation of perception with hallucination brought into the open something long feared and sensed. The struggle for truth is played out against and permeated by hallucination. Notions of lying and falsehood must be rewritten in a hallucinatory key. Freud's work is part of a wider cultural movement in which human beings imagine themselves on the verge of coming out of an age-old hallucinatory state. At least this is envisioned as a possibility, a wish. It lets us in on a bit more of what we are up against and perhaps also what we are part of.

PERFECTION AND PAINLESSNESS

In closing this section on Freud, it is important to draw attention to what I believe is a sleight of hand in his discussion of hallucination.

16. Freud, "Outline of Psycho-Analysis," p. 162.

Freud began by arguing that the overall and most basic function of hallucination is to reduce psychic disturbance and, in effect, to achieve a painless state. It accomplishes this by making the subject believe he is satisfied when, in fact, he is not. That is, pain is hallucinated as absent and pleasure hallucinated as present. But before one realizes it, one is speaking about bliss, well-being, a sense of perfection, not simply pleasure or pain. A minimum (absolute pain-lessness) becomes a maximum (a beatific moment), as if the null-point and infinite fullness were equated.

It is to Freud's lasting credit that he traced ways that ideals (here ideal or beatific moments) function as pain killers (as did Marx and Nietzsche, among others). To be sure, he also described how ideals, in the form of conscience, can induce pain. However, here we are concerned with bliss rather than impossibly perfectionistic ideals. Freud was right to link ideal moments with pain reduction, but does this function fully account for the origin of ideal states? Ideal states may be used defensively, but do they start as defenses?

If what we hallucinate is a past satisfaction, how is this satisfaction chosen? Freud called the earlier state, which we wish to reestablish, "the situation of original satisfaction."[17] Is this original satisfaction an "actual" one, as Freud suggested, or an ideal fantasy, a prototype (as Freud also suggested)? Past satisfactions are not uniform. Some are better than others. Which of the many gradations is hallucinated at a given moment? Perhaps it is enough for the infant to feel more satisfied than not, rather than perfectly fulfilled. Or perhaps the propensity to feel *perfectly* fulfilled (or miserable) is part of its basic equipment. Hallucinations tend to maximize experience in both heavenly and hellish directions and so cannot be clearly tied to pain reduction. Nor can we say that ideal moments always have pain reduction as their aim, although often they do. They also arise spontaneously and are enjoyable (joy, not simply pleasure) for their own sake.

The capacity to create and experience ideal feelings plays a formi-

17. Freud, "Interpretation of Dreams," pp. 565–566; idem, "Metapsychological Supplement," p. 231.

dable role in psychoanalytic theory. Libido seeks an ideal imago.
Eros idealizes. The "pleasure ego" seeks a state of perfect pleasure,
the "narcissistic ego" one of perfect self-fulfillment. The ego becomes (or wishes to be) its own ideal. Or, again, it is said that the
sense of ideal happiness originates in the womb or at the breast
(oneness with mother) or, better, involves fantasies of perfect bliss in
the womb or with mother. In all these instances, ideal experience is
exploited, but not credited in its own right. It is always treated in
terms of "something else" (womb, breast, epiphenomenon of a drive
or defense, etc.). However, the so-called "original satisfaction" (or
fantasy of blissful satisfaction) could not be what it is supposed to be,
if not for the basic tendency to experience in ideal terms. Ideal
feelings can inform many objects of experience and so cannot be
accounted for by any one of them. The capacity for beatitude creates
what mother can be and transforms sex into Eros. The propensity to
experience ideal moments is irreducible and constitutive, not simply
derivative (although, like any other primitive given, it can be used
many ways).[18]

We cannot call this fault in psychoanalysis an error. It was a far-
reaching decision. Freud knew exactly what he was doing. His was
part of a larger intellectual movement that turned the West upside
down and inside out. The systematic treatment of ideal experience as
a derivative of instinctual drives is part of what Freud referred to as
his Copernican revolution. He focused on how the ideal glow and
warmth of experience is an offshoot of repressed sexuality, a spur
and pawn in the conflict between desire and defense. Beatific experience or ecstasy is a hallucination meant to eradicate a lack, a lack

---

18. A sense of the ideal plays a role in structuring psychosis and perversion as well
as creative inspiration (e.g., Chasseguet-Smirgel, *Creativity and Perversion*, pp. 92–
100, 151–159). The role of ideal states in health and pathology has been portrayed
in a series of papers by Eigen: "On Working with 'Unwanted' Patients," pp. 109–
121; "Ideal Images, Creativity and the Freudian Drama," pp. 287–298; "On the
Significance of the Face," pp. 427–441; "Instinctual Fantasy and Ideal Images,"
pp. 119–137; "The Area of Faith in Winnicott, Lacan and Bion," pp. 413–433;
"Maternal Abandonment Threats, Mind–Body Relations and Suicidal Wishes,"

that recedes as it is approached. And the lack tied to desire—is that real or hallucinatory or both?

Freud attributed to Eros the capacity to make one's father God and one's mother heaven, slipping into sexuality a dimension which it depends upon as well as nourishes. He obscured the implications of the position that Eros requires ideals to be Eros or that womb and breast fantasies feed on the capacity for ideal experiencing in order that their very mixed environments be transposed to the key of perfection. Freud did not acknowledge that the capacity for ideal (beatific) experiencing can contribute anything to Eros: for him it was part of Eros (a wish).

Psychoanalysis makes a genuine contribution in showing how ideal experience becomes distorted or stillborn without a sustaining environment. Freud read significant portions of the biography of ideal wishes from the turns they take in psychotic hallucinations. Hallucinations depict the fate of ideal hopes vis-à-vis the hard facts of life, particularly as channeled through one's upbringing. In his case histories, Freud usually traced hallucinatory activity to a sense of wounded love. Hallucinations try to satisfy that love, act as substitute objects, and bear witness to the wound. Freud sees hallucination as both wish-fulfillment and distorted history (a history of wounded desire, bad objects, life's evils, psychic conflict). The real is treated as fantasy, the fantasy as real. From what has been said about Freud's thought, fantasy is an outgrowth of or euphemism for hidden hallucinatory activity (later in this chapter we will say more about how this is also true for reality). Freud depicted the ways the world is lost in psychosis, but returns as hallucination. It is part of Freud's wisdom (and reductionism) to see total bliss and hallucination as the same and to see in this totality a lack, a reference to a hidden wound, a biography of desire. We must be ready to find our psychic life stamped by this complexity and predicament and all the questions it raises.

---

pp. 561–582; "Creativity, Instinctual Fantasy and Ideal Images," pp. 317–339; "Dual Union or Undifferentiation," pp. 415–428.

Jung: Mythic Journeys

It is difficult to overestimate the role Jung played in twentieth-century psychology, countering Freud's role. His stress on the my-thic subsoil of experience informed workers in almost every area of human study. One might justly say that most depth psychological (as opposed to simply drug-oriented) approaches to psychosis today live in his atmosphere.

Jung maintained that the main impetus and direction of our lives are informed by unconscious mythic structures that have an objec-tive reality.[19] Similar archetypal themes and organizing patterns are found in virtually all times and places. Man is a religious animal. His gods and demons must not only, or even basically, be understood in terms of erotic and aggressive drives or the will to survival or power. Transcendent experience is valued for its own sake, although Jung tended to stress its healing and destroying aspects.

At his best, Jung stressed a binocular approach, with one eye on the patient's everyday reality and the other on underlying mythic themes. The individual's hallucinatory irruptions are related to uni-versal mythic themes in such a way that the individual may come to value what he produces. With the eye of myth, the patient comes to locate what he is undergoing in a larger framework of meaning. Jung calls this technique amplification rather than reduction.[20] The pa-tient's imagery is not seen only, or primarily, in terms of personal father or mother complexes, but is dignified by its links with a grand mythic heritage. Jung described this process as a kind of salutory dosing of "depersonalization," inasmuch as it enabled the patient to get outside himself.[21]

In Jungian literature, amplification was often used on initial con-tact with patients as a way of warding off an imminent psychotic episode or to structure such a catastrophe. Von Franz recounts a consultation with a woman on the brink of hospitalization who

19. Jung, "Approaching the Unconscious," pp. 1–94.
20. Ibid.
21. Jung, *Memories, Dreams and Reflections*, Chapter 4.

produced a dream of an egg with a voice saying, "the mother and the daughter." Von Franz continues,

> I was as happy as could be and went off telling her all the creation myths and of how the world is reborn from a world egg. I said that this showed the germ of a new possibility of life and that all would come right, that we only had to wait until everything came out of the egg, etc. I talked myself into a terrific enthusiasm, saying that "the mother and the daughter" naturally referred to the Eleusinian mysteries, and I told her about this and of the rebirth of the feminine world where the new consciousness would be a feminine consciousness, and so on.[22]

In this lucky instance, the woman felt it was possible for someone to understand her, that what she produced was meaningful and worthwhile, that her madness was not simply "crazy," and that its destructiveness, ultimately, had profoundly creative reasons of its own. She was, in fact, involved in the creation of herself and her world.

In the above example, the patient was able to relax her constricting grip on reality and allow her inner world freer play. Jung also used this approach to wean a patient from too great an encapsulation in inner space. By speaking the patient's language, he could enter the patient's world and thus be trusted. He recounted an example from early in his career, before his major contributions were explicitly formulated.[23] A patient lived on the moon, threatened by a monster. As her relationship with Jung deepened, she told him more about her moon life. Finally, she dared to look at the demon's face and to fly off the moon in his power. When, too late, she realized her error and tried to get back, Jung could say, "All this won't do you any good; you cannot return to the moon!" Her tie to Jung blocked the way and demoted her to reality. In this instance, Jung's contact with the mythic depths created an ambience that permitted the patient to disclose and unravel her inner drama so that she could be "tricked" into reality. His mythic contact short-circuited her fantasy with-

22. Von Franz, *Creation Myths*, p. 12.
23. Jung, *Memories, Dreams and Reflections*, pp. 128–130.

drawal by presenting begrudging points of contact. In Von Franz's case, the direction of the journey was inward, in Jung's outward, but in both cases the point of contact was with what was most potentially meaningful to the patient (or analyst).

Jung noted that he did not want to be pinned down with regard to therapeutic methods. He felt it necessary to retain the freedom of using all means at his disposal. He switched back and forth between mythic amplification of inner and siding with outer reality. In his own personal life, he more and more came to see the link between the two.[24] For many therapists today, this kind of double perspective is taken for granted, a matter of common sense (clinical common sense is not the same since psychoanalysis).

Both Freud and Jung took megalomania as their key phenomenological entrée to the psychology of psychosis. It is most impressive to witness human beings who believe they are God or who see devils and still more shocking to discover and begin to come to grips with just how inflated one is in one's secret (or not so secret) self. Jung detailed the oscillations in psychosis between inflation and deflation, since megalomania and the severest self-depreciation always go together. It is tempting to draw parallels between the psychoanalytic image of psychosis and Western religious tradition. In the latter, a similar polarity was fundamental: for example, original sin—humility (including the self-abasement and sense of worthlessness of the saint vis-à-vis the great God); Jehovah the omnipotent—Jesus the self-sacrificing; and so on. It is easy for psychoanalysts to trace in the Bible the vicissitudes of an infantile or archetypal self.

Jung believed that the patient's godlike feelings could not be understood solely or mainly in terms of sexual drives or the infantile psyche. The sense of self or other as god (or demon) is too universal a mythic as well as a psychotic phenomenon to reflect only the individual's experience with his own mother or father. Rather, such states draw on an underlying collective substratum of psychic life, a kind of phylogenetic unconscious, in which age-old forms and structures play a role in organizing our experience today. For Jung,

24. Ibid., Chapter 4.

numinous experiences created a frame of reference outside the personal and potentially gave the latter a deeper meaning.

Thus, if the patient sees the therapist as god, it may be that the unconscious is "trying to *create* a god out of the person of the doctor, as it were to free a vision of God from the veils of the personal."[25] In discussing one case, for example, he spoke of gross overestimations of the physician as part of an "unconscious development of a trans-personal control-point; a virtual goal, as it were, that expressed itself symbolically in a form which can only be described as a vision of God," and "which allowed the psyche of the patient gradually to grow out of the pointless personal tie."[26] "Pointless personal tie" refers to the patient's transference bind with the person of the therapist as father–lover, the Freudian dimension.

As with God, so with mother. For example, images of the anima, an unconscious feminine aspect of the male usually lived out through projection, must not be taken merely as "a substitute figure for the mother. On the contrary, there is every likelihood that the numinous qualities which make the mother-imago so dangerously powerful derive from the collective archetype of the anima, which is incarnated anew in every male child."[27] The anima incorporates material from the real-life mother, but as a formative principle, it cannot be reduced to the latter.

Hallucinatory experience grows out of and opens up toward mysterious levels of psychic life, in which the mythic or religious dimension has a central value. If properly addressed (e.g., if an adequate context of meaning is supplied), hallucinatory events can prove to be a gateway to the transforming power of the numinosum. For Jung, hallucination provided an entrée to dialogue with the collective unconscious and the most pressing of all psychic concerns, the evolution of the self archetype. When all is said and done, for Jung hallucination reflected an irreducible inner reality with its own claims and reasons. In a broad sense, such irruptions aim to compensate and

25. Jung, *Two Essays on Analytical Psychology*, p. 133.
26. Ibid., pp. 134–135.
27. Jung, *Aion: Phenomenology of the Self*, p. 14.

expand (or destroy) an overly constricted personal or ego-consciousness attitude toward life.

PERRY

Perry explored parallels between sacral kingship and messianic
imagery of the Near East and the manifest content of hallucinations
and delusions of a certain subgroup of schizophrenics.[28] He found
ten motifs that run through the ancient imagery and hallucinatory
content of psychosis (images concerned with the center, death, return to beginning, cosmic conflict, threat of opposite, apotheosis,
sacred marriage, new birth, new society, and quadrated world). The
most profound organizing theme is that of renewal. The king (or,
later, messiah) is mythically sacrificed and reborn in a drama through
which the whole cosmos participates in regeneration. The modern
schizophrenic individual reaches for this buried heritage in a desperate need for rebirth.

The personal self of the individuals Perry described is severely
wounded. They grew up in a milieu that disallowed the possibility
of good self-feeling. Their ego-consciousness seemed to be entirely
polluted by a sense of worthlessness, inferiority, and self-depreca-
tion. Perry views the flood of kingship and messianic imagery
from the collective unconscious as compensating for a self-deni-
grating conscious attitude. The individual's sense of worthlessness
would either be destroyed or transformed by his new sense of glory.

Perry stressed that the compensations offered by the collective
unconscious occur in response to a particular historical setting and
that the emergence of kingship and messianic imagery played a role
in externalizing functions and values that eventually entered a long
process of internalization, one still at work today. The potential
vision the king and messiah expressed in the ancient city-states is of
the worth and power of all individuals. This sense of supreme worth
and power (godship) was at first concentrated in the one for the all,
but gradually spread to maximize the possible integrity of all human
beings. Perry argued that the modern schizophrenic goes through a

28. Perry, *The Far Side of Madness*, pp. 1–79.

similar process, one which begins with what appears to be acute hallucinatory externalizations, but may end with a profound recasting of inner value and a new sense of self. He wrote

> It is my thesis that the visionary states we call psychosis recapitulate this entire history, as another instance of ontogeny recapitulates phylogeny. The renewal process attempts to evolve a new level of consciousness in the individual, and to accomplish this, induces an identification first with the mythology of sacral kingship, then with that of messianic democratization, and finally reaches a vision of the potential spiritual consciousness for life in the world of society today.[29]

The paradoxical result, as Perry described it, is that what begins as a breakthrough of collective masculine imagery (king and messiah) emphasizing logos and power, ends by building a better capacity for intimacy and relationship (Eros). The schizophrenic individual is greatly helped by letting archetypal affect-images evolve. By so doing, he tunes into a deep level of feeling and meaning, which ultimately is transformed (via the work and model of the therapy relationship) into a capacity for empathic contact with self and other.

Although Perry emphasized the turn from an orientation of spiritual power to empathic relationship, his account remains centered in masculine imagery. In Jungian terms, Perry brought out an archetypal basis for the masculine imagery of psychosis, but neglected the feminine. That there is an archetypal journey of the feminine aspect of the self is suggested by Von Franz's case vignette given earlier. Von Franz's patient repaired to archetypal world creation and Eleusinian mystery imagery: the cosmic egg, the mother and the daughter. Von Franz described her patient as "a walking animus," a person in whom "complete destruction of her feminine personality had gone on for many years."[30] The threat of psychosis brought with it a compensating feminine imagery, presenting in near-catastrophic form precisely what the patient lacked and warded off. Schwartz-Salant amplified basic aspects of the archetypal feminine side of the psychic journey (via the Demeter-Persephone mythos) for the nar-

---

29. Perry, *Roots of Renewal*, p. 195.
30. Von Franz, *Creation Myths*, p. 12.

cissistic personality, with some hint of what one might expect in psychosis.[31]

Perry's phenomenology of Eros as a loving or feeling relationship orientation is too simple. It almost entirely ignores the association of Eros with destructive aggression, an association Freud and later writers were only too well aware of. By emphasizing the contrast between a masculine spiritual power and feminine love orientation, he underestimated the role of destructive hate on a body feeling level. The clinical and social dangers of this oversight are far-reaching.

To be sure, Perry's results are highly qualified. His population was one with a fairly good prognosis—young adults undergoing an acute psychotic episode, particularly individuals who could sustain work with intense and meaningful affects. One would expect this psychic elite to "get better" in the care of most sensitive, competent clinicians today. Perry emphasized the *quality* of improvement. He felt that it made a difference whether such individuals are helped to shut out or go through what is happening to them. In the latter instance, one has a chance to truly grow and begin a life based on being in touch with one's psychic depths.

MEGALOMANIA

Freud and Jung took megalomania seriously in a way not ordinarily done today. Most often, clinicians stress the reactive aspect of megalomania symptoms (grandiosity, omnipotence, etc.) and suggest that self–god confusions would not occur except in response to psychic injury and neglect. That is, megalomania is treated as something that would be foreign to the human condition if only there were good enough parenting or a good society. It is treated as something that would not exist in a perfect world.

For Freud and Jung, the vision of such a perfect state of affairs would not be an antidote to megalomania, but rather another expression of it. Both Freud and Jung took the tendency toward megalomania as a primitive given, part of our basic psychic equipment. It might take different forms and be put to varied uses, but it never could (or should?) be eradicated. For Freud, it was built into Eros

31. Schwartz-Salant, *Narcissism and Character Transformation*, pp. 133–169.

and Eros' first offshoot, Narcissus. Kohut has shown how this basic grandiosity has its own developmental arc.[32] If met with a proper empathic response, it can mature into a sense of vitality and help give life meaning (e.g., it may take the form of creative ambition and ideals). If things go seriously awry, as Freud indicated, the megalomanic ego can split itself off and harden into a relentless Pacman bent on devouring the rest of the psyche and, finally, itself as well.

Jung believed that megalomania was an inflated state resulting from the ego's identification with archetypes. He stressed the ego's dedication to everyday reality tasks and the inevitable narrowing it must undergo to direct action. As the ego evolves to facilitate survival, it omits much that is not immediately relevant to its principal aim. The need to survive and the desire for psychic wholeness may not always go together. According to Jung, the collective unconscious tries to compensate (fill out, amplify, enrich) the conscious ego's more narrow focus. Paradoxically, it may ultimately aid survival, insofar as the ego's self-constriction has destructive consequences. On the other hand, the ego may be too weak to sustain and work with the affect-images created by the collective unconscious. Or even as a normal phase in this work, it may identify with these images for a time, and so feel larger than life as long as such possession is dominant.

PROBLEMS WITH JUNG'S BASIC TERMS

It is my view that Jung had not fully worked out the implications of his position. For Jung, whether the collective unconscious was constructive or destructive depended, in large part, on whether the conscious ego was strong, healthy, or responsive enough to synthesize what the unconscious brought up. Jung emphasized the dimensions of strength and attitude on the part of the ego. The following quote from Perry puts the problem in terms of the ego's synthesizing ability:

> Souls sensitive to the pressures and movements of the collective psyche feel these impulses toward renewal, and make the mystical journey, often in consequence transforming the religious authority or cultural canon.

32. Kohut, *Analysis of the Self*, pp. 106–109, 188–196.

Others who are not so vigorous or resilient in their capacity for resynthesizing go through such a turmoil in this journey that they become "psychotic" [psychoticoid?] along the way, before they can make of it something creative. And then again, there are the less fortunate ones who need more help to resynthesize, and unless they receive it, are threatened with submersion in psychosis.[33]

It seems to me that too great a burden here is placed on the ego. It was Freud's principal point that much of the psychic development goes on unconsciously, and this included ego processes. If psychosis occurred, ill must have befallen unconscious *and* conscious processes. The very ground through which the ego emerges and must look to for support also undergoes deformation in psychosis. Jung's insight that deep unconscious processes appear destructive in response to an overly narrow conscious ego is an important truth. But the ego is restrictive, also, because of the warped foundation of which it is part. In other words, conscious and unconscious functions are part of the same psychic fabric, and in psychosis, deformations spread through both, reciprocally or in a vicious circle. To place the burden of blame (causality) on either consciousness or the deep unconscious is too simple.

To be sure, Jung also referred to the spontaneous contributions of the collective unconscious, when it produces affect-images on its own, unprovoked by consciousness. In such instances, it may initiate compensatory activities of consciousness. Most basically, for Jung, consciousness and the collective unconscious compensate each other, although, in most of his analyses, he emphasized the compensating responses of the latter. Jungians, also, may refer to a weakness of the archetypal self as well as ego-consciousness.[34] The suggestion here is that the self is too weak to tolerate what it produces. This is much closer to the idea that in a pervasive psychic illness, such as psychosis, one might expect the person to be ill from depth to surface and not simply the reverse (often the therapist's ally is precisely what remains well in the patient's surface ego, which usually has roots in

33. From *The Far Side of Madness* by John Weir Perry, MD., p. 94. © 1974 by Prentice-Hall, Inc., Englewood Cliffs, NJ 07632. Reprinted by permission of the publisher.
34. Sandner and Beebe, "Psychopathology and Analysis," pp. 294–334.

unconscious pockets of potential health). In this regard, Jung defined the archetypal self as the center of the psychic totality, and the ego as the center of consciousness. He showed how ruthless and uncaring the self is of the ego as it pursues its own path, often permitting the destruction of the psyche itself. One would think that if the self were a good enough guide, if it truly had the interests of the psychic whole at heart, it would take into account the ego's wayward resistance and find a way to incorporate or work with it in the larger journey; however, if the unconscious foundations of psychic life are themselves warped, ego fragments that manage to survive may resist them for good reason.

An oversimplification of polarities runs through Jung's thought. The basic polarities that structure his overall work are (1) the impersonal collective unconscious and Freud's personal unconscious and (2) both of these, but especially the collective unconscious, in contrast with ego-consciousness. In Jung's work, both Freud's personal unconscious and ego-consciousness tended to fall together as preeminently extroverted, concerned with objects of erotic desire (or hate), the personal mother and father, surface adaptation to reality and survival. The collective unconscious, in contrast, is concerned with the unfolding of an inner self, a search for wholeness, which includes all aspects of psychic life, a psychic totality. Jung did not deal adequately with Freud's assertion that most of the ego is unconscious yet unrepressed or that it functions in hallucinatory, adaptive, and truth-seeking modes. Also, the formation and operation of Freudian drives and ego is anything but "personal." In Freudian psychology, Eros and Ananke are implacable forces or powers, types of deity machines. Similarly, the subject's relationship to Jungian archetypes and the archetypes themselves may be anything but impersonal (viz., a personal God).

An adequate analysis of consciousness and the unconscious would show personal and impersonal aspects to mental actions at all levels of psychic life. The very fabric of psychic life is personal–impersonal through and through. Jung has abstractly torn apart a co-constitutive reciprocity and assigned one or the other of these terms to different psychic levels, when both characterize all levels with varying shifts of emphasis (which must be determined in each context). That

neither God nor the anima are simply or necessarily mainly impersonal does not mean that what is most personal about them derives
from our parents: what is personal about our experience of God may
shape what is personal in our experience with our parents or vice
versa. There is likely much in our experience of our parents that Jung
would call archetypal or impersonal and much in our experience of
"archetypes" that is personal.

My suspicion is that Jung first went off by making his primary
dichotomy the collective unconscious and the personal unconscious,
thus foreclosing the personal at the deepest levels of psychic life. In
fact, his psychology does not include an adequate concept that con-
veys the full sense of what personal might mean. That he could
misname Freud's unconscious *personal* is evidence of this, since
Freud's unconscious is a kind of machine. Similarly, the distinction
between communal (a mutually generative relationship) and collective (a predominantly fusional relationship) was not properly developed in his work. It is doubtful that either Freud or Jung had an
adequate psychology of the personal–communal dimension. That
Jung attributed to the latter a mainly surface function suggests a far-
reaching distortion that permeates his work.

A secondary issue involves the question of origins. The origin of
the ideal remains as much a mystery in Jung as in Freud. If Freud
slips in the capacity for ideal experiencing as an offshoot of Eros and
Narcissus, Jung calls it numinous and associates it with archetypes or
the ego's experience of archetypal affect-images. The problematic
nature of his position can readily be seen when one asks where
archetypes come from or questions in more detail his phenomenology of the self.

When we try to pin down where archetypes come from, we
quickly enter a chicken–egg dilemma. On the one hand, Jung tells us
they are collective patterns from time immemorial.[35] We also learn
that they are acts of creative imagination (often of single persons,
mystics, or geniuses) in response to particular historical crises (e.g., a
sacral kingship mythology within the centered town and city).[36]

35. Jung, "Psychological Analysis of Nietzsche's Zarathustra," Part I, pp. 22–28.
36. Perry, *Far Side of Madness*, pp. 37–52.

Archetypes are innate structures that grow out of everyday experience and, presumably, must still be evolving. Thus, we may expect new compensations from the collective unconscious in new historical situations, yet something will also be age old about them (in Perry's terms, the new Eros orientation he saw emerging might, in turn, provoke a further logos compensation). Archetypes may also be residues of dangerous experiences. For example, in his Nietzsche seminars Jung spoke of a "fear of going over a bridge" archetype dating from a time when bridges were untrustworthy.[37] In this case, the difference between archetypes and complexes begins to fade, as both proliferate (like instinct theory at the turn of the century) to cover general patterns in personal relationships.

We are left with the inevitable circle that human experience is both structured by and gives rise to archetypes. The beatific (or horrific) vision, the vision of God (or the devil), which in one form or another is so fundamental in structuring religion and psychosis, is the result of an innate propensity of the human psyche, the result of age-old experience, the result of . . . , etc. We are reduced to saying that the Jungian archetype is one possible myth of origin (as Freud's metapsychology is a myth of structure) and must be judged as myth: that is, by its capacity to provide or express the living meaning and order of experience. More accurately, Jung offered his concept of the collective unconscious as part of a reflection (a cognitive filter) on the mythic dimension and as a way of approaching the latter experientially (a kind of second- or third-order myth). In looking for a starting or culminating point we are, finally, in the realm of value, vision, and taste.

This is never so pointed as when dealing with the relationship of self to God (or the devil), the most fundamental or archetypal dramas in psychosis. For Jung, Jesus is a symbol of the archetypal self (the guiding center of the psychic totality), and at times God seems to be equivalent to the collective unconscious.[38] A mix-up between self and god seems to be an intrinsic part of Jungian psychology. Jung's epistemological disclaimer was that we can only

37. Jung, "Psychological Analysis of Nietzsche's Zarathustra," pp. 23–25.
38. Jung, *Aion: Phenomenology of the Self*, p. 22.

know the numinosum as our archetypes structure it. The self provides our principal images of God and acts as a medium through which God intersects with psychic life. Jung also called the self a God-image.[39] We move in a conceptual circle, a kind of mandala: God is symbol of self and self is symbol of God. God, in himself, like the collective unconscious, remains unknowable. We only know, or believe we know, manifestations of the latter (in a similar fashion, Freud's unconscious can only be guessed at or gotten to via "derivatives").

In practical terms, in psychosis (or psychotic-like moments), the ego is identified with the self, lost in the self, as it were. The ego no longer is distanced from the manifestations of the collective unconscious. For Jung, the task of therapy, in part, was to help the ego gain distance, to disidentify with the self, to play its role in assimilating the meaning of what it is possessed by and enter a truly complementary and cooperative relationship with the psyche as a whole. In effect, this means learning to take one's God and demons as manifestations of a collective archetypal reality, as self symbols, at least until the capacity for ego distance has been integrated. If this can happen, one may begin to participate in a deeper unfolding of the self, a profound individuation process, as the self moves toward wholeness. For Jung, God, as manifested in the human psyche (as self-image), also moves toward wholeness. It is God's task to integrate the devil as a split-off part of his own self (God, too, has been mad, blind, and infantile).[40] We are in a house of endless mirrors.

One could easily depict Jung's vision of the self, center of psychic totality, as a hallucinatory wish. He tapped an age-old wish for wholeness. We are here in the realm of an irreducible mystery. We are divided and wish for wholeness and feel whole through our divisions.[41] The "wholeness" feeling itself belongs, in part, to the realm of ideal reality. In modern dress, it is transposed to a sense of psychological perfection; in earlier times, spiritual perfection.

39. Ibid.
40. Jung, *Answer to Job*, pp. 355–470.
41. Eigen, "The Area of Faith in Winnicott, Lacan and Bion," pp. 425, 429–433.

The sense of wholeness changes color with its context. It can take perverse forms as when, for example, it attaches to a woman's shoe or urine and feces or to a Nazi swastika (a perverse use of a mandala, symbol of psychic wholeness in Jung's writings). The Ku Klux Klan has its perverse ecstasies through the Cross as Death symbol. The devil, too, has his sense of wholeness. Indeed, the promise of certain kinds of wholeness is his greatest lure, although the very name, *diabolic*, means to tear apart (the devil's black irony).

Jung's vision of wholeness moves from an un- or predifferentiated phrase, through divisions, to an integration of divisions, the wholeness achieved through individuation. It stresses personal responsibility for working with the just claims of diverse psychic realities, an attitude of respect by consciousness for unconscious movements. The ego and self have their differences, but, finally, must learn to be partners. Hallucination must be turned into meaningful vision. Jung could be charged with a kind of psychological utopianism. Utopian visions have always inspired the capacity for limitless labor. It is precisely the link between vision and its lack that makes the most of both. When the fire dies down, we are still left with the question of quality. The stress on wholeness or the union of opposites does not in itself say what tone, texture, or inflection dominates the psychic totality. For example, I have suggested that Jung's misuse of the terms *personal* and *collective* reflects a serious defect in the basic makeup, style, and taste of his version of self, notwithstanding the seminal importance of his portrayals. A hairsbreadth turn takes us on very different journeys, whether through the wholeness of innocence or sophistication (division). Jung opened crucial vistas but the remaining questions are not answered.

Bion: Hallucination and Meaninglessness

Bion's work on hallucination is too complex to trace in all its ramifications here, but we can follow it in broad strokes with enough supporting details to make sense of the problems with which it is struggling. He raised the possibility that hallucinations are not primarily camouflaged messages about states of the self or the self's relation to reality, but rather attempts to cancel both self and reality entirely. They are offered as semblances of meaning, decoys, or bait behind which the self disappears or by which it is swallowed. The other (or self) may be sent on a spiraling search for meaning, in an attempt to make sense of hallucinatory content, and never become aware that the sense it finds is only a mirage, basically empty and without value. Everyday life is filled with empty words and gestures that, Bion would argue, function more in a hallucinatory fashion than we realize.

One way hallucinatory activity voids the possibility of meaning is by transforming life into death. According to Bion, the psychotic personality (or aspect of self) cannot tolerate a sense of aliveness or the complexities of living. It hates, envies, and attacks the sense of aliveness (whether in itself or another) because of the pain it must bring. Any living feeling can make us suffer (viz., we "suffer" joy as well as pain). To be alive is to be vulnerable, not only to others, but also to the ways our own nature can throw us off balance. Our own personalities provide endless and unfathomable difficulties.

From this point of view, hallucinatory activity is meant to destroy the possibility of contact with self or other. Bion notes that, in this regard, psychosis is anti-animism:

> Accordingly we hear of inanimate objects, and even places, when we would normally expect to hear of people. These, though described verbally, are felt by the patient to be present materially and not merely to be represented by their names. This state contrasts with animism in that live objects are endowed with the qualities of death.[42]

Bion also approached this "deathification" process by describing the attacks the self makes on links between thoughts, between thoughts and feelings, or among thoughts, feelings, and action. The attacks on linking processes ensure the collapse of meaning. The attitude here is one of anti-learning and anti-contact. For example,

42. Bion, *Learning from Experience*, p. 9.

Bion speaks of a −K (anti-knowing) attitude, in which one is set against discovering the truth about oneself. Instead of learning from experience (which requires experiencing or suffering experience), mental life becomes a kind of −K space, "the place where space used to be. It is filled with no-objects which are violently and enviously greedy of any and every quality, thing, or object for its 'possession' (so to speak) of existence."[43] A pantheon of beingless demons, corrupt vacuums, is substituted for the interplay between plenitude and its lack.

What is described is a state of mind (or anti-mind) that continuously converts being into nonexistence. "Possession" is in quotation marks because life cannot be possessed, only lived. Where life is concerned, one always meets with uncontrollable elements. The psychotic individual attempts a process of simplification in order to control everything, namely, by deanimating the possibility of experiencing and reducing all to the same deadness. Thus, any appearance of life in hallucinatory creations is indeed hallucinatory, a grim charade. For what prevails in the depths of these seeming sparks or efflorences is a monotonic blankness, a slippage to zero, a mad (hallucinatory) safety point.

Bion speaks of an original indistinguishability of psychic and material aspects of reality. In psychosis, the psychic and material split off from one another in such a way that psychic aliveness is lost. Insofar as the psychotic self maintains an attachment to objects, it does so as if the latter were material. Thus, it is able to obtain needed gratification "without acknowledging the existence of a live object on which these benefits depend."[44] Here the psychoanalytic habit of calling the other an object can be a bit misleading, for it is the living self of a subject that deanimating fear–hate aims at.

More pointedly, the psychotic self treats others as if they were its creations. As Bion writes,

> The general picture the patient presents is that of a person anxious to demonstrate his independence of anything other than his own creations.

43. Bion, *Transformations*, p. 115.
44. Bion, *Learning from Experience*, p. 10.

These creations are the results of his supposed ability to use his senses as organs of evacuation which are able to surround him with a universe that has been generated by himself: the function of the senses and their mental counterpart is to create the patient's perfect world. Evidence of imperfection is *ipso facto* evidence for the intervention of hostile envious forces. Thanks to the patient's capacity for satisfying all his needs from his own creations he is entirely independent of anyone or anything other than his products and therefore is beyond rivalry, envy, greed, meanness, love or hate; but the evidence of his senses belies his pre-determinations; he is *not* satisfied.[45]

For Bion, like Freud, hallucination functions so as to rid the subject of any sense of dissatisfaction. The psyche is aimed against irritants. This is a negative statement. Its positive form is that the subject desires a perfect state and hallucination is a way to achieve this ideal. It attempts this by obliterating differences. The difference between self and other is bypassed by making all self. The tension between memory and perception is destroyed by turning the former into the latter (or a hallucinatory version of the latter). The invariant through such hallucinatory action is the transformation of dissatisfaction into satisfaction by a magical mental gesture, a fiat.

Bion took the psychology of hallucination a step further than Freud when he sought to determine what happens to the psychotic individual when "hallucination is abandoned in consequence of the absence of expected gratification." Freud called attention to the education to reality that results when hallucination fails as a source of satisfaction. Bion noted that this is what can happen insofar as frustration is represented as such and somehow faced. However, the psychotic individual can or will not give in to representing an unsatisfactory state of affairs for what it is. It is here that hallucination ceases to become a representation of pleasure and becomes simply nonrepresentation. The individual is thrown into a desperate war between meaning and meaninglessness.

In the narcissistic moment, the individual hallucinates a perfect existence, his own creation. At this point, hallucination offers the

45. Bion, *Transformations*, p. 137.

subject a kind of meaning and consolation. Life is meaningful, sublimely and perfectly so. If necessary, gods will be created and invested with perfection so that the hallucinatory mode of satisfaction goes on without interruption. At bottom, of course, the gods are narcissistic excretia functioning as nectar. The shock of imperfection or the persistence of disturbance threatens to shatter the individual's hallucinatory regulation of existence, his self-imposed universe of meaning. This would plunge the psychotic individual into an experience of utter meaninglessness, since the hallucinatory mode of meaningfulness is all that he can bear. If he could sustain and represent his potential encounter with meaninglessness, he would be on the road to realistic living, as described by Freud. This is precisely what he cannot do. At this point, he must convert even meaninglessness into a hallucinatory achievement.[46]

Psychosis turns meaninglessness into hallucination by treating the former as a thing-in-itself rather than by representing it. For example, instead of representing mother's absence and in time learning to come to grips with the difficulties and opportunities it affords, the individual may predominantly and chronically treat the space (nothing) of loss as a persecutory thing, as no space at all, but as something filled in with malevolence. In this instance, hallucinatory activity avoids the potential loss of meaning by attacking meaning, thus bringing the dreaded meaninglessness under control and, indeed, turning it into another type of satisfaction, often more powerful than genuine gratification or even hallucinatory perfection. Hallucinatory meaninglessness is discovered to be a more effective way of eliminating disturbance than the risk of hallucinatory gratification, which can end (and so become meaningless). The psychotic self becomes a specialist in an instantaneous shift of key, a reversal, whereby all potential meaning (which may involve disappointment) is automatically short-circuited and turned into its opposite, a meaningless thing (no further fall possible).

---

46. Bion notes that the artist and the therapist also grapple with meaninglessness but sustain the impact of experience persistently enough to allow hallucination-like gestalts to evolve (e.g., *Transformations*, pp. 114–115).

Bliss itself can become meaningless. A psychotic individual may manage to hold on to hallucinated bliss through thick and thin and seal himself within it for long periods of time. At some point, in an effective therapy, hallucinatory perfection may begin to feel cloying. Individuals may brag or complain that they feel too good for too long a time. This is in contrast with the same or other patients who continuously harp on how terrible they feel and the miseries of living. One person who was very intent on working through his psychosis said, "I'm sick of feeling happy. I'm missing out. I'm not really feeling *me*." In this instance, bliss had become a monotonous enemy, a meaningless blurring of experiential nuances. The first years of his psychosis had been intensely painful, and the ensuing blissful phase (also years) a cherished relief. It was a testimony to his faith in life that he could wish to risk his "gains" for something more open-ended.

Bion's work dealt with the radical interplay of the torment, bliss, and meaninglessness of psychosis. He developed a profound phenomenology of the conversion of life into death. At the same time, hallucinations often heighten conflicts, and they themselves may be heightened forms of experience. Is the deadening process Bion portrayed the other side of psychotic sensitivity? Bion's own work suggested this. He counsels us (with Jung) that the inner world the psychotic stumbles into and tries to obliterate is quite real, so horrifyingly real that all his efforts are bent on hiding its reality from himself. We will study forms of mindlessness in Chapter 3. Here we only raise the question of what is left to the individual when hallucination fails (as it must) to reduce pain to bliss or to meaninglessness. Bion spoke of psychotic "nameless dread," the very edge of the psychically possible, before a mute obliteration of all psychic possibilities sets in.

Object Relations and Hallucination

What we call hallucination has always opened up for humankind a world of mysterious "objects," which are actually "subjects." Hallu-

cinatory objects often appear as numinous presences that exert force
and insert the one who undergoes them into compelling kinds of
relationships. The typical hallucinatory presence carries power and
frequently incorporates erotic and religious elements, together with
whatever national, social, or personal concern is at issue. It is thus no
accident that the foundational background texts of our universe of
meaning, the Bible and Homer, are preeminently concerned with
power, eros, and the gods. The questions we must ask of such
phenomena are What kind of power? What kind of god? What
quality relationship? What quality self?

A medieval text gives an account of a woman suffering from a
severe delirium that included wild fits.[47] She had gone berserk, a
phenomenon known even among animals. In the medieval context,
her madness occurred in an atmosphere of religious imagery. She saw
fiends and devils everywhere, and her hysterical thrashing and
screaming went on for over a year. She was frequently confined and
bound. One day while alone she saw (hallucinated?) a man who
appeared to be Jesus. He conveyed an ineffable goodness that formed
the basis of a conversion. In time she became a nun capable of
translating her illumination into practical achievement.

In instances such as the above, mad episodes seem to be part of a
religious journey that involves a basic reordering of the self. They
throw the individual into a kind of rock bottom reality, a totality of
suffering and relief that proves definitive. The psychic dramas are
enacted in an object-relational context. Western religion is structured
in object-relational terms. In the Judaeo-Christian tradition, what is
most pressing is our personal relationship to a mysterious other, who
is also the ground of our very I-feeling.

Clinical psychiatry tries to find secular ways of dealing with the
demonic. However, like religion, some notion of personal relationship is a primary concern. Thus, Janet[48] could deal with a man who
believed himself to be possessed by a devil by striking up a conversa-

47. "The Book of Margery Kempe." In *Medieval English Prose and Verse*, eds. and
comps. R. S. Loomis and R. Willard (New York: Appleton-Century-Crofts,
1948), pp. 405–421.
48. Janet, *Un Cas de Possession et l'Exorcisme Moderne*, as discussed in McCurdy, *The
Personal World*, pp. 222–230.

tion with the devil to see what it wanted. In time, it came out that the man began to see devils after a lapse into infidelity on a business trip away from his wife. He could not deal with his errant behavior or guilt. The devil was placed in the context of a personal (clinical) history and soon disappeared or, at least, became more manageable.

Freud formalized the radical importance of personal relationships and made them an object of systematic study. He traced the wounding aspects of relationships in the formation of mental illness. The psychoanalytic relationship makes its own formation and evolution a theme for explicit study. It constitutes a breakthrough in the concept of human relationships. From moment to moment we can experience and watch our story repeat and reform itself in relationship to another person whose primary function is to sustain our search.

In psychoanalysis, we learn that devils do not disappear so easily. They are ever-active as driving undercurrents and organizing structures. Id, ego, and superego may function as demons. Freud, like St. Paul, emphasizes how thoroughly we are stamped by our distortions. This, of course, is a theme of religion, philosophy, folklore, and literature. Psychoanalysis has its own particular way of engaging devils. The psychoanalytic attitude is one of open attention. The patient talks himself out while the analyst listens, interprets, or otherwise intervenes—a division of labor. Together they form a more whole personality, doubles of each other. As a result of this illusion, each may grow.

Psychoanalysis is a way of approaching how we are formed by our deeper wishes, our environment, and the ways we relate to these factors. At times, psychoanalysis becomes more real than life. At times, it is a nightmare. For some individuals, this may continue to be so for many years. Others may dip in and out of it at will, or as occasion dictates. Some may make use of it in well-dosed fashion without too many scars. Some simply do well with it and benefit easily. One ought not to underestimate the powers it tampers with and tries to influence. Biblical references to the destructive aspect of seeing or touching God (and his objects) are not lost (or ought not to be) on the modern clinician. Freud sought a way to handle God and the devil impartially, a way to approach these powers through a new conducting medium. Psychoanalysis is a kind of electric shock with open eyes, designed to benefit the one who goes through it, but not without unforeseen consequences.

The difference between nightmare and reality that disappears in the psychoanalysis of psychosis is part and parcel of our present age. Perhaps it was always so, but we are more acutely conscious of it now. The bloodbaths that characterize this century were foreshadowed in Jung's dreams and visions that preceded the First World War.[49] Alice Miller[50] has assembled documents that convincingly show how the physical and psychological cruelty of our childhood becomes the nightmare reality of adult existence. One of her case examples is Hitler, whose blighted childhood was objectified on the world stage. The hallucinatory quality of the holocaust is no mere attempt at defensive self-insulation, but suggests that such events grow from the same hidden realities as dreams. Freud warned us that dreaming is best confined to sleeping, when the body is out of play. The madness of violence is proof, if needed, of how dangerous it is to be in the grips of the dreaming process while awake. The latter may be a blessing when the dreamer is creative, but what untold horrors are daily unleashed in a waking trance. The spiritual adage that we are all sleepwalkers most of the time touches on a gruesome fact about our nature we try to make light of.

Robert Fliess[51] explicitly related the psychological horrors of subtle and gross child abuse to psychosis and dreamlike states. The psychotic behavior of parents has a dreamlike reality for many reasons. It is governed by the forgotten depths of their own childhood and evokes a sense of unbelief that such madness could really occur. At the same time, the abusive parent feels a sense of righteousness, which draws on his own history of accumulated humiliations and his belief that it is his right or even his duty to "correct" his child. The nightmare madness that stains a childhood is often the only or most powerful reality a growing mind has to hold on to. In order to survive, the child finds himself in a position in which he

49. Jung, *Memories, Dreams and Reflections*, pp. 175–176.
50. Miller, *For Your Own Good*, pp. 142–197.
51. Fliess, *Symbol, Dream and Psychosis*, pp. 243–261.

must wipe out the sense and remembrance of what is most real to him. He must hallucinate that the hallucinatory events that happened did not really happen, a blanking-out process Fliess calls "hypnotic evasion" (which we will study further in Chapter 3). The victim lives in a post-hypnotic trance; he is not allowed to recall what happened to him or to assign blame. In such a state of mind, anything can happen, for one remains vulnerable to appeals of voided roots, both good and evil.

There is thus good reason why Freud wavered between attributing psychopathology to actual parental behavior or to innate infantile wishes. The aggression perpetrated on the young in the name of upbringing is often tinged with or masks madness. Both parent and child live out this madness in a trancelike state akin to dreaming. In practical terms, the difference between dream (or wish) and reality, which Freud so tried to uphold, vanishes. In the madness Miller called "poisonous pedagogy," dream and reality are one. The invisible rape of infantile souls goes on daily, and, in some highly qualified sense, may be inevitable. We do not yet know whether or not it is possible to escape some degree of what Schreber called "soul murder" (cf. Chapter 7).

As we now know, Freud's seduction theory was right. Parents and children seduce and violate one another and do so as a matter of course. Most of the time this may not take the form of explicit sexual abuse (although the latter is more common than was once believed), but there seems to be no way we can escape all forms of seductive violence in our psychological upbringing. Nor do we know what kinds of beings we would be if we could. We can emphatically add that Freud's wish theory is right, too, in the sense that it points to the dream or hallucinatory plane of being that psychotic violence moves in and thrives on. The sense of rightness that characterizes the political or individual killer is never far from madness *and* the hard facts of life. In human life, madness and reality are so interwoven that each appears to constitute the other reciprocally.

By focusing on reality-testing as a central human problem, Freud drew attention to the radical symbiosis and enmity between hallucination and perception linked with common sense and judgment. He asked how hallucinatory beings become anti-hallucinogenic. He developed this theme abstractly in his theoretical writings. But in the analytic situation, it is part and parcel of immediate dialogical inquiry, an unfolding drama. The analytic situation itself is a quasi-hallucinatory ritual, two beings invited to explore a trancelike state together. Freud's great written cases raised the art of clinical narrative to a high form of biography precisely because of the wedding of delirium and analysis of delirium they achieve. The meaning of "object" (whether thing, function, or person) is always passed through the two filters of delirium and analysis, with these two finely interwoven. We recall that Freud believed he traced these strands to a point where they became indistinguishable, a point of origin that remains active throughout life.

Different Phenomenological Commitments and Psychological Invariants

The theoretical approaches toward hallucination outlined here present very different pictures of the meaning and value of hallucinatory states. For Freud, hallucination is a fundamental and compelling psychic operation, a kind of first-level cognition (or non-cognition), which aims at and is wish fulfillment. It is omnipresent in dreams and psychosis and works in hidden ways throughout mental life in what may be called man's propensity for unreality. Its most basic aim is to undo the possibility of pain and create ideal bliss. Man's striving for reality is placed against an overarching horizon of illusion. A great Freudian gambit was to define man as a hallucinatory animal, and to understand illusion, in its most basic terms, as madness. At the same time, hallucination contains relics of a history and messages of a wounded self and its relation to objects. It is even a way of holding onto objects now magnified into carriers of ultimate bliss or terror. Hallucination is a way of maximizing aspects of reality, as it wipes the latter out.

Jung found, in what Freud called hallucination, expressions of profound mythic structures that were the subsoil of meaning for man since antiquity. Freud would not disagree with this. However, his principal interest was in using mythic material to hint about the repressed instinctual unconscious. For Jung, the unconscious self was as concerned with spirit as instinct and neither was reducible to the other. Freud's principal fear was that his emphasis on the hidden ways instinct plays in spirit would be lost. Freud was intent on reserving a special place for the repressed unconscious as a spur and irritant in psychic life, from which no vision of wholeness can free itself.

Both Jung and Freud were personally involved in their encounter with the unconscious. Jung hoped to know his myth that he might live it better. Freud seemed to prefer to be free of collective myth ("where id is, ego will be"), while admitting that this probably was not possible. He seemed to be ready to settle for the hope that our awareness of our predicament might make a difference. His tone suggests that our roots are shackled by something that may forever entrap us. Yet he often advised living in accord with one's deepest instincts. He portrayed a situation in which we are in harmony yet in conflict with our foundations. His discovery of Narcissus and Oedipus in his life and the lives of others bore witness to his emphasis on the universal. He reworked this mythic and dramatic material in his own way, creating a kind of personal mythos, putting ego where id is.

Jung's dramatis personae (animus, anima, shadow, wise old man and woman archetypes, etc.) also constituted a colorful and expressive personal mythos (with no less objective reality for being personal). His emphasis was on wholeness, not compromise. Jung kept an eye on reality and the importance of disengaging ego from archetype. But when all is said and done, he invested archetypal reality (the evolution of the self) with a saving, religious significance. Freud, too, ultimately hoped that balancing the forces in the unconscious (eros over death) would save the day. But it would be a victory without religious significance, one in which Eros and science united. For Freud, religion was fundamentally hallucinatory, an opiate and error (madness). The overall tone of Jung's work valued religious experience positively. For Jung, not only was the religious unconscious fundamentally positive, it was also the ultimate psychic reality. For both Freud and Jung the so-called hallucinatory domain was the birthplace of meaning. However, for Jung, in contrast with Freud, it was not simply the link between science and Eros (knowledge and love) that saves. In his vision, science, too, had its roots in archetypal reality. There is a hidden unity between science and the deep unconscious. Science is also part of the evolution of the archetypal self and an expression of a collective mythos that goes beyond it.

Bion took us to the other side of madness, its *loss* of mind and meaning. Throughout the ages, madness has been seen as the gateway to a deeper wisdom, as demonic, but also as spinning into chaos or nothingness, into nowhere, gibberish, and nonsense: a disintegration. Hallucinations may not simply express distorted messages about the self and others, coded pleas for help or clues to an aborted inner journey, but they may also be mis- or anti-communications. Their aim may be to ward off the possibility of genuine communication of any sort, a smoke screen to throw self and others off the scent. A major difference between the ordinary view of hallucinations as basically meaningless (e.g., mere by-products of physical processes) and Bion's, is that Bion viewed the meaninglessness of such dramatic productions as intentional. Often the intention is malevolent, an intentionality that destroys all intentionality. The subject attacks mental links that tie him to himself and others. Or, again, the pain of living may be so great that the mind dismantles itself in face of the unbearable (we will take this up in Chapter 3). The subject here courts the zero point of meaning in order to undercut the possibility of being (Freud's Nirvana principle in a new key, an entropy model of meaning).

Hallucination is thus seen as a heightening and an emptying out, an attack and satisfaction, a purveyor and an underminer of truth on many levels. It might almost seem that whatever polar positions that might be taken are taken. In the above instances, each position has a ring of truth and seems to convey something about the ways hallucinations can function.

Nevertheless, it is possible to discern the basic invariants around which all positions rotate or toward which all positions are oriented. For example, the views of hallucination sketched above rotate around certain basic dimensions, so that bringing together opposite positions circumscribes their concerns. They are all involved with problems concerning self–other, in–out, psychic reality, meaning–meaninglessness and mind–body. They are thus united by common objects, although it may also be argued that the concept (and reality) of the object differs for each. All the authors studied take up hallucination as a fundamental mode of being (or non-being).

In this chapter I took up Bion's work with hallucination that focuses on his undoing of meaning, its function as a place where mental life disappears. More will be said in Chapter 3 of the relationship between hallucination and mindlessness. We will see how Bion treats hallucination as a prerequisite to, yet antithesis of, thinking, a kind of primitive sea from which meaning arises and to which it returns. Another image might be a spring with a vanishing source, with hallucination flowing toward thinking or the null dimension. For Freud, Bion, and Jung, hallucinations can play a role in germinating or destroying psychic life. They are part of a broad and deep imaginative capacity that helps make human life possible (the latter always includes the nullifying possibility). Perhaps the most basic invariant that unites these three is that for each the hallucinatory mode of being is constitutive for human life. It is no mere secondary offshoot of wounding (although it may also function this way) or epiphenomenon of physical processes, but rather a primary, determinative category of the human psyche. Like any human capacity, it acts in diverse ways.

Each author has his own phenomenological commitments. A critical task would be to study their assumptive grounds (more than we have here) in order to distill and refine their truths. However, enough has been said to appreciate what these workers tried to accomplish. Their emphasis on the hallucinatory mode of being as constitutive of the self in both positive and negative ways sets them apart from most clinicians who work with psychosis today.[52]

52. The usual tendency among therapists has been to judge hallucinatory material in terms of common-sense reality considerations and to try to get rid of the former as

Phenomenology and Evasion

Phenomenology is a loosely used term that can mean just about anything. For Husserl, the father of post-Kantian phenomenology, it meant the study of those structures that make consciousness possible. For classical gestaltists, it meant the study of everyday experience (loosely overlapping with Husserl's *Lebensweldt*). Both used the slogan "Back to the things themselves," although their analyses of experience took very different turns. In time, many writers used the term to refer simply to describing experience as it presents itself, at whatever level and however fragmentary the discourse.

Psychoanalysts have used the term to refer to the descriptive level of study, which is assumed to be a first-level approach to a subject. First one gives the "what" (phenomenology), then the "how" (psychodynamics), and, finally, the deeper and more ultimate "why" (etiology, causality, historical roots). Psychoanalysis worth its name aims at the "why," although by means of the "what" and the "how." Often, a depth psychological study is called non- or even anti-psychoanalytic because it is merely phenomenological. To be sure, analysts emphasize the interactive nature of these levels and note that the historical/causal assumes the psychodynamic and phenomenological (in clinical terms, work proceeds from more superficial to deeper areas, analysis of defense before drives). But the divisions themselves are granted a dubious validity and power.

When "what," "how," and "why" are closely examined, at least for psychological realities, their differences tend to collapse. An examination of "what" takes us deeply into "how" and "why" and

---

quickly as possible. The compensatory aspects of hallucinations are stressed. Hospitalized psychotic patients who get better are often aware of trying to control their crazy thoughts so as not to create a disturbance. They are helped in their efforts by medication but remain deeply afraid of themselves. The opposite approach is to view hallucinations uncritically as part of a self-building activity. A firm grasp of Freud, Jung, and Bion helps one thread a course between these extremes: hallucinations may reflect primordial creative, compensatory, and nullifying activities. A growing sophistication concerning the multiple functions of hallucinations characterizes the approach of many clinicians.

beyond these terms. We are very far from knowing what "what" is. Descriptions are interpretative approaches open to further shifts of meaning. They create possibilities of vision and are as inexhaustible as the capacity to experience anew. The psychoanalytic insistence that it gets to the "how" and "why" beneath the "what" is not only facile, but also an injustice to psychoanalysis itself. It gives the impression of dealing with known or fixed entities when, as a clinical method, it exists at the interface of shifting realities. A thorough exploration of the resources of psychoanalytic epistemology is beyond our purpose. For now it is enough to suggest that the false clarity uncritically embraced by many psychoanalysts tends to ward off a farther-reaching exploration of the meaning and function of the phenomenological dimension in psychoanalytic theory and practice.[53] It is hard to avoid thinking that the psychoanalytic insistence on the division between phenomenology and causal explanation, when psychic reality is concerned, is more a political declaration or wish than an actuality.

The general notion that phenomenology is a first or superficial approach to a subject has militated against taking hallucinatory productions as important in their own right. Since hallucinations are explained by "something else," one need not take their impact and claims very seriously. One of the most common ways to avoid the challenge hallucinatory experience raises is to view it as an unfortunate by-product or desperate result of an injured sense of self. If the wounded self is helped, the need to hallucinate will diminish and disappear of its own accord, or be confined to more normal functions like dreaming or loving or creative work.

There is no question that this is a great advance over the pre-psychoanalytic and still extant view that hallucinations are meaningless by-products of physical processes. To be sure, the "physical basis" viewpoint makes its valid contributions (many think it will

53. For example, I believe Frosch's tendency to jump prematurely from the "what" to the "why" mars the valuable explorations of psychotic processes he undertakes. His understanding is guided by the assumption that the ego is ultimately a body ego (Frosch, *Psychotic Process*, pp. 16–19), an issue I discuss in the present chapter and more thoroughly in Chapter 4.

turn out to be the key to mental illness). And many of its adherents would no longer think psychotic productions simply meaningless, but would see in them the outlines of psychic wounds or the failed pain of an individual not genetically equipped to handle the stress he encountered. The usual balanced view is that both situational and genetic factors are at work in mental breakdown.

An irony is that whether a practitioner favors "the wounded self" or "physical basis" hypothesis (or some combination), he can now, more or less successfully, treat a psychosis without ever having to know what any of the patient's hallucinations might mean. He may not even need to address hallucinatory productions in any of their specifics. Students are often taught to ignore hallucinatory content or at least not get bogged down by it. What is stressed is the therapeutic relationship, and if that develops well enough, the hallucinations will take care of themselves. For a time it became popular to treat hallucinations (and most dreams) as forms of resistance in the therapy relationship, emphasizing their defensive quality, a view still widespread. One need not even refer to the specifics of hallucinatory content in order to call attention to their overall function at any given moment. Function (whether defensive or reparative) is emphasized over content, as if the two are somehow independent of each other. A still cruder example of the tendency to downplay the significance of hallucinatory content, widespread in institutional, school, and day centers, is the well-nigh total ignoring of content in favor of techniques meant to wean patients away from pronounced dependency behavior.

To some extent, function was emphasized to correct an abuse of content, for example, endlessly interpreting content without taking into account the context in which it occurred. A more proper psychoanalytic stance is to treat hallucinations like any other "associative material" produced in a session, as complex compromise formations embedded in evolving transference–countertransference issues. Splinter groups veered toward one or another of the possible emphases to which this formulation can lend itself (emphasis on content, resistance, adaptation, etc.).

Special mention must be made of Kohut and his followers. Many

students of the self have reacted against a "defense–resistance" orientation and emphasize deficiencies (largely from environmental failures) in the early formation of the self. The work of forming a self
may suffer developmental arrest to such an extent that there is no
sense of cohesion, vitality, or affective tone.

From this viewpoint, hallucinations are messages that the self is
disabled, crumbling, and trying to hold itself together whatever way
it can. Hallucinations may function as a last way stop before the
abyss. In Kohut's *Analysis of the Self*, "the abyss" is a regression to
Freud's autoerotic phase of development, before the consolidation of
the narcissistic ego (which unifies diverse autoerotic currents).
Kohut states that insofar as psychosis is located in the phase of
autoerotic fragmentation, it cannot be treated psychoanalytically.
Not enough self exists to make treatment possible.

One of the oddities about his stance is that the primary material of
his developmental and clinical theory is what Freud called the "first
fact" about psychosis: megalomania or, in Kohut's terminology,
"grandiosity." Freud advanced his theory of narcissism (the ego's
basic self-cathexis, self-idolatry, grandiosity, cohesion) to account
for psychosis (Chapter 1 and earlier in this chapter). Freud's depiction of a primary narcissism is meant to handle, within a psychoanalytic framework, what Jung was to describe as the ego's self-inflation
because of enslavement by or identification with archetypes. Kohut's
starting point also is grandiosity, although he distinguishes a narcissistic from a psychotic personality.

Kohut emphasizes the evolution of ideal-feelings via the dual track
of grandiosity (self-idolization) and idealization, both of which ultimately function to uphold the integrity, coherence, and vitality of
the self. The nonpsychotic but still fragile self will form transferences
that express its developmental deficits and vulnerabilities. With
proper therapeutic responsiveness, grandiosity and idealization will
take more healthy turns, such as creative ambition and inspiration.

We will say more about the main forms of narcissistic transference
(mirror and idealizing transferences) and Kohut's concept of the
selfobject in Chapter 4. Here we only call attention to the hallucinatory dimension inherent in these transferences. In the mirror trans-

ference, the analyst is treated as support and nutriment for the patient's god–self; in the idealizing transference, the patient grows through abjectly idealizing the therapist and participating in his godlike glory. The same basic polarity Jung described in his work with schizophrenics, the swing from self as god to worm, provides the core material of therapeutic work. One can see in this sado-masochism (Freud), inferiority–superiority or power complexes (Adler), top dog–little dog (Perls), and so on. However, all of these are made more forceful by drawing on an underlying sense of divinity or diabolism. They participate in an ideal reality that, for better or worse, infinitizes experience. The patient acts as if he were, or wishes he were, or fears he might be God. Freud's narcissistic ego? Jung's archetypal self? Both and more?

Therapists easily have extended self theory beyond the clinical limits Kohut marked out since, as suggested above, Kohut studied forms of what Freud and Jung ultimately took to be manifestations of madness (the megalomanic self). In such a therapy, the positive value of hallucinations may be emphasized, inasmuch as they are able to provide a sense of coherence and vitality in a bleak and crippled existence. A therapist may or may not interpret content as seems appropriate. What might determine this is the therapist's empathic sense of how a hallucination (like any production of the patient) is functioning in the context of constituting or consolidating the self.

To an important extent, the direction and quality of therapy must be affected by whatever the therapist means by "self" (or his idea of a person, what "personhood" is). What we think and say about self is no mere superstructure, but part and parcel of who we are and who we may become. Therapists identify with different meanings and qualities of self, as expressed in varied languages and methods, and so embody different destinies. At this point, we can only guess about the different ways we affect each other, the variety of ways the self can act as a medium for the personal growth of another. We must trust that in therapy, as in life in general, these differences are truly profitable.

My use of *phenomenology* is informal and hybrid. It aims at bringing out aspects of psychological events that may evoke a more profound awareness of psychic reality. My hope, of course, is to get at the heart of a matter. This often means tugging at or teasing the periphery. The results may not be new, but it is hoped that some fresh awareness of significance or possibility emerges. My goal is less "explanation" than appreciation and the growth personal encounter brings.

The World of Hallucinatory Imagery:
The Extravagance of Hallucinations

Hallucination is a particular form image-making can take. It is part of the more general capacity to "see" and "hear" what is not sensuously present. When this capacity works properly, it brings a freedom from literalness that gives rise to the great achievements of culture. In psychosis, the image-making capacity runs amok. Images that might function symbolically are taken literally. Symbols become inspirited beings, yet without entirely losing their value as symbols. Often they express momentous dramas in which the life and death of the self or cosmos appear to be at stake. For the mystic, similar dramas ultimately are linked to a hard-won freedom, whereas the psychotic is chained by his images and held fast.

Hallucinations tend to make the abstract concrete and vice versa. This reflects the ambiguous position of image in Western epistemology, generally. Image has been assigned an inferior function, somewhere between sensation and thinking. On the one hand, images are the "dregs of sensation," carriers of information about sensations, on the way to the summation of sensations into concepts. If, on the other hand, it is realized that sensations cannot account for the formation of concepts, imagery may be granted the function of illustrating autonomous and immaterial concepts in sensuous terms. In a still more ancient antinomy, images were gods or messengers of gods versus sensuous misrepresentations of the unrepresentable. The status of image was much higher before the discovery of intellect. The idea of man as slave to his senses was a later transformation of the subject's enslavement to the power of the image. The dichotomy intellect–sensation became more basic than intellect–image. Perhaps this was necessary as a (long) transitional defense against the image. Distance was gained from the image by seeing it as immediate and concrete. Indeed, it is likely that the very birth of intellect was associated with the cognition of image as image (rather than, say, an idol). With the birth of the intellect, image, shorn of its power, might at best be assigned certain mediating functions (viz., between sensation and intellect).

In the eighteenth and the nineteenth centuries, the creative role of imagination burst out of its long repression, or, at least, was finally given its explicit due, often to the detriment of intellect. William Blake linked imagination with the visionary, the creative spirit. There is a long list of others who gave their lives for this vision, martyrs of the imagination. By Freud's time, one could easily catalogue the victims of the unconscious or supraconscious.[54] There were many casualties within the psychoanalytic movement as well, although these failed heroes usually preferred suicide to madness (an irony worth exploring).[55]

Jung, especially, was lyrical about the destructive and creative forces associated with the unconscious depths, which seemed to express themselves most naturally as or in images. Jung's own life bore witness to the hallucinatory vividness of his messengers from the depths. Freud seemed to handle these powers with kid (or rubber) gloves, usually keeping a careful distance, giving himself over to them through many protective filters (primal repression, secondary repression, the derivatives, sublimation; cf. Bion's *premo-*

54. A host of poets who died young come to mind, including a number of suicides, both young and old (e.g., Lautréamont, Novalis, and Höderlin).
55. Freud consoled himself and Jung over Honegger's suicide by remarking, "Do you know, I think we wear out quite a few men" (Freud and Jung, *Letters*, p. 413). A decisive account of madness and suicide in the psychoanalytic movement has yet to be written. Perhaps Roustang has made the best attempt to focus on this issue so far (*Dire Mastery*, pp. 36–54, 76–106). Psychoanalysis in the United States might have developed quite differently if Federn's ego psychology had won out over Hartmann's. Federn is doubtless one of the greatest of the early analysts who committed suicide, and the full impact of his work has not been felt.

nition). A very explosive pea to require so many mattresses. Actually, William Blake, too, had many intermediary spiritual agents (filters) transmitting Energy (Imaginative Power) from the numinous source to earth, a biblical tradition (e.g., the angels) expanded by the Cabala, and found in other religions and myths as well.

A genre of critical literature developed in an attempt to do justice to the "creative imagination," a typically modern compensation. For example, Barfield depicts how we creatively oscillate between intellect and imagination, each contributing in complex ways to the other. Ehrenzweig emphasizes the way both intellect and imagination, in their symbiotic tension, make use of more undifferentiated functions. Herbert Read offered a convincing demonstration of how "image precedes idea" in the great movements of cultural history, antedating Ricoeur's "the symbol gives rise to thought."[56] An entire field, academic and nonacademic, has grown up emphasizing the primacy of myth, which many philosophers, religious writers, and social scientists have made the basis of their anthropology. Articles in Freudian and Jungian journals are concerned with the relation of mythos to logos. It now seems that the dimension Freud called hallucination is here to stay, irrevocably thematized.

Any mental property can occur with hallucinatory vividness. Image, sensation, percept, thought, or word can be (combining Freudian and Jungian terms) numinously cathected. Hallucinations are nothing, if not extravagant. They are a kind of birthright, like everyday life. Everything is magnified or infinitized by them. We do not know how this is done. Often things are not only blown up, but also distorted, usually just beyond recognition. We know something about distortion through love and hate, primary process thinking, possession by (identification with) archetypes, social conditioning (including the condition of our culture, our place in history), and so on. We continuously decode and mediate: we learn to recognize parents as God, and God in parents. Drama would not be what it is

56. Barfield, *Poetic Diction*, pp. 183–211; Ehrenzweig, *Hidden Order of Art*, pp. 20–46, 132–133; Read, *Icon and Idea*, pp. 17–20; Ricoeur, *Freud and Philosophy*, pp. 494–551.

without hallucinatory disproportion. It is a treasure house and a house of horrors. Instead of pleasure, bliss. Instead of pain, hell.

Whatever accounts are given must do justice to the world hallucination opens. One cannot explain heaven and hell simply on the basis of pleasure and pain. The sense of perfection and glory that moves Eros is far beyond considerations of pleasure. Jung was not fooled by Freud. But his own gestalts acted as boxes to trap the numinous and assume what they try to account for. He himself seemed to be aware of this and gave warnings against his views for those who would hear, while he gave in to his nature and annexed dependents.

One could well imagine beings who can experience pleasure and pain without having to create gods and demons. What type of being must do precisely this? Why does ego or self or, more broadly, mind, spirit, or psychic life have this odd capacity? Is this surplus really necessary? Is so much needed just to make sure there is enough? To make sure *something* would not get lost? Why must children dream of witches and hideous snakes, when they may simply have horrible parents, dangerous life conditions (from time immemorial), fearful wishes, warped selves, the overwhelming hardships of smallness and not knowing how or being able to do what others are doing, etc.? Pieces of the puzzle change, but the puzzle remains. We are hallucinatory beings and must come to grips with this fact for better and worse. Freud's defining polarity of human subjectivity—hallucination/perception—will continue to exert a challenge long after other aspects of his work become museum pieces.

Case Examples: Some Basic Features of Hallucinations

Although a catalogue of hallucinatory imagery would be vast and changing with the times, it would show enduring themes and structures. For the remainder of this chapter, I will draw on two cases that give a sense of some aspects of psychotic experience, with special emphasis on mental and physical dimensions. No attempt is made to

be exhaustive or definitive. My sampling dips in and out of a number
of themes and psychic levels and will be supplemented in later
chapters. For the most part, I am underlining what is in the common
domain. Most workers with psychosis are well aware of its salient
features and have been so since the idea of madmen as patients
emerged in medical history. It may thus seem odd to end a chapter on
hallucination with what ought to be a starting point—another partial
overview of phenomena. Yet, as I suggested earlier, the reality and
claims of these phenomena tend to slip away in actual clinical practice. Psychotic phenomena are open to varied approaches, each with
its own virtues and limitations. My presentation is only one of many
possible. My belief is that a firm hold on the structures (and sense of
texture) that emerge here can enrich the empathic and creative background "feel" of workers of all persuasions.

THE SOILED PENIS AND NOSTALGIA

   Frank insisted that his penis fell into the toilet. This was a persistent hallucination (one among others) for him before he began therapy, and it continued to occur intermittently for many years. It had
the force and tenacity of a fixed idea. There were a number of
distinct variations, which tended to blur. In all of them penis, feces,
and toilet were hallucinated elements. That is, he saw and believed
(or acted as if he believed) in their prepossessing reality whether or
not they were actually present. There were feces in the toilet. His
penis might become feces or might already be feces coming out of a
misplaced and invisible anus (a male schizophrenic version of "floating uterus"?). In rarer moments, his penis would preserve some
integrity by remaining a penis, but one that was irremediably and
continuously soiled (a part–object version of burning in hell). His
tone ranged from great agitation to a kind of provocative resignation.
The former expressed a state of impending catastrophe, the latter,
doom.
   The gap between our ways of approaching his predicament was
enormous. He was gripped in something that seemed eminently real.
It simply happened, was happening, continued to happen. To him it
was all somehow obvious: It should happen, it would happen, it *had*

to happen. The recurring scene possessed an inevitability and finality. Yet not entirely, or there would be no room for occasional terror (although terror also left no room). In contrast, my own mind inevitably reeled off a train of possible meaning contexts. His home life is dreadful and the loss and fecalization of his penis dramatizes it. Identification with his mother's fecal genitals, his mother's power. He is his mother's shit. Castration wishes, fears, enactments. Where is the father? Enshrouded in shit, too? Frank turns everything to shit. He turns his mother's breast into a toilet bowl. His mother is a bad container. Is the toilet bowl his anus? He is showing his lack of and wish for active power. A sado-masochistic expression of needing to assimilate anal and phallic power. He wants to be reborn. He needs to return to earth and water on the way to redemption. The archetypal journey is spoiled. He is caught in a deformation of a transitional phase. And so on.

Frank was one of my first patients and I regaled him with all that I could. He thus became the proud possessor of my thematic productions. In itself this was not curative and possibly contributed to a false self. But, finally, it seemed to do more good than harm, for it provided a meaningful point from which to jump off, a nest of possibilities previously totally unavailable to him on a conscious level. If they became part of a false self or resistance, they made for a culturally richer failure, so that his tone was a bit less tinny, shrill, and bitter.

The real work was the overall holding environment, staying with Frank and trying to let go of my stereotypes, using words as gestures that leave room for feelings, the moment-to-moment surprises in an appallingly dim atmosphere, and just sitting. "Sit," a Tibetan Buddhist master told his pupils. "Just sit." The quiet aliveness of just sitting was novelty enough in Frank's life (his mother was unbearably yacky). Yet aiming for verbal accuracy presented a challenge to come alive more thoroughly, and worked best when it seemed to be part of the silence.

Silence for Frank was associated with nostalgia for "the good old days" before *this* happened to him. *This* was his illness, his madness, his spoiled state. He claimed it was not always so. Once he was like everyone else—normal, an ordinary person. He longed for this again. He wept when he heard the song, "Those were the days, my friend." Over and over he would tell me, "Those were the days."

In time it became clear that his picture of halycon days was a wish, a delusion. His days had always been marked by psychic assault and seductive insensitivity. There must have been good moments, perfect moments, for him to build his wishes on. But they were golden moments carved out of a mad world. His story revealed that what he called his past normalcy was a lucky ability to coast over or blunt his difficulties, combined with the collusive support in unreality he received from those around him. As often happens, when it was time for him to make a living and build a life, he found himself entirely incapable of it. He could not find a place in the world comparable to what his family offered, yet his life with family continued to maim and poison him. His sense of the ideal became structured by his wish to be normal and by his delusional belief that at one time he had known this precious possibility. This ideal possibility acted as a backdrop for his sense of having hopelessly fallen or, rather, these two ingredients (golden and fecal ages) formed part of a pattern or system, one as old as human memory.

For a time, with much help, he found a formulation that seemed to say something to him, one that assessed and expressed some aspect of his psychic reality. While one day staring into his (hallucinated) toilet bowl as if it were a crystal ball, it turned into a stage and the thought formed: a shit production for a shit audience (I will use the vernacular here as we used it). He meant the two of us, therapy. But also his family as shit-producing, shit-applauding theatre. An obvious but important turn of mind, followed by a period in which he hallucinated puking. Soon dreams also occurred in which he puked shit (he evacuated words like shit, but he also was cleaning himself out). In Frank's case, the movement from hallucination to dreaming was a step forward in the capacity to have an internal world. He then went through a period of vomiting in reality. Something from inside his own actual and fantasy body was responding to a therapy event, a genuine psychophysical happening from the inside out. This primitive in–out movement was very different from his presenting hallucinations, which were mired in elements forever placed outside him (external penis, toilet bowl, feces). He was puking his life up, perhaps puking life itself up. What a relief this must have been, yet with what anxiety and chagrin. He had to admit there was something in him he wanted out.

His penis continued to fall off, but one day it fell off into clear water—no feces. He reported this with a kind of triumph. It seemed a sign that he was not all bad. It was a gift for me (a real one, a seduction, a compliance?). If he looked in the toilet bowl he might see his face, not only shit, although still a toilet bowl world. The water was finally capable of reflection. Apparently the puking helped to purify it, a kind of human cesspool pump. His feces were reborn as a (live) fecal baby and further dramas unfolded concerning the baby self. A transitional world that straddled the animate and inanimate was emerging. The feces entered into a series of transformations rather than simply vanishing (which would have been pure conceit).

The puking ended for the time being. Frank remarked that seeing his insides did him good, it made him feel he might have insides, that his head, chest, and belly were connected. A sense of cleansing touched his disgust. Some kind of back and forth flow between in-out seemed dimly possible, although it was here first enacted in a raw and disjointed way. It was not yet clear what remained inside, what his insides were made of. More toxic or spoiled substances to get rid of? Something more substantial? A chasm? To some degree, all of these? Perhaps his principal discovery was that he could make something go outside of him. His hallucinated feces were stillborn, outside facts, just there. His penis dropped off like a dead weight. They did not seem to have any links with a genuine organic process. Therapy created a situation in which some movement in hallucinatory experience could be tolerated. In Frank's case, hallucinated movement (puking from inside out) was a welcome advance. That it led to actual puking suggests (in this context) that some elemental bit of psychosomatic connection was achieved.

This short and highly sketchy example covers a lot of ground. It illustrates the theme of contamination which is typical in psychosis.

It focuses on the penis as part–object or condensation, and plays on a penis–feces opposition and fusion. A correlate of contamination is confusion. In this instance, there are confusions between body parts (penis–anus; mouth–anus), body parts and functions (penis–feces), body functions (vomiting–defecation), and more general self- and world-forming psychic representations (clean–dirty, front–back, top–bottom, inside–outside). Such confusions are typical in psychosis. These are affective pollutions. The psychotic individual usually can tell the difference between his actual penis and his feces, although occasionally this is not the case. Such pollutions occur in the unconscious body-image or body-sense of many people, although they are more readily thematized in psychosis.

In this example, the process of contamination–confusion is linked with the theme of the fall. The person and life as a whole is spoiled. Things are not what they used to be. The golden age is lost. For the patient, this universal theme is played out in a sentimental way, a primitive nostalgia. A pop tune makes him cry. His present fecalized existence recalls a bygone (delusional) beatitude. An ideal moment is remembered, or created, and fixated on. Shall we say, with Plato, that it is a reflection of the Ideal Good that ultimately grounds us? Is it a memory or vision of God? Of a primary bliss with mother? Womb? A fantasy or reminiscence? An original creation? Primary love or primary narcissism? Identification of ego with archetype? That the ideal moment itself acts as a frame of reference or criterion for measuring experience is a fact. All interpretations that move around or bounce off it are profiles.

THE DEVIL'S FAILED COMMISSION

Carl suffered a psychotic breakdown in his early twenties, which required four months of hospitalization. Like Frank, he had been unable to negotiate the shift from adolescence to adulthood, yet how different their failures were. One felt Carl tried to fly but was shot down; Frank never left the ground. He could not get through college and was lucky to be able to hold a post office job, although he was very intelligent. Carl loved college. Contact with literature and the arts made him feel free. He seemed to start life on a higher level.

Carl's psychosis took the form of a hallucinatory spin, in which God and the devil vied for power over him, and he was terrified of both of them. His primary therapy in hospital was sixty insulin coma treatments, which greatly helped him. The loss and return of consciousness, characteristic of an insulin shock treatment, fit the death-rebirth experience Carl underwent in wrestling with his psychosis over a long period of time. When he left the hospital he was ready for intense psychotherapeutic work.

For the moment, I will describe facets of Carl's hallucinatory spin and an early turning point in the gradual reconstitution of his sense of self. Additional aspects of our work together appear in Chapters 3, 4, 6, and 8.

Carl *saw* devils. He *heard* God. The devils were inscribed on persons, particularly on faces. They did not appear in empty space. Nor did everyone appear a devil all the time. The devils showed on certain persons' faces more than others. In contrast, God's voice was not spatially localizable. Technically, Carl could locate it inside himself—perhaps in his head or chest, although it could as easily be under his skin. Even broadcasting inside him, it came from and was nowhere. It was invisible and intangible. The devils were manifestations of a single power, the devil, who appeared in and ultimately governed all of them. In the grand scheme of things, the devil's power was circumscribed. He and his followers appeared in, as, through, or on people. God had no face or form. He was not confined to material appearances. The devil may have been pure spirit, but he appeared only in the human face.

Carl's battle was a rather traditional one. God ultimately was the greater power in the cosmos, but God and the devil battled for his soul. Which would be the greater power in his life was at issue. That God was the ultimate power was scant comfort, if Carl failed to side with him. God's voice commanded Carl to follow wherever it might lead—to follow with blind trust. Carl had visions of it leading him into the traffic on a highway or a vagabond existence that would ultimately destroy him. The main aim of the voice was loyalty, at no matter what cost. Nothing less would break the devil's hold. If Carl failed to follow, hell was the long-term outcome, but there were other unspecified and more immediate dangers, including being alienated from God and, therefore, out of sync with the universe.

Carl loved God, but was horrified at his demands. If he followed God's voice he would die. If he followed the devil he would go to hell. Both threw him into panic, doubt, and resistance. He did not want to believe he saw devils, nor did he want to believe he heard God. He searched for a way out, trying to find some way to discount the claims made on him. But the claims were being made and these presences possessed a power and vividness that nothing else could compete with. The issue was one of will and fidelity, and it rendered him entirely will-less and paralyzed. He went back and forth between God and the devil's way, caught in a steady state of vacillation. At times, the vacillating attained such a speed that existence stood still and became horribly silent.

Carl fought hospitalization, but when his parents took him he went quietly. Inwardly, he heard himself thinking that if he were hospitalized, it would not be his fault if he did not follow God's word. He had an excuse not to. Of course, he could (and should) try to escape, but he also knew he would not. He did not want to. It seemed that an instinct for self-preservation was working. Yet he condemned himself for being weak and giving in. If he were stronger, he would follow the voice wherever it led. He did not like believing he was a coward.

Once in the hospital, he became violent and fought the devils he saw. Perhaps he sensed he could do little harm in this containing environment and felt free enough to let himself go. After he was subdued, medicated, and placed in a padded room, the realization that he was not in control of what was happening hit him for the first time. It dawned on him that all along he had thought, without realizing it, he could control what he was going through if he really wanted to. In a way, it was like a movie and he could turn the projector off any time he wished to. Now he knew he was wrong. There seemed to be nothing he could do to stop the flood of tormenting powers. The thought came to him that he was crazy, that there was such a thing as madness, and this was it. "So this is what madness is?" he heard himself think. There was no fighting it and he finally gave in.

The world seemed to break into small pieces. He stared hard to refocus, but again it was clear there was nothing he could do. He had to let go and simply stare or close his eyes. With his eyes closed, he continued seeing bits and pieces and the thought eventually came that it was his own disintegration he was witnessing. In one of his descriptions he said, "I saw my own I falling apart in front of me. My ego was breaking into so many fragments. The breaking went on and on until little was left but crushed powder in blackness." It was an event repeated daily in one way or another for many months, and continued in residual form for years. When he left the hospital he found the term *disintegration of the ego* in psychology books and held on to it. It fit this aspect of his experience perfectly.

We must omit much of what Carl went through now. For present purposes, suffice it that this "blackness" was a profound turning point. Many new visions grew out of it. It became a kind of base of revelation. While fading in and out of this state, he heard the devil in God's voice, and saw both his father, himself, and much more in the devil. The idea that not God, but the devil had been speaking to him from the inside as well as impinging on him from the outside led to the profound awareness of just how godless he had become and how easy it was to misjudge spirits. In time he had to confess to himself that he was not capable of telling God from the devil or either from his father or his own ego. The voices and visions he heard and saw were complex amalgams of all of these and much else as well. It was only through many years of deep therapeutic work that he was able to begin to allow his psyche to work in a more viable way.

At this point I wish to stress some similarities and differences between Frank and Carl's psychoses. The confusions that most readily became manifest in Frank's case tended to be on a body ego level. That is, his hallucinatory imagery was predominantly involved with physical objects: penis, feces, mouth, stomach, and so on. True, his nostalgia for a lost ideal points to a transcendental element. In actuality, however, the kind of well-being he yearned for felt more like a material substance than of the spirit. If spirit, it was buried in body parts, functions, and material objects, in so many tombs. The affective atmosphere in Frank's case was heavy and thick, suffocated by feces. His fecal penis functioned almost like a fetish, something to hold on to for dear life (or death).[57] He was loyal to his fecal penis as to a god. Yet it did not save him, this idol, but mocked his addiction. He was doomed to a toilet bowl world and his only solace and triumph was reducing the rest of his life to its terms.

Carl, by contrast, did not seem to know he had a penis or anus, or that feces mattered. His drama was lived out in almost purely transcendental terms. True, the devil appeared only where there were bodies, thus the body must count for something. Most important, something prevented him from following the words of the spirit, which might have led to his destruction (salvation). This implies a strong unconscious attachment to the body, common sense, and life in this world. But the explicit terms of his hallucinations were transcorporeal: God and the devil are pure spirits battling for his immortal soul. Eternal life or death was at stake. Space was more than space, not simply the space of everyday perception. Nor was it reduced to the circumference of a toilet bowl, as with Frank—a most material reduction. For Carl, space was the backdrop for a menacingly vibrating and unearthly scene. What was important about spatial objects was the chance they gave a more primary world to manifest itself. Human faces and the devils that nested in them possessed an intimate affinity for each other, a hidden bond. The fit was seldom perfect, although usually face and devil remained fused. Carl often saw the bleak and burning stitches that linked and separated everyday from transcendental horrors.

Carl's affective presence was more mercurial than heavy. He danced around the world of meaning. The core transcendental con-

---

57. For a complementary discussion of fecal imagery in perversion see Eigen, "Creativity, Instinctual Fantasy and Ideal Images," pp. 317–339; for a different but overlapping treatment of the fecal penis, see Chasseguet-Smirgel, *Creativity and Perversion*, pp. 68–69, 75, 81–82, 96–100, 152–155.

fusion that eventually surfaced (and made a momentous clinical difference) was that between God and the devil. It would not be an exaggeration to say that the discovery that he could not really tell the difference between God and the devil led to an entire recentering of his existence: he had to find himself (and God) outside the terms he had believed were final. It was discovering the mix-up between God and devil that led to his ability to see how (for him) both were composite images drawn from many sources, including his father's and his own agonies and grimaces. This is not simply a reduction of the numinous to the personal, but rather an expansion of his field of interest to include both. Carl may well discover that the devil, his ego, or parents cannot exhaust the meaning of God for him. If he goes far enough, he might find that God and self, parents or others, can enter into a preeminently enriching rather than destructive connection. To face distortions between and within the foundational presences of one's being may be the beginning of a journey in which one's relationship to what is most basic in life is transformed.

Is there a sense in which we can say that together Frank and Carl constitute a kind of distorted whole? Frank was mired in the physical, while Carl was mesmerized by the psychospiritual. Are they under- or oversides of each other? Can one reach the need for spirit in Frank, the need for embodiment in Carl? Or, again, perhaps Carl is attempting to work something out on a mental (or transcendental) ego plane, albeit distortedly. That is, the form his psychosis took may not simply be a sign of disembodiment, but rather a message that his psychic task is to work out fundamental confusions with mental–spiritual "materials." Correlatively, Frank may lack spiritual imagery for good reason. Perhaps his temperament best suits him to work out his problems more physically. It is easy to fall into stereotypical thinking about cases.

Hallucinations swing back and forth between mental–spiritual and body–material imagery. From moment to moment, mind may be treated as body and body as mind. Either mental or body ego can be hyperanimated or deanimated, often in complex ways. The subject spins in a world overfilled with meaning, or languishes in one in which meaning atrophies and dies out altogether. Either body or mind (or whatever combination) is experienced as too full or empty. Mental or body ego functions are hallucinated as present or absent (the idea that the devil has no face in a mirror is an example of a negative hallucination). Possibilities proliferate. What is crucial is to try to see how hallucinatory networks function in given instances. This includes what mental/transcendental or body ego capacities specific hallucinations magnify or nullify. What is being broadcast so loudly so as to finally be heard? What has reached a vanishing point so as to finally escape notice? What is trying to be born? What is trying to die?

We have said very little about the specifics about Frank and Carl's relationships to other persons (including myself). We will focus more on self–other relationships in other chapters and here say only that mental–physical self-relations are profoundly influenced by and even modeled on self–other relationships, as well as providing a structural setting for the latter.[58] As Bion wrote, "The earliest problems demanding solution are related to a link between two personalities."[59] The mental and the physical self often act as parent–child to one another.[60] There are many other variations as well. Most generally, mind–body and self–other relationships help structure each other. Any clinical account that does not portray self–other relationships from the perspective of both mental and physical self and vice versa has missed multidimensional patterns of essential importance.

In this regard, my clinical sketches are lacking. They are meant to play a sensitizing role and open the way for work to follow. Thus, in Frank's case, we would not be surprised to learn how his connection (or disconnection) between himself and his fecal penis caricatures what has happened (failed to happen) between himself and primary others. His hallucinatory anxiety provides him with an object of

58. Eigen, "Instinctual Fantasy and Ideal Images," pp. 119–137; idem, "The Area of Faith in Winnicott, Lacan and Bion," pp. 413–443; idem, "Maternal Abandonment Threats, Mind–Body Relations and Suicidal Wishes," pp. 561–582; idem, "Creativity, Instinctual Fantasy and Ideal Images," pp. 317–339.
59. Bion, *Transformations*, p. 66.
60. Eigen, "Maternal Abandonment Threats, Mind–Body Relations and Suicidal Wishes," pp. 561–582.

obsessive concern, a mixture of substitute satisfaction and image of lack. The sign of his (non)relationship is spoilage, and we must wonder whose feces (tongue, phallus, baby, body) he hopes will conform with the standard he has set. Whom is he trying to control? Is there anyone he once hoped to free? What type of psychic adventure would his penis point to if it could point? He has carefully kept his spoiled parts in a hallucinatory storage bin, mute offerings of what once might have functioned as possible linking elements. What intensity and rage has gone into the inertia and perseverative insistence of his toilet bowl mirror?

Carl's God and devil function as others or horrific self-objects or mad aspects of the self. The link is annihilation, loss, dread, "almost," "not quite," the eternally imminent—the mirage of final catastrophe. Who, if anyone, has made this threat? Is the catastrophic threat meant to fill a gap left by no-threat? Do such horrific threats at least offer the solace that someone was there enough to be threatening? Surely, someone in Carl's life must have been tantalizingly menacing or, at least, domineering. What intrusiveness is in his images, yet what lack of contact.

Carl "solves" the bind he is in by living forever, win or lose, in God's or in the devil's party. Whom is the ego modeling itself upon— who in Carl's life lives forever? Perhaps many images, many voices, and so many dislocations between voices and images. An unraveling process begins. First the advent of the most frightening beings or non-beings imaginable. Carl's God and devil *must* be taken seriously. Whatever else might be said of them, they forced him to see and hear them. They refocused his attention and propelled him into a realm of ultimate concern. They began as no monkey business attention grabbers who, in time, also revealed themselves to be great globs and sources of energy to be broken down and reworked. They showed themselves as raw materials and transforming presences. A close look (one must look in Pandora's box, at Medusa, Eurydice, Amor, the naked Father, the face of God) and more stories begin.

CHAPTER THREE

Mindlessness

INSANITY IS commonly described as "losing one's mind." As is often the case, the vernacular touches a profound, if one-sided, truth. The human capacity to blank oneself out and inwardly vanish as a form of protection is widespread. It may be that the capacity to blunt pain and anesthetize oneself is a general characteristic of living beings. In human existence, this elemental capacity is raised to a new power. It can vary from a momentary going blank to a vast nullifying of the self.

A patient, Leila,[1] speaks about her "oblivion machine." She vanishes in the face of life's difficulties. She is "not there" when she most wishes and needs to be there. It can happen with the seemingly simplest situations. She arrives at my office and the door is locked. Usually it is open. Should she ring or wait? She goes back and forth until her mind starts spinning, and she blanks out. After a time I go out to see what has happened to her. She is pale, in a cold sweat, dumbly tense, and fit to be tied. She cannot make a sound. She cannot find herself. Later, she said she wanted to cry when she saw me, but she was paralyzed. She saw me as from under water, or from

---

1. An earlier version of material related to mindlessness, especially concerning the cases of Leila and Lenny, may be found in my paper, "Aspects of Mindlessness-Selflessness: A Common Madness." This paper was published in *The Psychotherapy Patient*, vol. 2, 1986, pp. 75–81 and *Psychotherapy and the Selfless Patient*, pp. 75–81, ed. J. Travers, New York: Haworth Press, 1986.

inside her "bell jar." My absence opened up an endless hole in her being through which she disappeared.

This particular episode was mild and easily gotten through. She began to find her voice after we were alone. Startled to find a locked door, she had then felt stunned, and starting to go under. She remembers a whirl of thoughts and feelings, her immense need for me. How dare I not be there? Fury at her need and me. Horror at her demand, and fear of fury and fury at fear. Partially vanishing, partially mesmerized, transfixed and staring blankly at and out of her vanishing.

The unexpected paralyzes her. Surprise, loss of control, and cataclysm go together, as they do for brain-damaged persons (she often refers to herself as brain damaged, although she is not). Here the loss is associated with me. Any kind of social exclusion (whether an attack or a slight, or being ignored) provokes a sense of isolation, a numbing pain that ends with a dying out of herself. My absence, a sign of her deficiency, makes her more deficient. In the instance just described, she is able to say that her not ringing the bell is already a kind of choice, an expression of not being there. She wanted me to find her on my doorstep. Simply, she wanted me to find her. But by the time I did she had forgotten what she wanted, remembering only her urge to cry. She wants me to see her paralyzed and to feel it my fault. In general, I ought to feel it my fault for the way she is or isn't. Yet such blaming is already an ascent from oblivion, the beginning of a return, the mark of presence recalling her to herself. The moment before there had been nothing.

This relatively simple example mixes up a number of phenomenological and dynamic states and levels of being. For example, she and I speak of startle, fear–fury, blaming (hostile self-pity with an attribution of causation), loss, deficiency, isolation, weeping, cataclysm, spinning, paralysis, mesmerization, numbing, fading, blanking, dying, oblivion, and nothingness. These states vary in degree and quality of awareness of self and other and in the way mental and physical aspects of the self are organized. They form a complex and dynamic network of mindfulness and mindlessness.

It is important to focus on some of the principal ways mindlessness occurs and to study the basic issues this primitive deficiency–defense raises. Although speaking about mental states is always difficult, it is never more problematic than when we ask how the mind can be mindless.

Mindful Mindlessness and the Zero Point

The possibility that multiple centers of subjectivity could exist in a single personality and function independently deeply fascinated nine-teenth-century philosophers, psychiatrists, and artists. There was a general preoccupation with dissociative phenomena during Freud's lifetime. In his case histories, Freud described how a single personal-ity split itself into what appeared to be a multiplicity of subjects, each acting as if it possessed a separate mind with a separate agenda, and he stressed the difficulties inherent in speaking about such a state of affairs. Ought one to call each of these "inner personalities" an unconscious consciousness or can one do better understanding them as unconscious mental systems of a single subject? Both conceptual paths are extremely difficult. One of Freud's greatest achievements lay in his recognition of the radical challenge the phenomenon of dissociation presents to a science of mind.

Freud opted for a single subject with multiple unconscious sys-tems. These systems appeared to be both mindful and mindless of one another. To give coherence to this state of affairs, Freud postu-lated a theory of repression, which he called "the cornerstone of psychoanalysis." In this theory, repression does not account for all the unconscious, but only that aspect of it implicated in specific forms of neuroses, and helps to organize conflicts between cultural and instinctual drives. Most of the unconscious, however, is not repressed and may operate via other principles.

Repression (primary or secondary) is ambiguous in that it is an unconscious ego function that maintains itself, other aspects of the ego, and other psychic systems as unconscious. The repressing ego is an active force pitted against other, primarily sexual, active forces. At a minimum, it assumes mental operations that register, scan, select, and oppose specific mental contents without reaching conscious awareness. The ego must know and at the same time forget or not attend to what and how it knows. What is relevant for our purposes here is the *caesura*, gap, or blackout in our mental life, as the ego covers its tracks.

For Freud, repression was only one way the psyche could split itself, and was most characteristic of the neuroses. Freud also wrote of dissociation or ego splitting in perversion, wherein incompatible attitudes or beliefs exist side by side without seeming to modify one another. It is as if the subject sustains contradictory elements without being aware that they are mutually exclusive or without attending to their contradiction. He seems to be oblivious as to what is going on inside him and to what governs his actions. In psychosis, the stakes are even higher. The psychotic individual not only created alternative scripts for sexuality, but can also refashion the appearance and meaning of reality itself. In psychosis, crucial aspects of external and psychic reality can be blanked out or distorted, nulled or feverishly heightened (e.g., by denial, disavowal, or hallucination). Reality, as a whole, undergoes a radical malformation or transformation.

Freud depicted various modes of obliviousness—repression, ego-splitting, denial, or disavowal—as active processes, and emphasized dynamic psychic activity in which the conflicts were between unconscious psychic tendencies or between the self and reality. Libido is conceived as inherently active, a driving force, the activity of desire. Passivity also plays an important role in his clinical psychodynamics, and Freud depicted both men and women as afraid of their passive side (men of their "homosexuality," women of their "femininity"), although passivity may be clung to out of fear of activity. The subject is afraid to be either passive or active. Castration, separation, and annihilation anxieties permeate the subject's being and doing. The subject is afraid of loss of control and of self-assertion, all the fervent movements of life.

Perhaps the most formidable of all defenses Freud described is decathexis, which is a withdrawal of energy from or loss of interest in objects. In his writings on psychosis in 1914 ("On Narcissism,

p. 74), Freud noted that this withdrawal is accompanied by an increased cathexis of the ego, expressed in megalomania. Thus, the energy that is withdrawn from objects is invested in the ego, a protective reaction to life's difficulties that, at the same time, is a return to an earlier narcissism (see Chapter 1, pp. 6–10). He subsequently realized that decathexis may be more extreme,[2] and that psychic energy may be withdrawn from all life feeling, including the I-feeling. The psyche may so deplete and collapse into itself that it approximates a "return" to an inorganic (insensate) state. Freud depicts this as a death wish, a dying-out of investment. As long as one is in life and desirous, one is in danger of and vulnerable to pain. Absolute decathexis is absolute painlessness, which, in phenomenological terms, represents a loss of vitality and affective coloring, a self-deadening, a dropping out of psychological and possibly even biological existence.

Whatever the current status of Freud's concept of psychic energy, decathexis, death drive, and his mythic–mechanistic metapsychology, the psychological realities he pointed to are crucial. He attempted to deal with a tendency to numb or deaden oneself by postulating an urge to return to a zero point. In effect, the subject commits a kind of psychological suicide by emptying or denuding experience, by becoming inanimate. More than a return to the womb and primary narcissism, it is an undoing of all psychic aliveness and all that might keep one in existence.

Although it may not be possible to achieve an absolute zero point of psychic activity and remain alive, various mental states approximate such a hypothetical position. An extreme example is the "blank psychosis," in which the subject's psychic life is radically impoverished. He has very little ability to tolerate neurotic fantasy, perverse illusion, or psychotic hallucination and appears to operate by massive denial. Nothing bothers or grips him or has any real meaning. He imperturbably goes along with his day-to-day routine.

I met one such man, I will call him Lenny, after his release from a mental hospital. Once every so many years, his implacability breaks down and he threatens to become violent. His violence seems to

2. Freud, "Beyond the Pleasure Principle," pp. 9–45, 62–63.

occur without any accompanying mental content, although this last time it had been directed against the milkman and his mother. No fear or rage is reported, but his fits follow a breakdown of his usual behavioral routine. He starts to mumble to himself. He and those around him say they do not know what he says. His life is a mystery to everyone in it, but he does not think it is unusual.

When I saw him he looked like a vacuous Buddha. Chronically overweight, his color tone was cherub-like, and his fat seemed a comfortable cushion, a cosy life jacket. If I let myself go, I could feel a warm, quiet ecstasy while staring at his face. It was a stillborn ecstasy because I have no evidence that he ever felt it. He tended to sit without initiating conversation and to reply monosyllabically or with simple sentences if I asked questions. Within this framework I could detect subtle variations in quality of mood and attitude. At times his expression and tone were slightly disdainful and he shrugged me off as if I should know better. At other times he was complacent and tolerant of my presence. If I tried to stir him up, he looked at me with a benign, quizzical, and unblinking gaze, as if waiting for my madness to run its course. He remained more or less unruffled throughout the year (it felt like five years) I knew him.

Nearly 15 years later, what is most memorable is his mysterious maternal warmth and its blankness. It was as impersonal as Mother Nature, and as silent, yet it lacked the fecundity and variety of the living Mother. It was steadfast and unreasoning.

Anything could have been read into his Mona Lisa–Cheshire Cat grin. He was like an old lady who knows everything and sits and rocks as life goes by. Often I felt nothing at all was going on inside his mind, but the little he said showed me he was not retarded. He seemed just as happy when I spoke or didn't speak or whether we saw or didn't see each other. He came because his father brought him, and about a year later he stopped coming. Was he back in enough of a routine for his father to stop worrying? Was he on the way to another spell in the hospital? He was unshakeably friendly with me to the end.

In Lenny's case, it mattered little if I could detect oedipal or preodipal elements in his milkman–mother duo/trio. In a sense his whole existence was womb-like. He had an aura of prescience, but appeared to be out of contact with it. His eyes might sparkle, but like the stars, they were mute. Perhaps this is some kind of early identification with the breast or the mother's reverie, the cushion and omniscient know-nothing mother. Even his appearance was breast-like. From time to time did the suppressed active body ego break through with baby fits? No hint of a spontaneously active baby appeared in the time I knew him. One of my fantasies was that I might be of use to him if we were in a hospital together when he was violent, with no conspiratorial effort made to whisk his violence away as quickly as possible. He did not need medication because his whole state of being was tranquil. Perhaps, from time to time, this self-administered well-being wore off, and unconscious rage built up, cycles of inhibition–disinhibition, denial, and irruption. Was this rhythm (if it was a rhythm) governed chemically, psychodynamically, environmentally, or at all?

What came through most of all was that Lenny, in some important sense, was not there. Flickers of life rose and fell out of and back to a baseline numbness. He had fallen out of play and out of reach, vanishing in the cherubic glow on which he floated. He had no thought about himself he wished to articulate. In his absence, psychic growth passed him by.

Was Lenny's solution active? Passive? We are at a border where activity and passivity blur. Aspects of Freud's decathexis seem to shade into Breuer's "hypnoid state" and Janet's "weakness of integration." Breuer[3] postulated a blank state he called "hypnoid" as a factor in the origin of mental illness. This is a state in which the individual is radically passive and vulnerable to impressions. At such moments, bizarre images expressive of traumatic events and feelings can stamp themselves on the subject. Remaining dissociated from normal waking consciousness, they exert an unconscious influence. Lenny's blankness, however, made him invulnerable. It was like a thick coat around him, one that psychic contents could not get

3. Breuer and Freud, "Studies on Hysteria," pp. 215–251.

through. Instead of blankness acting as a medium for hysterical hallucinations, it led, in his case, to more blankness.

Janet has emphasized such an individual's tendency to fall away from himself because of an innate personality weakness. The subject is unable to integrate the diverse aspects of psychic life, which dissociate into subsystems that compete to dominate the relatively passive (weak) individual. Some contemporary research has been done on the psychotic's inability to synthesize or integrate experience.[4] Does it make much sense to call Lenny's problem lack of integration or is it more accurate to say that there was not enough of his personality? From time to time, however, Lenny's blankness broke into bits of hallucinatory violence. The absent self, perhaps, became present in a fragmentary way as the milkman–mother called to some old, but faded desire.

Freud began his career as a psychoanalyst by differing from Breuer and Janet in his emphasis on the unconscious subject's *dynamic activity*. But as he developed his notion of decathexis, it swept past the types of passivity touched by Breuer and Janet. For Freud, the deepest passivity of all was the pull toward death. He understood instinctual life as basically conservative, aiming to restore an earlier, inanimate state. In clinical terms, a subject in the grips of a death wish often seems to be demonically possessed, clinging and demanding to an extreme. Even an autistic child who whirls and squeals and will not or cannot speak is possessive and controlling. There is a fierce willfulness in the paralysis of will and a languishing passivity in the tyranny of demand. The subject holds onto his own untenability as he slips toward his null point.

Freud described the work of the death instinct as "silent," but it is an ominous silence. For Freud, masochism ran deeper than sadism and behind it lurked a need to abandon psychic sensitivity altogether and to become as stone. The death instinct refers to a dimension of psychic functioning earlier than the pleasure principle and hallucinatory wish-fulfillment. Metapsychologically, it is a going back to an earlier state. It depicts life as ultimately collapsing into inanimateness,

4. Shakow, *Schizophrenia*, pp. 4–144.

as if biological and psychological existence were too great a strain. In concrete clinical terms, the death drive is meant to deal with such phenomena as the tendency to repeat painful patterns, stubborn masochism, relentless guilt and self-persecution, and the negative therapeutic reaction (getting worse after getting better). Freud emphasized multiple tensions within and between psychic levels. The nucleus of psychoanalytic theory continues to be the conflicts of instinctual drives, ego, and reality. But all psychic levels are conceived as permeated by the antagonistic operation of life (Eros) and death instincts, the former building and the latter destroying unities.

The death instinct itself is polar. On the one hand, its basic work is to reduce all stimulation to zero, yet it is partly diverted and directed toward the outside world where it takes the form of an aggressive drive, sadism, or the will to mastery and power. Freud's attempt to explore the psychological link between our aggressive drive toward mastery and the need to undo ourselves was radically germane, in that his insight that the path of aggressive mastery is a circuitous route toward death must be studied in detail in an age when our power to "control" destruction has been raised to new limits or to limitlessness. Lenny's slowing down and Leila's speeding up reflect two paths that invite us to oblivion. They are the underside of mastery, the vast, numbing paralysis that awaits us when pain passes a certain boundary.

The Death Wish and Object Relations

Winnicott reworks Freud's concepts of narcissism and the death wish in terms of self–object relations. In Winnicott's[5] vision, the early self experiences a creative, rich, yet ambiguous omnipotence. Does it find or create the "object" that appears when it wants it? For Winnicott,

5. Winnicott, *Playing and Reality*, pp. 11–14; Eigen, "The Area of Faith in Winnicott, Lacan and Bion," pp. 413–418. See also Eigen (in press), "Aspects of Omniscience."

this is an unaskable question. It infringes on the paradoxical nature of the self's ability to be. The self lives and thrives in a dimension in which creation and discovery are one. Insofar as the rich play of ambiguity between self and other is damaged, the subject's creativity can sour and freeze into the more malignant types of megalomania that characterize psychosis. Or, worse, the self's sense of existence may disappear. Winnicott's clinical portrayals are concerned with the sense of unreality and the struggle to feel real. He is concerned with what therapeutic conditions will best permit a sense of the reality of experiencing to emerge in an individual whose self-feeling has disappeared or never developed.

Guntrip[6] abandoned Freud's mechanistic energic theory for a depth phenomenology of the self's relation to others, emphasizing a needy aspect of the self that, under extreme duress, might give up and die out. If the other it seeks is not there for it, it may finally stop seeking. It may passively "seek" the womb to escape the pain of a failed existence. Withdrawn and out of contact, it ceases to be.

Guntrip's most sensitive descriptions emphasize what can happen when the contact-oriented self meets with a blank other. He resorts to some of the same imagery (e.g., return to womb) Freud used to describe narcissism (a state of perfection) and the death wish (a zero point). But Guntrip believed that such states are most basically reactions to the other's failure to support the self's value and need for healthy contact. For Guntrip, megalomania and the urge toward non-existence would not arise with perfect parenting. Although Freud also studied reactive (secondary) megalomania and masochism, he could as easily have said that perfect parenting is impossible in face of the psyche's inbuilt (primary) narcissism and immobility.

Guntrip distinguishes between activity driven by internalized bad object-relations and activity driven by a dread of nothingness. In the former, part of the subject becomes a hating, attacking other, caught in an eternal battle. It struggles with the psychological rapist or killer within. One may become psychically (and sometimes literally) murderous in order to avoid being murdered or to protest what one has

6. Guntrip, *Schizoid Phenomena, Object–Relations and the Self*, pp. 1–114, 243–364.

undergone. We try to kill our killer and become one with it in doing so. Activity alternates with emotional paralysis in the endless battle.

The will to power may ward off a dread that there is not and never was a present enough other for the self to be supported. Beneath clinging and demand, blankness. A hate relationship is then better than no relationship, a deformed self better than no self. Hate-oriented activity maintains one's existence. Should this activity fail, one risks a fall into nothingness, so one grabs on to whatever one can. Addictive scenarios may be substituted for or alternate with the thrust toward mastery.

Kohut and Fairbairn have suggested that Freud's descriptions of the death instinct represent what can happen when relations between self and other go wrong.[7] Under certain unfavorable conditions, the life of the self may deteriorate, but usually the damage is partial. The self may mobilize itself, and thrust forward, in an attempt to ward off further deterioration and to compensate for damage. Creative work often is reparative. Active attempts at a mastery of the psychic damage, however, may harden the self. The personality becomes tough in a way that makes it impossible to address the splits in it. One learns to "get over" problems and to go about the business of living, only to find that a secret madness plays a role in the course of events and tinges the quality of being. One's hidden madness may involve both a deformed self and no self.

Meltzer et al. distinguish between hate-driven schizophrenia and a pre-hate autism.[8] The schizophrenic child appears to have developed a tougher shell than an autistic one, even if the latter may seem less accessible. Meltzer sees in the emotional sensibility of the autistic child a "gentleness of disposition."[9] The autistic child is extremely possessive, but not sadistic, and the therapist is not as apt to feel as wounded as with a schizophrenic. The schizophrenic's defenses are more encrustedly obsessional and split; there is more weaponry and

7. Kohut, *The Restoration of the Self*, pp. 116–131; Fairbairn, *An Object-Relations Theory*, pp. 78–79.
8. Meltzer et al., *Explorations in Autism*, pp. 6–29; 216–218; 241–242.
9. Ibid., p. 9.

armor. It is as if the autistic child fails to develop adequate psychic skin and thus is closer to the massive emotional upheavals of early infancy. The schizophrenic child handles this basic oversensitivity with more rigid defenses. He reacts to vulnerability with fear–hate. The autistic child, in contrast, may collapse into a spineless, motionless ball in the face of loss. It is as if he just dies out if he cannot control, be part of, or feel a nearness with his support object. He is also capable of molding himself to the contours of another. The schizophrenic's body is rarely so lacking in resistance; it is more apt to show the effects of a fierce hallucinatory struggle. An alertness to the enemy seems much more a part of the schizophrenic's stance.

Meltzer understands the autistic's ability to vanish as a "dismantling of attention."[10] He points to the mind's ability to stop attending to outer–inner events and go blank, appearing to drop out of existence. It is not clear, from Meltzer's description, whether this void state involves numbing, stupor, or emptying, or whether it is more akin to staring at a blank wall when one shifts one's gaze away from specific objects. Is the subject turning his attention from foreground to background or undoing the possibility of attention entirely? Where is the subject when he is nowhere? What kind of nowhere is it?

Is the null point for the subject who is sucked into a black hole the same as for the subject who fizzes out? The former seems to fly apart into an unknown, electrifying density; the latter may be as inert as an airless balloon. What dynamic principle underlies each? The nothingness reached by a Leila or a Lenny, for example, is not the same. The depth phenomenology of zero points is just beginning.

Fliess's "hypnotic evasion" referred to a somewhat later phase of development and emphasized actual sexual abuse by a psychotic parent.[11] He found that going blank helps repress the sexual arousal associated with such traumatic events. The introjected parent commands the child to excuse him (or her) and so the child ignores his own perceptions. The ego partly hypnotizes itself into blankness, while its real observations, together with dangerous instinctual reac-

10. Ibid., pp. 11–12, 23, 25–26, 40.
11. Fliess, *Symbol, Dream and Psychosis*, pp. 50–51, 267–291, 351–352.

tions, remain in the unconscious. Fliess encouraged his patients to abstain from blank states and build up a tolerance for body feelings and imagery.

The phenomenon of going blank, as described by Fliess, involves and reinforces a double split within the ego: a transverse split between introject and partial subject and a longitudinal split between that aspect of the ego that succumbs and that aspect that continues to exist. The capacity for blanking out is taken for granted in Fliess's analysis. He showed how it frequently functions as an adjunct to or "casing" for repression and stated that it must be addressed before repression can be worked with. The possibility that repression is superseded by a more thorough and devastating dissolution of personality did not play a significant role in his thinking. Fliess's work focused on patients who were intact enough to enter into a therapeutic alliance vis-à-vis repressed psychotic elements. For these patients, splitting operations provided a stable base. The blankness that swallows up repression, or the slide past repression into a world in which splitting operations proliferate, opens up more ominous vistas.

For Freud, the mind seeks to create and, simultaneously, undo itself. The return to an absolute zero point is a wish or desire or fantasy, although at times such a hypothetical state seems to occur. Sometimes, suicide may be the only way of making the mind blank or of dramatizing blankness. However, Freud's depiction of a death wish not only refers to the tendency to null oneself, but also suggests that one was never properly born. The failure of the self to have come into existence adequately is scarcely distinguishable from a collapse to a null point. The self hovers over zero. In Freud's energic terms, decathexis presupposes cathexis. But what if cathexis of other and self is extremely weak or partial? The individual who bitterly complains about losing his I-feeling and who is pained by a sense of numbness (e.g., Leila) is not the same as the individual whose I-feeling and affective density were never strong enough to be missed (e.g., Lenny). In the latter instance, one hopes to stimulate a sufficient self-feeling the individual will find worth struggling for. We may need to trace either a subject's lack or loss of self, the movement out of or lapse into nothingness.

Freud's association of the death instinct with repetition underlines just how difficult and unfinished the creation of self necessarily is. The psyche remains riveted on the traumatic event that blocks its coming into being and distorts its development. It must deal with pain before it can accept pleasure. We are unconsciously obsessed with and seek to master disturbances insofar as the latter disrupt our continuity of being. We are tempted to fall back into nothingness when the pressures that prevent and attend our psychological birth build up.

Constitution of the self and other is always partial. There are blank spots throughout and perhaps in the heart of self-feeling. Presence presupposes absence, gaps, something missing—and vice versa. In various ways, our sense of self bears the imprint of its prenatal void. As children, we teased ourselves by asking where we were before we were born, but that vast emptiness is part of what makes us possible. In psychosis, in part, we cling to this formless background in order to remain impossible.

The Sense of Catastrophe and
Doodling in Sound

Bion used a modified "Big Bang" image to try to depict the starting point of human psychic reality.[12] He imagined the origin of affective thinking as a catastrophic explosion and used psychosis as an example. He assumed that psychosis reflects, albeit perversely, the catastrophic foundations of human existence.

Bion depicted the first thoughts, which he called beta elements, as "objects compounded of things-in-themselves, feelings of depression–persecution and guilt and therefore aspects of personality linked by a sense of catastrophe."[13] The first thoughts or beta elements are

12. Bion, *Elements of Psycho-Analysis*, Chapter 9; idem, *Attention and Interpretation*, Chapter 2.
13. Bion, *Elements of Psycho-Analysis*, pp. 39–40. This section also draws on Eigen, "Toward Bion's Starting Point," pp. 321–330.

indistinguishable from body sensations and outer objects. They constitute hallucinatory raw material, which must be worked over in order to become part of a thinking process (we will say more about this later).

At the minimum, thoughts are persecutory and depressing because they must be tolerated. One must suffer the buildup of tension for thoughts to become part of a genuine thinking process. One must work them over and be worked on by them without knowing where this will lead. The discovery of thinking opens one to the siege of emotional truth, which has its own requirements and which may conflict with one's ordinary needs and wishes.

Yet primordial terror is something more than the tension between the requirements of emotional truth and survival or the break of thinking from oblivion. Something more pervasive and nameless is at work. Bion wrote that the sense of catastrophe *links* aspects of personality. It is the cement that holds the personality together, a primordial forming principle. Personality is bathed in the sense of catastrophe, as its sea and atmosphere. For Bion, there was something terrifying in the very birth of the self and the latter's inextricable tie to the oblivion that is part of it and that it is part of. In psychosis, it is personality itself that is the ongoing catastrophe. The sense of catastrophe straddles oblivion and form, a unity–disunity mixture. It seems already to have had a history when the infant first screams, and perhaps it is older than birth and even life. Emotional life bears the imprint of the combustible/conservative universe in which it occurs. Given the nature of our universe, it seems inevitable that cataclysm is a formative pole of our beings.

Whether or not Bion was right to view the sense of catastrophe as *the* primary fact of our emotional lives, it is a basic fact and in psychosis often the central one. It is an invariant that includes a range of more specific contents: dread of birth, death, change, boundlessness, sameness, the predator, isolation, castration, drowning, falling. Bion tracks a free-floating sense of catastrophe that grounds (or undermines) our existence. Its pervasiveness goes beyond any specifics we can name. Most of the time, we ignore it. But the psychotic individual can think of nothing else. He is propelled beyond ordinary thinking toward the thing itself.

In one of his accounts, Bion suggested that the earliest thinking involves the production of signs that point to an underlying and pervasive sense of catastrophe.[14] The psychotic patient he had in mind utters what sound like meaningless phrases. Yet the subject believes he can see these phrases because they are embodied in objects in the room. That is, his patient is convinced that somehow his sounds are connected to or even create the objects he sees ("in the beginning there was sound"). As Bion put it, this person utters actual objects, not simply phrases.

The objects he observes represent unseeable objects and so function as signs. An unseeable object may be the absent mother, but may also be something unnameable. For the psychotic person (or the psychotic aspect of self), visible objects are part and signals of an ongoing catastrophe. The catastrophe itself is invisible and ineffable. Tangible objects are its more or less momentary compressions. As noted above, the unnameable catastrophe may be conceived of in several ways, but it remains nameless. It may be dread of somethingness–nothingness, creation–destruction, oblivion–aliveness, or the cipher beyond.

If the patient is trying to seal himself off or maintain a nonposition in the null dimension, he is doomed to partial failure. Bion attributes at least a minimum of meaning to the patient's incoherent utterances. He likens his client's gestures to doodling in sound. Bion writes,

> In his case "writing" preceded not talking only but thinking. His actual speech was incomprehensible if I tried to unravel it by applying my knowledge of ordinary words and grammar. It became more meaningful if I thought of it as a doodling in sound, rather like tuneless and aimless whistling; it could not be described as speech, poetic speech, or music. Just as aimless whistling fails to be music because it does not obey any rule or discipline of musical composition, just as doodling fails to be drawing because it does not conform to the discipline of artistic creation, so his speech for lack of obedience to the usages of coherent speech did not qualify as verbal communication. The words employed fall into an undisciplined pattern of sound.[15]

14. Bion, *Elements of Psycho-Analysis*, pp. 37–40.
15. Ibid., p. 23.

We do not know whether the patient really was doodling in sound or whether this is only Bion's imaginative invention. It is likely that Bion did not know. His own sensitivity produces an image that has ordering value for him. We can guess that this thought made the patient's wayward meanderings bearable. Seeing the patient as doodling in sound lets the therapist remain empathic, yet maintain a certain distance, even humor. Supported by such a thought, the therapist may not only survive the session, but find himself quietly enlivened and perhaps of use.

Who orders whom? In this instance, Bion not only perceived the spewing of incoherent beta elements, but also could not avoid acting as a rudimentary maker of sense. It is Bion's psyche that develops the patient's invisible "writing" (Bion calls the birth of thinking a kind of "writing," here a signature of chaos), but it is the patient's impact that stimulates him. The patient is "seen" to utter objects in the room with the possibility of finding or disorganizing the shape or shapelessness of his existence through these objects. The therapist's inspiration acts to disclose or invent the patient's unborn or misborn world. The patient's incoherence expresses the zero state he attempts to achieve, and, at the same time, it is more than zero. The patient retains the possibility of learning what he means by observing the objects he speaks. He retains the possibility of meaning something by noting the nothing he tries to create.

We cannot tell from the data how Bion's patient reached the point of making meaningless patterns of sound. Is the person's apparent incoherence an attempt to reduce meaning to zero in order to enter into an invulnerable position? Or is it an attempt to return from zero and create or participate in an alternate reality? If the former, does the patient null meaning by hostile attacks on linking, or are his sounds the residue of a massive dismantling process in which mind and self fall away? If the latter, does catastrophe, as link, also drop off the end of the mental universe and into nothingness?

We can imagine how frustrating the therapist's organizing thought must be to the patient bent on sealing himself off from meaning. Where he would finally achieve a universe of absolute meaninglessness (painlessness), he is thwarted by the therapist's pigheaded stumbling on to sense. By entering the consulting room, he has tacitly consented to the intermixture and play of psyches. His space is not his own. He is prey to the other's visions and impulses. We would like to know whether the patient is bothered or relieved by Bion's conclusion. Is he reassured by the thereapist's interest that follows upon the latter's surprising and pleasing idea? Does he increase his efforts to jam meaning-producing gestures? Does he try to step up from or burrow more deeply into zero?

Bion relates the patient's movement within, toward, or out of the null dimension to a "failure" or "lack." In the previous quotation, he stresses the patient's lack of discipline, his inability or refusal to conform to the rules of discourse and discovery. Again, we cannot tell from this sketch what this lack owes to destructive hate and what to a sense of deficiency. This very inability suggests how profoundly linked these two elements often are. In psychosis (but not only in psychosis), a profound sense of deficiency may generate hate-filled processes and vice versa. It is precisely the individual's felt inability to participate in ordinary human interaction that drives him to set up alternate realities in which he reigns supreme and is victimized. From a seemingly inviolable position, he can attack threatening reality and spin it out of existence. He is left with a kingship of a nonexistent kingdom in which he, too, disappears.

In one way or another, we see similar processes every day. For example, a grade-school student may cover up his inability to read and write with toughness and bravado, or even violence. But underneath, the sense of deficiency festers, and in psychosis, it permeates the subject's psychic universe. It cannot be properly admitted, tolerated, and represented as such and so becomes a gulf that swallows up or taints everything the subject is and does.

It is an odd characteristic of the sense of catastrophe that it can be associated with something and nothing. A patient says, "I hold on to the ghastliness that grips me. It is my life. Without it I would be nothing," Another says, "I provoke catastrophes to feel alive. I don't know if I could live without feeling something terrible was about to happen. I make terrible things happen. I am a terrible happening." And yet when the catastrophic moment is upon him, the patient says,

"Now I am nothing but horror. Now I am nothing." Or again, "It is like being electrocuted forever. I vanish in the current. At first I am afraid of the shock, then become one with it. I am a shock going on and on in nowhere." Recall the blackness Carl fell into when catastrophe struck (Chapter 2, pp. 92–99). For Carl, a collapse into nothingness led to renewal. The saving darkness he found seemed to move him beyond the catastrophic moment, but it was a radical catastrophe that brought him there.

To speak of a zero point of mind takes us to the edge of meaning and perhaps over that edge. Yet the Zen master, as well as the psychotic, speaks of no-mind. Something very basic is meant when one speaks of nothingness and we have seen that there are many forms of nothingness. The nameless sense of catastrophe Bion points to moves between nothingness–somethingness–everythingness. It threatens to hurl the personality into an unimaginable abyss beyond oblivion, a horrific spacelessness in which there is no direction or valence other than horror itself. It fuses chaos and nothingness, scattered noise and blankness. This happens because the personality is in the process of disintegrating, experiencing and representing its disintegration, representing the disintegration of representations, and undoing itself and its representational capacity as far as inhumanly (yet all too humanly) possible.

Yet one wonders if the self is ever fully one with its sense of catastrophe. Bion begins his description by calling the patient's meaningless sounds a kind of "writing." And writing always involves some modicum of differentiation and deferral.[16] Although early expressive signals (e.g., screaming) are part of the catastrophic reality they point to, they also carry an implicit distancing element that can evolve (e.g., scream as evacuation, projection, communication). As the self goes under, it signals its dissolution in progress. It can do so only from some remaining quality of difference. Perhaps in the end, a difference remains between oneself and zero, and although it may be minuscule, it is infinite.

16. Derrida, "Freud and the Scene of Writing," pp. 196–231.

Blanking and Blissing Out

Tracing the primordial moments of consciousness and the birth of the self in infancy is a bit like the proverbial dog chasing its tail. An image of a triangle has sometimes been used to express the ambiguous structure of consciousness. The apex represents the sharper focus of consciousness, the broadening base is the field of awareness as it becomes fuzzier and disappears into an infinite subhorizon. To what extent the infinite subhorizon is characterized by a pervasive sense of catastrophe is debatable, if it is so characterized. At what point, and in what way, does the catastrophic sense become critical?

A traditional view is that catastrophe takes it subjective meaning from well-being, as evil does from good. What is felt as catastrophic is the breakup or loss of a prior goodness. Winnicott's[17] account of psychic development is firmly rooted in this optimistic outlook. He depicts an early sense of "going on being." The baseline of experience is a kind of moderate arousal level in which the infant has a playful interest in its world. Its "continuity of being" may be disrupted by drive pressures or the failure of caretakers. The infant maintains its continuity in face of or through good and bad feelings, up to a point. But if a breaking point is reached, the sense of continuity is lost. This rupture of continuity is associated with such primitive agonies as a return to an unintegrated state, falling forever, loss of psychosomatic unity, and loss of the sense of reality and the capacity to relate to objects.[18] In psychosis, the subject tries to find some way of organizing himself in the face of an unthinkable agony, in which the personality is threatened by a fate worse than nothingness.

In one of his descriptions, Winnicott expressed this break in the infant's sense of ongoing being in terms of a time element. He writes,

> The baby is distressed, but this distress is soon *mended* because the mother returns in $x + y$ minutes. In $x + y$ minutes the baby has not

17. Winnicott, "Mind and Its Relation to the Psyche-Soma," pp. 243–254.
18. Winnicott, "Fear of Breakdown," pp. 103–107; idem, "Ego Integration in Child Development," p. 58.

become altered. But in $x + y + z$ minutes the baby has become *traumatized*. In $x + y + z$ minutes the mother's return does not mend the baby's altered state. Trauma implies that the baby has experienced a break in life's continuity, so that primitive defences now become organized to defend against a repetition of "unthinkable anxiety" or a return of the acute confusional state that belongs to disintegration of nascent ego structure.

Madness here simply means a *break-up* of whatever may exist at the time of a *personal continuity of existence*. After "recovery" from the $x + y + z$ deprivation a baby has to start again permanently deprived of the root which could provide *continuity with the personal beginning*.[19]

Thus, in Winnicott's account, there is a primacy of continuity. Discontinuity takes its meaning from what happens to a primary sense of continuity. It is a fissuring, dissolving, or breaking process. For an evil eternity, the infant's ability to experience and symbolize life enhancing connectedness with its supporting milieu is lost. Winnicott writes that even $x + y + z$ degree of deprivation can be "cured" by the mother through selective spoiling behavior.[20] The mother nurses the baby back into existence to the point where separation and discontinuity can once more be tolerated and used for growth purposes. Winnicott stressed the primacy of the link between self and other and between self and self. Separation separates within a broader context of union or sense of connection. It is the sense of interweaving that makes separateness tolerable. He even writes, "this is the place that I have set to examine, the separation that is not a separation but a form of union."[21] In contrast, the separation that is part of too great a loss of continuity marks the self with a sense of unreality, spuriousness, and unthinkable catastrophe.

We can partially unify Bion's and Winnicott's concerns by understanding the sense of catastrophe as inbuilt, but not necessarily primary. The first catastrophe may not be the infant's dawning awareness of his psychic reality, but rather his early fears of losing it. The infant's sense of being is time and again threatened by on-

19. Winnicott, "The Location of Cultural Experience," p. 97.
20. Ibid.
21. Ibid., p. 98.

slaughts of stimuli for which he lacks a frame of reference. A sudden rush of blood through his head or intense pangs of hunger can disrupt and overwhelm his sense of continuity. The infant may scream out of fury and panic in the face of such uncontrollable upheavals. If help is not sure and quick enough, he may become stuporous and lose the consciousness he enjoyed moments earlier. A state of stuporous mindlessness replaces the sense of ongoing being.

The supportive intervention of the other brings the infant back to life and restores his sense of continuity. In time, the infant trusts the other will try to help him, and his sense of continuity becomes firm enough to encompass a certain degree of discontinuity. He learns to maintain his sense of being in the face of a potentially catastrophic anxiety. If, as time goes on, the mother chronically fails in her life-supporting function, the infant's sense of being may collapse or become damaged. The stupor that once relieved him in face of catastrophe becomes part of a debilitating attempt at self-repair or, finally, a giving up, a lapse into unintegration. What begins as a pleasurable, even joyous aliveness ends in a hopeless blanking out in the face of unrelieved horror and incapacity. We are all marked by dead or numb spots that, at the deepest levels, bear witness to a loss or lapse of existence that once seemed endless.

The blanking out pointed to here is more primitive than denial. An elemental response to agony, it threatens to continue endlessly. To various degrees, the infant tones down, shuts off, and dies out. The infant does not yet know about physical death. What is lost is his implicit sense of ongoing being, his psychophysical aliveness, his dawning awareness of being there, his primordial self-feeling. Over and over he goes through the experience of dying out and coming back, the most ghastly horror and the saving bliss.[22] If, however, the infant repeatedly returns from its lapse into nothingness to the same torment it left, it may come to mold itself more and more around the need for self-obliteration. His sense of aliveness is equated with hopeless misery and gradually dissolves into an encompassing blank-

22. Eigen, "The Area of Faith in Winnicott, Lacan and Bion," pp. 413–433; Elkin, "On Selfhood and Ego Structures in Infancy," pp. 57–76.

ness. He is encased in a self-numbing process, which may harden and become even harder as the years go on.

In many instances, this blanking out process underlies or is part of a chronic depressive atmosphere that can inform a life. In this context, depression has a self-soothing function. It may be so much a part of the background of existence that an individual scarcely notices it. Or it may signal that something is wrong. Even when depression is painful, it tends to reduce the impact of stimulation. Its presence usually suggests that some state of affairs has proven too much for the subject.

On the other hand, bliss can also lead to a loss of personal self-feeling. In normal infancy, pain is often blurred by blissful feelings. The infant's screams and its tears inspire the mother to embrace and comfort it. The baby's troubling feelings are soothed away and vanish in an erotic heaven. Its fear and rage are not so much solved as dissolved. Troublesome feelings may fall back into an unstructured state or become structured by such later defenses as splitting and projection. In time, the baby may come to identify with the mother's well-intentioned soothing and bliss-inducing activity. It will learn to dissolve bad feelings with good ones. The price paid for this maintenance of well-being is the tendency to lose the many personal feelings that are difficult. In effect, one feels good by sacrificing psychic complexity. The distance element in therapy helps bring out the feelings lost in fusion with the good side of mother, but also shows the hole left by too great an absence of holding.

The sense of catastrophe may not only be linked with loss of self, but also a sense that the self is starting off wrongly. Very young children often are aware that something has gone wrong, and it is not unusual for an adult or teenager to say, "I have felt something off ever since I can remember. Something was wrong from the beginning."

The sense of catastrophe may be part of a feedback system that mirrors how poor a start the self is getting or how skewed a direction its development is taking. It is more than a warning. It has vectorial properties that direct the personality to reset itself. Often, the subject fails in his attempt to right himself and to establish the proper links with himself and others. It may be that no matter what one does it is not possible to generate the kind of relationship that would help correct matters. The self keeps trying and failing, until the sense of catastrophe begins to lose its value as signal and becomes the subject's authentic reality. The sense of catastrophe is no longer a transitional part of a broader and ultimately corrective process; rather, it blurs out all possibility of being. It threatens to be everything forever, a menacing cipher. It is a dreadful nothingness, as opposed to the stupor or bliss that brings temporary relief.

In time, the subject adapts to it and the sense of catastrophe becomes dull and blank. One loses one's sensitivity to catastrophe and no longer experiences its increasing horrors. It may be possible for a culture to do this on a grand scale. We lose our sensitivity to our most pressing dangers, much as the toad boils to death without noticing that the water is gradually becoming hotter.

Mindlessness, Hallucination, and Creativity

How mindlessness is related to hallucination raises difficult questions. Often the two seem to converge. There is a kind of mindlessness in the hallucinated state of satisfaction that replaces a painful situation. And there is perhaps something hallucinatory in mindless bliss. Negative hallucinatory processes may help the ego cover its tracks in repression and keep dissociated personality systems seemingly oblivious of one another. In both repression and dissociation, the personality "knows" what it is about. It knows what, when, and how to repress and dissociate. Yet an essential element of the subject's psychic operation is a quasi-obliviousness to the true predicament. It is as if the mind keeps out of awareness precisely what would give the show away. The trick or the "lie" or *méconnaissance* is hidden. One is scarcely aware that the trickster self, fighting for its life, leads the personality on with hallucinatory scenes and mindless chasms.

Lewin[23] suggests that blank dreams give the subject a glimpse of the "dream screen," the blank screen or space on which dream contents are projected. He finds that this hallucinatory blankness often represents the breast or the final moment of the "oral triad." In feeding, the baby is supposed to have unconscious fantasies of devouring, being devoured and, finally, blissful oneness. If the nursing sequence is successful, the infant and mother are felt to penetrate–permeate one another actively and passively. They "eat each other up." Under good circumstances, the baby falls happily asleep, fulfilled and nourished. His blankness symbolizes this climactic oneness. Total satisfaction and a happy oblivion are one.

When the outcome is poor, unmitigated destructiveness may prevail. The subject vanishes into a wretched hallucinatory chasm. In the most severe cases, hallucination and mindlessness may seem to intersect as the subject approaches zero. It would appear, though, that when there is not even enough energy for hallucination, the subject collapses into an obliterating and final mindlessness.

Mindlessness and hallucination are frequently distinguishable in terms of subjective time and velocity. Hallucinations often involve a speeding up, and mindlessness a slowing down of experience. In hallucinations, the speed tends to bring experience to a standstill, and one small portion of experience is heightened to an extreme degree. The subject is hypersensitive in a highly selective way. Everything seems to gain its meaning from this small portion of experience. Yet this very smallness seems to add to the intensity of all experience. The individual's hallucinatory concerns dominate the psychic field and draw all meaning into their orbit; thus, things may appear more vivid, or be seen as more menacing or blissful, than in ordinary life.

One individual put it this way:

Things raced, leaped out at me. It was as if I were being attacked by the sight and sound of things. There was a heightening of everything, a glistening, a landslide. Things went faster and faster and angles were sharper. Faces were pointier—cut into me. It all had this incredible speed

23. Lewin, *Selected Writings*, pp. 87–163, 261–267.

yet was so endless. Not that there wasn't any time. It's just that time stood still it went so fast.

When the individual approximates states of mindlessness, things may also reach a standstill by slowing down. As one person described an experience:

I felt I was under water. Things were thick, heavy, in slow motion. It was like yawning and stretching for a long time but it didn't feel good. I felt my mind had been injected with novocaine. At first I tried to shake the numbness off but it spread through me and took me over. I was like a lizard without feeling. I knew it was a protection and would go away. But it didn't. I was paralyzed. My thoughts ticked like a metronome going slower and slower. I feared my heart would slow down so much it would stop beating. My eyes closed for long periods and I saw dark masses, black, amorphous clouds. I felt them with my eyes open. A nowhere forever. I remember thinking, "I'm going away." Now I think I tried to vanish and couldn't quite make it—yet came very close.

Although I have often found slowness and speed, respectively, to be phenomenological characteristics of mindlessness and hallucination, this stereotypical formula is too simple. For example, Carl's hallucinatory struggles and Leila's spins into mindlessness seemed quickening processes, whereas Frank's hallucinatory world seemed closer to Lenny's numbness. One could characterize Leila and Carl as searchers; Frank and Lenny seemed less touched by a heroic drive. However, at present little is known about such phenomenological and functional speed differences.

Mental processes can go on with incredible rapidity in autistic states. Meltzer[24] speaks of the "dazzling display of the speed and complexity of the mental apparatus" of autistic children, which alternates with a "suspended mental functioning" resembling a petit mal attack.

The notion of a mindlessness, in which the mind works with incredible speed, is paradoxical. Ehrenzweig[25] depicts the "vague

24. Meltzer et al., *Explorations in Autism*, p. 7.
25. Ehrenzweig, *Hidden Order of Art*, pp. 21–46, 95–109, 171–256.

stare" of the artist, a kind of blank state of mind in which unconscious scanning processes work at high speed. He hypothesizes an "unconscious undifferentiated ego matrix," in which the usual structural and semantic differences dissolve and new patterns of relationship emerge. Many mythic and fantasy images depict this dissolution and return (e.g., dying god–resurrection imagery). It is a state in which passivity and activity seem to meld. The personality gives up control, yet quickens by "vaguing out" surface levels of attention and perception. In this context, self-destructive imagery may represent the ego's attempt to break down formal structures that impede unconscious scanning processes, so that it may approach a kind of zero point that leads to renewal. Hallucinations or hallucinatory-like imagery can mark various stages of the ego's journey toward and back from the "mindless" moment.

Matte-Blanco distinguishes between differentiated (conscious) and undifferentiated (unrepressed unconscious) modes of being.[26] The undifferentiated mode overlaps with Ehrenzweig's undifferentiated ego matrix, with important differences. Matte-Blanco suggested that in unrepressed unconscious processes the members within a class are treated as equivalent and so can substitute for one another (e.g., all women are mother). If the tendency toward undifferentiation wins out completely, everything is equivalent to everything else. One may hypothesize such a moment as a limit concept insofar as it helps in the study of the tension between differentiation and interchangeability. In Matte-Blanco's scheme, Ehrenzweig's unconscious scanning registers and utilizes the spread of unconscious equivalences that approaches infinity, a basic homogeneity in which differences are reshuffled.

Milner writes of a "pregnant emptiness," a no-mind state of being that allows the new to enter.[27,28] For Milner, such a state may seem catastrophic to surface functions, but, paradoxically, she describes the emptiness as a plenitude. It is a kind of psychic orgasm in which

26. Matte-Blanco, *The Unconscious as Infinite Sets*, pp. 80–186.
27. Milner, *On Not Being Able to Paint*, pp. 104–105, 148–167.
28. Eigen, "Dual Union or Undifferentiation," pp. 415–428.

the oneness of time and timelessness is heightened. In this emptiness, one is fully alive.

For Milner, emptiness is a method and a goal. It is through emptiness that one learns to still surface functions in order to be empty. One empties oneself of extra baggage. The resulting emptiness has diverse meanings. It represents a presumed infant–mother oneness before the separation of subject and object. Yet it also is and represents the sense of psychic creativeness in raw or pure form. Milner feels that art most basically seeks to symbolize our underlying and ecstatic sense of creativeness. The sense of creativeness embraces the whole range of human experience, from joy to terror. The hallucinatory vividness that sometimes characterizes perceptual and symbolic experiencing hints at the power that an openness to expressive qualities may discover. For Milner, perception is a form of imagination, and the latter is renewed through a return to and from an inspired mindlessness.

Winnicott's creative "chaos" and "unintegration"[29] are related to Milner's "emptiness." Winnicott is concerned with the individual moving past his defensiveness to a sense of his true self. For a person to do this, he may have to let go of the usual ways of organizing the self and tolerate living in "formlessness." He may have to reach and tolerate periods of seemingly aimless psychic puttering about (Bion's "doodling with sound"). Winnicott expresses this by saying that, in therapy, a setting is provided in which the patient may learn how to play.

In this process, a person may fear breakdown. Winnicott suggests that the breakdown feared is probably one that has already happened, but was covered up.[30] In infancy, one's sense of being is disrupted in various ways. The infant passes through states that it lacks the resources to process adequately. At such moments, it passes from being to mindless unintegration, a kind of chaotic oblivion. One task of therapy is to help an individual allow such moments of unintegration to emerge. At such moments, one has nothing to hold

29. Winnicott, *Playing and Reality*, pp. 38–64; see also Chapter 1 in this volume.
30. Winnicott, "Fear of Breakdown," pp. 103–107.

on to. One starts anew or aborts the venture of self-discovery by prematurely organizing defenses. The latter puts an end to one's fear of nothingness, but at the expense of a kind of hardening of the psychic arteries. One closes oneself to the regenerative possibilities of loss of mind and self.[31]

Which is more basic—emptiness or chaos? In Winnicott's terms, both are formless. Chaos certainly feels noisier and seems to appear against a background or horizon of emptiness. That chaos seems to have more figure properties than emptiness is doubtless one reason Green associates the former with intrusion and the latter with separation anxiety[32] (although anxiety itself tends to be intrusive). Nevertheless, as gestalt psychology shows, although a background may be experienced as more homogeneous than a foreground, it also has some differentiated properties. And as we have seen, emptiness, nothingness, and mindlessness have many "forms" and functions.

I do not believe the issue of whether chaos or emptiness is more basic is resolvable. I suspect that assertion of primacy is a matter of temperament. Emptiness refers to a passive aspect of human experience, chaos to "mindless" activity. Either may be vividly life-enhancing, or deadening. One moves back and forth between chaos and emptiness, between more or less activity and passivity. The formless dust kicked up in chaos settles in emptiness, yet both generate forms. The patient Bion heard as doodling in sound expressed the life or death of the self in chaotically active terms. One can paradoxically say that mind was giving birth to itself by a process of mindless signaling—an active process. Winnicott's drop into chaos involves a kind of formless activity, yet it also requires a passive element, a just being. Are chaos and nothingness a reversible figure-ground for each other? Do both arise from a more unknown dynamic ground in which opposites are one?

We are left for the moment with a Chinese box situation, a situation long ago represented by the Taoist *T'ai- chi tu* figure, which

---

31. This basic theme runs through nearly all of Winnicott's clinical writings.
32. Green, "The Analyst, Symbolization and Absence in the Analytic Setting," pp. 1–22.

portrays the interaction of Yin and Yang. Activity is in the passive
and passivity in the active principle and they interface at a dynamic
boundary. The figure is meant to point to a basic order in the
unorganizable, a unity of opposites. The greater part is empty space,
encircled. One may object that this figure is too geometrical to
represent chaos or emptiness, that its function is just the opposite—to
wrest a starting point from the abyss. But with such an image, we
gain a toehold in openness, a place that enables us to take further
steps, and leap. But this circle appears on an object beyond it, perhaps
a page or painting, itself a figure in a larger horizon, and so on to
infinity. It points to what it is and is not. It is a figure that evokes a
sense of its relationship to non-figure (formlessness) through many
levels of psychic meaning. As a circle, it is one. Its contents are more
than one. Its ultimate background is zero. The one, the many, and
no-thingness are all involved with infinity.

The question of the one and many haunts psychoanalysis. Balint
speaks of one-, two-, and three-person formations.[33] Three refers to
the Oedipus conflict, two to the mother–infant dyad or, more
broadly, the "harmonious interpenetrating mix-up" of infant and
surround. By a one-person relationship, Balint wants to suggest an
area of the mind in which no external object is present. He writes,

> The subject is on his own and his main concern is to produce something
> out of himself; this something to be produced may be an object, but is not
> necessarily so. I propose to call this the level or area of creation. The most
> often-discussed example is . . . artistic creation, but other phenomena
> belong to the same group, among them mathematics, philosophy, gaining
> insight, understanding something or somebody; and . . . the early phases
> of becoming—bodily or mentally—"ill" and spontaneous recovery from
> "illness."[34]

Our language and social life exert pressure to turn this one-person
into a two- or three-person relationship. Most often, we use the
language of childbirth to describe it, a language oriented toward the
object rather than process. Balint understands Bion's beta and alpha

33. Balint, *The Basic Fault*, pp. 3–31.
34. Ibid., p. 24.

elements and alpha function as attempts to find a way to study the area of creation. Balint proposes the terms *pre-object* or *Objeckt-Anlage* as possible points of entry. One might say that the person is not alone at this level of being or that he is alone with his pre-objects. The latter "must be so primitive that they cannot be considered 'organized' or 'whole.' Only after the work of creation has succeeded in making them 'organized,' or 'whole,' can . . . interaction between them and external objects take place."[35]

Balint's area of creation seems to be connected to Winnicott's play, unintegration, and creative chaos. Both involve letting go of the usual ways of organizing oneself until a kind of primordial openness appears. Balint emphasizes that we know very little about this area. What do pre-objects look like? How are they transformed into objects? Why does this happen with lightning speed in some cases and take so long in others? How does one communicate with pre-objects? At times, the silent patient (like the silent analyst) may be doing much more than "resisting."

One can scarcely call the area of creation mindless. If it resembles a blank autistic state, it is often a subtly populated blankness. For example, Einstein wrote that he thought with vague muscular sensations and inchoate bits of image.[36] When things felt right and came together he translated his "felt meaning" into something communicable. It is as if one can almost see what goes on in the dark, but not quite. There are stirrings and promptings, a blankness yet intense absorption and a sense of something deeper at work. What is mindless? What is at work? It would seem that a bipolarity characterizes absorption: an openness, letting go, and immersion, on the one hand, a heightened activity, on the other, an intermingling of "passive" and "active" gestures, a state in which there is both nothing and something.

Is there an isomorphism between absorption and the structure of perception? That is, is no-thing the encompassing background or surround and vague stirrings incipient movements toward form? Are

35. Ibid., p. 25.
36. Einstein, "Letter to Jacques Hadamard," pp. 43–44.

these intimations already forms of a sort? Are they perturbations of
no-thingness, comparable to what might be the case if ripples of
darkness could be felt? Or is the formless darkness a medium for a
deeper activity? Are we at the edge of the experienceable or entering
a "territory" we can speak from and about as other horizons appear?

William Blake used the image of pulsation to evoke a sense of the
area of creation. In "Milton" he wrote,

> Every Time less than a pulsation of the artery
> Is equal in its period & value to Six Thousand Years,
> For in this Period the Poet's Work is Done: and all the Great
> Events of Time start forth & are conceiv'd in such a Period,
> Within a Moment, a Pulsation of the Artery.[37]

In contemporary psychoanalysis, Lacan speaks of pulsation to
describe the relationship between unconscious and conscious fields of
experience.[38] Unconscious and conscious dimensions communicate
through "rhythmic pulsations of the slit." For Lacan, the "slit" is the
hole in nature occasioned by the advent of the signifier. The human
subject is made possible by the discontinuity or split the bipolar
emergence of conscious–unconscious symbolic life is witness to. In a
sense, the human subject is the discontinuity that inaugurates him;
lack, his own elusiveness, is part of his defining structure. Lack and
signifier are aspects of the same constitutive stroke. The cry makes
silence emerge as silence, "the stroke of the opening makes absence
emerge."[39]

Signification gains its power by pointing to what is not there. A
cry may be an outward signal of invisible events that represent the
absent mother, or absence as such. A gap or lack is created, expressed, and filled in by crying. Demand testifies to lack as it tries to
foreclose it. The background is absence, the foreground signifier.
The unconscious is absence, the "thing that isn't there," which
spreads everywhere, like death. Part of the ability to signify involves

37. Blake, "Milton," ll. 28.62–29.3, p. 516.
38. Lacan, *Four Fundamental Concepts of Psycho-Analysis*, p. 43.
39. Ibid., p. 26.

slipping away, the signifier's built-in capacity to cancel itself, to signify itself as missing. We try to fill in for it or create substitutes, but in one way or another, the pulsations of the unconscious surprise us and for a moment we catch a glimpse of a founding gap.

The notion of no-thingness in the interstices of language and language itself as elusive lacework is part of French poetics, at least since the nineteenth century. It haunts Rimbaud and is explicitly celebrated in the prose poems of Mallarmé. Silence and mystery, love and death are interwoven associations. For Lacan, in part, the void that empowers or eviscerates human existence is created by the birth of language or, at least, is analogous to the sound–silence relation intrinsic to the life of meaning. Lacan repeatedly insists that his is not a psychology of the ineffable. He is a psychoanalyst, not a mystic. Freud irrevocably placed psychoanalysis toward one side of mysticism. For Lacan, the psychoanalysis of mysticism is an attempt to understand illusion, and one does this, in part, by discovering how human beings live (or fail to live) through signifiers.

Bion stresses the importance of developing a psychology of signs before symbols.[40] He notes that psychoanalysts (perhaps social scientists, in general) tend to speak of symbol when they really mean sign. The psychotic patient signals rather than symbolizes his ongoing sense of catastrophe. The materials he uses may resemble symbols, but they are used to point to an unnameable psychic reality. Similarly, the borderline patient must often be taught to link up words and feelings. He often lacks the verbal labels for elementary emotional states and thrashes wildly about or sinks in kaleidoscopic confusion. This basic creation of link between word and affect is not so much the use of words as symbols than as signals for imminent psychic events.

It is difficult to determine where the break with oblivion came for Bion. As mentioned earlier, Bion described the first thoughts, which he called beta elements, as mindless hallucinations. Beta elements loom as "objects compounded of things-in-themselves, feelings of depression–persecution and guilt and therefore aspects of personality

40. Bion, *Elements of Psycho-Analysis*, Chapter 9.

linked by a sense of catastrophe."[41] The first thoughts are non-thoughts, raw materials that must be reworked before they can become part of a thinking process. They grip the subject with catastrophic intensity. One might depict them as raw affective states that fuse image–sensation–perception. The personality has no frame of reference for them, so that they spread through the infantile cosmos with infinite horror, a kind of electrocution from no tangible source.

For Bion, the catastrophic nature of its own life is the first and most basic task the psyche must take up.[42] A toehold is achieved in catastrophic oblivion and the oblivion of catastrophe by the growth of elemental signals for one's predicament (e.g., screaming as expression, evacuation, projection, communication). It is the psyche's basic job to transmute initial catastrophic globs of experience into psychically soluble events. Bion calls the capacity to do this alpha function. The great creation–destruction myths, so basic a part of religious and psychotic imagery, express this transformational work. They act as signals for the sense of wonder, curiosity, and catastrophe that are part of the advent and evolution of the self. Beta elements are gestated by alpha function into an alive affective thinking process (e.g., dream work, mythic systems, signs into symbols, and, finally, reflection on signs and symbols). Bion uses such terms as beta and alpha elements and alpha function, in part, as reminders that our picture of the birth of our psychic universe is still open. We need to keep revisualizing our beginnings. Such terms gain meaning as we go along.

In psychosis, the transmuting of beta elements into food for thought runs amok, and the process may even be thrown into reverse gear. The personality may collapse to a point at which raw beta elements run wild. The latter now assume the more malignant status of failed thoughts, rather than merely unborn ones. In effect, the "pristine" catastrophe of our psychic origins becomes demonized. In such an instance, one seeks to deny rather than affirm the possibility of psychic birth.

41. Ibid., pp. 39–40.
42. Eigen, "Toward Bion's Starting Point," pp. 321–330.

Bion's picture of our psychic beginnings raises many questions. What mental acts give rise to beta elements in the first place? How do these mindless, hallucinatory globs link up with thinking? Is this linking already a thinking? Do beta elements act as stimulus releasers for thinking? Or does their origin involve an infinite regression, a primary process of primary process? If so, is it all right to break off this redundancy after, say, the third cycle (along the model of consciousness of consciousness of consciousness)? Are we creating subhorizon after subhorizon or discovering how we are made? Isn't such creation/discovery part of our make-up? And so on.

Whether or not the problems in Bion's thought are insuperable, it is important to bring out the governing vision. For Bion, the self is born, evolves, and dies with a sense of catastrophe. Catastrophe may not be the only ingredient, but it is a fundamental one. Psychosis brings out elemental catastrophic states that implicitly permeate our consciousness. The question that arises is whether anything exists in human nature to offset the sense of catastrophe in a fertile rather than a palliative way. What enables us to face and work with catastrophic reality in freeing ways? A capacity as deep or deeper than the sense of catastrophe must be called forth if healing or true maturation is to occur.

Bion's "solution" is a radical one: the proper response to catastrophe is faith (F).[43] To be sure, faith of a sort can be used as a self-soothing opiate, but this is not what Bion means. He tries to point to an attitude that opens one to the impact of psychic reality. In a developed sense, faith is *the* essential quality of the psychoanalytic attitude. For Bion, the latter (Freud's "free-floating attention") requires one to abstain from expectations, memory, desire, and understanding. It leaves one nothing to hold on to. We suspend our attachments and allow the play of psychic reality to evolve.

Bion uses the sign "O," to stand for the emotional reality of moment or, in general, ultimate reality as such. In itself it is unknowable, but the analyst opens himself in the faith that he will meet it. He

---

43. Bion, *Attention and Interpretation*, pp. 31–61, 92–105; Eigen, "The Area of Faith in Winnicott, Lacan and Bion," pp. 413–433; idem, "Toward Bion's Starting Point," pp. 321–330.

aims at the emotional truth of a session. The impact of the patient is translated into guesses or convictions about what is happening. The situation is both Kantian and mystical. The analyst aims at ultimate reality, but must work with hypotheses. Yet the personality change that occurs is one of being, not simply knowing (K). It is not that memory and knowing are lost. Our psychic life could not exist without them. Rather, Bion attempts to place our capacities in a broader context. A primacy of faith enables us to know and remember less dissociatively, as part of a fertile growth process.

Thus, F in O approaches an attitude of pure receptiveness. It is an alert readiness, an alive waiting, akin to the biblical tale of the soul who must stay awake at night lest it miss its Bridegroom. Bion describes how uncomfortable one may be in this open state. One must tolerate fragmentation, whirls of bits and pieces of meaning and meaninglessness, chaotic blankness, dry periods, and psychic duststorms. Yet Bion also suggests such states can be trance-like and akin to hallucinosis. He writes,

> Receptiveness achieved by denudation of memory and desire (which is essential to the operation of "acts of faith") is essential to the operation psycho-analysis and other scientific proceedings. It is essential for experiencing hallucination or the state of hallucinosis.
>
> This state [hallucinosis] I do not regard as an exaggeration of pathological or even natural condition: I consider it rather to be a state always present, but overlaid by other phenomena, which screen it. If these other elements can be moderated or suspended hallucinosis becomes demonstrable; its full depth and richness are accessible only to "acts of faith." Elements of hallucinosis of which it is possible to be sensible are the grosser manifestations and are of secondary importance. To appreciate hallucination the analyst must participate in the state of hallucinosis.[44]

Apparently the momentary vagueness or clarity of F in O is incidental to the basic attitude of readiness without hooks or supports. Bion depicts F in O as a gateway to hallucinosis. The temporary suspension of attachment to mind allows an underlying hallucinatory di-

---

44. Bion, *Attention and Interpretation*, pp. 35–36.

mension to appear. Much of our everyday behavior is governed by hallucinosis without our knowing it. The essential contents of hallucinations are beta elements, our point of origin. F in O opens us up to the pristine catastrophe of psychic birth.

If a growing individual learns to attend to what menaces him, he may be rewarded by the rich elaboration of a perceptual–conceptual network in which the meaning of things evolves. A paradoxical result is that faith enhances rather than mutes precision. One's contact with subtle nuances of experience deepens as one develops an appreciative sensibility for what remains out of reach. The very taste of experience gains new meaning. The subject learns the gesture of repeatedly starting from scratch, of living in a wallness moment and sensing his walls in a way that makes a difference.

However, when the psyche works in reverse, beta elements portend, not new beginnings, but rather the end of the psychic universe. The rebirth archetype degenerates into demonized repetitiousness and finally vanishes in a mindless sea of catastrophe. Bion offered many descriptions of how an originating sense of catastrophe goes awry. The psychotic individual often falls upon the raw catastrophe of our psychic origins only to turn it into a permanent anesthetic. He learns to administer doses of catastrophe as needed, in order to blank out aspects of himself and external reality.

The psychoanalytic attitude, too, involves a certain "mindlessness," a letting go and clearing out. The psychoanalyst makes productive contact with the domain in which the psychotic person vanishes, freezes, or drowns. Hallucinosis is employed as an empathic method, a method of discovery, whereas the psychotic is lost or sealed off in it. One might call the psychoanalytic attitude a scientific use of faith. Through F in O, one allows experience in hallucinosis to evolve. One grows through hallucinosis. Insofar as the psychotic individual forecloses faith, he gets caught in his hallucinations. It may turn out that, even in psychosis, hallucination has some relationship to faith, inasmuch as both hallucinosis and faith have been warped. The psychotic patient who, in time, develops a taste for the psychoanalytic attitude, may begin to put the capacities he has stumbled upon to better use.

In a sense, faith fights catastrophe with catastrophe.[45] It can shatter our attempt to cling to well-intentioned security systems. Contact with a castastrophic reality shatters the lies we have built up to protect ourselves. To blunt our awareness of catastrophe is to lose or never gain a sense of who we are. Faith thrives at our cutting edge. It sustains our approach to and our tolerance of ourselves. It keeps our sensitivity to ourselves alive. Our personality deepens when we are led by F in O.

Bion notes that the human race is ill-equipped to tolerate its own experiential capacity. It naturally orients itself toward external objects and the tasks of survival. The grim paradox is that insofar as we cannot admit and work with the sense of catastrophe that constitutes psychic reality, we may heighten external catastrophes as a way of objectifying ourselves. We may finally know ourselves through the dramatizations that hurl us into oblivion.

The "mindlessness" of catastrophe is met by the "mindlessness" of faith. Hallucinosis vanishes and returns through the open attitude of the mindless moment. Through specific hallucinations, bits and pieces of an unknowable catastrophic psychic reality are brought into focus. In time, the analyst creates/discovers interventions that make sense of them. If his sense is deeply rooted in the non-sense beyond knowing, his work may have a resonance that makes a difference.

45. Ibid., pp. 41–54, 98–105; Eigen, "Toward Bion's Starting Point," pp. 326–330.

CHAPTER FOUR

Boundaries

ONE OF THE FARTHEST reaching mysteries of the human self is that its sense of boundaries shifts in radical ways. The sense of self can expand to include all existence or shrink even to exclude itself. Animals, also, are concerned with boundaries and may fight over territory. But in human life, the stakes are raised to a new level. The very fit between the self and its sense of space and time can be thrown into question and well-nigh obliterated. Psychotics are riddled with profound boundary problems, which raise basic issues concerning the nature of our relationships to ourselves, others, and the cosmos.

Everyday Experience and Boundlessness

Human infants often behave as if they inhabit the same world we do. When alert, their behavior seems spontaneously in tune with an organized perceptual field. They show interest in objects, track movements, and prefer certain configurations over others. They develop attachments and, in general, act as if their world is not chaotic. There are, of course, important differences between infantile and adult reality. The infant undergoes a dramatic maturational unfolding. The quality of his existence will shift in surprising ways. He learns how to learn over and over again. But, to an important extent, he begins life as if it fits him and he fits it. In itself this is not surprising, since animals, in general, seem to be born into a structurally coherent world. Ordering processes permeate life and there is no reason to suppose they do not characterize infantile experience from the outset.

However, the infant does not always act as if he inhabits the world we do. At times, we are at a loss to understand what an infant is going through. His distresses and pleasures are not connected with anything we can pin down. Momentous upheavals seem to come out of nowhere. His reactions are unmodulated and unbounded. Perhaps he sees something nightmarish. Or perhaps a sensation (e.g., blood coursing through his head) for which he lacks a frame of reference overwhelms him. We cannot know, but we can guess. We feel there must be a reason for what we see. At such moments, we glimpse a world in which feelings and visions are magnified beyond all sense of proportion. Affective images and sensations, infinite and gripping, spread across the universe. Perhaps the infant then lives in a world that approximates what we later call hallucination. The coordination of everyday perception with fantastic experience is one of our fundamental developmental tasks.

Psychosis brings home how difficult it can be to relate our different worlds of experience adequately. One world seems to superimpose itself on or swallow up another. Often the psychotic, like the mystic, feels he has pierced the veil of appearances and reached the thing itself. In William Blake's phrase, "perception appears as it is, infinite." In psychosis, however, the key is usually one of infinite horror.

Carl (Chapters 2 and 3) spoke of the juxtaposition of line and color in his perception of physiognomy. In a description of a turning point in his hospital stay he said,

> The world was in Rembrandt colors, rich and darkly glowing. Miss Sharp [the head nurse] never stood still. She was tall and thin and walked briskly. From a distance she looked like a devil and I was surprised to find how nice she was when I spoke to her. The lines in her face stuck out like big, skinny bones but she wasn't sticky or pushy. I felt she wanted to help me. I felt bathed by the colors of her skin and her bony lines made

me feel alive. They were spikes and spurs to climb with. She was a mountain. She popped out of the picture. I remember the first moment I thought, "Why she's a real person." It was the first time I saw someone who was not mainly a devil. For days I stole glimpses of her to check if it was really true.

Here Carl recounts a moment in the middle of his hospital stay when things began to clear a bit. The world of everyday perception resurfaced through his hallucinatory spin. The claims of Miss Sharp as person and devil competed, with person once more in ascendency. Yet everyday perception was never totally lost. It provided the frame that supported his hallucinatory drama. Even if the world seems to fall apart or end, the psychotic subject still walks about and talks in it. He does not walk into trees. The girders of ordinary perception function as a staging or launching area of hallucinatory boundlessness, while this boundlessness threatens to sweep perception away.

In Carl's case, hallucination continued to saturate perception. Everyday perception had a hallucinatory glow. Prominent points of interest in ordinary physiognomy were magnified and put to special use. Miss Sharp's facial lines and psychophysical activity became bones, spikes, and spurs. She was at once a stimulating and comforting presence and an energizing mountain (a fusion of phallic and nurturing qualities). Something about her personal being was able to support hallucinatory play without caving in. For the moment, perception and hallucination achieved an uneasy but workable alliance. Although their boundaries blurred, they reinforced rather than tore each other apart. Carl was able to breathe a little easier. His interest in another human being was aroused. The experience of the human as a valid dimension showed signs of taking hold.

Implicit in the above discussion is the profound difficulty inherent in coordinating our sense of immateriality and materiality. In psychosis, these two experiential dimensions split and fuse in ways that focus the practical importance of this problem. For example, during his therapy, Carl oscillated between feeling he had no body and feeling that his body was the only thing that counted. Leila (Chapter 3) reported seeing her body from above. When she tried to reenter it, it felt oddly rubbery and dull, like dead skin. She was repulsed by the idea of putting it back on, much as one is disgusted by ejected spittle. When questioned she could not say whether it ejected her or she it. Neither seemed at ease with the other. In Frank's world (Chapter 2) spirit seemed to vanish altogether in a fecalized material universe.

When Carl was a child he often dreamt of flying through the air or riding on secret underground trains, performing heroic deeds. In his flights he felt boundless and airy, but with a dread of waking up and falling. He preserved some sense of airiness underground, although his movements were constrained. He went along train tracks until he found a cosy room or other secret hiding place from which to surface. He marveled at the miracle of his ability, but feared the walls would collapse and bury him. He moved from boundless expanse to containment to boundless expanse. In his psychosis, he often felt the world was made of a transparent immaterial "tissue," but at the same time he could not shake off a conviction that everything was encased in stone. Spirit and matter could not get together. They swallowed one another up, competed for dominance, and failed to modulate each other's swings.

In ordinary life, our implicit sense of immateriality blends in with our sense of material reality in a relatively smooth, seamless way. In psychosis, a misfit between the invisibility and intangibility of mind, as such, and everyday reality becomes paramount. In certain instances (Carl, Leila), the psychotic person cannot bypass or take for granted his discovery of the immateriality of experiencing. He magnifies his contact with mental presence. His discovery of immateriality takes precedence over ordinary spatial limits and makes possible the sensation that malevolence is omnipresent or can instantaneously spread everywhere. In other instances (Frank), evil is more limited and must devour its prey bit by bit. It must overcome material resistance with material might. In the latter case, physical, and in the former, mental, power is emphasized (brute force versus mind over matter). However, the victory of either is frightful.

Bipolar capacities, such as everyday perception–hallucination and a sense of immateriality–materiality, pervade our existence. Boundaries between them may be too rigid or weak. They may shift or lift in unexpected ways. All human capacities are subject to the play of boundaries. Our very I-feeling incessantly changes "shape" and "color" as it moves through many dimensions.

Federn: The Spreading I

In normal circumstances, our I-feeling waxes and wanes. It shifts in intensity and quality, seeming to vary from moment to moment like barometric pressure. In states of absent-mindedness or creative absorption, it may fade for a moment. It may grow keener when caught in conflict. In the case of prolonged psychic stress, it can become numb and die out. In physical illness, I-feeling may contract to exclude the body. In health on a sunny day after a swim, it may include not only the body, but the entire universe as well.

Federn,[1] an early psychoanalyst who focused on psychosis, tried to chart the vicissitudes of I-feeling in structural, dynamic terms. He was struck by how often a loss of I-feeling, a type of depersonalization, precedes psychosis. In studying this phenomenon closely, he observed that body ego feeling was frequently lost before mental ego feeling. Similarly, after sleep, mental ego feeling often awakens before body ego feeling. On the basis of phenomenological considerations, he concluded that "[m]ental ego feeling . . . is the first to be experienced by the child; ego feeling related to the body and to perceptions conveyed through the body comes only gradually."[2]

This is an astonishing remark for a psychoanalyst and has radical consequences for a theory of mind and self. It reverses Freud's declaration that "the ego is first and foremost a body ego," a fundamental tenet in virtually all psychoanalytic thinking. Federn reasons that if the I contracts and expands to include or exclude the body, it cannot simply be derived from body states. In infancy, I-feeling only

1. Federn, *Ego Psychology and the Psychoses*, pp. 25–37, 227–260.
2. Federn, "Some Variations in Ego Feeling," p. 442.

gradually encompasses the body. It takes time and development to discover I must be where my body is. The I-feeling, as such, has a certain primacy. It permeates the body and stamps it with I-ness, but it may withdraw again when unduly threatened. I-feeling nourishes and is nourished by the body, but its relationship to the latter is complex and problematic from the outset.

Federn's orientation allowed him to emphasize issues that were peripheral in Freud's approach to psychosis. In discussions of psychosis, Freud tended to emphasize the subject's megalomanic withdrawal from objects. Federn's starting point is the subject's still deeper withdrawal from or loss of his own sense of self (in Freud's later terms, an aspect of the death wish, decathexis of the self; see Chapter 3). The two are by no means mutually exclusive. The subject often alternates between megalomania and loss of self-feeling. The relationship between these states still provides a fertile area for exploration.

Federn starts his developmental account by positing a boundless ego- or I-feeling. This primary I-feeling is supposed to exist before a sense of spatial boundaries develops, and so can be anywhere and everywhere. Primordial I-feeling drenches the entire cosmos. Everything is invested or imbued with I-feeling. Original I-feeling is infinite.

The everywhereness of I-feeling comes up against the hard facts of life. The subject often encounters pain when he acts on his sense of boundlessness. He meets the resistance of spatial realities and other I-centers. In time, he is forced to rein in his I-feeling more in accord with his body boundaries. It seems less painful to respect such built-in physical limits than to continue as if one were immaterial. The ego shifts from a primordial cosmic I-feeling to a more circumscribed, adaptive attitude. It constructs a map of the world and learns to test reality. It learns it is more practical to be coextensive with one's body than with the universe. The subject builds a second nature. One must contract to fit the body one is part of. One can only be where one's body is, although it feels otherwise. A smaller I, more successful in material terms, becomes dominant. But a nostalgia for boundlessness lingers.

For certain individuals (and perhaps, to a degree, everyone), one's double sense of boundlessness–limits is too much to handle and is a source of unbearable pain. One may try to find a way out, through more loss of I-feeling. This may vary from mild self-anesthesia to a complete loss of self-feeling. In the case of hospitalized patients, we find individuals who could not successfully squeeze into an effective practical self. In the "hospital" of the world, we find others who have done so only too well.

Federn did not fully exploit the clinical implications of his vision. He, like Freud, adopts a worldly posture of acceptance of everyday misery as an inherent part of life. His practical work relied on the patient's positive attachment to the therapist to help the former tolerate the frustration of real-life boundaries. In Federn's terms, we must learn to give up our original, larger I for our smaller I in order to survive. We must be malcontents by the nature of things. We must live partially depersonalized and transfer some portion of our origi- nal aliveness to compensations. The therapy relationship acts as a psychic life support system, which takes the edge off depersonaliza- tion and facilitates some workable modicum of alive I-feeling. We must deal with our discontent as creatively as possible. At this juncture of history and potential destructiveness, it would be mad- ness to feel otherwise.

Nevertheless, Federn's theory also suggests that it may be possible again to contact our sense of boundlessness and use it creatively as well. We may have to know how to shrink ouselves to get along, but we must also know how to stretch, to let our self out for air. This involves more than pleasure and destruction. It is a matter of repeat- edly discovering who we are and are not. We live through the tension between our larger and our smaller I.

Today, the conventional clinical therapist tends to take the psy- chotic patient's deficiency in reality-testing as the most essential trademark of psychosis. Exploration of the meaning and function of an alternate sense of reality is usually skirted or prejudiced. The practical issue is usually how to adapt the larger to the smaller I as quickly as possible or to shut out the larger I altogether. However, if Federn's formulations are taken seriously, therapeutic work should help the individual interact with and build a creative tolerance for his dual sense of boundlessness–limits or cosmic and practical I-feeling. One task is to allow the larger and smaller I to "adapt" to one another, to give each its due. Each has a story to tell, a life to live, and much to contribute.

As is usually the case, Federn's phenomenological truth is beset with basic, theoretical problems. Federn's primordial ego-feeling is a reworking of Freud's primary narcissism. I-feeling occurs if the ego is invested with libido. The withdrawal or loss of libido from the ego leads to the loss of I-feeling. Federn's attempts to work out the relationship between originary libido and an originary ego face problems similar to Freud's. Who is the subject who gives and takes away libido to and from an orginary ego? In what way is the ego both a center of subjectivity and an object of still deeper psychic processes? How is the ego first a "mental" rather than a "body" ego, yet dependent on libido for its origin and sustenance? Federn's accounts of the interplay between Ego and Eros are better as clinical portrayals than as metapsychological explanations.

Federn seemed to be afraid of the originality of his own work and tried too hard to make it sound like Freud's. The implications of his work took him to a somewhat different territory. Freud tended to study the conflictual basis of depersonalization of an ego already attached to the body. Federn raised the possibility of the ego's refusal to enter the body in the first place. In both accounts, the problem of pain is central. Identification with the body increases one's vulnerability. One risks mortality and the vicissitudes of finitude. In Federn's framework, a psychotic individual may not have left his body so much as never really had a body to begin with. He may have called a halt to embodiment as soon as he understood its dangers. In this context, Freud's psychosexual stages (oral, anal, phallic, genital) represent ways the ego spreads through the body, a journey one may undertake or try to prevent.

In the light of ancient archetypes, Freud's psychotic seeks a return to the womb, whereas Federn's never entered it. Traditional folklore and mythic imagery depict the soul's decision to enter the womb and be born as a fall or descent. Its original home is immaterial heaven. It leaves its cool, dry abode for warm, moist climes. In contrast, the Freudian psychologist sees the womb as a heaven an individual may never wish to leave or seeks to return to. The first great separation is from the mother's body rather than immaterial heaven. In one tradition, heaven is home, the womb alien. In the other, the womb is home, earth's surface alien.

These views may represent different points of entry to an eternal circle or different moments of the developmental journey. In psychosis, as in life in general, both play a role. The subject swings between experiencing embodiment and disembodiment and a seemingly endless variety of mixtures. Our experience would not be what it is without a double sense of materiality–immateriality. It is part of what gives our experience its resonance, depth, and elusiveness. We move in and out of ourselves as if we were air, yet we also meet with resistance. Our thoughts are at once clouds and stones. Our flesh melts, but our muscles hold their ground. We are one, two, three, . . . infinity. Our mysterious I-feeling spreads through earth and heaven. For Freud it comes from the body, for Federn it moves toward the body. Where is its point of origin? We grow and fade in the mystery of doubleness.

Mahler: The Permeable Self and the Concept of Undifferentiation

The mystery of doubleness is nowhere more intensely encountered than in our sense of self and other. We feel both connected with, yet separate from ourselves and others. In mystical communion (co-union), the self feels wholly in union, yet distinct at the same time. At deep levels of our being, we feel part of others and others part of us, yet we also maintain areas of difference. We may swing back and forth, now emphasizing the dimension of union, now that of difference, whereas the two belong together and make each other possible. Distinction–union appears to be a constitutive structure of our beings. Take away either, and the self would disappear.

The psychotic individual seems to approach zero or infinity by trying to separate union–distinction. The psychotic self may approximate moments of absolute fusion and/or isolation. In either case, the psychological structure breaks down or becomes grotesquely distorted. The individual lives in a swamp or vacuum. The self becomes sponge-like and spineless, or brittle and rigid. More often the self goes both ways at once and is confused by its mixture of nettle and putty. It is scant comfort to realize that the bizarre fragments of psychotic reality are deformations of universal structures.

Psychoanalytic theorists who have had to struggle with radical boundary shifts of psychotic patients have attempted to view these states as miscarriages of more general developmental phases. One of the most formidable and influential of these attempts is Mahler's. Her account focuses on the problem of boundaries in human development. The problems inherent in her formulations help us appreciate more vividly the knots we must untangle in tracing our beginnings.

Mahler's theory of the earliest phases of human life posits two principal boundary shifts.[3] She describes the first stage of the infant's existence as one in which the psyche is a kind of self-sufficient or self-enclosed system. Following Freud, she likens this stage to that of a fertilized egg. She calls this a normal autism and writes that in it "the infant seems to be in a state of primitive hallucinatory disorientation [wish fulfillment], in which need satisfaction belongs to its own omnipotent, *autistic* orbit."[4]

In Mahler's account, the infant soon moves to a state in which he and the mother form "an omnipotent system—a dual unity within one common boundary."[5] This is the beginning of what Mahler calls a normal symbiosis. The infant moves from an autistic state, in which he cannot tell the difference between need and object, to a state in which he feels boundlessly one with the need-satisfying object. In the latter state, "any unpleasureable perception, external or internal, is projected beyond the common boundary of the symbiotic *milieu*

---

3. Mahler, *On Human Symbiosis and the Vicissitudes of Individuation*, pp. 7–13.
4. Ibid., pp. 7–8.
5. Ibid., p. 8.

interieur."[6] The self, immersed in a nurturing symbiotic field, begins a long psychological hatching process. Mahler charts aspects of the emerging separation–individuation process in which the child's awareness of the separate reality of self and others grows.

The starting point of Mahler's theory leads to basic difficulties. According to Mahler, the newborn infant cannot distinguish between pleasureable or good and painful or bad experiences, yet tries to get rid of bad feelings by "urinating, defecating, coughing, sneezing, spitting, regurgitating, vomiting," etc.[7] Correlatively, he cannot tell the difference between his own attempts "to rid himself of unpleasurable tension" and his mother's. All efforts that make him feel better are taken to be his own. However, Mahler's account omits the question of who the omnipotent author of experience might be and how experience is separated into pleasure and pain if originally all is undifferentiated. Areas of homogenization of pleasure–pain–self–other may exist. But in order to maintain oneself in a sea of pleasure, elemental distinctions between pleasure–pain and in–out (inclusion–exclusion) must be made. The processes Mahler describes involve more divisions than her terms "autistic" or "undifferentiation" suggest.

Similar problems characterize her formulation of the second type of undifferentiatedness she takes up, the symbiotic phase. Mahler believes that the infant becomes dimly aware of the "need-satisfying object" and includes it within "one common boundary" at about the second month. That is, he and the "good" object exist together within a common boundary vis-à-vis all that is painful and "bad." The subject has moved from an objectless autism to merger with a satisfying object, from one form of boundlessness to another. Again, who is the subject who becomes aware of a "need-satisfying object"? Can the infant ever tell the difference between himself and the mother within the common boundary? Mahler's statements suggest not. She describes this state as one of "undifferentiation, of fusion with mother, in which the 'I' is not yet differentiated from the 'not-

6. Ibid., p. 9.
7. Ibid., p. 8.

I'."[8] But if there is no distance between self and object, it is hard to see how one can even speak of an object.

In sum, Mahler describes two types of primary "undifferentiated" states: an autism in which a subject exists without an object, followed by a symbiosis in which subject and object are fused. Her discourse brings us to a strange and difficult place. We begin as one with ourselves, with no other, and progress to oneness with one who is no other. Who are we through this progression and who is the other who is not there? To put the absurdity or paradox succinctly, in Mahler's account we begin as one with ourselves before we are and move to oneness with the other before it is. Mahler's descriptions fit, up to a point, the zero–infinity of psychotic states. In clinical terms, her work captures extremes of isolation and fusion, when the self and/or other is everything and/or disappears. But whether she has done justice to the basic structure of the self, upon which such extreme states depend, is a fundamental issue.

All positions that start with undifferentiation have similar problems. If there is no difference between self and other, then self and other cannot yet have arisen. Before self–other awareness is the blankness of nothingness or just being and varied forms of consciousness. All forms of self–other awareness involve some kind of differentiation. If this were not so, who, in Mahler's terms, could be aware of the "need object"? To speak of a symbiotic or need object presupposes the possibility of an object-constituting capacity, of which need object is a special subset.

Strictly speaking, to exist and be undifferentiated is not possible. Anything that is, must, in some way, be differentiated. Otherwise, it could not be noted, addressed, or engaged. Gestalt psychology suggests that perception requires a differentiated field and this includes self-perception as well.[9] A self with no object or reference point outside it would vanish. Pure merger and isolation are abstract terms that do not characterize living experience. Areas of union and distinction occur together, with one or the other emphasized in a given

8. Ibid., p. 9.
9. Koffka, *Principles of Gestalt Psychology*, pp. 39–46, 110–125, 319–342.

situation. Later developmental stages build on elemental capacities to distinguish and unite.

Objectlessness versus Infinite and Realistic Objects

OUR AMBIGUOUS STARTING POINT

The problems Mahler encounters by dividing the elemental distinction–union structure plague psychoanalysis in general. Most psychoanalytic accounts of the birth of the self begin with some kind of objectless omnipotence. Even as thoroughgoing a relational theory as Winnicott's does.[10]

Research on early infancy suggests that at least an area of differentiation exists from the beginning. During the time period Mahler calls autistic, the infant perceives and tracks objects, shows object preferences, and interacts with its milieu in finely tuned ways.[11] The infant seems both separate and permeable from the outset.

Many parents report difficulties in dealing with the infant's contactful *and* contactless moments. The following is an excerpt from a session in which a parent with strong psychotic elements strove to deal with the panic her newborn infant aroused:

I keep trying to make her smile. I know I'm crazy. I want some sign from her. I want her to acknowledge me. Yet I feel she does and that scares me too. She is so herself, her own person. She just is. She looks at me quietly. I can't look at anyone like that. I would have to be strong to do it. She just does it. At those moments she is so relaxed. Everything is in order but I can't take it. I want to make waves. I want to tickle her. I want to stop her from being there.

10. I have discussed Winnicott's starting point and this issue in several papers, including "Instinctual Fantasy and Ideal Images," pp. 119–137; "On the Significance of the Face," pp. 427–441; "Guntrip's Analysis with Winnicott," pp. 103–117; "The Area of Faith in Winnicott, Lacan and Bion," pp. 413–433; "Dual Union or Undifferentiation," pp. 415–428.
11. For example, Stern, *The First Relationship*, pp. 33–69.

At other moments, the mother is frightened because the baby makes noises or smiles for no apparent reason. The baby then seems in her own world, out of contact or in contact only with herself. When the baby seeks eye contact or when the baby gazes seemingly nowhere, this mother is anxious. She is afraid of contact and lack of contact and the baby affords the opportunity for both. The mother is afraid of the baby's lack of seductiveness, its just being what it is.

In this case, the mother related her anxiety to the hysterical intrusiveness of her own mother. In such an atmosphere, the mother is greedy for a certain type of contact with the baby, one in which the baby exists as a satellite support object. But it is a blind contact. The mother cannot *see* and tolerate the infant's alive presence. She is afraid of the seeing and feeling of simple aliveness. The mother blurs the infant's reality as her own has been blurred. This is as true for the infant's real pain as for its calm gazing. The baby's screams of distress tended to throw this mother into a hysterical and paralyzed frenzy, just as its peacefulness tempted her to be disruptive.

The question of who the infant is and when the self arises keeps us wondering and stretching. We see so much and so little in the newborn. We speak of the infant's intunement, interactiveness, freshness, sweetness, obliviousness, ugliness, activity, passivity, Buddha-likeness, pain–pleasure orientation, archetypal bliss–agony, Job-likeness, infiniteness–physicality, and so on. Experimental research leaves most basic questions open. The fact that the baby can be interactive says little about the origins of the self as such. Newborn animals show intunement and interactiveness, too. A certain fit and non-fit between organism and environment is a fact of life, in general. Simple perception involves separateness and permeability. Does one have to postulate more than animal consciousness to understand the interactive order of the first month or so of infancy?

ELKIN

Elkin views the infant's smiling response by two or three months of age as a sign of self–other awareness.[12] At some point within the

12. Elkin, "On Selfhood and Ego Structures in Infancy," pp. 389–416.

first several months, the infant will smile upon seeing a face or a face representation (e.g., a mask with eyes and nose marks). This smiling response is not due to gas discharge, a transient spectacle, or stroking. It requires distance (seeing) and re-cognition. It betokens the advent of a symbolizing consciousness. Yet, Elkin emphasizes, this self–other awareness arises before a coherent body image is worked out. The latter, signaled by eye–hand–mouth coordination, is consolidated by about six months of age. A question then is, What kind of world does the infant live in, if he is aware of self–other before he knows he has a body?

Elkin discusses four main stages of infantile development: (1) birth–3 months, collective–erotic sensing;[13] (2) 3–6 months, primordial self and other awareness; (3) 6–8 months, a transitional period in which the primordial self is encompassing the body; and (4) 8 months on, various ego structures arise as the infant's relationship to embodiment evolves.

I will not give a detailed exposition of Elkin's work here, but rather will use its general structure to underline issues usually bypassed in developmental research and by most psychoanalytic theories. First, Elkin systematically distinguishes between consciousness (a phenomenon we share with other animals) and self–other consciousness of a sort unique to humans. As noted above, developmental research that discovers orderly patterns of perception and behavior does not in itself address the issue of when in interactive consciousness self–other awareness arises. Second, the general assumption in psychoanalysis that the "ego" is most basically concerned with body states (pleasure–pain) and the external perception relevant for regulation of the former mutes more subtle dramas of self–other awareness, particularly vicissitudes of the self before awareness of the body as such.

The infant lives from and through the body before the body is represented as a physical body with specific limits and functions. However, once self–other awareness emerges, body feelings become

13. Ibid., pp. 392–399. Although Elkin calls the state of mind of the infant from birth to three months "preconscious," he likens it to animal consciousness or "vital sensing."

a part of momentous dramas beyond them. For example, at some point, pain becomes a powerful element in an intersubjective matrix. In the context of primordial self–other awareness, hunger assails the sense of self as if it were, or were visited by, a menacing other. The other is feared as an attacker or a depriver. Pain is not anonymous or just a fact of life, but rather expresses intentionality, subjective presence. Since the body boundaries are not well developed, self and other approach infinity. Animal pain becomes dire agony, a hell. Hallucinatory imagery embroiders and magnifies it beyond all proportion. The primordial self may well live in a world structured by God and the devil.

In primordial self–other awareness, the infant lives in immediate contact with the intentional field of the other. Self and other vibrate and resonate to one another with transparent immediacy. The subtly shifting expressions and actions of baby–mother reflect their differences and intertwining. They seem to exist not simply as "baby" and "mother," but rather as connected subjective presences sensitive to infinitesimal (or infinite) shifts in the co-intentional field in which they live. Subject is linked with subject, psyche to psyche, a self–self relation with areas of union and separation. Felt body events feed this psychic interplay and gain their meaning from it.

Over and over, primordial self-consciousness is threatened, dies out, and returns. The ministrations of the other support its being. In time the primordial self learns to trust in the merciful interventions of the other. Without help, it cannot face the pain of its needs and after initial wrath–panic, drops into stupor. It is resurrected through the other's care. It repeatedly goes through this cycle of distress, wrath, fear, dying out, and return. Since there is as yet no well-developed body image, and so no mind–body split can occur, the drama takes place on the plane of pure self–other feeling. One's whole being is involved without barriers against oneself or chronic self-hardening. The primordial self moves from its initial sense of other as background or encompassing field or void, through intermediary phases of a devil menacer or depriver, to the culminating moment of divine, sustaining presence. The foundation of one's self-feeling gradually becomes established on a trusting sense of rebirth through the other.

At about eight months, the infant's representation of his body is developed enough so that mind–body splits can occur. Primordial self–other consciousness gives way to complex relations of mental and physical aspects of self-feeling vis-à-vis the mother. For example, when physical size differences become important (big mother, small baby), the infant begins to inhibit spontaneous expressions of rage. A split between a mental ego, which sizes up the situation and withholds aspects of body ego, ensues. The infant becomes worldly wise. The infant, too, feels guilty about wishing to hurt one he loves and tries to rise above his ruthless ways. In a subtle sense, he may play god to the infant mother, but at the same time adopts his goddess's ways.

As the infant's self-consciousness extends to include awareness of his body and physical reality as material, a natural division between mental and body ego occurs. This division is reflected in Federn's distinction between psychic and body ego feelings, the dual structure of the I. Jacobson distinguishes between a "mental and physical self," Kohut a "mind-mind and body-mind," Greenson an "observing and experiencing ego," and Elkin a "transcendental and body ego."[14] Each of these overlapping sets of concepts covers somewhat different territory, a worthwhile study in itself. Here we simply note a widely made distinction.

In Elkin's scheme, the emerging transcendental ego has roots in the now repressed dramas between the primordial self and other, and echoes of this earlier stage help organize the infant's conflicts with the mother. The infant may manipulate and fuse with the physically more powerful giantess. Various ego structures—autistic, schizoid, psychopathic, collective—with characteristic ways of relating to mental and physical aspects of experience develop. Similarly, insofar as the mother has qualities that support the infant's authentic psychic being, a communal (co-union) ego structure can grow. These various ego structures resonate with earlier God and devil images, so

14. Jacobson, *The Self and Object World*, p. 6; Kohut, *Analysis of the Self*, pp. 214–218; Greenson, *Technique and Practice of Psychoanalysis*, p. 47; Elkin, "On Selfhood and Ego Structures in Infancy," pp. 389–416.

that everyday tensions and the ways one copes become the foreground of an underlying sense of boundless drama.

The personality now learns to stiffen in response to threat. One
learns chronic ways of getting above oneself and others and of
shutting out feelings. Because one now knows what the body is, one
can begin to telescope and packet it. One gains control. One tri-
umphs over threats by one's own machinations. One learns to hide.
Rage may sour and turn into hatred. One may get stuck in manipulative fear–hatred insofar as the mother aspires to omniscience–omnipotence. Or one may allow one's fear–hatred to enter a more broadly
affirming relationship, a communion in which mutual forgiveness is
possible. The threat of loss of self is countered by controlling ego
structures. Yet through communion, genuine risk and rebirth continue. One reenacts with mother and life in general the loss and
rebirth of the self on new planes, a thread that connects with and
carries forward the primordial drama of early self–other awareness.

One always faces problems when trying to date the birth of the
self in infancy. The infant cannot speak for himself and if he could,
there is no reason to suppose his testimony would be any less subject
to doubt than anyone else's. One attempts, at best, approximations.
There are always more data and alternate interpretations. For example, the infant prefers face configurations much earlier than once was
suspected. It may even be that it is not the face the baby is programmed to be sensitive to, but certain types of line–angle relationships. Similarly, the development of a body image at about six
months of age may be connected with myelinization in the brain.
However, issues involving dating and the relationship of physiology
to psychology do not change the basic structure of the problem.

Whenever self–other awareness arises, such natural processes as
perception, cognition, and coordination take on new meanings.
They become part of the life of the self, materials through which the
self is born and with which it struggles. Perception occurs before
self-perception. But once self-awareness enters the scene, a whole
new world of perceptual nuances is possible. An infinite exponent
enters experience. The self must grapple with, and be inspired by or

broken on the fit and disproportion reflected in its sense of finitude and infinity.

BALINT

Numerous psychoanalytic investigators have tried to credit the sense of the infinite as nourishing and threatening the infant self. Balint writes of a "harmonious interpenetrating mix-up" between self and "open expanses and substances."[15] The infant begins at one with its surround, as with a boundless expanse like air or water. Balint describes the self arising within the horizon of impersonal Mother Nature. His imagery is naturalistic. The encompassing medium he depicts is resistanceless, but lacks personal presence. My description above adds that the self arises in an intersubjective matrix characterized by the subtle play of co-intentionality. The boundless expanse Balint emphasizes may be part of the primordial other, which forms a background for the emerging sense of self.

KOHUT

Kohut describes a oneness with mother, a boundlessness that sustains the growth of the infant's self.[16] Infantile grandiosity and idealization are forms our underlying sense of boundless interweaving takes. As development proceeds, these currents are transmuted into psychic structures that enhance the sense of self. Kohut coins the term "self-object" (later, "selfobject") to express and explore the area of inherent continuity and interconnectedness between subjects. The other as selfobject functions to support and empathically value the growing self. The selfobject blends in or lends itself to genuine developmental needs of the person.

Kohut's account has the merit of studying positive aspects of "ideal feelings" in the birth and growth of the self. However, he does not get past the prejudice that the first "other" is the "mother,"

15. Balint, *The Basic Fault*, pp. 66–67.
16. Kohut, *Analysis of the Self*, pp. 9–34, 54–67, 296–328.

whether a cosmic or a personal mother. Correlatively, his starting point of psychic development uncritically remains Freud's autoerotic stage: the ego is still first and foremost a body ego. He thus views the most severe psychoses as regressions to a fragmented autoeroticism and, therefore, beyond psychoanalytic treatment. He apparently did not take the implications of his own clinical findings far enough. What most interested Kohut was the development and vicissitudes of self-feeling. For him the selfobject was, in the first instance, aspects of the mothering milieu that aid self-feeling. The gap and links between the primordial other and mother never emerged in his work as a fundamental problem. It may be common sense to speak of the first "object" as mother, but this concession can obscure important aspects of what pristine intersubjectivity is like. What in psychic life makes the emergence and use of a selfobject possible is an issue that may take Kohutians beyond their present limits.

WINNICOTT

Winnicott investigated a number of aspects of what may happen before a well-bounded unit self is constituted vis-à-vis a spatially delimited, realistic other.[17] He began with an omnipotent creative self with mother as a background medium of support. He soon saw how inadequate a term "mother" and even "object" is for the atmosphere in which the self is born and nourished. He struggled with this problem throughout his life, never really satisfied with his formulations. To get beneath the term "object," he spoke of the infant's early world in terms of "maternal functioning." At the outset, the contribution of the mother may be all pervasive, but remains phenomenologically acausal or causally silent. One cannot say whether the infant creates and/or discovers the objects (e.g., the "breast" or face) that become significant. For Winnicott, this is an unaskable question. At the outset, creation and discovery are one. Winnicott associates a kind of benign and creative omnipotence with what he

17. Winnicott, *Collected Papers*, pp. 243–254; idem, *The Maturational Processes and the Facilitating Environment*, pp. 140–152; idem, *Playing and Reality*, pp. 1–24, 65–94.

calls the infant's "vital spark," "continuity," "going on being," "psychosomatic unity," and "true self." At this point, the infant's feeling real evolves through the support his omnipotence gains.

Another dimension in the constitution of the self is what Winnicott called "transitional experiencing." He tries to get beneath the subject–object dichotomy by evoking a sense of the area "between" self and other. A "transitional object" carries the meaning of that which is, yet is not mother and that which is, yet is not self. It, like mother, mirrors the self, and like the self, mirrors mother. Yet it cannot be reduced to either. Language that stresses division or fusion misses the kind of experiencing at stake here.

Winnicott's attempts to explore the early generation of the sense of self and other often lead him to a seeming disarray of ideas. He speaks of the mothering and internal mother image necessary for transitional experiencing to emerge and be maintained, although, in his work, the mother as mother is not conceived by the infant self until later. In various descriptions, the first transitional object is the mother used as a self-yet-not-self symbol, the mother used as a symbol of other, and symbolizing experiencing emerging as such. Winnicott writes that the most important thing about the transitional object is its not-mother and not-self quality, its value as symbol and what symbolizing feels like. The sense of immersion in creative experiencing he describes is beyond and more fundamental than the usual categories of discourse.

Winnicott never quite lets go of the term, "mother," but he does not hold on to it either. As his work unfolds, he tends to see the category of "otherness" or "object" as a more general one, pertaining to an earlier developmental level than "mother." The infant's apperception of the realistic mother is a subset of more general processes that constitute object or other as such. The question that plagues him is what intersubjectivity is like before mother is seen as mother. He tries to evoke a sense of how personal presence is nourished in a milieu of personal presence long before knowledge of who "realistic" personalities are is possible. If his work sometimes mixes up levels and terms, it also furnishes tools to take this exploration further.

GROTSTEIN

Grotstein combines aspects of Winnicott's and Kohut's concerns in his investigation of what he calls "the background subject–object of primary identification."[18] For Grotstein, this is the initial mothering presence that supports the emerging sense of self. The self grows by identifying with the help and care it receives from mothering. The personality lives in the caretaking ambience. The latter pervades the very texture of the infant's being. Grotstein likens a warp in the background subject–object of primary identification to an odd movie screen that distorts all figures.

His term, "background subject–object of primary identification," is a rich one, which gets beneath ordinary dichotomies. It implies both division and indivision, boundlessness yet separateness—"dual tracks" or developmental lines. The term "dual track" sounds mechanical and rigid until it is realized that it refers not only to train tracks, but to footprints as well. Grotstein believes that the self begins as differentiated and undifferentiated and both dimensions mark its development at every turn. However, he fails to distinguish systematically between the infant's primordial consciousness, primordial self–other awareness, and the emerging awareness of embodiment and mother. He fuses and moves back and forth between these developmental phases or dimensions in a way that weakens the thrust of his major findings. He invents his term, background subject–object, precisely because usual meanings of mother would not do. This term does not simply refer to aspects of maternal functioning, but rather suggests a general experiential structure that provides a framework for the latter. His specific explorations tend to remain rooted in aspects of the self–mother relation, although his terminology opens up vistas that subtend it.

18. Grotstein's term has evolved from "Background Object of Primary Identification" (*Splitting and Projective Identification*, pp. 77–90), to "Background Subject and Object of Primary Identification" ("Proposed Revision of the Concept of Primitive Mental States," pp. 513–515), to "Background Subject-Object of Primary Identification" ("Newer Perspectives in Object Relations Theory," pp. 59–68).

The authors discussed above developed terms that express something about the first "object" that is more than mother: primordial
other, selfobject, transitional object, background subject–object.
Other authors could be cited as well (e.g., Loewald, Rycroft, and
Milner[19]). There is much in psychoanalytic thinking to suggest that
the first object is an "ideal object." The self is conceived as beginning
in a matrix of oceanic or ideal feelings. The mother, other actual
people, and one's own body come to be differentiated out of such
primary ideal states.

It is an odd property of psychoanalytic thought to confuse the
capacity to create ideal feelings with the objects idealized. For example, the existence of ideal states are attributed to the infant–mother
relationship (womb, breast, maternal functioning, etc.). However, if
the mother as mother is gradually discriminated from early ideal
states, the critical implication is that the creation of ideal states
precedes the perception of mother *qua* mother or, at least, cannot be
derived from her.

The basic structure of the problem is the same whether one begins
with primary narcissism or primary love. In the former, the ego is
the first ideal object, its own ideal; in the latter, the mother is. The
capacity to create ideal states is attributed to libido (ego as Eros' first
object) or moments of perfect fit between infant and mother. The
question as to why energy or intunement should give rise to a sense
of the infinite is not asked. It is taken for granted that this sense is a
part of human experiencing. Yet it is precisely its existence that is
inexplicable. Why we should be creatures capable of encountering
boundlessness is a mystery. Our capacity to do so must be grappled
with in its own right.

Psychoanalysis charts the vicissitudes of ideal feelings vis-à-vis the
hard facts of life. Its explorations of how the idealizing tendency
works throughout our lifetime constitutes a genuine advance in the

---

19. Loewald, *Papers on Psychoanalysis*, pp. 208, 398–399, 403; Rycroft, *Imagination
and Reality*, pp. 38–60; Milner, *On Not Being Able to Paint*, pp. 148–165; idem,
Hands of the Living God, pp. 269–412.

history of consciousness. Its depiction of the interplay of ideal feelings with energy and early parenting has profoundly sharpened our sense of how critical it is for us to come to grips with the inevitable illusion–disillusion cycles that mark our lives. It casts new light on our tendency to overestimate and underestimate ourselves. It refocuses our basic developmental tasks precisely because of the way it treats ideal states as derivatives of "something else." However, anything in our lives can be treated as part of or dependent on "something else," unless we stumble upon the Irreducible. The quality parenting and energy may assume depends on the fact that we are beings capable of ideal feeling at the same time that the fate of the latter hinges on our endowments, our milieu and the momentum of our lives.

We enter circle after circle. Some speak of a "separation which is not a separation,"[20] a "separation which is a form of union,"[21] a state in which I, undifferentiation, and the other are interwoven. Positions are taken in which mental ego precedes body ego and body ego precedes mental ego. Elkin portrays dramas of an originary immaterial sense of self and other.[22] Experimental psychologists suggest that the infant lives in an orderly perceptual world with built-in tendencies for specific object preferences.[23] Something that approaches everyday perception vies with, complements, and intertwines with ideal reality. We encounter the mystery of our doubleness very early.

The psychotic stumbles on this complexity and is pummeled by it. He is drawn to and pulled apart by the extremes of our nature. He is all head, all spirit, all body, all body products. He seems to maximize everything at once. Or he may become ossified in one or another extreme. In distorted fashion, he lays bare raw materials with which we must come to grips. The extremes of psychosis—hallucinatory struggle in an intensified reality, mindless vacuousness, relentless activity, vegetativeness, whirling abstractions, entombment in con-

20. Milner, "Overlapping Circles," p. 70.
21. Winnicott, "The Location of Cultural Experience," p. 98.
22. Elkin, "On Selfhood and Ego Structures in Infancy," pp. 392–400.
23. Stern, *The First Relationship*, pp. 33–69.

creteness—present us with indications of what in our makeup we must take into account if we are to be a viable life form. It is too easy for unity to become obliterating fusion or separation to become autistic–paranoid isolation. Both tendencies operate in varying balance and intensity throughout a multidimensional spectrum. For the human self to succeed, adequate ways of relating to the processes that constitute us must be found.

Identification and Boundaries

The sense of union–distinction permeates Freud's thought. It is vital to the work of "identification." For example, the self's identification with another is at once a kind of merger and an appropriation. We become one with qualities of the other we wish to possess or one with the other we wish to be. We grow through our identifications, yet we are not all fusion. Someone is identifying. A gap remains even while it is seemingly foreclosed. Can there be oneness without some difference, whether early or late, in the self's biography?

A process akin to identification governed Freud's primary process thinking. In the latter, many different items were treated as if they were the same (all women are mother, elongated objects phalli, etc.). But for this to be effective, differences between types of objects must be acknowledged (horse as father, church as womb or rectum). The profound order of unconscious meldings is based on an uncanny awareness of differences that are exploited or undone. Objects are brought together or split apart as the self swims from identification to identification.

LEILA

In psychosis, the individual is often caught in identificatory spins and hardening processes. At a sensitive moment in her therapy, Leila said, "I feel as if I'm hallucinating my mother. I'm trying to hallucinate my mother. No—my mother was—is—a hallucination." She stumbled trying to say that there was something hallucination-like about her mother, but she could not pin it down. She did not mean that she was hallucinating her mother, which may also have been the case, but that her mother really did possess a hallucinatory quality that Leila did not simply make up.

Leila's mother was a beautiful woman who, in Leila's words, "did not fill her body." Her body was beautiful, but somewhat empty. By the end of Leila's infancy, her mother showed signs of muscular deterioration and died during Leila's childhood. Throughout her life and illness she (her mother) had a kind word for everyone. She never was visibly angry. As she wasted away those around her did not acknowledge, at least to Leila, that she was dying. Death was taboo. Everyone was to keep up a good front. Yet Leila felt petrification everywhere and lived in unacknowledged confusion.

Maids took care of her. She could not play with uninhibited intensity with her mother. Her mother could not support Leila's child strength. As time went on, she could not lift Leila. The maids she had were not touch oriented. Leila was touch deprived, but did not know it. She assumed, or told herself, "This is the way it's supposed to be." In a session she said, "I never had skin. No one touched or held me. I envy women who have skin. People like being near them."

Leila got along without skin. Her body hardened. Her mind soared. She identified with, and fought identifying with her mother's deterioration—beauty mixed with decay. "Even before she was ill she was her own hallucination. She hallucinated me. I identified with her hallucination of me. Now I hallucinate her hallucinating me." By hallucination, Leila meant an uncanny, ethereal reality, grim and dreadful, but at times uncannily beautiful, as beautiful as her never-angry mother who weakened and, bit by bit, disappeared.

With no real skin boundaries to slow her down, Leila skidded back and forth between seeing mother and mother seeing her in a hallucinatory key. As suggested in Chapter 3, she resisted her hallucinatory spin by dropping into a deeper mindlessness. As often happens in psychosis, she identified with aspects of her mother's "unconscious," her mother's being (or non-being). In therapy, she could begin to allow the full brunt of her situation in childhood to hit her. She could begin to discover, relive, and reconstitute herself through the hallucinatory world that so confused her and that she had tried to push aside.

According to Bick,[24] one would expect "adhesive clinging" in lieu of adequate psychic skin. Leila did not seem to be a "clinger." She was a very active and dynamic patient. She free-associated, struggled with her state of the moment, and tried to give her soul expression. She fought to find herself in the oblivion into which she often sank. Her clinging was silent. It came out most fiercely in her clinging to therapy. In the beginning of Chapter 3, I brought out how easily she could vanish in the face of the unexpected or the catastrophic expectation of my absence. For many years she would have vanished if not for her adhesive identification with therapy. Her clinging to therapy kept her in life. It also kept her out of life. For a long time, her therapist was her only meaningful point of contact in a climate of desperate isolation. Bit by bit, as gradually as her mother deteriorated, her psychic tissues began to mend. The profound hardening and whirling processes she had endured became profitable.

It is not clear whether Leila lived in her head (e.g., her identificatory–hallucinatory spinning–hardening) because she never entered into or retreated from her body. Perhaps both. Clearly, she had enough of a body sense to stay alive. She had enough body to want more of it and, eventually, to mourn the loss of what was missing. Her mother, too, presented a complex picture of aliveness and absence. For years, Leila's myth had been that she had had to retreat from her body in the face of her mother's illness. It was a partial myth built on her family's insistence that her mother had been perfectly healthy and happy before the illness, that all Leila's problems began with that illness. In time she realized that her own and her mother's ambiguous position in relation to embodied life was a reality from the beginning. Her mother's later illness dramatized and intensified it. Leila oscillated between having lost and never having had her body. "I lost something I never had. I lost something I

24. Bick, "The Experience of the Skin in Early Object Relations," pp. 484–486.

almost had. I lost something I had a little. At rare moments I gorged myself on my body."

She never was comfortable with her body, but neither was she totally alienated from it. The distinctness–union structure ("I am but am not my body; I am but am not my mind; I am but am not my . . .") was not lost in her illness, although it became rubbery. It resurfaced in her journeys to and from oblivion. She became one with therapy. It was part of her life. For a time it was her life. She identified with it and its ways. She learned to think and to be "therapeutically." Yet she never quite gave in to therapy either. She envied me or the me she thought I was. When I made a helpful remark, she would say, "I wish I could do that." My life must be everything hers was not. The difference between us irritated her. Yet she exaggerated it by envious idealization. Her envy functioned both to differentiate and to unite us. It kept her in polarized contact with me. It is as if she were saying, "We ought to be one but we're not. We're different. We ought to be different but we're not. We're one." We are always somewhere else in relation to each other, never quite where we are supposed to be or want to be.

Identification is a form of self–other awareness, a way the latter works. The forms this doubleness–oneness assumes may, at times, be circuitous and hidden. However, as can be seen in Leila's case, psychotic processes exploit rather than dispense with this basic structure.

Boundaries, Hallucinations, and Mindlessness

Is boundlessness objectlessness? In my view, no. The self arises through the encompassing horizon of an infinite other. It exists in a bounded perceptual field permeated with a sense of boundless immateriality. How is this possible? We do not know. But both dimensions—boundedness and boundlessness—are given to us and give us ourselves.

Is objectlessness, then, just a fantasy? I think it is more. What seems like objectlessness refers, in part, to the time before self–other awareness arises. This time is infinitely busy and blank. It is filled with events that occurred before the self existed. The self can imagine or learn about them and make the teeming blackout that preceded it part of its history. No matter how many blanks are filled in, however, blankness remains. Blankness, too, is an infinite horizon or subhorizon. Self–other awareness, with all its mixtures of fin-itude–infinitude, grows out of and through an infinite blankness. The latter remains a permanent part of the atmosphere of mental life, a critical object and a haunting texture.

The self may respond to pain by trying to bury itself in areas of blankness. This may happen when the self is too weak to sustain itself in an overly horrific universe. However, as we have seen, the self may also blank out in bliss. As awareness of the other is lost, awareness of self is lost as well. A total dissolution of the self back to the darkness that preceded it is rare, perhaps impossible. It is part of the agony of life that we cannot quite succeed in absolutely disman-tling our sensitivity. Even when this seems to have happened, as in the case of Lenny (Chapter 3), the apparent stupor achieved be-comes a source of pain to others. It is as if the subject transfers his vulnerability to the universe around him, a division of labor that often goes undetected. Blankness and sensitivity support each other. It is precisely self–other awareness that makes blankness real.

Hallucinations feed on blankness and self–other awareness. The self can spill its horror and bliss into the blackout from which it comes. Darkness becomes a mixture of menace and ecstasy. Waves of horror and bliss or simply non-being (relaxation, empty-minded-ness, absorption) bathe the self through the blankness that is part of its heritage and makeup. Similarly, aspects of self and other can be experienced as demonic or divine presences. An electrified blackness and self–other awareness pass into one another. It is as if a horrific darkness crystalizes into personified images, and the latter presences turn into darkness. Although psychoses diverge in their use of mind-lessness and hallucinations, at bottom one supports the other and, in varying proportions, both threaten to run rampant through psychic life.

In general, mindlessness impedes hallucinations, whereas hallucinations translate formless affective qualities into images and personal
presences. Mindlessness and hallucinatory self–other awareness are
complementary infinities. In psychoses, the inherent tensions between the limits one infinity places on another become excruciating.
The subject collapses under the strain or cannot endure the birth that
such a strain requires. More likely, he is caught between not being
born and the forfeiture of what has managed to come through.
Dimensions that should nourish each other, even through conflict,
become dedicated enemies. The subject is stuck between alien infinities.

In many instances, finitude is held onto as a last resort, and
everything is reduced to concrete banality—monotony as refuge.
Here, it is as if boundlessness disappears through an aperture in the
universe that someone inadvertently left open. One marvels, however, at the precision and thoroughness of the accomplishment. With
the surefootedness of a phobic cat, this psychotic subject steers clear
of all signs of the ineffable, often employing a bizzare version of
"common sense" as an ally. Meanwhile, his brothers on the other
side of the coin wave to him from the wings of a world that threatens
to blast them beyond space. We are all projects in between these
extremes, and the extremes as well.

CHAPTER FIVE

Hate

SOME MIXTURE OF fear and hate is almost always involved in the distortions and deformations that characterize psychotic experience and behavior. The work of hidden fear–hate can often be read in the person's body, which may be twisted and bent over with the rage he is out of touch with. One patient's (Ron's) gnomish appearance and bulging eyes reflected the chronic pressure his unconscious fury exerted upon him. He looked as if he would burst or become lame at any moment. On the surface, he presented himself as a charitable but maligned victim. He assumed his ugliness was purely physical. It would be years before he could see that his face and body were the wretched end products of silent and tortured yearnings. His character rigidities had crystallized out of a plethora of shifting states of being.

Babies pass through all manner of emotional storms without being damaged by them, since their temperament and style do not cut them off from the flow of feelings. In time, however, the personality congeals in certain positions, and an individual may become entombed in fury and fear, with which he has lost conscious contact. How does this happen? When? Can we really say?

Hate in Therapy

From his early psychoanalytic writings to his last fragmentary notes, Freud linked hate with thwarted love. In one of his last notes he wrote,

A sense of guilt also originates from unsatisfied love. Like hate. In fact
we have been obliged to derive every conceivable thing from that material: like economically self-sufficient States with their "*Ersatz* [substitute]
products."[1]

Everything is derived from the vicissitudes of love. This is the
informal and final Freud, the man who, at the end, linked up with his
beginnings.

In light of this, it would be a mistake loosely to equate hate with
the death drive, as many do. In Freud's clinical writings, hate is
almost always portrayed as reactive, a response to slights, wounds,
unsatisfied longings, and desires. The fundamental love Freud speaks
of is demanding and implicitly aggressive. People try to get their
way, aiming to fulfill their wishes, but they must learn the art of
indirection. Freud speaks of an erotic drive seeking sexual satisfaction, an ego seeking self-esteem, a multidimensional self seeking its
way amidst its own complexities and the resistance of reality.

The self is born and grows in a matrix of intersubjective desires,
and what a rich, conflictual matrix it is. A mother, worn out after a
few hours with her baby, wants to rest or take a walk. The baby
screams. She stays, although she is tired. She forces herself to keep
going. She identifies with the child and sets herself aside, but not
without repercussions. She loves and resents the child; she is not all
there. Or someone helps her and she goes for a walk. The baby
screams for a little while and "adapts." He makes his way in a milieu
in which he is wanted and not wanted. He grows up in an atmosphere marked by self-sacrifice and self-assertion. The mother is
empathic to her baby and herself. The baby must come to grips with
this tension. It is part of the richness of life and the soil of pathos and
tragedy. In so many ways, our desires run up against and/or fit in
with the desires of others, and their quality is affected by this
interchange.

We are beings rich in love, anger, and fear. But the death drive is
something else. It is not simply love gone wrong, but rather a pale
inertia on the other side of love and her sister feelings. It is not simply

1. Freud, "Shorter Writings," p. 300.

a rest and respite from sentience, but rather a mute collapse of the possibility of emotional aliveness. As Bion writes, it is "anti-": anti-life, anti-rage, anti-knowing, anti-faith.[2] It undoes what life does.

And yet, life produces and contains death as much as it is swallowed up by it. In Freud's formal terms, the death drive is the conservative principle operative in all instincts, a tendency in every impulse to return to the time before its birth, a time before all birth. Yet Freud also writes, "The individual perishes from his internal conflicts."[3] Does he mean we are worn out by the processes that constitute us? That we die of despair of ever really solving the problems our own complexity causes? That the struggle to live is, finally, self-consuming?

"Rage, rage against the dying of the light," the poet urged his father, and perhaps himself.[4] The rage of the poet cries out on the side of life, even as he is caught in a vicious whirl toward death beyond his control. Wrath affirms. Hate fuels. Anger or fury or rage quickens. Why then, in the life of Dylan Thomas, did it also help lead the way to death, as if it were an arm of death? Why does it play such a role in making the human soul and visage grotesque, even grotesquely beautiful?

If development takes a mad, sociopathic turn, a hating individual or group can ravage whole pockets of civilization and nature. Masses of individuals may be ravaged and consumed by hate, which is often the hate of injustice. Textbooks of psychopathology carefully catalogue the monstrous mutations psychic life can undergo. And, so far as I can tell, hate almost always plays a crucial role in the warped fragments of mental desolation. One does not have to be in total agreement with Freud's psychobiology to see how, under certain conditions, life shatters itself.

In her novel, *I Never Promised You a Rose Garden,* Hannah Green wrote that violent patients often stood a better chance of recovery

2. Bion, *Learning from Experience*, pp. 10–12, 28–30, 95–99; idem, *Attention and Interpretation*, pp. 22, 108.
3. Freud, "Shorter Writings," p. 299.
4. Thomas, "Do not go gentle into that good night," *Collected Poems*, p. 128.

than compliant ones.[5] Expressions of hate can enable persons to experience themselves more fully. But hate, like the death wish, is often silent. In mental hospitals one can see craters in which human beings once might have been. Occasionally, as from ancient volcanoes, screams erupt. They occur and fade, seemingly at random, vestiges of living flame, a prolonged dying out. It is not unusual to see an abandoned human tenement walking down a city street staring blankly, mumbling swear words beneath a stale breath, which is, perhaps, all that is left of the rage to live. Poor devils—or what remains of devils, for even devils need nourishment.

The devil has long been associated with hate and evil. Religion and psychoanalysis speak of many kinds of devils. In psychoanalysis there are id, ego, superego, oral, anal, phallic, mother, and father devils. Among Freud's early followers, Abraham[6] undertook a detailed and far-reaching study of aspects of the infantile microcosm in which the devil thrives. He stressed the dramas the infant undergoes in association with teething.

With the coming of teeth, the infant has at his disposal a way in which he can physically hurt the mother when she nurses him. Even if his initial use of teeth is a spontaneous and joyful exercise, he soon learns its complex consequences. The toothless sucker can enjoy the breast without reservation. The biter must exercise restraint or lose the breast.

Such a pivotal experience is maximized in unconscious fantasy. Biting, chewing, and swallowing the nipple–breast–milk–food–mother becomes associated with devouring urges and fears. When angry, the baby now has a weapon that can produce results. He can make the mother wince with pain; he can express his anger with his teeth. He can bite lovingly and furiously at the same time. Abraham describes this as oral sadism or cannibalism. The baby is caught between his wish to bite and his need to hold back. He can no longer take the mother into himself by uninhibited sucking. In unconscious

5. Green, *I Never Promised You a Rose Garden*, pp. 81, 262.
6. Abraham, *Selected Papers*, pp. 248–279, 418–501.

fantasy, he incorporates that which she has to offer by chewing her substance into bits and pieces. He makes her part of him by annihilating her. At the same time, he must save and protect her from annihilation. He must be "care-full."

Anxiety and guilt help maintain a balance between self-expression and inhibition.[7] The baby is thrown into an ambivalent situation: He may use his teeth in pleasurable or angry self-expression, or not use them out of anxiety, guilt, or love. The stage is set for a chronic division within the personality, between perception–cognition and motor behavior. The baby learns he must control his impulses or risk annihilation and loss. The infant becomes capable of splitting off from himself, rising above his feelings, and, if necessary, "losing" them (e.g., via repression, dissociation, decathexis). The chronic self-suppression and armoring described by Reich[8] becomes possible. The baby can now smile when he is fearful or angry. In part, he becomes a "tricky little devil."

Fairbairn[9] describes the schizophrenic individual as one who feels his love is bad, whereas the depressive psychotic feels his hate is bad. Feeling bad about oneself before one becomes a biter appears to be associated with a more massive wiping out of the self than problems organized around causing pain.

A patient who dreams of (or hallucinates) teeth rotting or falling out may have castration anxiety. But he may also be dramatizing

---

7. A critic of psychoanalysis may ask why it is necessary to suppose the influence of unconscious cannibalistic fantasies, repression, or dissociation, and the like. Animals also learn to inhibit themselves and act according to the requirements of situations. Inhibition and expression seem to be part of life processes and work together.

While such criticism rightly points out the continuity between human and other life forms, it does not do justice to the complexity of the human situation. Our mental equipment both magnifies and infinitizes experience, and perceives and thinks about events in careful, realistic terms. The fantasies that psychoanalysts observe, project, or postulate concerning infants are related to themes that recur in age-old myths and folklore. If psychoanalysis is wrong, something like it would have to take its place. If psychoanalysis itself is a mutation, it still is a phenomenon worth exploration, a clue to who we are and of what we are capable. What does the creation of such an art or science say about the creature who creates it?

8. Reich, *Character Analysis*, pp. 145–179, 218–247, 369–508.

9. Fairbairn, *An Object Relations Theory of Personality*, pp. 46–58, 155–156.

an earlier depressive problem with assertion–aggression or mirroring an even more serious process of self-disintegration and the inability to be.

BEN

One patient, Ben, had numerous teeth dreams over the years. Early in therapy, images of rotting teeth recurred. They varied from bare stubs to elongated fangs. They were part of a series of images of desolation and decay, as is often the case in the early stages of work with psychotic breakdown. Feelings of power and powerless were linked with his teeth images. He was tiny and rotten or huge and rotten, a rotting weakling or a rotting hulk.

As therapy unfolded, visions of childhood helplessness flashed through his mind. He recounted endless episodes of being force fed by a cajoling, domineering mother who only meant well. She was the most beautiful and the most ugly woman in the world. He loved her and wanted to please her. He hated her and wanted to foil her. It was as if he were being toilet trained through the mouth. But instead of gaining control over holding back and letting go, he was involved in shutting out and letting in.

At crucial moments, who won or lost hinged on how effective his teeth were. As his teeth grew in, he could use them to keep her nipple–spoon out. In effect, he tried to make his teeth function as iron gates, clamping down and relying on them for protection. He could try to control how much was allowed in and when. However, when his mother tricked him, or pushed past his teeth, his and their existence were nullified. At such moments, his teeth did not count. His will and sense of power became inextricably tied up with his ability to use his teeth to shut his mother out or to let her in.

As life went on and he came closer to the breakdowns that characterized his youth, his psychic teeth rotted. In reality, his teeth had some cavities, but they were basically normal. Only his dream and hallucinatory teeth were affected. He developed an annoying habit of baring his teeth, as if he were showing all the putrid power they possessed or reassuring himself that they were there. After baring them, he sucked his mouth in, as if he were swallowing them. He loathed his putrefaction and hated himself. He could not bear any show of power.

The collapse or inadequate birth of his capacity to use psychic teeth to regulate in–out corresponded to a failure in the development of a contact barrier between conscious and unconscious functioning. In good development, the mind spontaneously distributes the work to be done between conscious and unconscious systems. It is as if a permeable barrier maintains contact and respect between psycho-physical levels. Diverse tendencies modulate rather than swamp or neglect one another. In Ben's case, too great a burden was placed on teeth as a model for regulating psychic flow. Teeth are rigid and unyielding. That Ben had to rely on them as an in–out barrier prevented the development of a proper permeability.

Teeth should mainly be used for biting and chewing. They can also be tools and weapons, but they are mainly adjuncts to digestion. In Ben's case, a secondary function (i.e., barrier) was overused, thus making genuine psychic digestion impossible. He oscillated between too great a rigidity and malleability. As his breakdowns approached, his ability to use teeth as a psychic regulator lessened. As they rotted, his psychic systems became contaminated. He became excruciatingly sensitive to bursts of emotion and images, as well as to external presences. At times, he screamed as a way of trying to rid himself of massive streaming. At last, in a mental hospital, he exploded in peace.

One of the turning-point images in Ben's therapy was a saber-toothed tiger. Its first appearance in a nightmare terrified him. With encouragement, he accustomed himself to living with it. For some time, he experienced its coming with fascination as well as dread. I told him to try to keep his eyes open in the dream and watch the tiger, no matter what. It was incredibly graceful and powerful. Above all, it was unspoiled and pure. It had no defects. It was uncontaminated. Its teeth were clean, sparkling, and undauntable. Everything about this tiger was alive.

In part, it suggested what must have been best about his mother's activity and, perhaps, once his own—a deep body ego aliveness, an embodied sense of power. In actuality, his mother's active power had a spoiling effect and became, in his mind, associated with feces. In oral terms, her rotten phallus[10] was mirrored by his teeth. His weakness was the other side of her strength. The phallic side of life was spoiled or spoiling rather than invigorating. Yet even annihilating oral rape had its stimulating quality—it set into motion the precocious development and defeat of his will and helped to inaugurate the art of evasion and collapse.

As his psychosis worsened, he fell into a toothless abyss, the world of a debased sucker. The toothless mouth fused with the anus as a black hole which swallowed up existence. In health, a black hole may have a positive function in terms of compressing and destroying waste products. But in Ben's case, as often occurs in madness, it perversely threatened to turn all of existence into a psychic wasteland.

How far from such a state of affairs was the saber-toothed tiger? Even as a nightmare, it carried a promise of saving grace, although it would be years before Ben could begin to appreciate all it had to offer. It referred to a vital spark that even the worst in life cannot quite destroy. The therapy situation allowed it to resurface in a potentially useable form. A good therapist has bite. He uses his teeth as well as his receptiveness. Therapy becomes a vehicle for tiger-power: keenness of mind, spirit, and speech in a responsive context. For the desperate and desolate soul, therapy becomes a model for what is possible, a place to flex psychic muscles (what is left of them) and to taste a personal freedom scarcely thought possible.

Envy, Hate, and
Separation–Individuation

KLEIN

Melanie Klein emphasized the importance of envy in the way that unconscious hatred works.[11] Not only is the child envious of the

---

10. Eigen, "On Pre-Oedipal Castration Anxiety," pp. 489–498. The phallus, as distinct from the simple, anatomical penis, has long been a symbol of active physical-

paternal penis, but infants are envious of maternal power as well. For Melanie Klein, early hate dramas become organized around the infant's reaction to dependency. The infant envies maternal creative power, the capacity to give birth and nourish. The mother's inherent creative power seems superior to the infant's. He did not create, nor can he nourish himself. He is the lesser and his mother the greater god, an inequity that precipitates anxiety and depression.

Melanie Klein tends to equate hate with Freud's death drive and sees it at work at the beginning of life. The psyche at first tries to handle painful feelings by expelling (projecting) them. This strategy tends to boomerang insofar as the infant is faced with taking in (introjecting) objects he has spoiled. The mother must detoxify and rework the bad states the infant casts into her, so that the "milk" (psychic and physical nourishment) she gives remains good. This is not always possible. No matter how good a job the mother may do, it is difficult to stay one jump ahead of the infant's spoiling process. For one thing, the infant puts its own creativity envy (attacks on the breast, the womb) into the mother and feels the source of his life turned against him. The state depicted is an envious war between hostile and greedily loving powers.

Melanie Klein's views have come under attack for their use of Freud's death drive and their view of psychic life as basically paranoid. In work with psychosis, however, the power of her vision must be appreciated. The psychotic often experiences himself as caught in a struggle between competing gods or demons. Whatever problems one may find with Freud's formulations of a primary megalomania or narcissism, a megalomanic self versus a megalomanic other must be faced in work with psychosis. And in most individuals, the megalomanic sense of self and other is tainted with hate.

The Freud–Klein line of thinking sees the devil in unconscious ego operations. This is not only a matter of possession by an ancient

---

mental-spiritual power. For the phallus-penis distinction see Laplanche and Pontalis, *The Language of Psycho-Analysis*, pp. 312–314.

11. Klein, *Envy and Gratitude*, pp. 23–24; Segal, *Introduction to the Work of Melanie Klein*, pp. 24–53. For Klein's equation of hate, destructiveness, and the death drive, see Klein, "Notes on Some Schizoid Mechanisms," pp. 292–320. Also see Chapter 3, this volume.

archetype. The way the psyche slants in on experience at any level can have a demonic edge. In Freudian–Kleinian terms, the attempt to maintain a "good feeling" by trying to make believe (e.g., via projection, dissociation, externalization, repression, decathexis) that pain is somewhere else or nowhere, leads to a life of evasion and deceit. An ideal reality is used as a substitute for real living rather than as a part of what makes life full.

In Klein's terms, the infant overcomes his unconscious diabolism by entering the depressive position. In the latter, he learns to tolerate bad feelings as part of a relationship. Both ego and internal object become more complex, and introjection rather than projection is emphasized. That is, one holds fast to the goodness one has taken in instead of spoiling it. One tries to make up for rather than project hateful urges. Gratitude for the object's helpfulness rather than envy wins out. Dependency is lived as part of a humanizing process and not simply retreated from with annihilating fury.

In work with deep disorders of the self, one must be careful that useful theoretical schemas do not offer the devil another home. For example, Klein's positive valuation of the urge to make reparation as a healthy response to the urge to destroy may be on the side of a sound realism. But it grows from and reinforces a vision of the self as basically bad, something that needs making up for. This often is true enough in daily life and expresses a very real practical morality. We would be the poorer if we could not make up for our destructiveness. Yet is the basic "answer" to the problem of hate the need to always be making up for who we are? Are we most basically monsters making up for ourselves? The Kleinian view gives original sin its due, but leaves us in its shadow. It contributes to the splitting process it is meant to overcome.

MAHLER

Klein's depressive position is often associated with Mahler's separation–individuation stage and the gradual movement toward self- and object-constancy.[12] Mahler's[13] depiction and positive valuation

12. Grotstein, "Newer Perspectives in Object Relations Theory," pp. 59–68.

of the move toward self- and object-constancy entails similar dangers. Her descriptions capture important facets of the child's triumph over dependency urges, the fear of, yet wish for, separation and individuation, and a gradual consolidation of self- and object-representations with which to organize the self. What seems to be lacking in her work is a critical assessment of the resulting normal psychic structures and the internalization process as such. What is given up, what is gained in establishing a stable identity of self and other? What sorts of self and object are constituted and consolidated? The basic intentions of the self-in-process Mahler describes must be questioned. Is a sense of mastery and relief, concerning who one and the other are, bought at the price of a deeper alienation? To what extent are "constant" self- and object-representions life rafts? In what ways do our representations imprison us? Is the resulting self a necessary disease, as well as a chance to be? Neither Klein's nor Mahler's views are self-critical. They lack an exposition of the problems their solutions raise.

Fury Deeper Than Hate

WINNICOTT'S I DESTROY YOU–I LOVE YOU

Winnicott's formulations of the function of rage or fury[14] act as a foil to Klein's and Mahler's. He tries to point to an early fury, which is not simply or mainly defensive or reactive. Its main function is creative. For Winnicott, there is a sense in which rage helps to create the sense of the otherness of others or, rather, a new and fresh sense of self and other. The individual learns to "use objects" for growth purposes after discovering that the other survives one's destructive attacks and fantasy control attempts. A kind of psychic explosion takes place in which one lets go as fully as possible. In the other's

---

13. Mahler, *On Human Symbiosis and the Vicissitudes of Individuation*, pp. 7–31, 219–236.
14. Winnicott, "The Use of the Object and Relating Through Identifications," pp. 711–716.

survival, otherness is born (or reborn) and the self quickens. In such an instance fury or rage is deeper than hate and can undercut hate as a frozen attitude.

Perhaps Winnicott's most memorable expression of this process is the following:

> The subject says to the object: "I destroyed you," and the object is there to receive the communication. From now on the subject says: "Hullo object!" "I destroyed you." "I love you." "You have value for me because of your survival of my destruction of you." "While I am loving you I am all the time destroying you in (unconscious) *fantasy*."[15]

The notion that aggression can further differentiation is not unusual. Violence often characterizes hatching processes,[16] and Winnicott's treatment of this insight enriches it. In particular, Winnicott is concerned with finding a basis for true self-feeling deeper than or beyond introjective–projective fantasy operations. However important the latter are, they tend to keep the subject trapped in subtle forms of psychic web-spinning. The subject puts himself into others or others into himself and is caught in a kind of fantasy bubble. The baby's wrath plays a role in exploding fantasy and reaching the realness of himself and others. An explosion clears the air. The discovery that the other continues to be alive in spite of one's fantasy of destruction creates or ratifies a joyous shock of difference. One is liberated by the other's survival and aliveness. We survive the worst in ourselves. Spontaneity *is* possible. We are not simply monsters who must feel guilty and make up for ourselves or deny guilt and remain insensitive—at least not most basically. We come through and become more real together. Our sense of what *real* is keeps shifting.

A new dimension of experiencing opens up in which genuine self–other communion becomes possible. In this interplay, fantasy and the sense of the real require and feed each other. A new sense of the real is born through the destruction of fantasy, while the real invites

15. Ibid., p. 713.
16. Greenacre, *Trauma, Growth and Personality*, pp. 162, 171, 182.

fantasy and further attacks, a continuous cleansing, breaking down, and restoring process.

In Winnicott's terms, the destroyer is one term of a complex drama in which love has primacy. Both the "I destroy you" and "I love you" are valued inclinations of the human heart. They are spontaneous feelings toward others, not discharge mechanisms. The "I love you" doesn't make up for "I destroy you," but turns the latter to good account. In this context, destructiveness makes love real, and love makes destructiveness creative. Winnicott tries to evoke a sense of relationship that is not primarily characterized by defensive manipulation, adaptive control, or mastery. He tries to evoke a sense of the *intrinsic quality* of experience. He depicts something that *can* happen between persons where empathic comprehension and self-expression meet.

How easy it is for the other to make a false move that spoils the situation. A mother or father or therapist may react to infant fury in a retaliatory, masochistic, or controlling way. The infant then feels that he actually destroyed the other's integrity. He forces the other into a corner and pushes him over the brink of his resources. The parent cannot truly meet or cope with the infant in an intrinsic way and begins pulling rank or collapsing. The child becomes addicted to ommnipotent fantasy control of the blundering, wayward parent or mired in fear–hate of the parent's self-righteousness. Fury turns to hate. He learns to hide and manipulate feelings. The serpent in Eden begins to compart-mentalize the psyche, and builds many nests.[17]

Mind–Body Splits and Anal Metaphor

One of the devil's favorite hiding places is the "asshole."[18] No body area is a more highly charged pivot point for associations, especially in pathology, than the anal. Oral and genital meanings tend to

17. Much more could be said concerning the biography of hate in psychoanalytic theory and work; for example, Hartmann, "Contribution to the Metapsychology of

channel themselves through the anus, even more so than through each other. For example, some common symbolic equations are: tongue–nipple–feces–penis–baby; face–breast–buttocks; teeth–feces–penis; breasts–buttocks–testicles; mouth–anus–vagina. The various aspects of anality appear to play an extensive role in knitting the body together in the realm of meaning.

In structural terms, the anal area lends itself to organizing more "undifferentiated" psychic processes than either the oral or the genital areas. Anal identifications involve greater ambiguity than either oral or genital models with reference to self–other differentiation. For example, oral fusion tends to explode itself with the inevitable discovery of the breast outside. Anality lacks such clarity, hence, its basic doubt and obsessive strivings. The subject must tolerate the basic ambiguity that pervades anality and find creative ways of making use of the associated identity feelings.

The quandaries are many for the growing ego. Are feces part of the body self? How can the ego coordinate their initial overvaluation with subsequent repudiation? Where do they come from? How? They invade the passive subject from inside, yet the active subject has a say over their passage. At times, it is impossible to know whether the anus is expelling or taking in, inasmuch as shitting can feel like sucking (viz., the yogi may recommend breathing from one's anus). The baby fluidly displaces top–bottom and in–out. Demonic inclinations feed on this potential for confusion.

In psychosis (and in deep pathology, in general) anality tends to

---

Schizophrenia," pp. 177–198. Hartmann speaks of the diffusion of drives, a preponderance of aggression and ego weakness in psychosis. In his terms, therapy requires the "neutralization" of aggression as a step toward transformation of the latter into energy useable by the ego. Since I myself do not want to be "neutralized," I find his terminology uncongenial. My aim is not exhaustive treatment of the subject, but rather evocation of some of the most important states, processes, and issues.
18. Parts of this and the next section incorporate material from the following papers by Eigen: "On Demonized Aspects of the Self," pp. 91–123; idem, "Creativity, Instinctual Fantasy, and Ideal Images," pp. 317–339; idem, "The Area of Faith in Winnicott, Lacan and Bion," pp. 415–418; idem, "Aspects of Omniscience" (in press).

assimilate orality and genitality, rather than the reverse, although the influence is reciprocal. Anal images tend to function as signs of spoiling, stain, toxicity—of evil itself. For example, when Weil[19] tried to express features of the repressed bad self, which he theoretically located in early oral mirroring, he spontaneously used anal language (a shit or garbage self, self as asshole). Often patients who exhibit ravenous oral traits tend to view their body in anal disposal or toilet terms.[20] Food is spoiled as fast as it is consumed. The fecalization of oral and genital aspects of the self-image has often been described by psychoanalytic authors.[21]

Anal signifiers have long been favorite tropes of the demonic. The psychophysical experiences of anality give rise to expressions that reflect demonized ego operations. The sweet, innocent buttocks present themselves as soft and indefensible, an ideal front for hidden, filthy operations. The sphincters operate, hidden from view, within, under the auspices of an invisible, controlling mind. The brain–asshole connection is reflected in many common expressions, for example, "smart-ass," a trait long associated with the snake and the devil. Some of these features are reflected in the following dream. A woman sits next to the subject at a bar, then gets up to leave. As she walks away her whole head and body appear to be buttocks on legs. The buttocks have a face, and they give the subject a startling, knowing wink. The subject was catching on to anal omniscience.

Potential explosiveness is coupled with an innocent front and hidden control. One cannot sit on life indefinitely. The phallic power of planes and bombs or missiles are colored by anal meanings, flying shits ready to lay waste to populations. Similarly, the nipple–phallic aspect of weaponry ("I'll feed you full of lead") refers to a fecal feed, unmistakeable in its result, a person "wasted." A pan-fecalization of values underlies the megalomanic superiority demonstrated through weaponry. Addiction, the underside of explosiveness, is similarly

19. Weil, "The Origin and Vicissitudes of the Self-Image," pp. 3–19.
20. Eigen, "On Working with 'Unwanted' Patients," pp. 109–121; idem, "Creativity, Instinctual Fantasy and Ideal Images," pp. 317–339.
21. Meltzer, *Sexual States of Mind*, pp. 68–73, 92–98, 110, 175–176; Chasseguet-Smirgel, "Perversion, Idealization and Sublimation," pp. 349–357.

steeped in anal imagery. The language of murder and addiction share many common terms. One is "blown away" or "wasted." Dope is shit. One cleans oneself out with shit ecstasies, just as murder or tantrums (individual or societal) try to get rid of hated contaminants or dreaded spoiled–spoiling elements.

The ancient image of the hooped snake—the snake eating its tail, symbol of eternity in time—succinctly summarizes the structure of anal pathology of concern here. The snake's coiled body partly externalizes the controlling sphincters. The snake's oral–anal contact expresses tendencies toward oral–anal fusion, while its eyes remain transcendent, overlooking the scene. This neatly expresses the typical pathological structure of our times: The body ego's wish for fusion, coupled with a detached, impersonal mental ego. Both body and mental ego are tyrannical. The once flowing and flexible tongue-like snake has become relentless, rigid, and diffuse, a noose tightening toward explosion or the inert leveling off of a cynical self.

Jungians, in accord with an ancient tradition, see in the hooped snake a mandala, a symbol of wholeness. The Age of the Circle arose with the spread of mother goddess figures, the centrality of fertility dramas, the barnyard, the farm, and, finally, the city-state. The circle was womb, but more than womb. It heralded the birth of geometric thinking and its decisive epiphany: man's eventual awareness of mind as such. Geometry pervaded life, from handicraft to a vision of heavenly bodies and the very form of the earth.[22]

The Age of the Circle (and its partner, the cross) portended the growing geometrization of life out of which we are now beginning to burst. The Industrial (and now Nuclear) Age is perhaps its most recent epiphany, although one that seems bent on spoiling the processes that produced it. What may have begun as an age of the womb appears to be culminating in a journey through the asshole, a possibility encoded in the encircled serpent at the outset. In this regard, a patient once dreamt of an encircled snake trying to disappear head first up its own anus, an apt, if vulgar, image for our present cultural impasse.

22. Campbell, *The Flight of the Wild Gander*, pp. 120–192.

Contemporary Devils

There is no history outside the self-feeling of persons, no history without self, no self without history. Demonized ego structures found in individuals reflect the texture of the times and have their own historical input. Case material, if well chosen, touches torments that go beyond the particular individual. It catches areas of ferment through which an age moves or dies. We glimpse threads of where we have come from or where we are going in fragments torn out of context.

The stakes were never higher. We have available unprecedented means of destruction. If we persist in not coming to terms with the megalomanic aspect of our sense of self, whether in its innocence, or warped by hatred, we will not know what hit us or why when we blow ourselves to oblivion. In the consulting room we study processes that can save or sink a civilization; we slow them down so as to see in fine detail what usually rushes by.

We learn and relearn that madness in individuals can operate invisibly. It is often undetected by the untutored eye. If therapy is uncompromising, the psychosis that secretly threatens an individual may finally appear. It may turn out that he knew it all along, but did not want to or could not admit it. Some individuals seek to shut their madness out at all cost. Many say, "Yes, I'm crazy. But if I ever gave in to it, I'd be lost." Often the words, "I'm crazy, but . . . ," are meant to lessen the impact of a grim and unmanageable reality. They are an excuse or an evasion, although occasionally a person screws up courage and turns them into a launching pad. Often those who evade the requirements their madness makes of them open themselves to physical dangers or inflict illness on others.[23]

In therapy, there are people who will or who are forced to meet

---

23. For a portrayal of the hidden relationship between somatic ills and madness, read Marie Cardinal's *The Words to Say It.* (Cambridge: VanVactor & Goodheart, 1983). For an example of evasion of madness by making others ill, see Jule Eisenbud, "On the Death Wish," in Nelson and Eigen, *Evil: Self and Culture*, pp. 227–238.

their madness. The compromises they have made with themselves egg them on. They cannot live with anything less than the most thoroughgoing self-confrontation, and even that will not do. A dragon has them by the tail and their search is relentless, if often grown in on itself. One patient's mother had told him since child-hood, "You'll get hurt if you go too deeply." Her Tiresias-like warning sealed a destiny. His madness fed a life bent on creatively–destructively wrestling with itself.

Others are anything but heroic, but do what they can. They seem to slip into insanity slowly, and do not face themselves so much as live through what they have to. They would have avoided their madness if they could. For them therapy can make the difference between fading away and turning one's life to good account. Such a person once said, "I always knew I was insane, but no one ever believed me. I daren't listen to myself. I wouldn't know what to do. I kept hoping it would all finally just go away. But it never did."

One type searches, the other waits. Either may get better or worse. If we take up our madness we find ourselves at any moment in distortions we would like to wish away. If we are lucky, what is most alive about us develops through a detailed appreciation of the illness that refused to go away.

SMITH

A highly successful professional man who began therapy in the wake of a heart attack, Smith himself had no history of hospitaliza-tion for mental problems, but his children and grandmother had. He came from a mother-dominated, fatherless home. His hard-working mother behaved bizarrely, for example, exhibiting chickens she had decapitated as if they were penises. His father insisted that Smith's mother was killing him, and he committed suicide when Smith was five years old.

Smith early realized that life was brutally crazy and he determined to rise above it. At the same time, he found life extraordinarily rich and wanted to live to the fullest. His mother loved him boundlessly, but also terrorized him. She blindly idolized him,[24] because he would be the one to make all things good. Everything he did felt at once great and spoiled. He hated and admired his mother's power and he nourished his megolamania with polluted love.

Smith married young and maintained his family commitments for the next 40 years. His sexual interest in his wife quickly waned and he found himself generally feeling more and more like a dead man. He achieved success at the price of blunting his self-feeling. In time, he escaped his growing depersonalization by having affairs with younger men or boys. For moments his sense of unreality would be offset by his, and his young partner's, total idolization of the other. He was also aware, however, that there was something "unreal" about the world he entered with his lovers. He felt caught between prosaic and intense unrealities. A number of his lovers turned out to be psychotic or became so during their relationship.

He described himself as a parent to all his children (lovers, wife, siblings, actual children). He lived out his baby self in identification with others. He felt himself fused with his lovers, yet, in a corner of his mind, aloof. To some degree, he was able to live out or project good body feeling with or into them and rationalize their disorganization away. He ignored his growing somatic problems and dismissed his body with a trace of contempt. He did not change his habits after his first heart attack. It was as if he found a style of life he believed worked for him and he would rather die than give it up. To change was the death of deaths.

After a few months of therapy, Smith confessed that he sometimes saw devil images when he was weary and closed his eyes. A few days before one session, he glimpsed the devil in a store window, only to realize it was his own reflection. With encouragement, he tried to focus on such images and soon discovered that his awareness of evil presences went back indefinitely.

---

24. For an excellent description of the process of "idolization" as encapsulated madness in perversion, see Khan, *Alienation in Perversions*, pp. 12–16. "Smith" is also discussed in Eigen, "On Demonized Aspects of the Self," pp. 96–97.

When he looked at his devils closely, they manifested a mixture of agony and self-pity, but if he continued to withstand them, they became rageful and threw temper tantrums. The scenario varied. They might become limp, as if exhausted, or rise up in defiant and seductive torment. It was as if they, too, had lost their I-feeling and were trying to regain it through the intensity of pain. They mirrored a fiercely numb paralysis, a hopeless rage.

A series of significant dreams soon followed these reveries. One opened with the terror of burglar-killers. Ominous figures lurked outside his apartment, and Smith doubted he could keep them out. A baby began screaming, "Fire." It seemed almost a demon screaming. A woman in a nearby building opened and closed windows. She also kept filling her apartment with different objects, and then emptying it. The baby's blood-curdling scream faded.

Any set of dream images can be approached many ways with profit. Following was the main line we took at the time. The sequence starts with hostile dangers, followed by a baby's scream. Perhaps the terror and outrage suggests there still is hope in compelling a response. However, the mothering self cannot function as an adequate container for baby explosiveness, absorbed as she is with her own internal space and boundary problems. She is caught in an obsession, unable to coordinate opening–closing or emptying–filling, that is, in–out traffic. The baby's unmanageable feelings demonically spiral, then fade into nothingness.

In imaginative activity, Smith gradually opened himself to the scream of his baby self. To an extent, the devil was a frozen scream. Experiencing the sensations of screaming had a thawing-out effect. Smith wept uninhibitedly for the first time in adult memory. In general, he became more sensitive to the fading in and out of the sense of vital aliveness and the silent urges to scream that often passed unnoticed throughout the day. It began to dawn on him how much of his life was spent screaming without his knowing it. He became more aware of ways in which he fobbed such moments off—he had been afraid of his madness and of knowing just how mad he really was. He was finally able to give credence to a background sense that he had long been "as crazy as a hatter" (hater?) and could begin to trace the terrible scars his sanity–insanity cost him.

In fantasy, he saw his heart attacks as a baby screaming, a devil's fits. Devil images now made him feel mighty. They alternated with terror and helplessness. He felt in touch with the currents of a baby self. His chest, his breathing, and body generally had been constricted, tight-assed. He had been controlling and sticky. His feelings were messy and made messes. Perhaps, he mused, his heart attacks were a way of cleaning himself out.

He dreamt of a playful little girl who was a bit messy. When Smith focused on her, he felt a delightful sense of relaxation. He also felt an urge to tighten and keep a grip on himself. He could not imagine how this little girl could possibly defend herself against danger. Yet contact with her made dangers disappear. For a time he tried to see her as threat or dismiss her as merely passive, worthless, or seductive. With my firm backing, the intrinsic goodness of the little girl was increasingly recognized and owned. She learned to stand up for herself. Smith came to see her as the most undemonic aspect of psychic life he had yet produced. He saw more clearly how he had driven himself to his breaking point, partly so that acts of catastrophic self-violence might carry him past his lifelong numbing. The little girl was not numb, but she could only appear after a baby's paralyzed scream could be heard. As a practicing devil, Smith really heard no one, least of all himself.

Smith was aware that too much physical damage might have occurred for psychic work to save him. Yet, the discovery of the screaming baby and the little girl in the wreckage of a lifelong madness opened new directions, a new sense of self.

PAUL

Paul felt on the verge of a breakdown several times in his life. He periodically sought help through drugs and supportive psychotherapy. He was helped to function, but also to avoid coming to grips with himself. "I just want to feel OK again," he said. "I'll do anything." Then as if to placate me, he added with a sincere expression. "I really want to work on myself."

His most intense life experience had been manipulating his wife and best friend to make love while he watched. The marriage broke up soon afterwards, precipitating Paul's closest brush with a full-blown psychosis. Suffering overwhelming panic and depression, he could do little but stay at home. He was suicidal. In time, medication blunted some of his anxiety, but he never fully recovered. He tried to get used to living a chronically depressed and fearful existence and hit on various perverse routines for minimal relief. He masturbated for hours with women's stockings, panties, and shoes—his ex-wife's or his daughter's. The ritual culminated in what he described as "explosions," intense orgasms that left him drained, a relief that made him feel "great," then "shitty."

Paul was raised by a physically ill mother who used her illness to dominate the household. He was tantalized by three older sisters. When he was four, one sister initiated a game in which she tied him on a bed and did a striptease. After her interest turned to boys outside the household, the sight of her stocking was enough to send Paul into a frenzy.

Since early childhood, Paul was also repeatedly given enemas. The ritual consisted of his being held firmly by his mother across her lap while his father or his mother gave the enema. Paul's penis pressed upon his mother and this pleasure fused with anal sensations culminating in rageful, humiliating ecstasies. He felt he would die in the midst of orgastic explosions. Paul became addicted to perverted rebirth experiences.

He imagined or recalled splitting into two demons in these scenes. One was a body demon madly exploding. The other was a head demon, a grimacing onlooker chuckling, "Heh, heh." Throughout his life he tried to throw off one or the other side of this split, but ended by being ripped apart.

A related feeling was his disgust with his mother's display of her ruptured navel. It infuriated him that his mother repeatedly rejected her doctor's advice to remove it surgically. Paul wanted to rip it off, but her masochistic exhibition stifled him. As he eventually could say, "Cutting her belly-cock would cut my lifeline." As often happens, maternal castration fused with separation fears.[25]

Paul's father was kind and mild, but he lacked the strength to set this wayward household in order. Paul's awareness of his father's weakness intensified his underlying despair, but his father's quiet warmth supported some ability to soothe himself with depression. His persistent, unsuccessful efforts to help his father help him played a significant role in consequent breakdowns.

In the enema scenes, the father was the mother's helper. Paul would stare at him in pleading disbelief: "Surely you'll turn against her and save me." In one fantasy, Paul imagined his father turning the tables and giving *her* an enema or a spanking. This wish was translated into the primal scene enactment in which Paul's friend "fucked the shit out of" his wife (Paul's language). Following this act, his wife (mother) vanished like feces, ushering in his breakdown.

Such events are not narrated to "explain" Paul's lifelong problems, but rather to suggest the atmosphere in which he grew up. The sexual clarity of such scenes helped Paul to organize his rage and diffusion through perversions. They gave him something to hold on to. His fetish objects functioned as highly charged packets of maternal power. Their small size (panties, shoes, etc.) and well-bounded form made them easy to control and set limits to permeability and fusion. Fetishism is an attempt to externalize and gain mastery over the mother's phallic power or to mitigate one's crushing sense of helplessness. In Paul's case, the fetishism was not so much a denial that mother has no penis, as Freud suggests, but rather a dramatization of just how powerful her phallus really was. In families like Paul's, the mother's "phallus" is apt to be the only effective one.

Paul's perversions also expressed the wish that his father subdue maternal power, while Paul merged with it. By containing mother's power in an object at his disposal, Paul achieved, by way of perversion, what his father failed to achieve. Through perverse activity, he tried to make good his father's lack. He was both his father's proxy

25. Aspects of Paul's case are also discussed in Eigen, "On Pre-Oedipal Castration Anxiety," pp. 489–498; idem, "On Demonized Aspects of the Self," pp. 100–104.

and better, in part working at father repair through the self as double. The perverse subject goes about his father's business the only way he can in a mother-bound world. He is given over to collusion with mother, while transcending her with whatever father elements he can salvage or fabricate. The fetish becomes a weapon with which to beat mother at her own game.

In mind–body terms, the body ego loses and heightens itself through merger with the fetish (mother's power), while the mental ego hardens itself and is triumphantly controlling. The mental ego remains detached from the body ego's fusion. Paul's head demon may be driven to allow no mother at all within the circumference of its self-feeling. His body demon may allow no mother outside it. From time to time, the body ego tries to explode the trap in which it is caught. Rage tries to break through fusion. The mental ego is then confronted with whether or not it is willing to give up the spiteful, delusional control to which it has become attached. At such a point, Paul's entire personality lives in agony between despair and fear, and possibility.

DEE

Dee was a twelve-year-old girl diagnosed as epileptic and schizo-phrenic.[26] Her epilepsy became manifest after her first attempts at kindergarten, in which the separation was intolerable. When I met her, she was in a state of vegetative collapse, incontinent and unintel-ligible. Occasionally she masturbated while watching TV. Her *grand mal* seizures were poorly controlled by medication, and it was be-lieved that she was suffering from progressive brain deterioration. Her mother felt her problem was nutritional and could not give up trying to cure Dee with Tyger's Milk, bran cookies, and other magical oral supplies. Dee's father was a gnomic man who claimed he did not speak before the age of 18. He sometimes tried to play

26. The case of Dee was previously discussed in Eigen, "Breaking the Frame: Stopping the World," pp. 89–100; idem, "On Demonized Aspects of the Self," pp. 96–100.

cryptic games with Dee; one involving a snake going into a hole will be described later.

For some time I shadowed Dee silently and after awhile she began to notice my presence. I noticed her noticing me and felt she noticed that, too. Her eyes flickered with life, then went blank. Was she tuning me out, or was she simply unable to sustain a moment's semi-aliveness? At times, I imagined flickers of disdain.

Soon I felt she was looking even when she was supposed to be unconscious during her seizures. She was mentally alive in the midst of earthquake and paralysis. I saw a devil looking through her eyes, a malevolent core of consciousness at the heart of apparent oblivion. It was a searing look, pure hate, a mocking laser. As I stared more closely, I believed I saw malicious glee and ghastly suffering, but also something regal and haughty, even prankish, as though the devil were sticking out its tongue and saying, "OK—Let's see what you can do."

I discussed my feelings in supervision, but they persisted. Finally my supervisor and I decided I should let happen what may. Dee was one of my first "cases" at a treatment camp some 25 years ago. I was fresh and undaunted and would try anything.

One day as Dee started a seizure and flashed her devil look I heard myself scream, "You bitch!" The seizure stopped instantly, and she glowered. From that time on she noticed me more often, and differently. She had to put more effort into blanking me out. Our silences thickened, but her face had more color.

I dreamt that Dee was underwater without knowing how to swim. I was trying to teach her. Her parents pushed her under each time she tried to surface. They refused to let her swim or drown. She showed signs of decomposition, but reached out to me.

Since this was my dream, it used Dee to tell a story about my life, but I could not help feeling that I also dreamt it for her. My striving to build an adequate psychic life from the debris of parental failure was a drive that in Dee was stillborn. In such a situation, the therapist lends to the patient what the latter above all requires, a functioning psyche committed to developmental struggle.

After my dream, our silences became more intense and sly. I

fancied Dee felt vulnerable for appearing in my dream. It was as if I stumbled upon a secret broadcast system in which the devil, however delusionally, broadcasts news of self. On feeling the full impact of this new silence, I found myself wanting to put my hand in Dee's mouth. Her presence seemed to act like a vacuum, exerting a suction-like force on me. Again I spoke with my supervisor about it. We tried to analyze my impatience, my hostile sexuality, Dee's need to get stuffed, my inability to contain the anxiety of a void state, and so on. My hope was that my urge expressed a linking gesture, however tainted, and I gave in to it.

Dee eventually turned her head to look at me with dismay, the most direct and emphatic look of recognition I had yet experienced from her. She tried to collapse and ignore what was happening, but I kept my fingers in her mouth. Almost without warning she stood to her full height, stared at me with outrage, and screamed. I maintained my hand in position as best I could without choking her, and she hit me. She was hitting me with all her might, but I didn't feel any pain. After all the time I spent banging against the wall of her unrespon-siveness, I felt only joy. She reared up in indignant majesty and beat me to her heart's content, pummeling any part of my face or body she could reach. She looked righteous and queenly and radiant, a mixture of imperious credulity and chagrin: "How dare you affront Her Majesty!" It was the first physical exercise I had seen her take outside her seizures. After this episode, tangible progress in her treatment began to be made. It was a kind of spontaneous/compul-sive exorcism that dramatized the force Dee exerted and her parents' relentless exploitation of it. However, it was probably the first time her explosive hunger could surface in a situation in which respectful comprehension was possible. Her seeing met with seeing.

Her seizures diminished, and her skin tone continued to improve. Although all life processes were rusty, within a month she spoke understandably, largely fed herself, and eagerly walked with help. Her features and body began to soften. At times, she glowed. When she rested, her limbs were more sensuous, as if she could now enjoy the languorous spread of body sensations. She was more active and noisy and also quietly alive. Needless to say, all this progress, momentous and uplifting for the young therapist, was scarcely a drop in the ocean in the life of the patient. But, we like to think, the ocean is the better for it.

Was Dee's illness basically physical, psychological, or both? Did psychological problems trigger a weak physiology? Did a weak physiology stimulate psychological difficulties? In Dee's case, I felt that something was off throughout the entire psychophysical spectrum, as if psyche–soma–family–culture were cut from the same fabric. For example, the hand-in-mouth episode reflected and reworked a pattern that ran through Dee's life in many ways. A chilling variation on this theme occurred in a letter her father sent to her during the first month of camp. I will recount it without comment as it speaks for itself.

The letter was a series of pictures with captions: (1) snake on left, hole on right with the caption, "The Snake and Hole"; (2) snake approaches hole with caption, "The Snake Goes toward the Hole"; (3) snake enters hole with caption, "The Snake Goes in the Hole"; (4) snake vanishes, but bit of tail still visible with caption, "The Snake Disappears into the Hole"; (5) a hole with caption, "The Hole"; (6) chaotic lines trailing off on blank page with caption, "And Then There Was Nothing." At the bottom, "Love, Daddy."

The "Unwanted" Patient

Some persons have undergone such spoiling processes that their presence in the therapist's office is unappetizing.[27] In extreme instances they may actually be grotesque and smelly. Everything about them exudes a bad self-feeling. But even when physically tidy, they may be psychologically incontinent/constipated and behave so messily or withheld that the therapist is inclined to feel like a latrine. Such patients often drive therapists away, as they do people in general.

27. This section is adapted from Eigen, "On Working with 'Unwanted' Patients," pp. 109–121.

They may oscillate between an overcloying and obnoxiously negativistic manner, in apparently endless repetition of extreme forms of hostile dependence. They can appear needy and demanding, yet present intractable resistance if one tries to help them. In some instances, they may appear snake-like and cynically chilling. If they are vegetative, they are also willful and proud, although in seemingly masochistic and silent ways. They are very sensitive to slights, but seem to have long ago accepted that the best they can do is just manage to get through things, and many give up this hope, too. Often they carry a hope tinged with resentment, made heavy with an accusing sense of deprivation and self-pity. They seek relief from pain, but have a high tolerance for feeling that things will never change and nothing good can happen to them. All this despair seems part of an atmosphere of muted want and rage. There identity is formed by a chronic sense of injury, together with a primitive union with those who injured them.

The therapist must become adept at sustaining and processing negative feelings. If he is careful, a world of subtle nuances of negativity gradually becomes visible. The work is very like cataloguing and exploring varieties of fecal odors, as if such discoveries were valuable. In time, the therapist may have as many names for shades of darkness as an Eskimo does for snow. And yet, if the therapist is respectful of the patient's illness, however intolerable this may be for patient and therapist alike, sometimes light also comes. Several illustrative sketches follow.

ELLIE

An unpleasantly obese woman, whom I shall call Ellie, scarcely seemed to take care of herself. She initiated her therapy with complaints and demands concerning everyone around her. She lived a vegetative existence filled with self-pity and chronic hatred toward herself and others. When she was not in the hospital, her husband no longer approached her sexually and she put on more weight, feeling deprived and resentful. She seemed to cover herself with fat in passive defiance, and frequently smelled. It was not her obesity itself that was disgusting, since fat women can be vibrant and appealing. It was her spirit, limp and decaying, which had turned her body into an oppressive mass. I had the vivid impression that she experienced herself as feces and that the food she fed herself was a form of feces and she the sewer.

After several months of sitting through a verbal barrage and constant complaints, something genuinely interesting happened. Ellie revealed that although she knew she was nauseatingly fat and put off others with her appearance and behavior, she did not really believe she was fat. She carried a picture of herself, taken 10 years earlier, when she was 19 years old. Her hair was a wavy strawberry blond (not the straw sticks she actually displayed) and her figure was well within normal range and attractive. This, she claimed, was the real her, the person she saw in her mind's eye throughout the years and who she still felt she was. She disclosed that when she was certain she was alone she often would open her arms and gracefully dance about the room, spinning and swaying. Only in those moments could she feel truly herself.

Her wish to show me her dance grew and soon she did. Her dance was as graceful as she boasted, poignantly so. Yet, for a moment, I could not help thinking of Charlie Chaplin as Hitler performing a ballet holding a globe of the world. She danced on and I allowed myself to be drawn in, so taken with her expressive gestures that I, too, forgot she was fat and saw only a thin, young woman. She turned into her fantasy, which, for a time, became reality for both of us.

Afterwards, Ellie broke down and wept. She could not admit the pain of owning her bodily distortion. She feared she could not tell the difference between what was real and what she imagined. To complicate matters, her "unreal" outer form conveyed important inner realities. Her obesity gave expression to deep narcissistic and exhibitionistic needs. It was something everyone could see. It expressed ugly feelings she could not deal with and tried to hide. Her fat was insulation, but also ooze. Through her unkempt obesity, she was calling attention to the fact that her feelings about herself and others were in danger and that she needed help.

PAT

In another case, the patient, Pat, withdrew from contact in an accusing, suspicious manner. She looked at me disdainfully as if I were beneath words. Her face had an unappealing embryonic quality, as though she were a baby in a test tube, distorted by the glass through which she was seen. The sharpest quality about her otherwise amorphous face was an expression of distaste. The only sexual act she ever enjoyed was cunnilingus, in which she relaxed and felt powerful and loved. In her case, I took this as a positive prognostic sign. At least sometimes, she could let someone make her feel clean and valuable.

Much of the time Pat felt I wanted her to be subservient, and in lucid moments, she called me a "male chauvinist pig." I felt she wanted me to lick the shit away and clean the wound of her self-hate. She endlessly attacked me for my callousness and threatened to leave, frequently storming from the room. For a time I hoped she wouldn't come back. We did not pretend to like each other, but did begin to develop a mutual patience or tolerance of a sort. She said she put up with me because other analysts were no better and she had to let someone help her sometime.

She blamed me for everything wrong with her. I was responsible for her collapse, her womb-like life, her bad feelings about herself and others. I was making her dependent and using her. I made her hurt her parents. I was the bad one. I suffered her hate for years. But her face filled out. She worked, dated, and started school. Bit by bit, she approached life's starting line.

Much later Pat disclosed she had liked as well as hated me, but knew if she expressed her liking therapy would be spoiled. She had come to feel a secret gratitude for my holding together in face of attack, but did not want to ruin it by saying so. She felt a certain purity by being able to hate without having to counteract her hatred with displays of love. At those moments, the love she felt without risk of intrusion was hers alone. My patient dreaded having good feelings stolen. She felt her mother had always done so by force or seduction. It was important that I did not try expressly to divine what she was feeling beyond her expression of hate. Had I done so, I would have been like her mother, picking apart her innermost being against her will. My taking her hate allowed her to move beyond the mutual terrorizing that characterized her relationship with her parents. As in the case of Ellie, longing and destructiveness went together. Therapy was a situation in which the full force of her hate could be sustained without polluting her love. The hate in her system could be gathered together in a strengthening way, rather than continue to spread in all directions and eat up her life like a cancer.

RON

A third example is the analysis of a middle-aged man who had passed through six therapists, one of whom he had seen for 10 years. Ron had a gnomish appearance. His body was somewhat bent and twisted, so that he seemed shorter than his actual size. His trunk and pelvis were pinched together and his head squeezed into his shoulders, although medical examinations revealed no evidence of physical deformity. His chronically spastic body had become grossly distorted because of his severe anxious–rigid character structure and related body armor.

Ron spoke in a non-stop, repetitious fashion, and most of his verbiage centered around his illness. He now feared he was totally giving in to it. He was too tired to put up a fight any longer. He had always been able to come out of the hospital and work at some menial job. According to him, his past therapists had marveled at his vast store of energy and told him, "If only you could channel it positively, what you couldn't do." He felt he had enormous powers of intelligence, which remained blocked. The fatal flaw of his life, he said, was that his energy was trapped in "negativity" (his term).

To me he seemed far from "giving in." I even felt some certainty that he could not possibly know what "giving in" might mean. Ron's images were hydraulic: vast energy needing channeling. Were they his, a past therapist's, a teacher's, his mother's, the culture's? He spoke loudly and went around in circles. He knew what his trouble was, but he could not do anything about it. His windmill style was a protective shield around himself, as if announcing that neither he nor I would ever get near him and we might as well not even try. Better yet, we should try and then complain. He seemed addicted to a mood of grandiose exasperation, tinged with self-pity. In the end he put everyone off except his mother, with whom he lived, and lately her patience was also wearing thin. At times he would break his monologue by asking whether I thought I could help him. "I don't know," I might answer. "We can try. What do you think?" But even this question soon seemed part of the windmill.

Ron could not dream. Perhaps he feared nightmares. Patients going in and out of psychosis often produce horrendous images expressive of psychic devastation. What scraps of dream he produced were slivers, torn from everyday perception, that suggested extreme psychic impoverishment. No gods, devils, or witches in his world. He was a pure realist. He seemed to want to shock me with his plight. He wanted me to join him in his fight to realize his great potential and be sorry when he failed. I ought to cheer him on and be frightened when he threatened to give up. A self-critical voice in myself whispered that I ought to feel empathic: "Look how misshapen life has made him."

Nevertheless, without clearly knowing why, I experienced a certain amusement with his manner and style. He presented himself in an incorrigibly ill-fitting extroverted manner. His blustering, almost shouting style did not quite go with his dwarfish development, or perhaps it went too well. His eyes bulged and his ears extended from anxiety. As I viewed him, I could not suppress images of a kind of restless corkscrew turtle. In some sense, Ron presented himself as a morbid, comic figure. I was tempted to view my response as my own deficiency, but my need to keep distance proved valuable. It was important for me to have the right to my own perceptions.

Although my imperturbability frustrated and infuriated him, it also allowed a piece of "unreality" to enter his life. In time he saw me as the real him. My expression and tone felt more like himself than he was. I was an ideal he, a he he wished to be, his "secret, real self," distortion-free. That is, I was an impossibility. My godlike bemusement nourished him. Did it cater to his masochism? Would it further his debasement? Would he do better as my slave than as his mother's? What a giddy temptation for therapeutic megalomania. Yet "reality" had not helped him.

My reserved amusement was a form of self-protection. At the same time, he used my silent comic perception to help place his pathology in a larger perspective. Unlike his mother, I was quite happy to share my superior status on equal footing. If I were a god, why not he? Much later he could say that my attitude made him feel that his illness was a secondary offshoot of who he really was, a felt cognition that gave him faith.

In this case, the healing movement was initiated by my defensive persona, a dissociated system of feeling and behavior partly stimulated by the patient's developmental needs. Another type of patient might have induced a reaction of hushed reserve or a respect for fragility. In this instance, an unconsciously induced comic perception of Ron's physiognomy functioned to feed back to the patient a dissociated and poorly developed aspect of his own personality that had not had the opportunity to develop adequately. A latent, unacknowledged, clown-like self-image met with an appropriate bemused response. The self-hatred expressed in the image was reflected by the withholding aspect of my distance and the mocking aspect of my humor. However, clowning is also a cry for love, and in this light my feeling was experienced as a playful and respectful affirmation. The patient was able to create a response ambiguously fitting enough to satisfy multiple, but specific, therapeutic needs.

The patients in these case histories generally externalized their problems and showed very little spontaneous interest in psychic processes. When the latter occurred it was usually obsessive and used to reinforce a self-hardening process. Such persons have been forced to undergo gross personality distortions patterned after inordinately destructive early object-relations. The egos of these patients have a marked incapacity to process aggressive feelings in wholesome ways. The self's hate is aimed, in part, against its needs and love wishes and leads to a reproachful attitude toward an apparently ungiving or overwhelming world. If the therapist fully opens himself to the attitudes of these patients, he will tend to feel injured or drained. The patients themselves have erected barriers to influence this by repelling those who venture near. At the same time, the intensity of their deepest needs compels them to attempt to draw the other into their orbit and merge. Hence the therapist, like the patient, is in danger of feeling pulled apart by the patient's conflicting tendencies.

The patient may try to escape from the tension created by poorly managed antagonistic tendencies by collapsing one or other of the poles of tension or, simply, by leaving the field. He may, for example, try to become part of the therapist, have the therapist become part of him, or try to drive the therapist away. If the therapist is steadfast, the patient often drives himself away. The therapist's instinctive repulsion and indignation, which is often unconscious, with regard to the patient's style, products, and demands, offends the patient's narcissism and provokes retreat. On the other hand, a too-nurturant attitude may make the therapist appear too eager and needy and also drive the patient away.

Although the therapist's instinctive negative reactions cannot be avoided, they can help as well as harm. They invite and require the analyst to explore the disagreeable world to which they point. What makes therapy different from other frustrating situations in the patient's life is, for one thing, the therapist's sustained awareness of the process, or, at least, his expectation that there is, in principle, a process one might attend to if one could.

The patient who chronically tends to evoke distaste in others evokes tendencies one normally avoids. The therapist engaged in this work has unusual opportunities to work with phobic structures embedded in his psychic foundations. Whether or not this effort is worthwhile or desirable hinges, in part, on individual preferences, values, and ultimately, one's vision of life.

On Self-hatred

Self-hatred is a basic theme that runs through all the above case histories. There is perhaps no more basic theme in mental illness.

This includes hatred of self, whatever and wherever self may be—the self of others as well as one's own.

Bion expresses this by saying that the psychotic subject attacks his own and his analyst's ego functioning.[28] The problem is not so much the ego's conflict with drives, although this intensifies matters. The psychotic subject, according to Bion, reaches a point where he cannot tolerate alive and good functioning at any level. He disintegrates in the face of life. He disintegrates life.

To be sure, Freud's account of the ego's conflict with drives is important in understanding the work of self-hatred. Early in life we come to feel that our impulses are bad. We learn to hold ourselves in. We want what we ought not to want. We break things. We hurt people—we feel pain and cause pain. We are potentially destructive. We must take care and be on guard with ourselves and others. To a certain extent, we become our own watchmen.

Our situation is complicated by the fact that many of our impulses are inherently good. We break things and hurt people without meaning to. Our delight in hurting another (e.g., poking a finger in mommy's eye, stomping on daddy's belly) often has a good side. We playfully affirm ourselves in our vigor. No wonder it is so easy to get good and bad feelings and God–devil mixed up or use each against the other.

ALISON

In one extreme, but not very unusual instance, a patient forestalled awareness of her self-hate by holding onto good feelings with a vengeance. If one took her at her word, Alison felt good most of her life. Her mother might be psychotic, her husband angrily depressed—but she felt good. To hear her speak, one felt all hell would pay for it if she did not.

In analysis, she confessed that as a child she was determined not to give in to her psychotic mother as her sister had. She became like her witty, successful father instead. Together they looked down at the

---

28. Bion, *Second Thoughts*, pp. 86–89; idem, *Elements of Psycho-Analysis*, pp. 48–61.

crazy woman who stormed throughout the house and could not manage her elemental emotions. When her father died prematurely, she continued the fight alone.

Her first therapist (10 years earlier) sided with her good feeling, her professed love of life, although her life was a constant battle. She married a sarcastic man who maintained his equilibrium by lashing out at her. No matter how bad things got, Alison found a way of feeling good and had no idea why this maddened her husband even more. She could scarcely permit her children privacy. She was invasive to an extreme, which she rationalized as concern. She was a nonstop talker and doer. She felt wronged if her husband or children tried to get away from her and attributed it to their fragility.

During the first year of our work, she brought in a succession of dreams in which she bled profusely. She could not stop this outpouring and feared she would die. An image like this has many determinants, but what a fine expression it is of how she depleted herself by letting what might have developed into an internal world promiscuously spill out. Her dreams incessantly gave the lie to her good feelings, but she chronically attributed her dream wounds to her husband's or mother's attempts to injure her. For Alison, they were the concrete results of their destructiveness. Whatever bad happened to her was because of them.

The blood nightmares persisted for a long time, no matter what she said about them. They did not give way to her explanations. She had to admit she did not know why she had such dreams, although a sense of injury was involved. After she began to restrain herself and to feel some depression, the bleeding stopped. Several years later, she was able to link these dreams with the self-hate she feared would destroy her. She had taken in her mother's illness after all. The salvation she managed to eke out through her father now came back to haunt her. It was part of a split in which a smart, self-congratulating mental self (father identification) continuously bombarded a more obviously hating, invading–engulfing mass (mother identification).

Alison had been tearing herself apart and wearing herself down without knowing it. She was totally unaware that she seemed years older than she was. In her mind's eye, she was youthful (like the father of her childhood and early teens), yet in reality her face was marked with devastation (like her mother's). She lived out the attacker through her husband, which allowed her to attack the attacker self-righteously. That she was not simply the innocent victim in relation to him became clear when his behavior began to change as she acted less like her mother. The roots of her self-hatred went deep into her early life and were fed by the community of hate in which she was enmeshed. It was, of course, a subtle mixture of love and hate that kept hate alive. With no love at all, there would be no medium for hate to thrive in. In Alison's life, love and hate worked through self-deception. Yet, as often happens, she prided herself on her knowledge of her own and others' feelings.

In psychosis, one's relation to the capacity to know is as important as one's conflicts with love and hate. Psychotic subjects often feel they know more (or less) than those around them. They know so much they do not have to learn anything new. They feel they have heard within themselves anything the therapist might have to say. They see through the therapist's defenses and pretensions to draw the conclusion that such a flawed soul must be wrong or irrelevant.

Alison was a know-it-all. She went for years without seeming to be capable of genuine self-doubt. Her good feelings about herself were justified by and supported a sense of superior knowledge. She knew better than anyone. The eventual challenge that therapy presented to her sense of omniscience helped to precipitate her depression and a growing ability to hold things in.

A key to whatever help therapy was able to provide her was my unwillingness to give in to the sense of relief her feeling good induced in me (or her). My deeper perception was that Alison had a hell to go through and that she had prematurely found heaven. It was indeed tempting to side with her good estimation of herself and avoid possible disaster. Her dreams were fixed on disaster she seemed ill-equipped to suffer. To a great extent, my job was to delicately, but doggedly side with the message of disaster her dreams embodied. The fact that her dreams had not given up on her was a good sign. They had not succumbed to her omniscient goodness. They persisted in presenting another side. Her sense of being a psychic disaster refused to be erased, at least in her dreams.

Bion expresses the self-erasing function of psychic life with a minus sign. All capacities are subject to numbing and erasing. For example, $-K$, $-L$, $-H$ point to the ability of the subject to attack the linking activities of knowing, loving, and hating. In this context, hate is on the side of life. In Freudian terms, hate is part of the life drive. It contains a positive element. One hates a felt injustice. Hate is a testimony to the existence of value. One still values something enough to hate not getting it or being it. One has not totally given up or reached the point where nothing is worth getting angry about (a form of $-H$).

A death wish may erase any psychic activity. Hate may be erased by it, as well as love and the wish to know. A death wish tends to undo psychic aliveness in all its forms. It moves toward a maximum of inertia or entropy, a zero point of stimulation. In this context, life turns against itself. Hate in the service of the death wish undoes even itself.

On the positive side, our urge toward self-annihilation can be cleansing. In our self-attacks, we may try to get rid of what we feel has gone wrong about ourselves, and, in extreme instances, we try to wipe ourselves out in order to begin anew. If the right attitude can be adopted, self-hate can find its place as part of an overall growth process. If one fails to find a frame of reference large enough, the results are often crippling or even lethal.

CARRIE

In one instance, a woman's life severely deteriorated after she came from a small Western town to New York City. In short time, she fell into a drug and a borderline criminal existence. In her words, she "let herself go." She gave in to the worst in herself. She felt somehow nourished by danger even as she fell apart. At first she gave in out of a sense of excitement. Her new, free experience titillated her. But in time she found herself gripped by a process that might destroy her.

She was a religious woman who, for the first time, felt alienated from her God. She felt certain He could not love her because of how she had twisted herself out of recognition. In time, the idea took hold that she so distorted herself precisely to see if God could or would still see and find her. She courted dangers inherently repulsive to her in order to feel unrecognizable. Each time she performed some new act of self-obliteration she would feel, "Now I've done it. This time I've really gone too far. Now I've *really* lost Him." When the experience settled, however traumatic the aftermath, He would surface again, bobbing up from beneath the place she lost Him. What she was driven to learn was that there was nothing so revolting she could do that would finally drive Him away.[29]

The downward spiral in this woman's life was part of a drive for self-purification. She needed to throw off her persona, the plaster of Paris goodness in which she felt trapped. She felt her "evil thread" would lead her to her zero point by constantly overturning and burning her out. She became a kind of caricature or distorted mirror of her sick spot, with the hidden hope of getting back to the place her sense of inferiority emanated from. She tested God to see if He *really* loved her for herself alone. Each time she lost Him and He found her again, she wept and laughed with gratitude and lost Him again, until the reality struck home. I was reminded of a young woman I once knew who flunked out of college to see if her parents would still accept her. After convincing herself they would, she finished school.

It would be wonderful if people could find themselves with less waste and menace. However, long years of work with psychosis indicates that, for many, this simply cannot be done. There are those who scare themselves into and out of oblivion. They cannot settle for less than tasting everything they are. In Carrie's case, a woman was able to find a context capable of sustaining her need to lose and find her relationship to God and, consequently, herself. One can imagine how many others there are who fail.

29. This case was reported in Eigen, "Psychopathy and Individuation," pp. 289–290.

A person who hates himself often does so for good reason. He feels there is something very wrong at the bottom of his being. He has taken a wrong developmental turn. He is not the self he wants to be, could be, or should be. His self-attack is most basically an attempt to right himself. Through self-attack, he hopes to tear away what is keeping him from being more truly and fully himself.

Similarly, the patient's attacks against the therapist partly try to right what is wrong with the therapist.[30] Many psychotic, borderline psychotic, and narcissistic personalities cannot bear to be helped by someone as flawed as their therapist. They attack the therapist because of what is ill about him, as well as out of envy of his strengths. They often succeed in affecting the therapist's ability to function. The aim is not simply one of power. The urge to make the therapist impotent also reflects an attempt to annihilate his faulty ego and drive him to deeper levels of searching.

At times, idealization is related to self-attack. The patient may idealize the therapist and long to be him or be like him. Idealization often ties itself to good real qualities of the therapist, which both relieve and madden the patient. The patient may not be able to bear the idea that the therapist is better off, healthier, or further along. He both admires and is threatened by what he perceives as the therapist's superiority. He hates as well as revels in his own parasitic or dependent needs, which make the therapist seem even more superior. The patient attacks precisely what he longs for. In this position, self is envied and attacked wherever it is found. Love inflames hatred.

The hate can spiral, so that the patient's attacks against his own and the therapist's self become meaningless and chronic. Any attempt at contact triggers an unconscious annihilating gesture. The patient's and the therapist's goodness or badness become irrelevant. The patient no longer knows why or even that he is angry. He is cut off from the source of his hate, which loses its potential as a corrective message. It becomes an amorphous morass, a stale and dull atmosphere, a blind lashing out. The hopeful precision once attached

---

30. For work on the patient's need to cure the therapist, see Searles, "The Patient as Therapist to His Analyst," pp. 95–151.

to angry responses or a hating disposition is lost in a kind of self-obliterating chain reaction that leaves no trace of its origin. In this case, the egos of patient and therapist may indeed be done in, but with small possibility of rebirth.

Self-attack and Rebirth

Many cultural institutions try to organize self-attack tendencies with more or less effectiveness. As one example, I wish to mention the ancient mystery ceremonies. The initiate might pass through a night of terrifying disorientation in which he feared or believed he would die. In the morning, he would rise with the sun, one with the reborn god, a god among gods. He would be aware of his immortal, immaterial self. Such a triumph acted as a reference point. Forever after, he must learn to reawaken faith in the transcendent moment he experienced, true self-knowledge.[31] Attacks against the initiate's "self" constituted a necessary transitional phase in a larger movement.

In time, such attacks were internalized and became part of the individual's daily journey through hell to heaven. Various aspects of the death–rebirth archetype are expressed in such dying god figures as Osiris, Apollo, Prometheus, and Jesus. Through Jesus, we undergo our moment-to-moment crucifixions in the larger context of resurrection.

Madness capitalizes on the relationship between self-attack and rebirth. In psychosis, the individual may be lost in a senseless self-attack system, which both keeps him in and presses him out of life. He may be frozen, in terror of dying, or weep with pity and joy in sight of Eternity. These states can fluctuate rapidly and at times seem to occur simultaneously. They may be pitted against, merged with, or split off from each other. If left to themselves, they do not usually get anywhere. They go round and round, degenerate into more

31. For example, Schuré, *The Great Initiates*, pp. 75–128, 223–264.

vicious spirals, or die out with scarcely a trace. It is the rare individual who can go through such a tailspin by himself and then be made better by what he has passed through. Most people today lack a frame of reference with which to organize such states in a truly liberating way. Even in good therapy, it seems something of a miracle when the phases of a death–rebirth sequence come together properly.

Nevertheless, even when therapeutic or individual efforts fall short of the mark, good results are possible. The individual can often be helped to make better use of his need to attack himself and others. He can learn to listen to what his anger or hate is saying, what he or another really wants. He can appreciate, at least a bit more, what is noble as well as evil in his hatred. As one person said when speaking of an insensitive soul, "If I were him, I'd be ashamed not to hate myself."

Many patients benefit by having their self-hate respected. A well-meaning therapist who tries to reassure a patient that his self-hate is not really justified may buy relief at the expense of a deeper and fiercer search. Our culture is perhaps poorer, as well as freer, for throwing out the pilgrim's old prescription of hatred of self as a self-detoxifying method. We can and ought not go back to the way things were. But we can reclaim and rework tendencies that can no more be rooted out of human life than can breathing.

Shock of Madness and Multidimensionality

The death–rebirth archetype would not be possible without madness. We not only wish to live forever, but, in some way, we feel that we do. A sense of forever-ness traverses the spectrum of human experience. For Freud, forever-ness is an aspect of Eros ("there is no death in the unconscious").[32] It gains its full meaning in tension with

32. For example, Freud, "Negation," pp. 135–242.

an acute sense of mortality. In general, an idealizing feeling and the violence of life go hand and hand.

A moment of violence may be found in the act of creation (or recreation) in virtually all higher religions, East and West. Vishnu, the Destroyer, is part of the Hindu godhead. Buddha did violence to himself on his way toward Enlightenment. Jahveh is violent. The cross objectifies an inherent aspect of Jesus' attitude toward himself. And as he said, he brings a sword. His sword is a fiery dragon.

Aggressive components are well-nigh universal components of religious ritual. Rage can be a holy emotion: "holy wrath," "pure" hate. On an elemental level, rage, fury, wrath, or hatred carries a sense of numinous power. But neither God nor the devil has a monopoly on fury. We live in a combustible–conservative universe, and it would be surprising if cataclysm were not part of our nature. Mythology and science deal with implosive–explosive phenomena as part of the overall structure of existence.

To discuss issues of human aggression solely in practical, realistic terms is to miss the mystical, cosmic underpinning of affects. We are destined to fail in our management of ourselves as long as we downplay one or the other term of experience. It is as mad to disregard the numinous in daily affairs as it is to run away from the pressing requirements of social–political–economic factors.

When we hate we think we are or ought to be God. When we are angry, we feel we are right about something. We hate when we feel it is too difficult, if not impossible, to redress a wrong. We are impotent gods. However, hate is not entirely without hope, or it would die out. Stupor or compliance might take its place. When we hate, we want our will to be done.

Hatred simplifies. It splits the world into those who are with us and those who are against us. Even when our hatred is right, as it often is, it may lead to disaster because of the absolute, oversimplified terms it needs in order to thrive. Life will finally slip through its fingers because they are too stiff.

I have emphasized splits between mental–physical self and self–other in psychotic individuals. But we can trace toxic/explosive splits throughout the body politic, between nations, races, the sexes, vocations, and so on. We have barely begun the careful study of ways anger hardens into hatred. What we learn from psychological experiments is important, but it scarcely scratches the surface.[33] Our knowledge of the relationships between God-feeling and I-feeling from infancy on has largely been neglected by "hard" science. The need to learn more about the intricate comminglings of the sense of self, the Infinite, social, and materialistic realities invites reasoned vision and hard work.

That the depth psychologies may, in certain respects, turn out to be more imaginative fancy than hard science does not lessen their value. Even as art or myth, they heighten awareness of the ways imagination works. We see the same imagination at work in political, racial, and national crises. We become aware of the vast chasms self–other awareness brings and bridges. How easy it is for hate to close or to widen gaps. What cosmic as well as practical dimensions hate takes on! We cannot afford a naive approach to either the mystical or the practical sides of life. Neither is going to go away, not through analysis, not through any manner of national–international reform. The self-affirming/self-destroying aspects of self-hate exemplify the kind of beings we are and what we have to work with. We may or may not learn better ways of meeting and handling ourselves, but we are not going to wish our multidimensional nature away.

We are left with complexities that tease us. Hate is enlivening, a voice of affirmation and protest. Yet under certain circumstances, hate is deadening and a sign of death. We may hate and/or love death and/or life. We suffer massive self-erasure and desperate heightening of experiencing as a way of life. Mao Tse-Tung wrote that we grow through our internal contradictions and Freud said we die for "internal reasons."[34] Given the ways madness works in our lives, how do

33. For a good, popular account of anger as a learned response linked with the ability to symbolize and interpret experience, see Carol Tavris, *Anger: The Misunderstood Emotion* (New York: Simon & Schuster, 1982).
34. Mao Tse-Tung, "On Contradiction," in *Selected Works of Mao Tse-Tung* (Peking: Foreign Languages Press, n.d.), p. 313; Freud, *Beyond the Pleasure Principle*, p. 38.

we survive ourselves as long as we do? To what extent is madness fertilizing? The shock of how mad we are or can be brings us up short. Our glimpse of madness is perhaps more shocking than the fact of death. That such a thing as madness exists changes the tone of everything. It throws death into question. It makes of annihilation an ingenious and macabre toy.

The "beatific" moment can blunt or inspire. It can make the real more real or steal us away from ourselves. But it must not be overlooked or prejudged. It is no longer easy to separate madness from sanity, if ever it was. The reason–madness dichotomy, traditionally understood as reason versus the irrational, is breaking down. Our sense of the real is shot through with ideal feelings and vice versa. We may have to understand anew how they work together and find new ways of grabbing the devil by the tail. The depth psychologies enlarge our perception of how the devil drinks and breathes the beatific vision that informs our loving self. Whether we like it or not, we must incessantly grow to keep up with the demands such intertwining makes and learn what it costs to follow the paths that open and the ones that close.

CHAPTER SIX

Epistemology and Reversal

IS THE AVERAGE MAN today still a naive realist? Does he still *see* the sun rise and traverse an arc around the earth? Do what his senses present to him seem the same after he has learned about the infinities of space and microorganisms? We telescope so much of our experience today. The earth really does seem smaller and older than it used to. The whole cosmos taken as a single packet may be compressed by our minds to postage stamp size, and that blown up. The ancient notion that macrocosm and microcosm reflect one another has been made more precise by modern science.

For the modern sensibility, the entire object-world has a certain plasticity. Objects have size only in relation to one another. We grow or shrink depending upon the context in which we find ourselves. We are part of contracting and expanding networks of things, peoples, places and values. We can turn ourselves inside out, while coolly remaining hidden within a carapace. We become jelly or steel as the moment requires, and as we do this, we feel that all liquidity and solidity is reversible. We know we are mostly water, which freezes, melts, or vaporizes. The transformations of Lewis Carroll's fancy have correspondences in mathematics, physics, and our emotional life.

The voice of madness speaks to us today. An increasing number of people no longer feel a great gulf between themselves and the insane. Freud formalized this when he claimed that the difference between the normal, neurotic, and psychotic was merely quantitative, a slippery business. We share common structures, a common unconscious, and can hear one another if not ourselves.

Yet we are not simply all one. States change into one another, but qualitative differences persist. For Freud, the dynamics of paranoia are not the same as those of schizophrenia. Neurosis and psychosis are structurally distinct. Hysteria, obsessional neurosis, and melancholia all have special processes and patterns. Nevertheless, for Freud, quantity determines quality. And what determines quantity may be unknown or ambiguous, open to interpretation in any given instance. Always, a subjective factor intervenes at the moment determinism seems about to close all gaps.

The psychotic subject takes advantage of or is tortured by loopholes, the loophole of subjectivity. He may seek to close the gaps the possibility of interpretation opens or be unable to see anything other than holes where meaning might be. The subject disappears and reappears through loops of signifiers. But more than the dance of meaning is involved. Schreber (Chapter 7) tells us he lives through his "nerves." His "nerves" are excited and catch the "nerves" of God. He is an excited mass of torment and bliss, a delirium of discovery. As his delusions mature, he believes himself in direct contact with a voluptuous God and enters a realm in which spirit and eros fuse. He is no longer empty or dispersed. He finds a disquieting home, a more or less stable self, and space. He rides the snake of signification toward what, for him, is ultimate reality.

The movement from destruction to stability is but one of a series of reversals at work in psychosis. Self–other and mental self–body self provide endless material for the work of reversal. Freud noted that reversal is an elementary operation of the mind, one of the earliest defenses, perhaps preceding defenses.[1] In particular, he called attention to reversals of subject–object (turning against the self, turning against the object) and reversals of affect (love turning into hate into love into hate). The general ability of the mind to distin-

---

1. Freud, "Instincts and Their Vicissitudes," pp. 109–140; see also Green, "The Analyst, Symbolization and Absence in the Analytic Setting," pp. 1–22; idem, "Negation and Contradiction," pp. 318–339.

guish and unite is allied with an elemental capacity to reverse experiential perspectives.

In psychosis, reversal may spin everything out of existence or bring life to a standstill. Raw elements of personality kaleidoscopically whirl or loom as desiccated and terrifying figures without apparent context. The space and time we take for granted falls away or never was properly constituted. "I" and "You" become ciphers, menacing splinters, evil masks and presences, charred walls, and shrieking sirens. The psychotic is circled with questions and assertions that allow him no room to move in. He jumps above each swing of the cherubim's sword as it slices through mind and soul, one stroke after another. For the psychotic self, the Tree of Life and the protective sword struggle and turn into each other in macabre, grizzly ways.

The Fiction of Inner Space

In everyday life, "I" and "space" are taken for granted. Most of us tend to accept the fiction of an inner space for mental contents. We feel that there is a place inside us where thoughts, feelings, or motives can come and go. If we become philosophical or psychotic, the nature of this assumption may take on a central importance. The philosopher may investigate the principles that make such a phenomenon possible. The psychotic tends to become swallowed up in the startling perception that inner space is a fiction, and so not really anywhere, or he may try to literalize and freeze this "space" by filling it with grotesque creations. The analogical nature of inner space is lost or malevolently exploited.

The philosopher and psychotic may be obsessed with how we know or can know. Both may try not to take anything for granted. The philosopher, however, states his assumptions provisionally and explores their implications. The psychotic swings between not giving in to making assumptions (i.e., seeing through everything, never settling provisionally) or taking as fact the hallucinatory consequences of an unstated position. The possibility of having a world with an effective sense of inside, outside, and between is short-circuited. Nullity oscillates with nightmare. The psychotic becomes like the centipede who cannot walk, on counting his legs. In his vision, he is mesmerized by the building blocks of personality, obsessed by the naked materials themselves, which he cannot allow to come together and function appropriately.

CARL

Some time before the onset of Carl's psychosis (Chapters 2, 3, 4), he found himself staring at a tree for hours. A typical sequence would begin with his sitting in his room studying. The intensity of his work would mount. He might masturbate or feel like masturbating. He could masturbate two or three times a morning. An urge to go outdoors would overtake him. A voice might say that at a particular spot on a certain block he would meet the right girl for him. She was never there. He walked through the park and, without quite knowing when, fell in love with the bark of trees.

A ritual developed in which he first touched the bark, knelt before a tree quietly, embraced it, and then gazed at it intently. He felt awe and rapture. The tree blurred. He could see its insides and the roots beneath the ground. He never totally lost consciousness of its form, the tangled network below, the fan of branches above, the body. How did trees come to walk or crawl or fly? It seemed that all living beings bore the imprint of their tree-like origins. On the other hand, a tree was a blown-up cell, a magnified unicellular organism. All was one, one all. Yet the tree was upright, steadfast. It bent in the wind, but was hard. It was different. It was not simply everything else.

Nevertheless, Carl could virtually dissolve the tree by staring at the texture of its bark. The tree tended to disappear into its texture, swallowed up by it. It was an act of divestiture. All fell away. Naked being remained. The tree tended to become everything else. Staring at a wall or a road was not as good. Carl could dissolve a building into the pure texture of stone, but the living sap was missing. The sense that living sap was on the other side of the bark was crucial.

Carl used texture as a vehicle of dissolution, but what it disclosed was the indestructibility of life. The sap was part of the bark's porousness. The bark was skin-like, amebic, gooey, dry, teeming, elephantine. Bark was an antidote to consciousness. It was *his* consciousness.

During puberty, Carl would go to the cemetery at night and stare at the moon. He would make the moon come down to touch the tombstones. He did this by gazing at it until it got bigger and bigger. He focused on its texture until its form blurred and expanded, but his state of mind was clear. He exerted his power over the forces of the universe. He tried to reverse the order of things. Several years later, he recited the Lord's prayer backwards, and two years after that, the devil first appeared. But in puberty, his concern was control over natural powers.

Carl's tree was in stark contrast with his moon ritual. His feelings for the tree were softer and more undemanding, reverential, and grateful. His relationship with the moon had been one of mastery and power. One might say his attitude toward the masculine tree was feminine and the feminine moon, masculine. In Carl's life, these two attitudes were poorly coordinated. He had first tried to hold himself together with an attitude of dominance, but the pressure was too great. As his breakdown approached, his feminine side assumed greater importance. Masculine powers, God, and the devil, all whirled in futile, voracious conflict. It was, finally, the emerging sense of the importance of a world outside them—a soft, vaginal darkness, the unknown as such—that made the beginning of healing possible. The world vanished and returned through texture and darkness.

Without realizing it, Carl had treated himself and his psychic insides as objects he could seize and hurl, like pots or weapons. He did not recognize the space between or within his psychospiritual objects. His God did not have depth, but was as monomaniacal as the devil. It was, paradoxically, his relationship with the bark of a tree, a material object, that opened a depth dimension beyond the simply physical. Through texture, Carl bathed in a soft and delicately nuanced sense of infinity. No matter how much of the texture was filled and busy, more was open. This mixture of density and open-ness eventually spread through and encompassed Carl's God and devil as well. In this instance, a change in Carl's sense of the obscure background or horizon of experiencing eventually spread to include more circumscribed psychic figures as well.

JANE

Another example of the tendency of objects to usurp space in psychosis may be found in the obese person's confusion of food with air.[2] One patient, Jane, was forced into therapy by her husband. She had become vegetative and obese, but denied any difficulty. She tried to maintain a merry persona and thought, when her problems were hinted at, that it was silly. She just wanted to be left alone.

As the therapy relationship developed, a depressive distress began to surface. She voiced her anger at unmet demands. The distance element in therapy bothered her and brought out her sense of help-lessness. Our first serious round of tension together peaked with a dream image of an animated cloud that seemed to expand without limits, like a boundless balloon. Jane's sense of self was dangerously diffuse and potentially explosive. The overall feeling that emerged was one of agitation as long as anything remained outside her. Jane was trying to inflate her self-feeling so that otherness could not exist beyond her boundaries, but her skin would have to have been coextensive with the perimeter of the universe for this to happen. She felt weightless and overate to feel some solidity.

As she became more aware of these kinds of feelings, she thought herself odd and grew more anxious. This sort of "floaty" feeling had been part of the background of her life without her acknowledging it before. Her anger at me for making her feel "crazy" offered her momentary relief, but it did not alter her growing sense of "strange-ness." Her depression intensified and she reported suicidal thoughts. She could now begin to connect periods of gorging with intolerable

2. Eigen, "Reflections on Eating and Breathing as Models of Mental Functions," pp. 177–180.

depressive pain. Insofar as she could be encouraged to suffer pain, she found that her depression gave her a sense of being filled. It had weight and dragged her down. As an evasive reaction, she would try to reinstate her weightless oblivion, which gave her an illusion of wholeness. What was left of her being oscillated between these extremes. It now seemed that her vegetativeness and inability to function was a kind of lying low, waiting for the maelstrom to pass.

Jane felt rejected by her father and deeply merged with her mother but knowing this did not seem to make a difference. It was part of her personal mythology, a litany. In her dreams, toilets and feces began to appear. Several times she dreamed that feces came out of her mouth when she talked, a top–bottom mix–up. I told her she treated herself like a toilet and, through therapy, the feces were coming back up. Her gorging demonstrated her willingness to swallow anything.

Jane's depression now oscillated between feelings of disintegration and gluttonous numbness. The panicky disintegration was potentially cleansing, since during such phases, she lost all her urges to eat. At those moments, she contracted in order to hold herself together and so allowed more space outside herself. Her sense of disintegration led to elevator dreams, in which she was trapped when the elevator went out of control. She felt a fear of suffocation in relation to these nightmares. It was as if now she could not get enough air, whereas before she could not get enough food.

Our discussions led me to the thought that the elevator (whatever else it might be) dramatized her stomach, which, like the proverbial "floating uterus" of the hysteric, went wild. It ran amok through her insides and took over other functions. The elevator shaft was probably a fusion of air and food "pipes." I told her she had food and air mixed up.

At this point, background asthmatic symptoms intensified. She was literally starved for air—caught between eating and breathing. Her gorging had masked and tried to make up for a chronic insufficiency of air. Both food and air as symbolic systems (as well as literal functions) may be defensively employed against, or to a certain extent substituted for, each other. As Jane's overeating diminished, her chronic air deficit began to be experienced. I told her then that

she had air and mother mixed up. After some confusion and annoy-
ance, she felt great relief. She had thought mothering should be
present like air (her mother had colluded with this wish, both of
them against her father). Material and immaterial dimensions of
reality had been confused: Mother became air and air became food,
something to eat, not breathe. The result of such a mix-up between
the immaterial, the permeating surround, and the material figure was
that Jane could neither breathe freely nor be nourished emotionally.
As the felt distinction between breathing and eating (and their symbolic correlates) matured, Jane's asthma receded and her weight loss
was consolidated. She was able to tolerate more differentiated contact
with herself.

Carl's psychosis, in contrast, was more explicitly dramatic. His
insides seemed to hang outside him for all the world to see. In a sense,
he had to be tucked back into himself. Jane's madness had to be
slowly squeezed out of her. She had lost contact with how terrifying
it was to be a person and inured herself behind thick walls. She was
dissolving in fat and dullness. In both instances, the sense of psychic
space was foreclosed or preempted. In Carl's case, psychotic objects
and, in Jane's, the body proper, took over any possibility of spa-
ciousness. Psychotic objects or the body dwarfed, sucked up or
overstuffed potential space.

Space and the Psychical Apparatus

Freud made the seemingly absurd statement that our sense of external space is a projection of the psychic apparatus. In his last notes he
wrote, "Space may be the projection of the extension of the psychical
apparatus. No other derivation is possible. Instead of Kant's *a priori*
determinants of our psychical apparatus. Psyche is extended; knows
nothing about it."[3]

3. Freud, "Findings, Ideas, Problems," p. 300.

Whatever difficulties we have with this notion, it is in keeping with his view that the psyche begins as a self-contained system, out of contact with the external world, and that the unconscious is "the true psychical reality." It assigns an originating role to unconscious processes, with regard not only to inner, but also to outer perception.

Bion picked up Freud's suggestion and began a kind of visionary depth phenomenology of the originating space of affects. For example,

> I shall now use the geometrical concepts of lines, points, and space (as derived originally not from a realization of three-dimensional space but from the realizations of the emotional life) as returnable to the realm from which they appear to me to spring. That is, if the geometer's concept of space derives from an experience of "the place where something was" it is to be returned to illuminate the domain where it is in my experience meaningful to say that "a feeling of depression" is "the place where a breast or other lost object was" and that "space" is "where depression, or some other emotion, used to be."[4]

Although Bion could not have made his statement without the psychoanalytic atmosphere Freud created (it is steeped in psychoanalysis), it differs from Freud's in emphasis. Freud spoke of the structure of an unconscious psychical apparatus, Bion of early emotional experience. A feeling, perhaps depression, is the place where an object was. And space is where a feeling used to be. Implicit in this formulation is the importance of the experience, empty–full, for the constitution of the sense of space.

When I wrote that Carl had to be tucked back into himself I meant, in part, that he needed a container for his psychic life so that he could begin to work with it. However, we are only beginning to realize how complicated the development of a good container can be. Bion spoke of a permeable "contact barrier" that separates and allows communication between unconscious and conscious processes.[5] This allows the unconscious to contain and process psychic events (e.g.,

4. Bion, *Attention and Interpretation*, p. 10.
5. Bion, *Learning from Experience*, pp. 17, 27.

transforming raw sensory and emotional events into dreams, food for thought). In Bion's vision, a well-working unconscious continually evolves. The contact barrier not only plays a role in constituting the division between conscious and unconscious work, but it also helps to protect unconscious functioning from the tyranny of consciousness, and perhaps it protects each from the tyranny of the other.

In Carl's case, not only did the contact barrier break down—it was always deficient—but unconscious life also froze. His God and devil failed to evolve, remaining monolithic and stereotypical. Nor could they be metabolized or offset. In traditional depth psychological terms, they were mixtures of archetypes, complexes, and introjects; symptoms of an arrested or skewed development; unsolved problems; faulty psychic structures and functions. Carl's psychosis seemed a climactic outpouring of a blocked and malformed life. His conscious–unconscious evolution was initiated by his discovery of a wholly other range of experience: texture and darkness. These latter values expressed and took on the function of a horizon or "container" for the flow and processing of psychic life.

In Jane's case, the discovery of the air–solidity distinction was crucial. Food and her own body were substituted for mother. But mother was substituted for air. The lightness of being was lost. All collapsed into a mute *mater*ialism. Through therapeutic work, air and breath, like Carl's texture and darkness, became models for an unconscious container or horizon, a "ventilated space."[6] This involved some taste of the doubleness of experience, a beginning sense of the unseen and intangible, which offset Jane's addiction to what could be seen and touched.

In a sense, Jane's problem caricatured the materialistic aspect of modern science. Modern field physics began with the realization that all space was filled. The idea of space as empty (a traditional symbol of immateriality, an infinite container) gave way to a sense of physical forces everywhere, which could affect things at a distance. A

6. Green, "The Analyst, Symbolization, and Absence in the Analytic Setting," p. 8.

psychotic subject may treat space as immaterial, or act like the scientist who knows his ideas about space are convenient fictions, but he is not as objective about his ideas as the scientist is.

In hallucinations and dreams, filled, empty, or fictional space may be expressed in images of burial and flight. For example, an object that ought to function as a container is experienced as a tomb. In such an instance, the therapist is reacted to as a suffocating presence or as a sign of death. This may caricature the stifling wish of a parent to be all for the subject, as death is finally all. A person's space may become so constricted that he uses what is left of his freedom to turn the other into a place in which to die. An individual may feel so stifled as to be unable to use projections. Even bizarre or horrific objects stand no chance of leaking out. At first, one may feel buried alive, but, in time, suffocation becomes a respite. If one does not permit oneself the luxury of dying out, one may try to disperse or contract oneself to the point of rendering the entombing container superfluous.

On the other side of the coin, the psychotic subject who is obsessed with flying hopes to see through everything. The omniscient one takes no container seriously. It is obvious that identity is a matter of luck, a concatenation of chance factors that give rise to someone or anyone in this or any place. The panoramic vision of one in flight feasts on an unending spectacle. Space blurs and loses its meaning. It exists simply as an excuse, as something over which to launch oneself. Inner and outer are one as objects of exploitation. The one who sees through everything may ask, If mind is immaterial how can I give myself to the space that I construct? Self-possession and withholding in high-altitude flight become chronic, although the fear of falling keeps the individual in a state of incipient panic.

Bion relates the failure to develop or to make use of a sense of inner space to the failure to experience and represent an absent object as one once present and vice versa. In particular, both "entombed patients" and "flying patients" are unable to create and sustain a sense of the other as absent. Bion writes of the importance of tolerating a "no-mother" or "no-thing" experience. One must make space for the absent other, if one is to have any relationship to space.

Neither the object nor its absence must be compromised, if experiencing is to be respected. The entombed patient is engulfed by presence; the flying patient identifies with, rather than encounters, absence. In both, the ambiguity and tension inherent in the presence-absence polarity is collapsed or exploited.

Habitual spins between flights, in response to dread of engulfment, and fusion, in response to abandonment anxiety, are well documented in the literature on psychotic, borderline psychotic, schizoid, and narcissistic personalities.[7] These spins, in part, are aborted attempts to catch hold of opposite sides of one's nature. Such vertigo keeps one ill, but it also dramatizes possibilities. The healthier individual caught in this situation hopes that some day these "parts of himself" will come together. However, there will always be the ambiguous play of conjunctive–disjunctive profiles. In general, we work to sustain a space in which dualities thrive: "I am but am not my body. I am but am not my mind. I am but am not my. . . ." We arise between as well as through the categories that constitute us. We move in and out of our containers and live through the interstices of who we are.

I Am but Am Not My I

Our I-feeling is intimately related to issues of inner space. Questions concerning the meaning of inner space might not arise, if not for the "I" who asks them. But even this might be questioned. For I is not coextensive with conscious, let alone unconscious, life. There is far more to the field of consciousness than I-feeling. In Chapter 4, we have seen how I can contract or expand to exclude or include variable aspects of experience at different times. I have met individuals who claimed not to have an I-sensation. They insist that saying I is

7. For example, Guntrip, *Schizoid Phenomena, Object-Relations and the Self*, pp. 17–86; Khan, *Privacy of the Self*, pp. 13–26; Kohut, *Analysis of the Self*, pp. 1–34; Kernberg, *Borderline Conditions and Pathological Narcissism*, pp. 3–47; Schwartz-Salant, *Narcissism and Character Transformation*, pp. 9–28, 37–70.

merely a linguistic convenience. For them, consciousness and unconscious brain processes are enough to carry on the work that has to be done.

In psychosis, whether or not one possesses an I-feeling, may be experienced in excruciating ways. Carl's I-feeling was both intensified and lost at different phases of his journey. His I was heightened when torn between God and the devil and muffled when bathed in texture and darkness. During a phase of his recovery 10 years later, he went through an agonizing period during which he claimed to have lost his I-feeling entirely.

At this time, he was far enough along to keep some spark of humor alive in the midst of horror. In one fantasy, he imagined himself a detective searching for his missing I, only to find it mutilated and disposed of in the trunk of an abandoned car at La Guardia airport. He was better off without it, he thought, because of the condition it was in. Nevertheless, this relief was short-lived. A deeper sense of injury than he had ever known before had to be faced. He now functioned well in school and work, but was tormented by the sense that no I was doing it.

In time Carl recovered his I, but his sense of what it was like to be without it never left him. He was left with a dual sense of anonymity and personal uniqueness. He experienced an anonymity in the very depths of his I-ness and felt his I spread through processes beyond it. I and not-I seemed inextricably mixed in every pore of experience.

The past two hundred years have seen a burgeoning of interest in I/not-I phenomena. Egologies arose in German philosophy and were an important part of culture by the time Stirner published his manifesto, *The Ego and His Own: The Case of the Individual Against Authority*, in 1885. Stirner's work is an ecstatic celebration of the resounding glory of the I. He opposes the I-feeling to anything that would confine it, without adequately grasping the ambiguous nature of I-feeling itself. His own locutions betray him and set the stage for things to come. For example, Stirner's use of *His* rather than *My* in his title already suggests there is more to I than I. This usage runs through his work with overtones that are more than linguistic convention. He rhapsodically calls the I, "the unique one," "some one," "the third party," and other third-person epitaphs. His I affectively echoes the not-I that permeates it.

Some dozen years before Stirner's publication, Rimbaud had already written, "I am another," and earlier still, Whitman, "I am multitudes."[8] Heidegger expressed this tendency more formally with his development of the idea that identity is a relation.[9] He wrote, for example, "sameness implies the relation of 'with,' that is, a mediation, a connection." He remarks that Western thought required more than two thousand years to get to the point at which it could focus on "mediation within identity." For him, this "mediation" is not localizable but rather an "abyss" or "spring" in which man and being appropriate and deepen one another.

Heidegger's teacher, Husserl,[10] envisioned a "trinitarian egology." He postulated three major structural levels of the ego. The "empirical ego" tends to take the everyday world for granted. In this attitude, we are naive realists, lost in objects or simply in tune with the perceptual world as given. The "psychological ego" is aware of and may focus on the processes that give rise to our experience of objects. For example, in addition to the chair we become aware of our perceiving of the chair. We study the structure of perception or how the chair is given to us, as well as learn what we can about the chair (its use, composition, aesthetics, etc.). By an additional act of abstraction, we may ask not only about the object and the experiencing through which the object is given, but also what constitutes our *experiencing* as such. Husserl calls the attitude that characterizes inquiry into the possibility of experiencing as such, the "transcendental ego." In simplified terms, we can focus attention anywhere throughout our consciousness of consciousness of consciousness.

Sartre and Gurwitsch developed nonegological theories of con-

---

8. Whitman's *Leaves of Grass* was published in 1855. Baudelaire's *Fleurs du Mal*, published in 1857, was an important part of Rimbaud's readings in 1870, the year preceding Rimbaud's famous declaration in his *voyat* letters.
9. Heidegger, *Identity and Difference*, pp. 25–42.
10. Husserl, *Cartesian Meditations*, pp. 7–88; idem, *Crises*, pp. 103–268.

sciousness.[11] The I appears as part of consciousness as constituted and so cannot be understood to be its originator. Consciousness as such is characterized by an inherent transcendent function. Consciousness is always reaching beyond itself, and an implicit self-reflexiveness is part of its action. To postulate a transcendental ego needlessly duplicates the basic structure of consciousness.

Egological and non-egological views lend to important differences in emphasis. Husserl's vision of a transcendental ego constituting a psychological ego constituting an empirical ego is, I believe, important for an understanding of psychosis. One can relate psychotic experience and productions to dominant ego structures or attitudes, and determine how structural levels are constituted with reference to one another at any time.

At certain moments or in certain types of madness, the transcendental ego is quite real. At such moments, the psychic universe moves from top down rather than from bottom up. One *sees* an originary I, a pure I, giving rise to lesser ones. One does not start with sensations and build up ideal unities. One begins at the beginning of I-ness, with an I-ness that, from the outset, is a cornucopia of ideal possibilities (or impossibilities). The individual bypasses empirical and psychological attitudes and is mesmerized by an originating, transcendent I. In such a state, the transcendental ego is all and nothing can compare with it.

At other moments, the fact that the ego appears as part of a larger field is prepossessing. Consciousness precedes the I and goes on without it. Ideas occur to the I. The latter does not originate them. The I experiences feelings connected with its fate. A feeling may open unsuspected worlds. The I's jaw drops as it stands aghast at or in admiration of galaxy after galaxy of experiential possibilities.

Carl knew both extremes well: an originary, transcendental I that gives rise to and swallows up existence and an anonymous objective consciousness in which the I disappears from view. Often they are

11. Sartre, *Trancendence of the Ego*, pp. 93–106; Gurwitsch, *Studies in Phenomenology and Psychology*, pp. 89–106, 124–140.

reversible. In experiential fact, all combinations and shades of relationships between I and anonymous consciousness are possible.

The use I have made of Husserl's and Gurwitsch's theories must be qualified. Husserl was speaking of a structural condition for the possibility of consciousness as such. Similarly, Gurwitsch studied structures of consciousness, not contents *qua* contents or pathological perversions of structures. As an ideal possibility, the transcendental attitude does not swallow up existence or the I, but rather simply permits observation of what appears as it appears. My usage assumes a dramatization or reification of basic principles. Psychosis is psychosis precisely because principles are taken as things (and vice versa), as real, not provisionally, but absolutely.

The I and Anonymity

FREUD

The paradox of an "anonymous I" is a pervasive theme in Freud's work. An important example of this is the double language of psychological phenomena that runs through psychoanalysis. The ego is treated both as a center of subjectivity and a system of psychological functions. It is the living "I" that desires, wills, and finds ways of avoiding and defeating itself, of surviving and sometimes triumphing. And it is a mental system that includes such functions as walking, talking, and perceiving and common sense and logical thinking. The ego as a theoretical system and a center of subjectivity is the locus of such defensive gambits as repression, idealization, and reaction formation. As discussed in Chapter 3, the ego knows and does not know what it does. It must know what and how to hide, yet it must erase this knowledge if unconscious lying is to be successful.

The difficulties are compounded by Freud, who sometimes treated the mind as if it were the brain and vice versa, in spite of his determination to distinguish between the two.[12] He often spoke of

12. Sulloway, *Freud, Biologist of the Mind*, pp. 13–21, 361–392, 412–415.

the phenomenal body as if it were the physical organism and vice versa.[13] In part, this is because he assumed that the reflex arc theory made an appropriate model of the mind. Thus, he treated the mind (e.g., thinking, empathy, judgement) as if it were a machine made up of bundles of reflexes, a complex network of tracks, superimposed on one another, with nodes or switches. His uncritical use of association theory expressed a reflex arc view of sensations or ideas as strings of cars moving on complex networks of tracks. On the other hand, he would speak of the body in terms of will and passion, the phenomenal body in the mode of concupiscence. An imaginary physiology guided his vision of mental functioning, and his true feeling for the latter at times informed his view of the organism.

Freud used an *ad hoc* theory of the brain as a model of the mind. He might have used a field, rather than reflex, model, and, indeed, many of his informal descriptions do just that. But whatever model he might have used, it is likely that his tendency to treat the mind as the brain and vice versa would have persisted. It is fundamental to Freud's thinking, and not simply because he mixed mind and brain up. He knew the difference. His whole psychology is based on the distinction. Rather, it seems to be a part of his outlook to see structurally similar processes at work across different dimensions of being. Insofar as he applied concepts derived from physics, neurology, and biology to the psyche, a sense of an anonymous basis of subjectivity pervades his work.

MERLEAU-PONTY

Merleau-Ponty has further deepened our sense of the body as a center of subjectivity.[14] He refers to the body as subject. We are alive through the ordering processes of the body, given to ourselves through perception and movement. Whenever we pause, we can feel the breath of the anonymous subject who continues to keep us in existence. In his descriptions, Merleau-Ponty typically uses the third person, "one," to refer to the subject: one sees, one hears, one knows.

13. Henle, "Freud's Secret Cognitive Theories," pp. 111–134.
14. Merleau-Ponty, *Phenomenology of Perception*, pp. 67–199, 243–298.

Where Merleau-Ponty spoke of "one," Freud spoke of "it." Nevertheless, Freud's id and body ego and Merleau-Ponty's body subject are not identical concepts.[15] Merleau-Ponty's body subject is not founded on repression. Its emphasis is on the interweaving of subject and world that characterizes perception and behavior. For Merleau-Ponty, the I emerged from the one as from the ringing of a tuning fork, not by repressive fiat. Both touched the pulse of subjectivity at a depth where I–it–one fluidly transform into one another, although Freud's sense of origins was, finally, more combative.

FAIRBAIRN

The duality in Freud's thinking, expressed in the relationship between I and anonymity and in an anonymous aspect of the I, galvanized a succession of important psychoanalytic revisions. Fairbairn[16] went so far as to see the Freudian division, id, ego and superego, as three I's or ego fragments or split-off dispositions of the ego. His account begins with an originary, unitary ego, rather than a chaotic id. The ego is related to a confirming, good object (primarily, a good aspect of mother) who sustains and develops its inherent sense of value. At the same time, the ego gravitates to and molds itself around centers of anxiety production, preeminently rejecting and overexciting aspects of the other. It defends itself by incorporating, introjecting, and identifying with centers of danger. It installs within itself imagos of the bad object and dispatches aspects of itself to contain them. An inner (unconscious) world arises; it is made up of a central ego still related to the good object, a dissociated or split-off libidinal ego identified with the exciting object, and a rejecting ego identified with the rejecting object.[17] Fairbairn described the

15. See Eigen, "Dual Union or Undifferentiation," pp. 415–428.
16. Fairbairn, *An Object-Relations Theory of the Personality*, pp. 3–27, 59–179.
17. Strictly speaking, in Fairbairn's scheme the central ego is supposedly not part of the inner fantasy world. Its relationship to the external good object is not mediated by fantasy. For Fairbairn the inner world of fantasy is the result of a schizoid splitting of the ego. The central ego retains its more direct and open relationship to the external good object. Fairbairn seems to suggest that if mothering were perfect, psychic splits would not occur.

ego's actions in the face of a psychological threat as a divide and conquer technique. It builds a version of threatening reality within itself in an attempt at mastery and control. It sacrifices integrity for survival. And in the end, it is driven by the structural divisions it creates and compulsively repeats the patterns of excitement–rejection that form its inner world.

It is an odd trait of language to speak of *I* as *it*. But this locution reflects a conceptual and experiential blending of I and anonymity that runs deep in Fairbairn's thought. The libidinal ego is a needy baby I that seeks the mother. It wants the exciting other and keeps reaching for the mother. It is hungry for contact and needs related-ness, support, possession. It needs to be seen, cared for, and, above all, wanted. In dreams, it may appear as a weak, longing female. The latter cultural stereotype expresses a fundamental facet of the needy self.

What is personal and what collective in such need? Nothing is closer to the I than its neediness, yet nothing is more impersonal and obliterating. Need runs roughshod over the I, yet enlivens it. It can flood and drown the I, but the latter is flat and dull without it. Freud's term *drive* expresses the force of the matter. The vocabulary of need is replete with such adjectives as peremptory, tyrannical, imperious, abject, slavish, overwhelming, anxious, hopeful, and hap-less. When the needy baby screams demandingly, is it I or one or both who yells? Who or what floods? Who or what is flooded? Fairbairn criticized Freud for the way the languages of psychology (the I) and biology (it) cross in his work, but the problem is inherent in whatever psychic events one addresses. The I is personal–imper-sonal through and through. We have focused on Fairbairn's libidinal ego, but we could have shown this with his central and anti-libidinal ego structures as well.

Fairbairn viewed the therapeutic task as a kind of exorcism. The split-off ego structures and objects must be assimilated by the central ego. He spoke of psychoanalysis as a kind of modern demonology, as did Freud. However, whereas Freud tended to see devils in the passions (id) and malfunctioning conscience (superego), Fairbairn focused on demonized ego-objects. For him, Freud's id and superego are largely split-off aspects of an originary ego. They are degenera-

tion products, the result of a movement toward fragmentation, precipitates of dangerous situations. Fairbairn's vision is of an ego that
begins to fall apart in face of psychic threats and tries to hold itself
together by solidifying broken pieces into enduring structures. The I
remains precarious and, to a degree, alien.

JUNG

Perhaps of all depth psychologists, Jung was the most fascinated
by the observation that different aspects of the self behaved as if they
were centers of subjectivity with their own personalities. He could
not accept Freud's simple tripartite structure or the idea that behind
the multiplicity of masks worn by Imagination were only id–ego–
superego and their objects. In a succession of developmental spurts,
Jung attempted to do justice to his vision of psychic life as an
"archipelago" (the unconscious as multiple consciousness) rather
than a "flashlight" (consciousness as an ego function).[18]

In a beautiful passage, he describes the succession of images
thrown up by psychic life as "sparks" or *scintillae*.[19] In an older time,
these might have been viewed as manifestations of the World Soul
rather than as individual inventions.[20] Jung classified his visions and
dream images, those of his patients, myths, folklore, and the like, in
terms of their level of depth, overall character, and psychic function.
He especially used alchemical imagery to help organize his findings.
His description of the *dramatis personae* he encountered is one of the
most arresting portrayals of psychic life ever attempted.

Jung's basic conceptions are as problematic as Freud's. For our
immediate purpose, however, we need focus only on his most basic

18. Jung, "On the Nature of the Psyche," pp. 159–234.
19. Ibid., pp. 190–199.
20. A good example of the tendency of the modern temper to individualize "collective" experience may be seen in studies on William Blake. For a long time scholars
thought Blake's prophetic visions were merely idiosyncratic creations. Only gradually was the esoteric Platonic, as well as Biblical, tradition within which he worked
established as a context for his imagery (e.g. Kathleen Raine, *The Human Face of God*
[New York: Thames and Hudson, 1980], pp. 9–23, 267–298).

distinction, "collective" and "personal," with its broad correlates, "self" and "ego" and "archetypes" and "complexes." Rather than belabor detailed definitions of what is already common knowledge, suffice it to say that, for Jung, collective, self, and archetypes are deeper than personal, ego, and complexes. The personality as a whole is molded by a basic ground plan or overall archetypal structure, the self. The self is the center of the psychic totality and the ego the center of consciousness. In the course of development, many "sparks" stake their claims. They run the gamut on the collective/archetype–personal/complex continuum. All are able to contribute when journeying toward wholeness. Specific images are ultimately messengers of the self, which carry information about the course and requirements of development. The structural ground plan of the personality is expressed phenomenally in images and events that need decoding and amplifying. All life is suggestive; echoes of the *Spiritus Mundi* are everywhere.

In the end, whatever developmental specifics are important along the way, the basic Jungian drama is between ego and self. Jung envisioned the ego as more superficial. Like Blake's Urizen, it becomes tyrannical and tries to claim more space than it ought to. It tries to pass itself off as the center of the psychic universe, thus displacing the true center, the deeper self. The task of individuation is to restore a proper balance between ego and self and to allow the fundamental ground plan of the Self to evolve and become incarnate.

To be sure, Jung made appropriate disclaimers. A certain tension between ego and self is necessary. We could not participate in the life of the self if not for ego consciousness. And the self would not have a proper field for play if not for phenomenal time and space or everyday reality. The ego must take responsibility for itself and its relationship as a partner in a psychic movement with roots and aims beyond it. In optimal situations, ego and self are in a compensatory relationship, which offsets one-sidedness as the psyche moves toward wholeness.

Jung's vision brings out the ambiguity of the relationship between the subject, the I and anonymity with special intensity. Who is subject? Who object: ego or self? For Jung, each is both. The I is subject of consciousness, the self subject of the psyche as a whole. Self and ego are objects for one another. Yet each learns to respect the claims of the other as a subject to be reckoned with. Each may feel lacerated or supported by the intentions of the other and act accordingly.

A Chinese box or, better, a Möbius strip situation unfolds. Is the self an I? Is I-feeling part of the self, part of the transcendence of phenomenal time and space? Jung consistently describes the self as collective and transpersonal. Does the transpersonal subject say I? In what sense? Who calls the ego it? A divided ego? A greater I? A subject beyond I and you? Is the self anonymous or the most personal reality of all? Are Jung's most basic terms, collective-personal, misleading or inadequate? Is the self within or beyond duality? Is it, in part, a principle of the unity, or complementarity of opposites? Beyond opposites? In Jung, it is all of these and more. For it also opens up to the Unknowable Infinite beyond itself. And yet, for Jung, the unknowable as such appeared to be the self. Does this self, like Jahveh, say I? And so on.

We cannot expect Jung to resolve the unresolvable. His work is rich enough to give us a sense of the problem at hand. His simple polarization of the psyche into ego and self or the personal and collective unconscious itself suggests the depth of the issue. He reminds us that usual treatments of self as object of ego, as sum of social roles, as id–superego–unconscious ego, and so on, obscure as much as they reveal. The trail of the I vanishes into a deeper subject, the self, and beyond a darkness, a leap, the I is a self, the self an I, yet more than I. As far as we can trace, I and anonymity intertwine.

LACAN

For Lacan, the issue of an I deeper than the ego became the takeoff point for a scathing critique of the ego.[21] "I" (*je*) is identified with the deeper subject, whereas ego (*moi*) is the subject–object of the imaginary dimension. When the baby sees himself in the mirror, he

21. Lacan, *Ecrits*, pp. 1–7, 30–145.

experiences an exhilarating, triumphant sense of an externalized visual self-image that is under its perfect control (a coherent, bounded image instantaneously responding to its every gesture). The infant automatically uses this visual I to defend against helplessly identifying with his vaguer, more awkward, imperfectly controlled bodily sense of self. A wedge is driven between body feelings and an exteriorized visual self-image. The mirror or imaginary I (ego, *moi*) lives as an actor (performer) with an eye on the audience, the other, whose desire it seeks to stimulate. It is a narcissistic I whose agenda is self-worship or idolatry. Anna Freud's descriptions of ego defenses, Melanie Klein's portrayals of introjection-projection, and Hartmann's emphasis on adaptive functions of the ego, all touch on aspects of the imaginary ego bent on mastery or seductive control.

Who is the I bent on Truth? We do not quite know from Lacan's work, but it is a deeper I, bound up with the unconscious subject, a subject with a story to tell. The I has a particular history it seeks to express and know. Perhaps, above all, it is the story of how it enters a life of subversion by (re)constituting itself as the ego. The subject not only lives in the imaginary as ego, it can also know and represent itself as doing so, at least in a fragmentary way. It thus transcends the imaginary as it is simultaneously given to it. The subject symbolizes its rifts and deceptions as it creates and is created by them.

Lacan described the unconscious psyche as a knot in which the real, imaginary, and symbolic are interlocked like three rings. If one ring is broken, the knot breaks apart. Another way of representing this situation is as a Möebius strip, or three intertwined strips or a strip that knots over, under, and through itself.

The relationships within and between subject, I, and ego are steeped in ambiguity. The ego who captivates the other is its own best audience. It constitutes itself as performer *because* it already is audience to itself. As both actor and audience, the ego is other to itself. It gains a victory through an estrangement that, oddly, is addicting, a perversion that can feel like the most real thing of all. The ego is a twist of the unconscious subject, although the unconscious is more than ego. As a principle of subjectivity, the un(not)-conscious is the other *par excellence*. It is always other to the conscious subject. But it is also divided within itself. The real, symbolic, and imaginary are other to each other. Otherness is a principle within and between all psychic dimensions and is constitutive of subjectivity as such. The I on every level is touched by otherness—from its most intimate to its most objectified reaches. "I am I and I am another" echoes unendingly throughout the subject.

The writers above touch on divisions within the subject that are magnified, deleted, or otherwise wreak havoc in psychosis. In psychosis, subject, verb, or object may be reversed, as Freud noted in his discussion of Schreber. I may be substituted for one and vice versa. I-feeling, or anonymity, may be hypertrophied or hypotrophied, pitted against or fused with one another in seemingly endless ways. Correlatively, the space *I* lives in may be over- or under-personalized. Any imaginable combination of personal–anonymous I/self/subject/other may appear in someone, sometime. Theorists of subjectivity select from and build on various possibilities of experience. In psychosis, such abstractions frequently are experienced as gripping facts. We will now say more about symbolic expressions of the anonymous–personal subject–I–Self, space–spacelessness, and the play of reversal.

Beyond the Upright

Freud envisioned a self that moves from immediate to delayed gratification. The infantile self tends not to delay its pleasures. Action according to the requirements of reality makes delay necessary. Many see Freud's pleasure and reality principles and his emphasis on postponement as reflecting a bourgeois, now disintegrating culture.[22] Weber's "secular asceticism" as descriptive of the Protestant work ethic, Nietzche's depiction of what is weak and stupid in the

22. For example, Marcus, *Freud and the Culture of Psychoanalysis*, pp. 256–264.

Judaeo–Christian tradition (the dead rather than the living God), Marx's vision of the inauthentic life that characterizes a class structure in which the powerful few are parasites on the "enforced" labor of the many, all emphasize evil uses of an ideology of postponement. All express currents of or a longing for change.

Of course, Freud's pleasure and reality principles reflect an ancient dualism. Humankind has long constituted or found itself in a world with higher and lower psychophysical functions and structures. The upright posture ensures that vision is above, whereas other physical functions (eating, breathing, copulating, evacuating, walking, and so on) go on below. A hierarchical universe emerges in which heaven above and earth below assume paramount importance. For millenia, "lower" was viewed as animal, "higher," human or divine. The emerging *I* marveled at the upright space at its disposal, of which it was part, which was part of it. At some point it felt itself distinct from as well as part of everything else. It explored its panoramic vision, which it implicitly expressed in every aspect of culture: drawings, pottery, architecture, politics, religion, warfare, and sexuality. It eventually began to study its capacity to comprehend relations (early architecture, astrology, mathematics, and, finally, philosophy). A sense of going on forever (ever upward) contrasted strongly with observations of mortality (permanent loss of uprightness).

Today, we seem to have broken through our image of ourselves as upright. We identify with the streaming, spineless life of a universe we cannot see with the naked eye, an abundance that changes form or direction as fast as we try to observe it. We know ourselves or our bodies are that life and feel that our visible forms are somehow secondary to the swarming imperceptible sea of energy that makes us up. We let go of the once-formidable upright father image, the dying patriarchy, and see through the idea of authority in general. Writers emphasize how present-oriented, episodic, and fragmented our experience is. We no longer simply gain identity from well-defined social roles and institutions.

In psychoanalysis, the move beyond the upright has often been called "regression." Balint spoke of "progression for the sake of

regression."[23] Considering the realm of experience to which he
pointed, this locution is strangely linear and organized by the hori-
zontal–vertical polarity. When he wrote less abstractly and used
concrete images, the pyramidal, graph-like organization disappeared.
He described the infant's early experience as a "harmonious interpenetrating mix-up" of self and other and tried to evoke a sense of
such states by speaking of a "boundless expanse" or "resistanceless
medium," like air or water, the "oceanic."

   Balint focused on the space between objects, which he viewed as a
"pre-object" space, a "formless infinite." He asked how in this space
objects come to be formed. He did not explicitly ask—but might well
have—who is the infant of this infinite expanse? Who is the subject?
Is there simply undulating experiencing without I-feeling, with I-
feeling, or, reversibly, with and without I-feeling? Balint spoke of
moments in which I is everything, oscillating with moments in which
everything is more than I. My locution, "everything" is already misleading for this pre-thing world. This ambiguity itself is a principal
characteristic of the realm in question. He writes of a "one body"
situation, and his meaning shifts from the infant's own body, to all
life as one body, to both of these combined. The experience Balint
writes of involves a well-being and bliss that is a precondition for a
later sense of identity. Without it, a "fault" or rift is established in the
personality. An inability to establish and sustain a sense of the one-
bodiedness of being and the harmonious mix-up of self and other
leads to a deep and lasting sense of something wrong at the very core
of one's life.

   It is difficult to evaluate the play of imagery in Balint's thought
because he fused images that traditionally symbolize different dimensions. For example, he used water and air to express a boundless
aspect of the infant's experience with the pre-object mother. To be
sure, water and air often are associated with a sense of infinity or

23. Balint, *Thrills and Regressions*, pp. 86–90; idem, *The Basic Fault*, pp. 64–76, 79–
91, 159–172.

boundlessness. However, cultural symbolism from ancient times has more precisely linked air with the immaterial and God, water with gestation, birth, and Mother—infinities with different flavors. Balint described both air and water as "substances," thus losing the sense of immateriality that characterizes experience. Without explicitly recognizing it, Balint's depiction of early experience gives more weight to water than air.

Traditional symbolic uses of the fish, bird, serpent, and wind express various aspects of the melding and reversibility of materiality–immateriality in primordial experience. Fish and serpent symbolize sexuality, time, renewal, *and* spirit. They straddle or unite both worlds. Bird has been more linked with soul and wind with spirit. All share a certain unpredictability of movement, like the impalpable, lightning movement of mind. Their blending of logos–eros ensures that neither pole of experience is trivialized.

All the above symbols have ambiguous relations with the upright. The fish is a phallic creature; it may move in any direction. The phallic bird may fly in any direction, although we are most fascinated by its up and down movements. The phallic snake (upright in Eden before the Fall) suspends our sense of boundaries. The invisible wind bypasses time and space. Phallicity is usually associated with the stiffly upright, but in these images, it is flexible and evocative of a movement beyond form. With bird, fish, and serpent, a highly circumscribed, active figure takes on the qualities of its boundless surround.

In Freud, something of the reverse also occurs. He often spoke of libido as if it were a figure rather than simply a theoretical construction (he called it active, masculine, and sometimes personified it). At the same time, his images for it are relatively formless; he likened it to liquid, electricity, elastic, and glue. In his hydraulic, military, and governmental images, the ego (executive, general, transformer) channels, assimilates, and reworks highly "charged" libidinal "currents." Yet phallic imagery is also associated with libido. Fish, bird, and serpent express the basic phallic quality of the force that impels the personality and drives development on. Libido (in part) is like an omnipresent electrical or liquid flow with the monomanic intensity of a penis bent on orgasm. Freud treated libido as if it were as ubiquitous as air, except that air is conspicuously absent as a formative image in his thought.

The tendency of air to be fused with and assimilated by water in Freud's libido and Balint's primordial other (or self–other harmonious mix-up) is in keeping with the general tendency of psychoanalysts to emphasize the "oceanic" aspect of mystical experience.[24] This is consistent with the psychoanalytic tendency to see the first object as mother (*mater*). Traditional religion and folklore is emphatic in viewing the foundational object of human experience as God, an immaterial First Object. What was thought to be an advance in scientific thinking (understanding the roots of mysticism in the baby–mother relationship) appears, in part, to express a more general collapse of the essential categories that have ordered humankind's sense of world for millennia (the latter was mediated by the symbolic air–water distinction-similarity). The scientific materialism espoused by Freud and the swallowing up of the category of the immaterial by libido and the baby–mother relationship go together. God is not dead, so much as seen to be a baby (imperiously narcissistic) or maternal (giving birth, succoring, overpowering). Correlatively, a debunking of logos runs through the current cultural scene, a result Freud would have deplored, but had anticipated and inspired.

Our sense of being upright preoccupied us for thousands of years, but it now gets in the way. We must read our history in light of our concern with posture, but sense the new work our logos–eros makeup is undertaking. We cannot return to our old-fashioned sense of uprightness, used and abused by big-baby patriarchs. Mother worship cannot be substituted for father worship. New materialisms and a lopsided emphasis on eros will not do. Ways of life circumscribed by ancient symbolic systems can no longer satisfy us. But the play of opposites in these systems provokes insight into aspects of our beings we must address in changing ways.

24. See Chapter 2, Note 10.

A Note on Reversal

In order to fully use our mind's natural tendency to reverse perspectives, the raw materials for reversal to work with must be available. I have suggested that the symbolic world associated with air (spirit) suffered a serious reduction in Freud's system. At the same time, Freud greatly expanded our picture of the mind. He did so by putting eros–ego under his microscope and tracing tensions between these Siamese twins throughout personality. He expanded our sense of self by studying particular contractions. However, the contractions remain. His study was made possible by placing entire spheres of experience in brackets. We must live the Freudian universe, but at the same time remove the brackets.

In Freud's studies, reversal continues to work in a highly circumscribed sphere. The universe Freud charted thrives on reversal. We have mentioned turning into the opposite and the reversal of direction toward or away from the self. Freud's work is filled with polarities that conflict with, feed on, and turn into one another: active–passive, male–female, sadism–masochism, voyeurism–exhibitionism, life–death, ideals–instincts, and so on.

Jung was so impressed by the play of opposites in personality dissociations and mythic experience that he took a primary function of the unconscious to be compensation for conscious attitudes. He called the reversals that occurred because of the work of unconscious compensation *enantiodromia*. To an extent, his own work may be viewed as compensation of Freud's, inasmuch as he engaged spirit in broader terms (e.g., Jung treats air/earth/fire/water as complementary pairs of opposites, as ancient tradition did). Jung's work illustrates the centrality of reversal in depth psychological thinking and a certain uneasiness that is expressed by some workers such as Bion and Elkin at the cramped space spirit has in psychoanalysis.

Bion's belief that in primordial experience the sense of materiality and immateriality are undifferentiated opens a Pandora's box of possibilities.[25] Bion gave us many examples of how psychological reality is treated as material reality and vice versa. A psychotic subject may try to make everything animate inanimate and vice versa. Thus he may reduce the other to the status of a material object and substitute material satisfaction for intimacy. On the other hand (or at the same time), he may be unable to tolerate materiality because of the limits the latter places on boundlessness. In both cases, Bion stressed the subject's avoidance of or incapacity to tolerate the pain that development requires.

As noted earlier (Chapter 4), Elkin portrayed the primordial self and other as arising before awareness of physicality as such. In his account, immateriality is a basic category of experience and infantile development. A primordial immaterial other precedes awareness of the actual mother or maternal functioning and embodiment. In terms that blend Western religion and psychoanalysis, one might say that the basic issue for development is the tension between one's relation with God (primordial other) and mother. In this context, Freud studied, in detail, the processes involved in the work of embodiment (e.g., the building up of the body image via oral–anal–phallic–genital identifications). Bion's and Elkin's work, like Jung's, provides an expanded arena for the play of reversible perspectives. Unlike Jung's, their work is not limited by the simple division of psychic life into collective and personal unconscious, which I have criticized.

If Jung's view were simply correct (i.e., that the collective unconscious or self compensates conscious ego attitudes), one might expect that, in a materialistic age, the collective unconscious would constellate spirit archetypes. To an extent this is so, but hardly in any way that could easily confirm such a global formulation. One might try the opposite and say that today's rampant materialism is a compensation for the ages of too great an emphasis on spirit. Again, such a blanket statement could not stand up to criticism. In such formulations, one can see that thinking via reversals is often overgeneral, even stereotypical, and can be extremely rigid.

<hr/>

25. Bion, *Learning from Experience*, p. 29; idem, *Attention and Interpretation*, pp. 26–73, 87–96.

In psychosis, every possible mixture and dissociation of material and immaterial dimensions of experiencing are found. A psychotic individual raised in a materialistic milieu may or may not bring up compensating images. He is as likely to mirror or caricature his surroundings and ego attitudes as compensate for them. Often mirroring and compensating activity blend together in highly specific ways.

In one instance, a woman who murdered a friend's child and managed to feel self-righteous about all her actions, repeatedly dreamt of a man with a snake's head throwing snakes at her. For some time her therapist persisted in viewing this image as an expression of guilt, and the work went nowhere. Only when she realized that this patient's conscious and unconscious life were mirror images of one another did she begin to sense how thoroughly hardened and free of guilt her patient was. The latter indeed lived in a snake-headed, snake-throwing world where there might be fear but not guilt. If compensation was at work here, it was merely a shift from passive to active and vice versa, the reversibility of killer–victim roles. Whether active or passive while asleep or awake, the predator–prey structure remained constant.

The unconscious often dramatizes attitudes that run through one's psyche (and one's culture or subculture). In my experience, when the unconscious plays a predominantly compensating role, alternative models that once influenced the growing self usually are discoverable. For example, a man whose father was a lawyer who lived by his wits and common sense began to hear God and see devils when he had to make a living. As therapy unfolded, he began to feel how profoundly touched he had been by his religious maternal grandmother. She was a simple, good-hearted woman who took God seriously. He felt how precious he had been for her. She supplied him with a "higher" frame of reference with which to view his father's preoccupations. It was only much later that he could begin to value his father's achievements in their own right and begin to meet life's demands. It was also not surprising to see his father grow more religious with age, as he drew on the heritage of his own childhood, which he had abandoned for so long a time. In such an intertwining of factors, it is probably impossible to discriminate a spontaneous archetypal level from the play of bipolar ego ideals. What we do see are certain pairs of attitudes (e.g., idealistic–materialistic) that run through the psyche as a whole—divided, melded, and distributed in a variety of ways. Whatever theoretical perspective we adopt, we can conduct an endless analysis, since there will always be further reversals of positions to monitor.

Again, it is not the ability to reverse per se, but rather the network of attitudes that provides a context for such work that is crucial. Reversals are freeing and/or imprisoning, depending on a variety of conditions. An individual may spin out of existence when caught up in constant, high-speed reversals or come to a standstill if the reversal is too slow. In either case, as suggested in earlier chapters (1, 2, 3, and 5), self-world obliteration occurs. On the other hand, the subject's ability to persist in reversing experiences into their opposite can finally break through a sense of constriction and open new worlds. In therapy sessions, it is possible to study moment-to-moment shifts in the liberating/destructive movement of the self-reversing mind.

In one session, a patient saw himself swinging on a long pole. The pole was on a mountain and the patient found a way of attaching himself to it by making a cloth seat (very like a backpack in which a parent carries a child). Apparently the mountain was very steep and he had to use this pole to get down it. Each swing of the pole takes him to another side of the mountain and almost permits him to touch the ground at the bottom. He sees ravines and must be sure to land on solid ground. However, for a long time he cannot land. Sometimes he enjoys the swings, but he is also afraid. At some point he begins to see a penis (his?) on one side and feces on another and fears he will land in the feces. Now he veers toward one, now the other, now between, now away from the scene entirely. Eventually it becomes important to get down, no matter where. He lets himself off when he can and must now look around.

Clearly, such images have to do with top–bottom, front–back tensions, however one understands them. Even though the panorama is vast, the patient lives in a relatively narrow world, since the height–depth and front–back of it are defined by danger–safety.

Spirit–instinct, parent–child, facets of body image, inflation–reality and power–helplessness are some polarities with which the adventure is concerned. Of particular interest here are the penis–feces swings and the moment-to-moment shifts in mood of our therapy relationship. We had reached a point where our feelings toward one another changed quickly. Certainly we were trying to bring together previously split states. But something more was happening. We actually felt we were creating and being created by the affects that came and went. With each swing something appeared and vanished again. Each swing was both a discovery and return, a gain and loss. As we felt active and energetic and shitty together, we felt a universe being born in and through us, an emotional universe. My patient felt giddy with his coming on how thoroughly we move through each other, how we experience the high, low, front, and back of ourselves through a contact that is at once dizzying, threatening, and profoundly life-giving. We become more autonomous by passing through each other. The mountain becomes a transparent medium, a silent conductor, without losing its formidable opaque solidity. The air–ground polarity is other (aspects of other) and self persists through the ego's monkey antics.

Bion, however, taught us how devastating the capacity to reverse can be. We fight against the emotional universe that being in a room with another person (or ourselves) evokes. In such instances, as fast as affective meaning appears it is nullified, dispersed, dulled, or turned into a grotesque double of itself. Potential life dies as fast as it is glimpsed. Reversible perspective becomes a reversing perspective, in which the very capacity to constitute experiencing is thrown into reverse gear and undercut. True reversibility, the play of doubleness, is lost or compromised.

One patient spoke of "the shredder." As fast as anything might happen for her, an automatic shredder annihilated it. At first therapy was a haven, but as her love for me grew she came to see therapy as one of the biggest sources of pain in her life. If only I didn't exist, she would not know how terrible it was to be alone. She would not have to feel just how thoroughly she shredded herself and everything else. She and Shredder would live in peace. She envied my functioning in sessions, my success, my family. She could discount the superiority of most other lives by spotting the fatal flaw in others. Even when she freely admitted others were better off, she was far enough away for it not to matter. Our daily closeness, groping and playing together, fighting to get somewhere, seeing and seeing our seeing, made simple escape hard. Shredder—traditionally, the devil—stood out like a red skyscraper, an inflammation. He pointed out everything about me that was terrible, but that only made her love me more. She saw her love for me as the biggest devil's joke of all. Shredder's victory was love itself, for with love came suffering and his triumphant laugh. It helped to hear me say, "God is love? Ha! That's the most demonic proposition of all."

Bion noted that it is difficult to perceive growth when working at the level where the very possibility of constituting experiencing is concerned.[26] A person may seem to be growing yet not growing, seem not to be growing and growing, seem to be growing and growing, or seem not to grow and not grow. Similarly, one in pain or not in pain may be growing or not growing. It is no wonder criteria of therapeutic outcome have been so difficult to agree upon and assess. In one passage, Bion suggested that the use of the Eden–Babel–Oedipus myths can help determine whether growth is happening.[27] One can illuminate fragmented psychic products, especially "scattered components of a disintegrated ego,"[28] by passing them through these myths like filters and seeing how the bits and pieces are distributed in light of invariant structures (e.g., one may assess where the patient's productions fall with regard to the curiosity-striving–punishment motif).

A crucial characteristic of these myths is that they offer no solution. They express conflictual situations. Man is brought down by his striving to know, to be God. Reaching out or high or in brings suffering but there is no way around the tension of this difficulty. There is the pain of knowing and the pain of not knowing and

26. Bion, *Elements of Psycho-Analysis*, pp. 54–68.
27. Ibid., pp. 64–66.
28. Ibid., p. 67.

punishment suited to either condition. We reach out, we fall, we reach out. We become seasoned. Adam transforms into Jesus. Jesus resurrects. We hatch again and again. Something in us seems to be irrepressible—up to a point. We meet barriers. We are made possible by barriers, constraints, or limits, as we are by bones. We meet ourselves as we leave ourselves behind. A Sumerian proverb expresses this hard fact of life: "I escape the wild bull and a wild ox appears." This characterizes inner as well as outer reality, as ancient mystery ceremonies suggest.

An essential element in the myths Bion relied on is pain. Whatever else they are, the myths of Eden, Babel, and Oedipus reflect painful situations characterized by complex sets of relations. Through the lens of these myths our capacity to perceive and make use of pain grows. If we meet and dwell in these myths, we notice ourselves more. The fact that such myths exist means that we have begun to notice and pay attention, at least sometimes. These myths express the pain of knowing and themselves help constitute the capacity to experience hardships attached to the will to know. They allow us to experience and reflect on experience. Through them, we build a tolerance of ourselves.

The impasse and suffering met through the need to know propels the subject beyond knowledge to the point where knowing and faith intersect. The realization that we can never fully possess ourselves (or anything) leads us to explore the aesthetics of openness. We become artists of non-possesiveness, adept at permitting experiencing to build and speak. We learn to listen and reply. We become partners with our athletic drive toward mastery and the plenitude of unknowing, our need to control and our need to be reborn through mystery. Mastery and mystery—double poles of our nature. We have an infinite hunger for both. We grope for and are created through a "space" in which a greater and lesser subject, an I, a me, an anonymity come and go in all imaginable ways. It is a space pervaded by otherness incessantly in the process of being born, an other as intimate and far away as our own I-feeling. If we are mad, we make ourselves more so by scratching (zeroing or irritating) the terms of our experience. But if we do not follow the itch, we remain unborn, and if we cannot nullify who we are and what we have done, we remain shallow.

A two-and-a-half-year-old boy stacks blocks and knocks them down, urinates in the toilet or potty, but sometimes all over the floor for fun, acts perfectly in a restaurant, then impishly screams, drinks some juice from his cup, and spills the rest in happy defiance. He is triumphant in his mastery and undoing. He feels good about learning how things work, and fitting into a basic order. And he feels good dispersing the tension and constraints. He finds a certain freedom in form–formlessness. He moves back and forth and, if he is lucky, begins a journey in which both sides of life can evolve in all their hidden intricacy.

His parents are indecisive. They feel bad if they discipline him and bad if they do not. They, too, must do and not do. They lay down the Law, the Commandments. No meets no. They permit. They waver. Why haven't more poems been written about parent and child? The parent who is not totally cut off discovers there is nothing more delicate, resilient, or tough than a child's soul, than one's relationship with a child, one's own child. The term "own" will be blasted open in untold ways. The inevitable confusion of space and spacelessness ensues. One passes the barrier of blood to the place where souls are created. One almost tastes the blood–bloodlessness of one's own soul. We go past soul and return again. Where have we been? We go or are taken there as we can, as Scrooge is lifted above his life, as a child overturns a cup and laughs. The mess on the floor teaches us that anything can happen, but the cup, before it is broken, reminds us that we come and go through vessels.

CHAPTER SEVEN

Schreber and Rena

IN THIS CHAPTER, we will explore selected aspects of two cases in some detail. The first is Freud's Schreber case,[1] the other is drawn from my clinical practice. Schreber is one of Freud's great case portrayals, one of the writings in which Freud transforms case study into a new genre. It not only explores a clinical entity, but it also seems to illuminate and stretch the human experience. My own case is more modest, but has the advantage of being mine. I believe that the comparison of the psychotic Schreber who wished to be a woman, and a contemporary psychotic woman, may offer some fruitful parallels and contrasts. In addition to the more general goal of exploring psychotic experience and its implications for what it means to be a human being, this chapter suggests transformations for the phenomenological work of this book into clinical interventions.

Freud's Schreber Case

Daniel Paul Schreber was born in 1842. He became a judge in Leipzig, his birthplace, and suffered three mental breakdowns between the ages of 42 and his death at 69. During his second illness, he

1. Freud, "Psycho-Analytic Notes on an Autobiographical Account of a Case of Paranoia," pp. 9–820.

wrote his memoirs, an account of his illness in which he saw himself as destined to save the world by turning into a woman.

Freud never met Schreber, but used his memoirs to demonstrate the significance of psychoanalysis in understanding paranoia. Freud wrote this work as part of his beginning debate with Jung. As Jung's work developed, he emphasized parallels between psychotic imagery and mythology that could not simply be understood in terms of repressed sexual conflicts.[2] Freud tried to provide Jung with a frame of reference that included specific ways the ego structured sexuality in symptom formation. He did not think that the description of ageless complexes (or archetypes) could explain why an illness took one form and not another. Jung, however, felt that sexuality and ego mechanisms, although important, did not exhaust or perhaps even approach the core movement and meaning of psychotic processes. It would be too much of a digression to take up the terms of this dispute now.[3] For our purposes, we can loosely use Freud's and Jung's insights insofar as they enrich our discussion of the sort of world we would enter if we were to meet a patient similar to Schreber.

Perhaps, one of the most striking differences between a mental health worker today and one 80 years ago is how easily many of today's workers might respond to some of Schreber's productions. A contemporary clinician who met a sensitive man in a mid-life crisis speaking of "soul murder" or a "basic language," as Schreber did, might nod affirmatively with little sense of discordance. He might empathically feel that in some way we are all soul murderers and murdered souls, more or less damaged and damaging. Freud sensed

---

2. Jung, "The Psychology of Dementia Praecox," pp. 38–42, 99–151, "The Content of the Psychoses," pp. 163–178, *Symbols of Transformation*, pp. 7–32, 121–170, 441–444, "Recent Thoughts on Schizophrenia," pp. 250–255, "Schizophrenia," pp. 256–272, *Memories, Dreams and Reflections*, pp. 124–138; Freud, "On Narcissism," pp. 79–81; *Freud-Jung Letters*, pp. 186, 287, 307, 356, 358, 368, 378–380, 407–408, 421, 426–427, 441–443, 460, 469.
3. Freud and Jung offer coherent and fruitful positions with characteristic limitations and drawbacks. One can approach the human psyche from any number of starting points and explore modes of experiencing associated with each.

the diminishing gap between patient and doctor when he wrote near the end of his study, "It remains for the future to decide whether there is more delusion in my theory than I should like to admit, or whether there is more truth in Schreber's delusion than other people are as yet prepared to believe."[4] An implication of Freud's remark is that delusion and truth run through human discourse, psychosis or science. We are now very much in the process of discovering the depth of this intermixture in our lives.

The symptoms of Schreber's first breakdown included hypochondriacal and coanesthetic sensations, which, in time, were organized by feminine imagery. These included a sense of softening of the brain, physical decomposition, and hypersensitivity to light and noise. Eventually such sensations became part of feeling himself as a woman, a plaything of God, man, and devils, and, finally, a savior destined to restore to mankind its lost state of bliss. What began as a sense of disintegration and hypersensitivity became degraded, turned into divine whorishness, and culminated in the "spiritual voluptuousness," fulfilling God and man alike.

In Schreber's case, a sense of disintegration coupled with hypersensitivity became linked with the idea of becoming a woman. A heightening of body sensations went along with the breakdown of "masculine" control. Freud characterized this as "flooding," which he called the "primary trauma." In his early psychoneurological imagery, Freud described the stimulus streaming that results when cortical inhibition is lifted, a kind of stimulus rape. Following Freud's lead, later analysts related paranoia to anal sensations, which may be felt as alien and taken as assaults.[5] Alarms sound; the musculature tightens. The body becomes rigid. Danger is near and everywhere. In true paranoiac fashion, Schreber was "tight-assed." He dreaded, yet was fascinated by and delusionally courted, the idea of penetration. Soon before his illness, in an early morning state between waking and sleeping, he thought how nice it must be to be "a

4. Freud, "Psycho-Analytic Notes on a Case of Paranoia," p. 79.
5. Meltzer, "The Relation of Anal Masturbation to Projective Identification," pp. 335–342.

woman submitting to the act of copulation." Freud notes that
Schreber would have repudiated this idea indignantly had he been
fully conscious. Yet this is precisely what Schreber finally allowed
himself to experience during his psychosis.

It is an oddity in the history of the depth psychologies that
Jungians did not explore the Schreber case to the extent Freudians
did. Schreber's basic movement from a male position to death and
rebirth through the feminine seems made for Jungian analysis.[6]
Today, many speak of a breakthrough of the feminine as a compensating shift in an age overly dominated by masculine ideology and
power. In this and related ways, Schreber may be seen as a pseudo-
pod of evolution who lacked the psychological and cultural resources
to understand his experience.

Freud's treatment of Schreber's illness as repressed and projected
homosexual wishes has received a bad press. Authors delight in
showing how paranoia cannot simply be linked to repressed homosexuality. In so doing, the suggestiveness of Freud's work is reduced
to facile parody, which in some ways Freud himself invites. Yet one
sees in Schreber (and in Freud's treatment of him) the unfolding of
an archetypal drama, a visionary sequence with profound implications for us today. It is our job now to begin to carve out a frame of
reference that does justice to what Schreber stumbled upon and to
explain the significance of his experience in contemporary terms.

Epistemology and the Feminine

If, for Aristotle, what linked man to God was rationality, for
Schreber, the link was neurology. For Aristotle, the image of immediate contact was alien: man realized what was highest and most
uniquely human/divine through awareness and exercise of rational

6. For example, von Franz, *Creation Myths*, pp. 11–13; Neumann, *Amor and Psyche*,
pp. 57–161; Schwartz-Salant, *Narcissism and Character Transformation*, pp. 107–169.
See also Chapter 2 of this volume.

principle. For Schreber, man was locked with God in mortal struggle or eternal bliss. Schreber believed God was attracted to human nerves in a heightened state of excitement. God is all nerve, pure nerve. He cannot help but resonate and be drawn to man's nervousness. Schreber's excitement and hypersensitivity became the nodal points of cosmic drama. The pulsating awareness of raw excitability, sensory streaming, a flood of heightened experiencing seemed to feed Schreber's delusions. When such states died down Schreber felt that he and the entire universe had died. When the heightening returned, it brought with it ideas of personal and cosmic regeneration.

Schreber made use of and parodied the science of his day. Neurology was in fashion. The textbooks Freud grew up with showed the cerebral cortex as the seat of human intelligence and the subcortex as the source of emotions. The cortex inhibits, selects, and reworks man's animal drives. Nerves course through the body. Excitations build up and culminate in neural firings followed by recovery time: a pattern of incessant climax, dying out, and renewal. For Schreber, such ideas or observations became part of immediate experience. He envisioned and felt his nerves intertwining with God's. God's nerves shined like rays. At their best, God and Schreber shared an ecstatic, "spiritual voluptuousness," the proper experience of nerves working harmoniously. For Schreber, the nerves in scientific textbooks were not simply anatomy, but, rather, centers of subjective experiencing, akin to the ancient Hindu visions of nerves as centers of consciousness.

As Freud pointed out, Schreber's relationship to his God was as ambivalent as a child's to his father, alternately rebellious and reverent. However, it also shared and even caricatured a complex ambivalence associated with aspects of the experiential and epistemological revolution of modern and post-modern sensibility. Schreber's experience of nerves and Freud's libido theory are both part of a larger cultural movement re-evaluating the epistemological role of the body.

For the larger part of the history of Western thought, the body has been a second-class citizen. It was associated with the ephemeral, animal, or machine—to be used and transcended. In Descartes' system, mind is free and body a machine, radically different orders of creation. It was, paradoxically, the scientific investigation of the body as machine that played an important role in establishing the body as an organizing center of subjectivity. Spontaneous ordering processes were discovered at all levels of life. The distinction between Descartes' two orders of being was blurred: if mind was spontaneous, so was body; if body was machine, so was mind.

Schreber's journey, as Rimbaud's, demonstrates what agony a man may go through to discover and valorize his body. In this context, Schreber's salvific beliefs depended not only on his becoming a woman, but also on his astonishment at having a body at all. The breakthrough of body experiencing shattered his hold on reality, and his loss of control made space for the life of the body. He constructed his own psychotheology to give body experience its due. Given archetypal and cultural patterns, it was natural for him to experience the body in the mode of erotic sensibility as feminine.

Schreber's discovery of his body was first a source of torment, then salvation. At first, he believed his doctor wished to castrate him. Indeed, Dr. Flechsig, who saw him through his first breakdown, did castrate patients as part of therapy, and Schreber must have known this. Schreber fought against the possibility of castration, actual and imaginery. As often happens, delusion and reality reinforced each other.

Schreber dreaded and wished to become Dr. Flechsig's whore. The idea of being a whore partly reflected the unequal distribution of power in the doctor–patient relationship, but it also had an element of freedom and brought relief from an overly masculine persona. Such a fantasy, of course, is widespread in men and women alike and has many determinants. Freud's account is perhaps at its best in portraying how fiercely one fights against one's longings and how intimate wishes spring at one like alien intruders, endless sources of persecution.

In the recent literature, Freud has been criticized for underplaying the role of reality in the formation of personality and mental illness.[7]

7. Miller, *For Your Own Good*, pp. 3–91; Schatzman, *Soul Murder*, pp. 1–31, 88–109.

Although Freud sees Schreber's brother and father behind delusions involving Dr. Flechsig and God, he does not make anyone responsible for Schreber's problems. Indeed, he attributes Schreber's "cure" to the latent influence of a father worthy of his son's idealization. According to Freud, the main injury Schreber's father caused was his premature death when Schreber was 19. Freud emphasized a wounded idealization process, followed by Schreber's failure to become a father himself (in giving birth to a saved mankind he proved himself more fertile than his wife). It thus may be that Freud did not underplay reality factors so much as fail to use more of the right ones. We now know how cruelly inhuman Schreber's father was to the growing boy and can trace these cruelties in Schreber's delusions.[8] The influence of Schreber's mother has not been authoritatively portrayed.

Surely, it would have helped Schreber if he could have spoken freely about his father and the abuses he suffered in childhood. It would have taken an empathic and gifted listener to draw him out, since Schreber could not have guessed how ill he had been treated, nor could he have linked his father's inhumanity with his later illness. Schreber's well known, respected father systematically rationalized his behavior and the idealization he courted overcame all criticism.

Nevertheless, it is doubtful that an analysis of Schreber's father problem and the master–slave relationship that characterized his childhood would have exhausted the impact of the world Schreber experienced in his psychosis. Once he tasted the thrill of "spiritual voluptuousness" in wrestling with God, it became a reality. Analysis of his father relationship might have helped set things right, but Schreber still would have had to come to terms with God and father as realities with separate, if interlocking, claims.

Schreber's psychosis made rebirth the most prepossessing experience of his life. Everything else was redefined in light of it. Forever after he was concerned with being born again. Good therapy, however, could have helped mediate a better or different birth, one with a greater complexity of insight and a more probing interplay of delirium and self-correction. Analysis may help the "twice born" face the

8. Schatzman, *Soul Murder*, pp. 53–75.

question: "What quality of rebirth am I involved in? What direction am I taking? What follows?" But one can or ought not mitigate the breathtaking significance of the moment of re-formation. There are demonic as well as divine renewals, and people can be helped to work with the regeneration that comes their way. With help, one may learn to shape as well as be shaped by the quality of renewal.

An aspect of Schreber's tragedy is that he was left to his own devices in shaping his pattern of rebirth. He had no way of monitoring, correcting, or controlling it. Today he would have various body therapies, oriental philosophies, and feminist ideologies to help him. It might neither be necessary nor possible for there to be a Schreber today, or perhaps, in some sense, there are many Schrebers. But if we are Schrebers, we are more self-critical than he. We are Schrebers whose frames of reference have grown to include transverse sexual identifications. By becoming the other sex, we know, as Schreber could not, the vanity of this utopian fantasy.

We are no longer afraid, at least in theory, of being the opposite sex. Often current norms require us to be so. We are no longer even sure what sex means, an uncertainty which would have been impossible for Schreber. A man today may not be afraid to be a woman, but this will not help him resolve his sense of catastrophic reality. The sense of catastrophe remains permanently with us as critic of our renewals. We study how frames of reference evolve so that our quest for an adequate frame remains problematic. We analyze the specific qualities of alternate frames, insofar as we can apprehend them. We do not know where we are going, but take things a step at a time.

Schreber's solution was more traditional. The basic structure of his psychosis fit an essential element of the Hebraic religion. The religious Jewish man was in a feminine relationship to God: Israel, Bride of God. This age-old relationship is not confined to Judaism. In the words of William Burroughs, speaking of Arabs in Tangiers, "Allah fucked me, the All Powerful. . . ." Schreber found a sort of peace in his rediscovery of the ancient feminine relationship to the godhead.

His solution reminds us of a real, enduring strain of our nature, but our own relationship to the feminine is more complex and problematic. If we are religious in temperament or commitment today, we may have to realize that we are partners with God in mutual permeability and that all links involve movement. As we will see, such a realization was part of Schreber's experience, but he failed to situate his madness within a larger context of meaning. As far as his visions were concerned, he was on his own. In the end, Schreber remained mad because he used his madness as a solution, rather than a probe. A contemporary Schreber might be more apt to use the materials of his psychosis experimentally, as tools of research, a laboratory of the self. Or, at least, he might be encouraged to do so in therapy with a fellow traveler.

Structures of the Self: Above–Below, Front–Back, Distinction–Union

The psychotic self brings out the tenacity and fragility of our relationship to basic structures of experience. We take for granted that we order our world in terms of such relationships as above–below and front–back. The psychotic individual whose very sense of embodiment is in jeopardy must fight to hold onto the perceptual configurations that order our world. Buildings may seem to topple, vast holes in the earth may open up, or areas of a city may rearrange themselves cryptically. Often such experiences accompany and tug at common-sense perception. Sometimes an individual realizes he is seeing how the world feels to him. The boundary between one's sense of inner and outer catastrophe blurs.

Schreber's concern with the up–down and front–back of things was mirrored in his preoccupation with the higher–lower and anterior–posterior aspects of his God. Schreber envisioned forecourts or an anterior realm above which God hovered. This place of transaction between divine and mortal nerves was a necessary waystation in the ascent of souls. God's posterior was divided between a lower (Ahriman) and upper (Ormuzd) God, Persian deities possibly taken from Byron's "Manfred." Schreber's higher and lower Gods (or

aspects of God) were often in conflict, as, similarly, were the hap-
penings in God's forecourts and posterior. In Schreber's world,
divisions tended toward divisiveness, each part struggling with the
rest.

Schreber's thinly veiled references to higher and lower functions
were more explicit in his writings on God's ambivalent relationship
to defecation. At certain points in his psychosis, Schreber felt that his
excited nerves attracted God's nerves against the latter's will. Nevertheless, it also pleased God to be enmeshed with Schreber and, to an
extent, Schreber wanted to go on pleasing God. In order to do this,
Schreber believed he must occupy his mind with his relationship
with God or God would disappear. Also, he thought that he was
able to maintain some mastery over God by incessantly thinking
about their struggle of nerves. In this situation, God manifested his
villainy by making Schreber want to defecate. This was a clever ruse,
since as soon as Schreber turned his mind from God to feces, God
could free himself. At the moment of defecation, Schreber would lose
his mind.

God persevered in his villainy by stopping Schreber in the process
of defecating. Thus, God and Schreber were actors in an eternally
frustrating scenario. They could neither truly have nor truly be rid
of each other. Enjoyment was soured by a battle for control.

Schreber's excretory drama is one of proliferating dualities: mind
and nerves working with and against each other. Nerves mediate
voluptuous sensations, which run through literal and spiritual bodies. Mind uses these as a source of aliveness and food for thought, yet
keeps above them. Mind exercises a certain control over the agent
(God) who provokes and is attracted by such sensations. Mind must
not allow itself to drown in the sensory sea, which it can, however,
appreciate through the senses. There are times, however, such as
during defecation, when mind (self-control) will vanish. Schreber is
then threatened with a dual catastrophe of mindlessness and total loss
of power. God will be free to laugh at him; there will be no mind left
to oppose Him.

Defecation has a privileged place in Schreber's system. It is precisely through Schreber's excretory needs that God can prove Him-

self superior, since God does not have to shit. God is pure nerve.
Schreber is nerve, mind, and body. Schreber's mind acts as a locus of
power and autonomy. Schreber can see and chart what is going on as
it happens. He can hold out even as he is given over to a divine
enmeshment of nerves. God's strategy is to make Schreber lose his
mind through his body. If the spiritual voluptuousness of nerves
does not quite work, perhaps a natural function like defecation will.

It is as if God will lose if Schreber fulfills any natural function.
Anything mental or natural can defeat God. God apparently thrives
in the tension of irresolution (e.g., making Schreber have to defecate
and then stopping him). Schreber's mind and body offer a resistance
to God, something not given to nerves alone. Yet beyond this
common purpose, mind and body fight each other, since everything
is at war with everything else.

Schreber's world was highly differentiated, but profoundly hostile. His observing and controlling aspects of mind fought against
feelings. Phallus and anus were drawn to and repelled each other. A
deep antagonism permeated the very foundation and framework of
the universe. God and the Order of Things were enemies. Schreber
tried to ally himself with the Order of Things, but was drawn to
God. When he saw flaws in the Order of Things, as he did in God,
he had no recourse but to fight against the assumptive grounds of
Being.

Yet Freud claimed that all this hate was a sign of love. The paranoiac's "I hate you because you hate me" was a transposition of a
deeper "I love you." A wounded yearning found its circuitous path
toward realization in hallucinatory delusion. Hostile distinctions
were wedded to, disguises for, and transpositions of a longing for
union. Schreber's relationships with Flechsig, God, and the Order of
Things were nothing if not intense. He lived at a heightened pitch
wherein love–hate fused and de-fused, precursors of each other. A
longing for union with the Father underlay Schreber's paranoia.

For Schreber, a warp pervaded the distinction–union relation that
structures our psychic universe; distinctions were hostile; the pull
toward union threatened to be overwhelming. Each tendency was
played off against the other. Love offset total destructiveness and

hate warded off obliterating fusion. In Schreber's world, distinction–
union tendencies were antagonistic, or, at best, bizarrely compensated for the other's dangers. Hierarchical organizations were used to
bind damaging excesses and distortions of polar tendencies. Thus a
detailed scheme emerged in which, for example, higher–lower and
anterior–posterior "functions" could be sustained and, after a fashion, coordinated (higher–lower and front–back areas of God, cosmos, and Schreber).

A more seamless sense of co-union contrasts with the hierarchical
style of organization: the distinction–union structure of the Holy
Trinity, the Eucharist, and the philosophical sense of the One in the
Many. Here, a sense of division and union co-constitute and fulfill
each other. An example of this sort of thinking is Schreber's statement *"that each single nerve of understanding represents a person's entire
mental individuality"*[9] (Schreber's italics). Here, there is a concordance or intunement between distinctions. It is the mode of experiencing Schreber worked his way toward throughout his psychosis.
It was, for example, only after God and the Order of Things came
together and worked harmoniously that Schreber was "cured" and
released from the hospital. His fight of all against all culminated in a
vision of beatific harmony, in which distinctions enhanced and supported one another. God, the Order of Things, Schreber as savior,
the human race—all, finally, allies or partners in a grand redemption.
To be sure, there were still reciprocal antagonisms and power antics,
but for quite a while, a more favorable balance between love and hate
obtained.

Caesura

The achievement of harmony came after a gap or pause in which
Schreber believed he and everything else had died and returned.
Freud understood this caesura as the withdrawal of libido from

9. Freud, "Psychoanalytic Notes on a Case of Paranoia," p. 22.

objects to ego, expressed in a sense of world destruction and megalomania. He took Schreber's consequent messianic vision to be an
attempt at recovering the lost object-world in a new key. Libido
returned via hallucinatory delusions, which could express the latent
love wishes Schreber's sense of persecution had masked.

Although there is much that is valuable in Freud's account, he
appears to overlook or play down a central part of the death–rebirth
or loss–recovery phenomenon described by Schreber. For a period,
Schreber died or vanished, along with the world. His megalomania
took a new form following his return, but it cannot be said that it
characterized the moment of disappearance. In Freud's terms, libido
left the ego as well as the object-world and for a moment there was
total darkness.

Megalomania was part of Schreber's psychosis before as well as
after the blackout and return. It took the inverse form of hostile self-
reference. Schreber was the center of a hostile universe in which all
the efforts of demonic others were directed against him. It was
apparently of the utmost importance to others that Schreber be
abused, treated as a whore, castrated, and killed. The central difference before and after the blackout was the change from negative to
positive. Before the blackout, Schreber's relationship to Dr. Flechsig
and God was largely hostile; afterwards, his delusions were more
satisfying. Thus, Freud's depiction of the shifting balances between
ego and object in terms of the seesawing of libido seems suggestive,
but deficient, inasmuch as megalomania and concern with objects
characterized Schreber's states on either side of the chiasma.

For Freud, Schreber's achievement of beatific harmony represented the solidification of his delusional system, which became a
kind of encapsulated psychosis. Schreber was able to view his ideas
with the eye of common sense and live sanely among the sane,
although he maintained his visionary beliefs in secret. Such a consolidation and freezing of his madness into a workable packet followed,
according to Freud, a period of greater turmoil and irresolution.
However, Schreber's earlier period of tormented turmoil was just as
fixed as his later benign state. He, Flechsig, God, and the Order of
Things whirled and collided in constant fear and enmity. The details

changed, but the theme of attack and discord, the feelings of dread, hate, and horror, were constant. Schreber's negative state before the caesura was as fixed as his positive resolution afterward. That Schreber again required hospitalization late in life (after his mother's death and wife's illness) suggests the continuing reversibility of such states.

If Freud's account of Schreber's turnabout is deficient, what further thoughts can we offer that Freud was not in a position to make, owing to temperament, perspective, and, in part, insufficient knowledge? As mentioned earlier, Freud speculated that Schreber's illness had had a relatively favorable outcome because he was able to draw on a positive relationship with an admirable father. We now know how badly Schreber's "esteemed" father treated him, and we are forced to look elsewhere for what might have tipped the balance for the better. Freud might have been right to note the contribution Schreber's ambivalence toward his father made to the emotions that characterized the course of his illness. However, if Schreber remained within the arena of emotions aroused by his father, he might never have gotten out of his horrific battle with idealized devils.

It was, I believe, only because Schreber was able to go beyond the heritage his father left him that he was able to sustain his breakthrough to the beatific. It appears that the shift from hating to loving delusions came during his second breakdown (1894–1902), when Dr. Weber became his doctor. Dr. Weber respected Schreber and was interested in his ideas. He apparently liked Schreber and showed this in many ways. Schreber was a frequent dinner guest in Weber's home. Weber describes Schreber's spirited conversation and genial conduct with his friends and family. It seems likely that the good feelings and respect Schreber felt helped effect his profound transformation of thinking.

Schreber's relationship with Weber provided the impetus for Schreber's *Memoirs* (1900–1902), since Weber's care provided a holding environment that was safe enough to support Schreber's sustained efforts and engagement with himself. Schreber noted that many of his most freeing ideas came as he wrote, and it is clear that Schreber's exertion in his *Memoirs* was a form of therapy, a way of re-creating himself. He was not simply reporting what happened to him, but was also tapping into an originary dimension through which renewal became possible. What Freud saw as a final consolidation and petrifaction of a rigid belief system, Schreber felt as the passionate fire of the living Spirit, a surprising movement that lifted him out of the abyss. New worlds of experiencing opened up. What Freud saw as a closing, Schreber experienced as a beginning.

That Schreber began his *Memoirs* as part of his attempt to get out of the asylum suggests how far the restructuring of his ambivalence was able to go in relation to Weber. Although Weber's personal relationship with Schreber appears to have been relatively benign, he formally opposed Schreber's wish to be discharged. He may have found Schreber amiable and interesting, but still thought him crazy and perhaps feared for his welfare outside the protective milieu of the asylum. Schreber had to take legal action to win his release, but he and Weber remained on good terms. One might argue that Schreber was exhibiting the canniness of the experienced inmate who mimicked health in order to win release. But this would be unfair to Schreber's truthful nature, since there is no evidence that Schreber compromised his experience, as he knew it. Through all that happened to him, he reported his experiences as accurately as he could. It seems, rather, that his relationship with Weber was benign and strong enough to tolerate considerable disagreement. The two men went on exchanging views and enjoying one another throughout.

That Schreber had to fight for his freedom was therapeutically helpful. He further created himself in the fighting, no one was hurt by his efforts, and mutual good feelings prevailed. In contrast to his relationship with his dominating father, Schreber could assert himself without loss of integrity, which he fought for and won. I suspect Weber was able to provide Schreber with a taste of Winnicott's "use of object" situation.[10] Schreber's assertiveness occurred in a context that led to a quickening of his sense of self and other and increased his well-being. He found himself in a situation in which he

10. Winnicott, "The Use of an Object and Relating Through Identification," pp. 711–716; see also Chapters 4 and 5 of this volume.

was not injured by his difference from a power figure, but found a way of benevolently fighting for his own sense of worth and power. All in all, Schreber's fight to free himself was exhilarating, if nerve-wracking, and spurred him to marshal his strength and vision in new ways. Whereas his earlier fighting had been part of a self-defeating circle, this fight was part of a larger movement of renewal.

Under Dr. Weber's care, God and the Order of Things began to work together, so that Schreber was no longer torn between them. A partnership of tendencies and forces ensued. Freud's emphasis on the erotic relationship to Schreber's actual father prejudiced him against a more open conception of the primordial dimension involved. It may be that Freud could not have made his discoveries without the strict limits he placed on his investigations. We would all be the poorer without his insights, but a corrective amplification is in order if we are to do fuller justice to the shift of affect and image that character-ized Schreber's movement from war to harmony.

Weber provided the atmosphere in which a change of orientation was possible. A kind of "middle man," he allowed Schreber to move from a fight against a demonized Flechsig and God to a God to whom he could in some way say "yes." Through Weber, Schreber was able to escape the emotional bind that characterized his relation-ship to his father. In a larger framework, he was able to see God as better than he thought, perhaps even basically good, at one with the Order of Things. His fear that God was a disorderly devil was mollified, and he saw that the major forces of the universe were working toward a good end. He could, in some way, begin to give himself to his God. He could let down and be a woman without fear of abuse. Schreber's body soul became orgasmic. God ravished him. It was divine. He allowed God to do what no man could.

One can only speculate why Weber did not become a focus of Schreber's delusions. Perhaps this attests to a certain modesty or lack of megalomania on Weber's side. Perhaps he functioned as a back-ground object that affected Schreber's imagery without possessing it, so that an aborted or blocked archetypal drama could unfold. Schreber lived through his own pattern of self-attack and transcen-dence, tearing himself apart until he reached a kind of zero or bottom point, a nakedness that led to rebirth. Schreber sought a larger context than his own father. He not only transposed his father problem to God, he also tried to undercut it by tapping a deeper dimension. In Weber's care, Schreber moved from an evil to a benign primordial Other, working out his own personal version of the Song of Solomon.

That Weber's impact was not faced and worked over directly has a negative aspect as well. Schreber went deeper than his father problem by discovering a positive primordial Other. But he failed to work over oedipal currents vis-à-vis a real-life flesh and blood other. Schreber had no doctor who could work through the transference.

In a way, Schreber discovered an affective foundation upon which life could be lived. Life was governed by a benevolent rather than an evil primordial Other/Order. But for primordial reality to connect with everyday reality, one must wrestle with a real-life flesh and blood other, as well as God. Schreber's fight to free himself from Weber's care partly served such a function. In his case, however, either primordial reality absorbed real-life reality or the two split. Hence, Schreber's cure was fragile, and proved to be temporary.

Schreber enjoyed many years of good living between his second cure and final relapse. From our viewpoint, he could carry on as long as the positive primordial Other and everyday other remained connected. This mediating function was served by his wife, and it was after her debilitating illness that he was again hospitalized. In psychoanalysis, the therapist acts as a background object and focal figure who mediates contact between primordial and everyday dimensions. Like Weber, or Schreber's wife, the therapist is also a vehicle, a facilitator. However, in transference, it is mandatory that the patient gather up the polar threads of his existence and give each their due. The therapist is a mediator, but also a barrier that must be faced and overcome. He warns that the serious patient must not be released from his task before he develops a sound working sense of the ways the primordial and the everyday intersect. It is, in part, the therapist's presence as therapeutic conscience that keeps the patient locked into the task of discovering his own way of experiencing what must be experienced.

For a cure to be secure, the cosmic must work its way out, through, and be seen in relation to a particular person or persons. In psychoanalysis, this is effected by working through the transference. As Becker and Jung pointed out, the transference can be a gateway to the cosmic, through a flesh and blood person.[11] Schreber had little chance of meeting someone who could stand between the most basic polarities with a receptive working attitude toward each. Had he met such a person, he might not have required rehospitalization. But would he have written his *Memoirs*? Would he have written anything? Would he have written something even more telling?

In the above discussion, I have used the term *transference* loosely, describing it as a mediating vehicle between the primordial and the everyday. It is now time to examine its function in more detail and we will use a case of my own to do this.

Rena

Rena was the youngest of eight sisters and the only one who had not been sexually abused by her father. Her childhood had been marked by veiled talk about her father's carrying on, yet it was only in her early adolescence that he was taken to court and subsequently jailed. She remembers thinking he must have loved her most, since he harmed her least. He somehow protected her from himself and that granted her a certain privilege.

However, as therapy unfolded, she voiced a secret sense that she was odd or unusual and not simply more precious. She felt guilty that she was an exception, but also haunted with an inkling that something must be wrong with her, since he had overlooked her. Her exclusion from his abuses made her feel both better and worse than her sisters.

Her mother told Rena her father didn't bother her because she was too young. She was with her mother more than the other girls. This

11. Becker, *The Denial of Death*, Chapter 2.

enhanced her feeling that she was special. It made her feel that the other girls were much older than they were, and this enlarged the gap between herself and them. It was not until she was well into therapy that she could begin to ask if they had not been young, too. Rena grew up feeling she was mother's pet. At the same time, she felt lost in the large household. She could not keep up with the others; she was constantly brought up short by what she couldn't do; and she felt left out of her sisters' fights and shifting alliances. She often felt lost with her mother, as well, who was often distracted. From very early, she did not know what to do with the discrepancy between her mother's version of family life and the painful states she suffered. As she once put it, "I couldn't believe my family was unbelievable. I tried to prove myself wrong."

An undercurrent of strife and backbiting dominated the family mood. Her mother and aunt (the mother's sister who lived with her) treated her father as if he were subhuman and did not belong in the family. In one way or another, all the females in the family acted as if her father were an alien. That Rena also loved him left her with an unspoken conviction that, in her own way, she was as aberrant and beyond the pale as he. A small but important part of her therapeutic work involved her reliving the moment when she saw him in court and wanted to say, "I love you," but did not because this was the last thing she was supposed to feel toward the "animal."

Rena's first breakdown occurred after she and her husband went to a weekend encounter group sponsored by her church. They were encouraged to find and speak the truth to one another and to be as honest as possible. They emerged battered, but with the hope of an intimacy she hadn't thought possible. She felt "high" and in tune with everyone and everything. She was surprised when, several days later, she became extremely distressed over the hate she had felt during parts of the weekend. An urge to kill her husband flooded her, and she became terrified that she would act on her urge.

Bloody images alternated with her ecstatic sense of having discovered God. She saw Light. The heavens opened. She heared singing. God's voice spoke to her of the goodness of all things. She tasted peace beyond understanding. Yet this very peace became a source of torment. How near and far it was. Murderous images assailed her and threatened to obliterate any possibility of good feeling. She felt torn and diffused by extreme states. She was once more helpless and unable to keep up with what her own nature produced.

Her priest told her to let God help her, that it was all right to feel the garbage within, God loved her with all her feelings. He felt there was a sacramental element to her murderous feelings and that discovering them would make her a better person. Perhaps he was right, but she ceased functioning in worldly terms and was hospitalized. It was the first of her many hospitalizations throughout her twenties and early thirties. Her recoveries were brought about with medication, supplemental psychotherapy, and warm support from her husband. When I met her, she seemed to accept these relapses as part of her life and simply wanted to be helped through them as painlessly as possible. She had good periods between them.

After our first months of work together, it became clear that her good periods were not unmixed blessings. Apparently, she paid for her husband's warm support during her illness by catering to his need to feel in control. Although he did not make a good living, he would not let Rena work. He insisted on making the major family decisions and even oversaw many of the minutiae of daily household problems normally left to the woman at home. It was as if his own self-doubt and sense of smallness were alleviated by being big at home, and I wondered to what extent he needed his wife's dependence on him and perhaps even her breakdowns.

Her thoughts of murdering him may have been a response to her sense of suffocation and need for space and power, although they had roots long antedating her marriage. She married a man she could break down with and collusively live out the needs and patterns that marked her development. Perhaps she would have felt unreal with a man capable of sustaining more autonomy, even though she felt held back by their style of living.

Rena remembered first feeling unreal before she was five. It lasted only moments, but had a terrifying, fascinating impact. Her mother was speaking to her aunt about her father. Suddenly she turned toward Rena and said, "Don't you agree, dear? Or are you father's little pet?" Her mother's face lit up in an eerie grimace, an ugly happiness. Rena felt herself turn into a whirring fan. She spun into the air. There was a reddening, blackening, then colorlessness. Her mother went from huge to tiny with her voice coming from a great distance. For a long instant, Rena felt nothing was as it seemed to be. Everything was something else. When she returned things went on normally, but for a time she suffered from a sense that there was an empty space inside people. She would look at someone's "outside" and wonder what he was like inside. She wondered if the other had a fan inside that could whisk him away, too. In therapy she recalled that such states came and went in milder forms through the years, but she never focused on them. She thought of the forbidden rooms in fairy tales. As a child she was surprised that they contained evil, which turned into good in the end. She had always expected the heroine to find nothing in them.

The first dream of childhood she could recall was of whirring sounds, together with chaotic black lines on a blue–black background. It was as if she were trying to scribble over and blot out the sight and sound of something. In therapy, she imagined it was her mother's spiteful grimace. She had been too afraid to admit that she felt her mother tortured her, that her mother tortured anyone. As a child, she was torn between her mother and father, but lacked the resources to tolerate this. Now her murderous feelings and sense of unreality seemed to go together. She had gone on to take life as it came without clearly realizing how worried she was that something was wrong. Later she could say, "I think I felt that life itself was insane at its core, that a basic madness was at the bottom of things." The whirring and scribbles were perhaps the last marks of chaos before oblivion, or the first marks a child draws and calls a face.

Some Session Notes

One does not cover "everything" in therapy or writing. One always selects and forms. In therapy, who I am inevitably draws out aspects of the patient that fit my sensibility and abilities. Yet what happens is, finally, real and compelling for the patient. It is as if something a person feels is scarcely possible to know or say is addressed. A shift in the quality of self-feeling occurs. How is such intimacy possible in a situation as seemingly artificial as psychotherapy, with its time limits, behavioral codes, and fees? In Rena's case, a distance element was crucial for the kind of intimacy that would most help her.

Rena worked with me seven years, probably six more than she had intended. I do not think that with problems like hers seven years is enough time to achieve optimal results, but it is enough time to make a difference. Almost in spite of herself, she felt drawn to her warps and injuries, what Perls called the "sick point."[12] At first she was appalled by this urge and I reassured her that there was probably something in me that draws the worst in people out. In time, her contact with what was fixed in her illness became a source of relief. With selected session notes, I will trace some of the twists and turns of themes that helped make a difference. These sessions occurred in a two-month period during our second year of work. In my write-up, I have retained something of the fragmentary quality of my notes and sessions.

DIFFERENT KINDS OF DARKNESS, DIFFERENT KINDS OF LIGHT

Session A. [Rena had already begun grappling with her mother's anger toward her and her own anger toward her mother. Marital discontent surfaced and she met a woman, L, with whom she began an affair. My feeling was that therapy gave Rena permission to admit rage, but this admission was disorganizing as well as relieving. Our relationship was not strong enough to bind the feelings it evoked. Rena used L to explore and hold herself together. In a way, L was an extension of myself. Rena would never have had this affair without therapy. But at this point, how L was to be used and transcended remained open. It was an issue with which we struggled in these sessions.]

12. Perls, *Gestalt Therapy Now*, p. 18.

R: As I lie here, I feel I am effortlessly communicating with L. I have never felt so little resistance. We are communicating without barriers. I feel you are she. No, you are almost she but you fail. You are after all a man. You are evil. You are in the way. I dreamt of mixed up intestines, as if mine and L's were mixed together. What a wonderful feeling. I wish it could go on forever. I feel such a loss without it.

Now I feel my scalp being pressed. I want to bury my head. I want to crawl into the womb and feel enveloped. I don't want to be out there above ground where it's day.

ME: Aren't you mixing up two kinds of darkness—womb and intestines? You speak of womb only after your intestinal high starts to fade. You need the womb because you can't take being without barriers, you can't take loss.

R: I'm at ease with L. She doesn't threaten me. She's as afraid of her body as I am. She doesn't like herself either. I can understand her and let go. I can spread. She won't stop me. We are new together. We feel free.

ME: You can't take it—the freedom or its fading. So you make light your enemy and think womb your friend. You don't think darkness and light need each other?

R: I want to bury myself. I want to hide. I want darkness.

ME: What kind of darkness?

R: I feel cramped.

ME: By me or the womb?

R: Both. It's true I'm cramped in the womb. I want to be cramped. No, I'm afraid. I want my freedom. I want the other kind of darkness, too. I want the open darkness with L.

ME: A darkness with no bounds.

R: Yes, an open darkness, totally open.

ME: [So there are two kinds of darkness, boundless and bound. One is compatible with light, whereas light never escapes the other. Rena mixes and opposes them and pits this confusion–opposition against light.]

R: The other day I practiced looking at men on the street. If someone was attractive to me, I'd look. It's hard to do. I forced myself to let myself feel. It's hard to be out in the open with feelings. I said to myself, "Now is the time to admit them, to believe them." It was exciting. I have the same fears about angry feelings. About letting them out so I feel them. I felt I could get so excited by my husband I scared myself. It's hard enough with strangers. It's easier with L. I know I won't vanish forever with her. I'll come back. There's a time limit on it. She's more like me. I go dead with my husband. I start to turn on and then think "no, not him."

ME: You go dead with him like with me. You let yourself go with L like with me.

R: I die and go. Die and come back. I had a dream. I was keeping my eye on the baby of a friend who had it by artificial insemination. There were a lot of people around. I got interested in them, then wanted to be alone and went off to my room. I forgot about the baby, then suddenly remembered and ran to look for him. He was OK crawling around the floor. I was relieved. He ran away when he saw me, then playfully ran back and burrowed into my pelvis. We playfully cuddled. I felt great. It was so gratifying. He was so quick, playful, lovely.

I hadn't any legs for years. Now I exercise. I move them. I feel my legs. I've been spineless. This week I was erect. In another dream I kneaded L's buttocks. I could pick her up. I walked down the street erect as a red tipped building. Very vivid. That was the way I tried to be this week. I was out in the open, erect, strong. Buildings receded in size and I felt very tall. So much confusion over what I have for a body.

ME: Con-fusion. With fusion. You're probably trying to reconcile having intestines with an erect back.

R: Gut feelings, back feelings. Will I have feelings or not? My mother's on my back. I've carried her. I shut off to carry her. She stuffed herself into me through my back, my backside. I'm weighed down, filled by her. That's why I'm so empty. She's empty and I'm filled with her. There's nothing in me except the anger. My mother screamed at me. She was so kind and generous. I hated her when she yelled at my aunt. She seemed ugly, a witch, always angry. Emptiness and anger. Buttocks are squooshy like breasts. I feel erect squooshing L. I am erect with squooshy L. These sessions are hell. I go through snakelike contortions to get to another place. I go through my gut. But it's different than last week when I feared my head falling off. With Z [a man she knew] it's different. I felt in a crucible. My legs vanished in light. I never got past the blinding light. I might have been changed if I had courage to hang in. My insides would finally come outside. I could finally acknowledge my feelings. This is the big fear.

ME: [Fear of darkness, fear of light. The light has always been blinding, flooding, overwhelming, associated with certain men. The darkness too is flooding, overwhelming, associated with women. There are different kinds of darkness and probably different kinds of light. Many permutations of male–female tensions, fusions with darkness-light. Her aim: total insides out. Anything held back seems alien, wrong. As long as goal is total evacuation, expressing anything is threatening.]

R: L and Z are mother and father. I'm merging the two of them. I want to merge both. I want to be in bed with them, pressing Z with L's hands on me in back of me giving me her energy. They become a womb. I'm in the womb with them. Potent womblike feelings. Out in the open world I can't have any feelings. In this hermaphroditic mishmash I come alive in a special way. I feel longing. It turns me on. I float around in ooze with them timelessly. Z loves me as I press him. He is my mother. I can't get away from her. He has her face now. I see her in him. I can't have feelings away from her. I can't have anything that's not her. I'm furious at her sitting on me, inside me, blocking me. I had dinner with an older woman friend on Tuesday. She has plenty of drive, a successful woman. I admire her drive and the way she is still friendly to men. I can sometimes feel sexual with a man, but I don't have feelings for men. I feel my drive to be someone is damaging to men. Now I just feel hostile and maybe a little sad about it. There's nothing I can do about it. I'm just an angry person. A damaging person.

ME: [She tries to create a mother–father link, but can't sustain it. It collapses into mishmash and her mother takes over. She is afraid I will be as wounded as her mother if she has a male and female side, if she is someone. She is afraid of damaging me as she was damaged. She is afraid she cannot survive individuation. Polarities collapse or remain antagonistic. She is yearning, mad and sad. She seems to give up and return at session's end to a "safe" position, partly in response to the impending separation. She is angry I haven't helped her more and frightened at the possibilities tasted. Perhaps she feels attacked by me and attacks herself. But an active baby has appeared who can take separation and who can go on playing and being himself even in odd and difficult circumstances.]

THE GAP

Session B (a week later). [Rena begins speaking about her wish to discover whether she can be with a man or not. Her friend L apparently can be with men and women at the same time. Rena doubts whether this is her path. She feels she will have to choose one or the other as a lover. She fears she will be caught between these possibilities, unable to choose a man because of her hostility and unable to choose a woman because of the escapist element involved. She will, as usual, be left with nothing.]

R: I dreamt I was hugging and stroking L. She stiffened, pulled away. Her husband showed and touched his penis and L touched it too. I felt she did it to make me jealous. He looked like a little boy and I thought, "So that's why she likes him." Did he touch it because he was fearful of losing it? It's as if I'm his penis, stiff and erect. L was doing things to keep me away from him. She tried to divert my attention. In the dream L was impossibly beautiful. Her husband is not a good-looking man, but in the dream he was most attractive too. In another dream I was carrying my landlady on my back.

I want to clarify my relationship with men or accept I'll be with women. L's hands and gestures are a kind of veil that keeps me apart from men, a distance that can't be dodged between me and men. I'm an emotional blank without her hands. I can't communicate with you. I connect through touch. Here there's a gulf, a gap. There is a wedge between myself and a male body. L is the wedge. I am alive in L's hands yet I am blocked by her. I drew pictures of L this week and of a man's body. A man's body is a tomb between me and him.

ME: What would happen if you chopped it [the man's body] up into little pieces first?

R: I like picturing doing that. But I feel I'm a little girl playing with food to delay eating. [She plays with idea of chopping and eating a man's body, L's husband's body, Z's body, my body.]

Mother is crying. Father's angry. Hollow empty space inside me.

When I see an attractive man I feel instant, delirious joy. I think of his leaving and turn off and become distant. Can't joy last? To have it is to lose it. Because my mother stayed around I don't feel that way with women. I'm not afraid a woman will go away. L goes away but I'm not afraid of it. But even if a man stays, I feel he is going. I feel he is away. I hated Christmas. Once when I was writing I wrote Christman. The bubble of Christmas. All that death, fragmentation, decay, chaos—then the bubble of Christmas.

ME: [Rena understands the penis in her first dream literally, as a particular man's penis rather than as a symbol of active power. She dissolves the gap between herself and the penis by being the latter. Yet she makes symbolic/experiential use of the phallus in feeling strong and erect. A polarity exists between L's hands and the phallus. Rena is helped and blocked by both. In the dream, contact is made between them (L and her husband touch his penis together), which makes Rena anxious and evokes fascination and flight. A kind of primal couple is constituted who agree that the phallus exists. It is as if the dream is trying to show Rena this. She notes various feelings that interfere with her assimilating phallic power. Again she polarizes male–female realms.

She turns the gap into something physical, a physical barrier: woman's hands, man's body (tomb). Yet with me the gap also remains something immaterial, a distance between us, a lack of physical connection. She tries to fill this in with physical imagery, with things familiar. For the moment

I allow this, but suggest she chop up the body to make it digestible, a movement in incarnation. She likes this as it seems to affirm her on her own terms. In the present context, her father's anger and mother's tears suggest his ability to make her respond. It affirms his power. Indirectly, it suggests a potential increase of Rena's phallic power. She is not so helpless with mother. She not only carries mother like a steadfast camel, but can also frighten and perhaps torture her. Of course, she is each partner and is groping to make space for both sides. Her emptiness or hollowness may yet take on a containing function rather than remain a blank menace.

I might have suggested she enter and stay in the tomb of the man's body rather than chopping it as food. Creative burial would then be the transformation theme. I chose to stay with the eucharistic component, but recognize alternatives. I felt this the more wholesome path without quite knowing why. The session winds down with her staying on the theme of male–female difference at one level or another. She traces various convolutions of the distance element, which she associates with man and expresses as his leaving. In her actual family, man was the alien other, as brute and pariah, as the criminal sent away, the one who finally leaves or is disposed of (a fecal penis, spoiled and spoiling). But what is most important here is that the distance element survives and therapy revives, preserves, and exacerbates it. She tries to equate the gap in our relationship with all other gaps, gaps she can fill in or maintain with bodies. However, the therapy gap cannot be exhausted in this way. She ends the session with a recitation of the vanity of false hopes and litany of destructive states as often happens when we are about to say good-bye. The distance element here is equated with loss, but this is a serious reduction of its meaning.]

SOFT AND HARD

Session C (two weeks later). [Rena enters looking at me in a new way, much more softly and openly. I feel a sensuous twinge in response to her. She seems more solid, less hostile and brittle. She took a week off during which time she visited a nude beach.]

R: I feel a buzzing, spiraling energy with you. In a way this is odd because I feel you have a patient, quiet energy waiting for me. But your comfortable energy spirals are more intense than I imagined. Last week I dreamt of a beautiful man without genitals. I desexualize everything. I want to be sexless and comfortable with you men. Naked men on a beach are not attractive but exciting. They are not comfortable. The other week I dreamt of a knife flying past my head illuminating something. Something black turned to white. I'm afraid of a man killing me. Now I'm not as upset by a penis. I see more softness, more flesh than steel. Men on a beach are vulnerable. Rear ends can't be hard. They're very mortal, just people, human beings, not magnificent in any way. I connect these feelings with you. I feel less hostile and withdrawn.

I had a pleasant day yesterday but wasn't nourished by it. I was cut off, no sense of connection.

I'm trying to get ahead with my work. I've felt imprisoned. I'm opening up more. I yelled at someone for boxing me in. It turned out fine. At first she got mad and defensive, then apologized. My mother took away my anger, my body, pleasureable feelings. She was always on top riding me. I saw two columns in a dream. A sexual image? Decay? I feel more tender movement. I'm evolving in some way into something else. Something is happening. Something is blocked. I'm blind. It's all happening blindly. I feel I'm reaching a place where there's some space, where there can be some movement. Something about joints in a dream. Can they move? Do they hurt? Arthritic? An elevator has problems with its joints? New direction?

ME: [Her week's vacation did her good. Instead of falling apart, she felt and used more space. Did my initial sensuous feeling provoke her session themes or anticipate them? I certainly felt I was responding to something new in her. In session she tries to knit together more heightened and peaceful states. How can sexuality and comfortableness exist in the same universe? She is afraid of being killed by phallic energy yet goes some way toward linking soft and hard. She can come through her anger at work. Her anger was effective rather than making a mess, a gain in assimilating phallic energy, whether her own, her mother's, father's, or mine. She can admit she is changing. Two columns and elevator joints appear with some decay and a sense of impeded movement. Perhaps she can feel and recognize softness because of assimilating phallic power. She is not manic. A sense of difficulty remains but she does not have to entirely spoil her gains at session's end.]

SNAKE HAIR

Session D (one week later). [I do not feel the sensuous feeling of last week or, at least, it is not center stage. Rena seems more self-contained, tightly controlled, and self-occupied. I feel she is trying to hold back and contain anxiety and is actively trying not to allow herself to become dispersed.]

R: I dreamt that a wild looking man with locks of hair like snakes leaned over and kissed me. There is something between us, a table perhaps, so a kiss is as far as we can go.

I got into fights at work and with L. I need to fight with women. I get angry and I see the face in front of me bulging and angry. L's face was a vagina with bulging eyes, mushed and mangled, angry at me, looming. I cringed. My own eyes bulged with anger. I feel a membrane over my head which shuts my eyes, nose, mouth and ears. My body is a big penis, my head the tip. I tilt forward and try to break through this membrane. I try to stick myself up that vagina [L's, colleague's, mother's vagina-face] and disappear. Now the vagina is back down and I see it as mangled, a distortion, bloody. I see my mother on the toilet menstruating. A penis comes out of my forehead and I put it between my mother's legs and do it. I stick my head in and disappear like an ostrich. I don't want to see or hear or know what is going on around me.

ME: Two kinds or uses of penis? Hiding and breaking through? Linking, fusing, breaking apart.

R: Yes, I come out or disappear. I come out on top and disappear in the bottom.

ME: You can't get close enough to the man? You can't get far enough from the women?

R: Men are always too far. You're too cold and far away. I can't get inside you. There's always something between us. I can lose my head with a woman. I can stick my head inside her.

ME: A man's head is crawling with snakes.

R: Your therapy ideas are snakes. My head is filled with snakes too. Snakey head and mangled bottom.

ME: [Does the distance between us drive her to women or is it protective? Both? Perhaps the distance element enables her to fight more safely (she never fought so successfully). It gives her a frame of reference outside the mother realm she is obsessed with. Yet she must retreat. She fights and vanishes. She experiences phallic power in a literal way with her body as a kind of penis. She is afraid of head or snake power. The penis head breaks through the membrane but is terrifying. She tries to get rid of the top–bottom tension by losing her head. At the same time she is trying to make a top–bottom connection. In general, the problem is how to get a decent enough working relationship between above–below, mental and physical consciousness. Various experiments are tried: extreme polarizations, fusions, antagonisms, fragmentary glimpses of coop-eration. She concludes with a clear image of how mental ego and body image are warped and wounded. The snakes refer to mentalized hate, a penis–phallus confusion, a thwarted but still writhing gnostic dimension and a determination to exhibit deformation wherever it is found.]

EXCITEMENT

Session E (one month later). [Rena started body therapy (Rolfing) in addition to seeing me and is reading Wilhelm Reich and Alexander Lowen. She is experimenting with periods of living apart from her husband and teenage children and periods of living with them.]

R: I have a fixed idea that you're mean. Z called and said he missed me. I felt a more open feeling for him than before, then closed up. How much I've reacted against the danger of being overwhelmed after going to bed with him. I ran to L soon after. Rolfing—muscles around clavicle/arms, excruciating pain, cried. When he let up and did a softer massage I had a marvelous orgasmic feeling. I was so relaxed and warmly glowing. Precisely the opposite with Z. I feel battered beyond endurance by him. I have sex and pain totally mixed in my head. Yet I go for these totally painful massages which seem pleasurable afterwards. It's not pain I'm afraid of but the imagining of pain. Is it Z's penis or Light I most fear? The light is most intense around his face. It comes from his face or somewhere inside his head. Sometimes I see it above us high in the room. If I saw Z now I would run away. I feel I'd be damaged, torn apart in intercourse. My mother talked about going blind when I was born. I experience my birth as violent. We were at war even then. We were locked in cosmic struggle in the womb. I came out angry. I see myself as a destroyer. I feel incredible rage at her now. It was her or me. Now I'm the penis trying to get back into mother. All this mayhem going on. I'll be mangled like I mangled her. Mangling and safety and pleasure are all mixed up with the penis. But maybe I blinded her with my light. My Rolfer is attractive. With him it's sexual feeling in agony. I've been getting sexual feelings of one sort or another for different men. My Rolfer doesn't go inside. He stays on the outside of my body. I guess that's safer. He doesn't batter me inside like Z with his penis. He isn't light. With Z it's all imaginary pain. In Rolfing the pain is real.

I spent the weekend back home. When I left I wanted to cry at tearing myself away from my children. I felt like a kid on a schoolbus leaving them. I feel terrible leaving them, but I can't help it. I've no choice. It's something I have to do. I missed L terribly. I was low and feared I'd never stop being depressed. I banged on the couch and felt better. Banging made me more in touch with sexual feelings, then the wish for L vanished. I run to mommy everytime I get involved sexually with a man. I can't get it together. Either I can't have an orgasm or can't have feeling. I have an image of doubling over and hiding. Walking down the street is unpleasant lately. I shut off feelings if someone comes toward me. On the way over here I tried not to and was able to feel a warm connection with people around. I was able to let that happen because I do not feel so undefended. I could let the armor down because I am not so afraid of being totally overwhelmed. I do not have to give myself up when I open. I experience myself and others as more human. Connecting. It scares me to let too much of that happen.

These last few days I've related to everyone with my body. Now I'm closed. I'm defending against opening up.

ME: You felt depressed when you left your kids, then got out of it by anger and sex. Now you feel better, more yourself. But I wonder if something wasn't short-circuited.

R: No. First I felt sexual feelings then depression. Feeling needy debilitates me. I feel terribly scared around attractive men. I run to mother to shut off my sexual feelings for father. L is a wonderful choice as she's afraid of sex. I keep sexuality for my husband under control by fighting with him and leaving. I keep excitement down. I go around with penises inside me these days. Penises everywhere. I'm always on the verge of being stimulated. I'm always aroused and torn to shreds. I'm damaged inside. It's mayhem. The Rolfing pain I experience almost as tenderness. It's all in Lowen and Reich. If I have any feeling for you I turn it into something negative. I feel frustration at your not being aggressive enough to force me to endure feelings for you. This could go on all my life. It's like holding onto a safe job. I feel like an alcoholic personality running away from experiencing feelings. I'm afraid of being out in the open. I can't risk your scorn. I can't risk your seeing all kinds of things wrong with me, all my armor, my blocks in my body. You'll see something is wrong and out of joint and have contempt. You'll see how distorted and ugly I am. My head is elongated. Everything is twisted out of shape. My feelings put me out of shape. You'll look at me and turn me to stone. I am Quasimodo, a real freak, a penis person.

There's a big difference in my life. At work a woman's eye popped out at me but I showed her another way of doing something anyway. I didn't just get mad. I was able to suggest something, an alternative. She looked relieved and thawed out. A big difference from last year. More real, human. I wasn't just fighting monsters. I was living in a situation and working with it. I was staying with it and feeling it out and getting ideas about it. I wasn't stopping. I didn't keep reacting at the same level. I was matter of fact. I felt relief that she wasn't just a mother figure. She wasn't as frightening as last summer.

ME: [Penis and light continue to be linked with and differentiated from each other and dark maternal terrors and pleasures. Head and below the eyes/below the waste feelings compete and fuse with and complement each other. Distinctions are fought for and abandoned. Rena finds an ideology and therapy (Reich, Lowen, Rolfing) that fit her work of discovering and having a body. Her new ideas and therapy complement and conflict with mine. Rena has fought hard to find her body. An issue on the horizon is how body life is to be understood. At present she tends to interpret experience as furthering or defending against excitement. Thus she and I are definitely at odds in evaluating her depressive reaction to leaving her children. She views depression as a defense against excitement and I suspect an element of escapism in her sex and aggression. We each can marshal substantial evidence for our positions. At this point it remains to be seen if and how body feelings will be used as resistance as well as revelation. Often an advance is used as a barrier to further work. One holds onto and fears losing one's gains in face of more subtle demands.

Rena has found a way of feeling good and acting effectively. She moves through mood and image swings to a relatively new and reliable sense of well-being. She is more autonomous. She sustains distance between herself and her identifications (with L, Z, mother, me). She is more able to examine and evaluate what we make her feel without cutting herself off from her experiences. Nevertheless, it now seems as if experiencing is evaluated mainly in terms of excitement, an expansion compared to where she once was, but still a reduction. A costly struggle for a larger frame of reference may be necessary. Perhaps our disagreement is part of a larger circle, a more encompassing perspective. But it does look like a new type of battle is at hand.]

Rena and Schreber:
The Kernel of Psychosis

It is difficult and perhaps unfair to compare Schreber and Rena, but it is a useful exercise. Both are concerned with what it means to be embodied, the difficulties of being one sex or the other, and the role of embodied being in transcendent vision. One difference is that Rena came to know that she was concerned with constituting a viable relationship to body experience. Therapy was a frame of reference that let her consciously use her psychosis to constitute a fuller sense of self. Schreber, too, got to a larger sense of self. However, a basic split between everyday life and his cosmic vision remained.

Rena was born at a time when there are therapists at home in conversing with madness. Schreber's doctors never ceased to view his productions as alien, however fascinating. Schreber learned to circumscribe his vision and keep it neatly packeted. It was his private affair. On a deep level, it united him with humankind and the cosmos. But on the plane of daily living, it made him freakish and he had to guard against its intrusion. In the end, this split did not work. He succumbed and ended his days in an institution.

Rena could allow her "inner life" to pass through another subject. Her thoughts and feelings intermixed with mine for better or worse. A gap remained between us, a distance she often experienced as mean. But in her case, the distance was felt acutely because intimacy was also possible. In time, a more difficult, but psychically sophisticated appreciation grew of just how profoundly intertwined distance and intimacy can be. For her, the cosmic reality and the everyday reality became ever more closely connected. She did not have to watch out for herself in the same sense Schreber did. Her watchfulness took on a different meaning, allied with receptivity to what may happen next.

In part, Schreber's sense of freakishness was centered on his becoming a woman, whereas Rena's involved her masculinity. The image of being a freak was Rena's rather than Schreber's. She could live out her sense of freakishness and be a penis person with me and her friends. In the end, Schreber could be a savior for no one. Each had to seek salvation through becoming the other sex. But Rena could find a cultural and therapeutic ideology that took her imagery metaphorically. Schreber never ceased taking his imagery literally. No one showed him how to do it otherwise. He lived out his femininity with people who did not fully appreciate it and ultimately it could not support him.

For the remainder of this chapter, we will more explicitly take up aspects of Schreber's and Rena's worlds with reference to the six elements of psychosis explored in previous chapters: (1) hallucination; (2) mindlessness; (3) boundaries; (4) hate; (5) epistemology; and (6) reversal. Some redundancy is inevitable, as these areas overlap. Finally, I will underscore some basic principles that underlie interventions with Rena and, where possible, suggest corresponding ones for Schreber.

Hallucination

Both Schreber and Rena were concerned with alternate realities. Schreber more obviously built a personal and cosmic drama between good and evil into a system in which the salvation of humankind was at stake. Rena was caught between blinding Light and visions of bloody horrors. On the physical side, Schreber organized his anxiety in terms of castration and his wish to be a woman. But he also had more global fears of physical disintegration, which eventually spiraled into a sense of actually having been annihilated. The final structure of his psychosis pivoted around his feeling that the universe suffered destruction and rebirth and that he was intimately implicated in perfecting its restoration. He compensated for being physically passive by taking an active role in universal salvation.

Rena's annihilation horrors tended to be organized around her active side. She was terrified of grossly injuring loved ones. Active murderous urges were quickly converted into a sense of being irredeemably lost, falling apart forever, and an overwhelming helplessness. Rage oscillated between a sense of worthlessness and physical disgust. Her sense of being harmful was generally associated with phallic imagery, inferiority with femininity. The womb as a source of power was carried by her mother image just as facets of Schreber's dissociated active side were reflected in his murderous God, although both were androgynous.

An essential theme in the phase of Rena's therapy recounted above involved making a distinction between phallus and penis. Following Lacan, Laplanche and Pontalis[13] view phallus as the more general term used as a symbol of active, transcendent power, in contrast with the simple anatomical penis. They quote Laurin who, as did Freud, linked this distinction to ancient initiation ceremonies.

> In this distant period, the erect phallus symbolized sovereign power, magically or supernaturally transcendent virility as opposed to the purely priapic variety of male power, the hope of resurrection and the force that can bring it about, the luminous principle that brooks neither shadows nor multiplicity and maintains the eternal springs of being. The ithyphallic gods Hermes and Osiris are the incarnation of this essential inspiration.[14]

In the sessions above, Rena struggled with penis–phallus–womb–vagina–anus–face fusions and oppositions. A central area of confusion–distinction was Light–penis and this oneness–duality was contrasted with woman's darkness below. Her male lover's (Z's) head and, particularly, face were associated with light. She herself, her female lover (L), and her mother were associated with the creative values of interior darkness, but also with the ominous pull of a fusional swamp and the safety of inert depression. In her secondary associative networks, Rena's own head was the tip, her body the shaft of a penis. Her female lover's face was, at times, seen as vagina and anus. The softness of buttocks was associated with breast and spread to include the non-erect penis, flesh, and vulnerability. She was torn between coming to appreciate her own female body, being a penis, and assimilating phallic functions.

Her path was to assimilate phallic capacities by being a penis and identifying with phallic aspects of her lovers, mother, and therapist. The paradoxical result was an increased appreciation of her actual female body and what it symbolically expressed. As she experienced her active might, she could also become more open, softer, and more

13. Laplanche and Pontalis, *The Language of Psycho-Analysis*, pp. 312–314; Eigen, "Female Sexual Responsiveness and the Therapist's Feelings, pp. 3–8.
14. C. Laurin, in Laplance and Pontalis, *The Language of Psycho-Analysis*, p. 313.

tolerant of annihilation anxiety. The blinding light gradually became a source of inspiration and energy rather than of abasement and decimation. Increased anal–vaginal softness went with a better ability to see. This growth went on amidst continuing conflicts between the terms involved. As the mind becomes freer, it spontaneously zigzags between all the experiential combinations it throws up. However, the main lines of a basic order gradually emerge.

It could be argued that what I call Rena's need to assimilate phallic power is actually a form of capitulation to an ideology of male dominance, penis envy, or identification with the aggressor (including the phallic mother). We can trace the effects of a controlling mother, an abusive father, and a male-dominated culture in her symptoms. However, these factors do not exhaust the transformation work here. Making the phallus–penis distinction and having an exhilarating sense of her own phallic power (for a time by enacting an image of the actual penis) liberated facets of her own femininity. Her capacity to be active had long been associated with the fear of inflicting injury or being injured. In therapy, she began to allow the free play of activity along cosmic, social, and physical planes. She began the work of distinguishing and interrelating these levels. Like Schreber, she found herself thrown between seemingly irreconcilable worlds of experience, which required a larger perspective on the whole of existence.

Mindlessness

We cannot enumerate here all the ways that Schreber and Rena exhibited "mindlessness," but we will stress some of the main ones. There is the mindlessness of disorganization and the mindlessness that gives rise to new ordering processes. Schreber and Rena often suffered the disorientation related to the advent of surprising and shocking experiences. Both were stunned that what happened to them could happen. A soul cannot know what it means to be mad until it happens. One does not think it can happen to one, and if it does, one cannot believe it would be *this* way.

For example, Carl, in Chapter 2, did not believe what was happening to him was happening. For some time he thought he could control his hallucinatory spin. It took time for him to realize he was caught in something stronger than his own will or, at least, the will he was used to. He began the long journey of discovering another way of relating to what befell him.

Before such a turnabout, one thrashes in terrified attempts to keep above the bombardment and dispersal. One grabs whatever scraps in the turmoil seem useable as a life raft. Schreber and Rena felt they were going under. They felt a tormenting sense of helplessness and had no adequate way of understanding what was happening to them. They grabbed onto and ran away from the hallucinatory images that ripped them apart. Both the fragmentation and the lack of effective orientation toward that fragmentation are aspects of what it means to "lose one's mind."

Freud suggested that Schreber's hallucinatory delusions were part of a reparatory phase of his illness, an attempt to reconstitute objects previously lost. Apparently, it was preceded by a more massive obliteration of self and cosmos, a caesura in which all of life died out and returned in a new guise. One wonders if Schreber ever truly allowed himself to experience and dip into that mindless moment. My impression is that he was always busy. He could not allow himself to slow down enough to dwell in a moment of unknowing. He was always fighting and controlling. Even when he finally let go and luxuriated in his discovery of "spiritual voluptuousness," he surrounded the latter with ideas of mutual control and power. God was still attracted and tied to man's heightened sensibility and vibrating nerves whether He wished to be or not. Schreber still could not stop thinking about his hold on God for a moment, or all (his own mind and mankind's salvation) would be lost. The difference now was that the hold God and Schreber had on one another was more gratifying. Schreber's thinking was devoted to how he could add to God's pleasure, rather than merely avoid catastrophe. As God's

woman, his job was to please God, not simply fear Him. An explicitly ecstatic experience—spiritual voluptuousness—became the center of his obsessional activity.

It is doubtful that Schreber ever allowed himself to feel alone. He
went from hostile fighting and dread of submission to a kind of
sensuous surrender without giving the caesura between these states
its due. He went from one hallucination to another, horrific to
beatific, a kind of mentalized "fight and fuck" syndrome, without
adequately crediting the gap between dominant positions. He acknowledged that there was a gap in his experience when everything
was annihilated and then returned and that this gap was a decisive
turning point in the nature of things and course of salvation. But in
his fully developed vision and way of life, he skirted an encounter
with the gap itself. He occupied himself with the products produced
before, after, and through the gap and so did not allow himself truly
to taste what it means to stop. As fast as possible, the gap in existence
through which things come and go was converted to a saving vagina,
filled with ecstasy, fully occupied, and endlessly busy. Schreber
could not be alone in the mindless moment through which hallucinatory projects surface and disappear. Schreber's psychotheology takes
note of a pivotal moment of unknowing, but it does not occur to him
to dwell with or in it, and in the end, his intuition of the Void is more
catastrophic than creative.

Rena's concern with excitement was akin to Schreber's spiritual
voluptuousness, although with important differences. That she could
have an alive body and live an alive life was a revelation for her. Her
first adult foray into the realm of heightened existence came in the
form of dreaded murderous urges. In time, the intensity of her
aggressive feelings partly transformed into generalized psychosomatic excitement, a sense of vital aliveness and sexual involvement.
She came to view her moods, thoughts, and disposition in terms of
how they furthered or defended against an alive self, and for her, the
latter meant a self absorbed in primal excitement.

For some time, Rena sought to achieve a certain mindlessness in
excitement. In mindless excitement she could throw off the tension
of mental conflicts and feel whole. The excitement she was interested

in veered between images of phallic light and intestinal/womblike darkness. The former was associated with differentiation, the latter with fusion. However, either extreme veered toward mindless obliteration. She was battered and blinded into mindlessness by phallus and light. She melted into sticky, adhesive formlessness through belly and womb. Between the two, her excitement was optimally manageable and enjoyable, yet she was fascinated by the pull of both. In the end, her excitement itself forced her to sustain tension. For, if she fully gave in to the power of light or darkness, she would break or collapse into a mindlessness beyond excitement, a zero point from which she feared she might never return.

In their own ways, Schreber and Rena sought salvation in some type of sensuousness. Both bound themselves to existence by violent visions and sensuous openness. In a broad sense, sex and aggression were nodal points of their self-experience and self-organization. It was almost enough for them to clear a path for body experiencing and find a serviceable way of relating to bodily experience. For Rena, a danger existed that self-maintenance through variable doses of excitement could become subtly addictive and act to block a more profound and flexible development. Unlike Schreber, she lived out her sense of aliveness with sexual partners who expressed the polar gradients of her nature. Schreber finally settled for a more transcendent awareness, his fully developed delusional system. However, it is not clear that Rena's ideology of excitement was any less delusional. Both Rena and Schreber used one form of mindlessness to fend off another. For each, sensuousness, whether in the form of excitement or spiritual voluptuousness, was a genuine achievement. But sensuousness gave each something to hold on to. It fostered a kind of secret controlling possessiveness. The possibility of entry into the mindlessness beyond the erotic–aggressive twinship was largely foreclosed.

The sensuous grace upon which Schreber and Rena alighted indeed brought relief. It was a kind of area of mindless expansion safely circumscribed by alert mental exercise. Given the limitations discussed above, Rena delighted in the discovery that letting go her mind made her more mindful and, circularly, greater clarity allowed her to let go more. For both Schreber and Rena, the ability to tolerate an area of mindless sensuousness was linked with a new clear-mindedness. Both experienced a new conjunction between self-surrender and self-assertion. However, neither journeyed into the vast formless background of experiencing as such. Each specialized in a particular subsection of sensuous experiencing. Both avoided the point where maximum light and darkness intersect. Neither dared to sustain contact with or creatively dip into Rimbaud's vertigo or Keats's silence beyond the reason–sensuousness duality. Yet each intercepted messages from the light–darkness beyond control and funneled them through particular mastery systems in ways that made a difference. Most higher religions depict mediating agencies that funnel messages from one level of being to another. Perhaps in this, Schreber and Rena had an appropriate modesty. They continued to storm heaven, but in tolerable doses and with a style each felt was congenial.

Boundaries

There are always boundary problems in psychosis and, as discussed in Chapter 4, they bring out basic questions concerning the nature of boundaries in human relationships in general. Schreber simultaneously fought and attracted God. He dreaded losing God because of a break in their contact, and he dreaded losing himself in the depths of this contact. Both fusion and separation seemed total and absolute to him. Both tendencies were allied with mutilation and annihilation anxieties. Contact was a war in which threats of attack and ravishment chaotically mingled. Loss of contact resulted in the destruction of the universe. In either case, obliteration or maiming of self and other was at stake. As his psychosis developed, he found a better way of coordinating distance and closeness factors. He found a form of union in which his and God's identities were sustained or, correlatively, a sense of distinction compatible with mutual intermingling.

Schreber's psychosis seemed to work toward a sense of the reciprocal, co-constitutive nature of distinction–union tendencies in human life. At every point in his psychosis, we see these two tendencies at play. As Freud pointed out, Schreber's "You hate me" is, in part, a transformation of "I love you." Schreber's predicament brings out how ambiguous and ambivalent attack can be. God attacked Schreber in order to satisfy a wish for union. His attacks tried to undo the distance between them. At the same time, God's attacks bore witness to an intimacy: He and Schreber must be close to fight so intensely. On the other hand, his attack tried to halt an underlying pull toward union. It separated and cemented, annihilated and created distance. Attack bound God and Schreber together and kept them apart.

Similarly, their sticky drive to undo distance was testimony to how far apart God and Schreber were from one another. In part, God and Schreber were glued to each other as a reaction to too great a distance between them. A tenacious wish for union grew out of this distance. In general, if we look at union, we see distance at work and vice versa. Although the precise function of distance and union factors must be defined in a given context, both are always at work and take their meaning from one another. Whether twisted or wholesome, distinction and union reciprocally constitute one another, and their dual presence is a defining structure of the human self.

Rena oscillated between extremes of intestinal fusion and phallic differentiation (her own images). However, at each extreme, a remnant of its polar twin remained. No amount of fusion could throw off all sense of difference and no amount of differentiation could undo an underlying sense of union. In one form or another, both tendencies played themselves out with reference to one another.

As we have seen, extremes of light and darkness led to loss of mind and self. Light was associated with division, darkness with loss of distinctness. But at the extremes of intensity, both were blinding. When governed by fear–hate, division became divisiveness and could become fragmenting. Similarly, a hostile darkness swallowed up division rather than functioning as background or foil. In general, one of Rena's tasks was to build a tolerance for the swings of polar tendencies and discover how they enhance rather than defeat each other. As with Schreber, boundaries between top–bottom, front–back, male–female, active–passive and self–other were often excessively blurred or rigid. How to value and properly situate whatever agglutination or dissociation of tendencies appeared was a constant challenge.

Rena developed her own version of what Schreber called the "basic language." For example, she spontaneously experimented with many possible combinations of upper–lower aspects of anatomy and male–female genitals. She saw anal, vaginal, and phallic faces, amalgams of and unbridgeable distances between vagina/womb and penis, fusions of womb–belly, anus–phallus, anus–vagina, and the like. What was above appeared below and vice versa. What was in front appeared behind and vice versa. Distinctions blurred or were exaggerated in a kaleidoscopic swirl of body parts and psychic capacities. She was trying to establish a sense of mind outside of and one with body together with a fuller sense of body. In general, she was struggling to move more effectively through her entire psychophysical field. Confusions and dislocations came to play a role in expanding her sense of what subjectivity can be.

In particular, I wish to emphasize the importance of the face as an organizing center of the imaginal flow. In the sessions recounted here, Rena associated the face with hard phallic light, soft buttocks, the penis–vagina combination, and the anus. The light involved the eyes and the interior of the head, the softness included cheeks. Penis, vagina, and anus also involved nose, chin, and mouth.

A question was whether the face could sustain its integrity through such fusions. Of all areas of the anatomy, our face most betokens personal identity. The basic language spoken by Rena and Schreber suggests that when personal identity is gravely threatened, the centering role of the face is usurped by lower parts and functions. The usual boundaries give way or are experimented with in order to express a critical situation. For example, a face may appear as a soiled and soiling anus, indicating a spoiling process. The self may be felt as worthless as garbage or feces, or it may undergo ruthless, hostile attack. Rena fought for her ability to see through the shit that flooded her. For a time, seeing itself became a relentless persecutor. Everything was seen as shit.[15] The perception of flaws outweighed her sense of the valuable. In one fantasy, she placed shit over her eyes like salve. Her thoughts were like bugs. Even shit might be valuable if it slowed her down. She was most concerned with seeing and letting go of seeing, a struggle with light and body darkness.

The lower body areas and functions fused with the face often express an attempt to link top–bottom, mind and body. For example, a face inscribed on a penis or buttocks might be an attempt of consciousness to suffuse the body. Similarly, a penis or an anus inscribed on the face may be an attempt of body to make itself known. In such instances, psychic life is trying to create a freer upward–downward flow of consciousness and energy. What seems like a spoiling process can be an attempt to put mind and body together in whatever ways are possible under the circumstances.[16]

Rena's tendency was to pit eyes and body against each other and then break the tension by dissolving their difference. She would oscillate between antagonism and collapse. Fierce and rigid boundaries dissolved into a sea of jelly, much as Sambo's tigers melted into butter (one of Rena's images). The basic distinction–union structure was abused. At the same time, she was trying to bring together anonymous, collective, and personal elements of experience. It remained to be seen what meaning the basic terms of her experience (such as light, darkness, phallus, penis, womb, intestines, anus, vagina) would assume. It could be hoped that their relationships would continue to evolve. Perhaps they would find ways of distributing

15. For a further discussion of the face as an organizing image for Rena, see Chapter 8 (pp. 348–357). More generally, see Chapters 4 and 5. For examples of face-anus fusion also see Eigen. "Creativity, Instinctual Fantasy and Ideal Images," pp. 317–339, idem, "Dual Union on Undifferentiation, pp. 415–428. Freud noted that an image of the face or head may appear as inscribed on the bottom part of the body, particularly abdomen, penis, and buttocks. "A Mythological Parallel to a Visual Obsession," pp. 337–338. Milner and Meltzer also explore top–bottom confusions. Milner, *On Not Being Able to Paint*, pp. 150–157; Meltzer, *Sexual States of Mind*, pp. 68–69, 72, 118–119.
16. Eigen, "Creativity, Instinctual Fantasy and Ideal Images," pp. 317–339; idem, "Dual Union or Undifferentiation," pp. 415–428.

themselves as distinct and united in increasingly enrichening ways. Would the face emerge as a coherent and moving center of personality that could act as a frame of reference for the free play of disparate impulses? When Rena left therapy, these issues were still very much in the process of opening up. She was no longer in danger, in the old sense. She would never need institutional care again. But there are more subtle ways of being in jeopardy, and some of these are lifelong friends and enemies.

Hate

Freud took the problem of hostility as central for Schreber and suggested how "I love you" can become "You hate me." Schreber's battles with Dr. Flechsig and God were permutations of forbidden erotic urges. Although Freud connected the figures who played major roles in Schreber's psychosis with his family, he was not able to link Schreber's self-hate with his father's inhumanity and madness (the latter's obsessive system of physical purification in the name of health bordered on madness). Freud realized that one could feel bad about oneself because of one's impulses, but in Schreber's case, he did not see how thoroughly self-attack was tied to a mad parent.

As Freud portrayed it, hate is used as a defense against love. It is tied to wounded, frustrated, or forbidden love. It has its own rightful sphere and is part of our basic equipment, which can be exploited for a variety of purposes. In part, Schreber exploited it to keep the other close without losing himself beyond a certain point. As implied in the preceding section, he used hate to modulate closeness–distance relations.

For Schreber, the battle with Dr. Flechsig and God was prepossessing. He was attacked and had to defend himself, but no defense was adequate. Yet he warded off greater powers with a mixture of his own devices, God's stupidity, and the Order of Things. A great struggle ensued, which tested mind and body and ultimately led to a breakthrough to a new dimension of experience. The struggle between God and Schreber was mirrored in a war between mind and body, which, in time, culminated in a kind of mutual appreciation.

In Schreber's symptoms, his hate seemed almost entirely directed against himself. His hate assumed the form of great, attacking powers he must outwit and cajole. The sense that all is fair in war allowed him to justify whatever hostile mental control and physical seduction he could exert vis-à-vis the enemy. His hate was able to move out and in, via his imaginary reworking of objects and impulses. He was able to distribute his hate in such a way that his sense of self and other was maintained.

A loss of self and other was experienced in the move from hate to bliss. Everything died out when hate ebbed before the new era of spiritual voluptuousness began. A caesura existed between hate and love in Schreber's salvific journey (see the sections on the caesura and mindlessness in this chapter). It was not a gap or death that Schreber was able to sustain. Although it was part of a process that allowed him to turn from attack to pleasure, Schreber never transformed it into a true "dark night of mind or sense." It was a moment to be gotten over as quickly as possible and filled in later.

It was because of this haste and inability on Schreber's part that spiritual voluptuousness not simply succeeded hate, but rather was used as a way of handling it. To an extent, voluptuousness blurred hostility. His hate was "blissed out" rather than truly "solved." An archetypal sequence unfolded, but was also partly aborted. A dark night of mind and sense did not culminate in an appreciation of the Other's goodness or profound *personal* communion. God and Schreber remained as unknown to each other as ever, but they erotically enjoyed each other more. They turned a miserable relationship into a pleasurable, even ecstatic one, but in a pre-eminently anonymous, sensuous way.

The gains were profound. Schreber discovered his body and a whole new dimension of possible experience. He partook in a genuine sense of loss, death, and rebirth. He came through an extended phase of tearing himself apart. But he and God did not stare at or even glimpse each other's face. He did not seek God's face and God retained a certain stupidity to the end. God did not seem really to want to know and understand real men. Schreber insisted He was and remained incapable of doing so (according to Schreber, God only understood corpses). In a kind of mad and spiritually transposed way, Schreber (and his God) was a sort of Madame Bovary. He fell apart in the end. His "solution" was not based on a primacy of the face. To be sure, God must remain unknowable. But one relates to and intersects with the Unknowable in a profoundly personal way. One may not be able to look at God's face (any more than Medusa's) and live, but one seeks that face with all one's heart and soul and might. Neither God nor Schreber cared what the other looked like as long as each kept the other going in an erotic heaven.

For a time, mind and body came together. But without the face as a primary center for the cross-weaving of impulses and archetypes, mind and body must split again. Even at Schreber's best, the outline of his basic split could be seen. He and God still battled for mental control, although the power struggle was muted by the pleasure they gave each other. In his remission, splits functioned more like natural divisions, but they were not decisively undercut.

Perhaps Weber's care made a more benign outcome possible. Weber's intelligent and friendly interest in Schreber may have created a setting that allowed the rebirth archetype play. However, Weber did not really understand Schreber. He may have liked, but he did not *know* Schreber, at least not in a profound sense. His care was, in some way, blind. The percipience needed to support the primacy of the face was missing or inadequate. Schreber went from a God filled with blind hate to one filled with blind bliss. The comprehending vision necessary to support the personal element, a face with eyes that see and are seen, was not a sufficient enough part of the holding environment. Schreber contacted feelings that were good enough to dissolve his fear–hate to a point at which sane living was possible. But his underlying fear–hate did not undergo the kind of critical restructuring needed in order to withstand the shocks and losses that lay ahead. Like his God, a certain blindness and stupidity remained in Schreber. He did not really seek to know himself. And in the end his soul slipped through his fingers.

Like Schreber, Rena used hate to keep excitement down. In the sessions described, she was concerned with her use of hostility as a defense against sexual feelings. However, she also worked hard to tolerate seeing just how thoroughly her mother had exploited loving feelings to blur anger. Love and hate were used as defenses against each other. One of Rena's main complaints in these sessions was that she warded herself off. She either experienced too great a distance from herself or collapsed into a swampy morass.

In her psychosis, her head and womb/belly seemed to explode with rage. Her head was shattered by hostile, battering light and her womb became a bloody tomb. She was flooded with murderous feelings, which both obliterated and exploited top–bottom differences. In time, the tide of terrifying imagery released by an explosion of hate was worked over into a more firm and flexible sense of distinction–union across a number of dimensions: top–bottom, front–back, self–other, personal–anonymous, mystical–everyday, and so on.

Her rage had a cleansing effect. It made her feel more powerful and freer. This was possible insofar as it became part of a relationship that could situate it. Her rage at me for my "cold distance" broke through her "good girl" persona. She wanted me to be as terrified as she of being "bad." My preserving my own space gave her permission to have space, too. Her head became a place through which light could come and go; her womb a place to experience fertile darkness. In part, her breakdowns occurred because she did not have room for herself. Insofar as therapy functioned as a larger and sustaining frame of reference, conflictual feelings could make contact in ways that amplified rather than simply tore at each other.

As with Schreber, the advent of good feelings played a double role. Most importantly, it expressed and added to her sense of the basic goodness of existence. For her excitement went along with a profound well-being. But years of "good enough" feeling preceded her breakdowns. Her psychosis involved fragmenting murderous urges and imagery that for years had been handled by drugs, supportive therapy, and everyday life. Apparently, good feeling was not good enough. It was only after her murderousness found a home in her body that the good feelings her body gave her could be properly valued. The affirmation inherent in her good feelings became more believable and effective after positive elements of her hate found room in her life. In Rena's case, this did and could not happen without the kind of therapy that valued and understood both the power and weakness of hate. Without the alternate frame provided by therapy, her murderous urges would have been destructive and unmanageable. In a sense, she was right to dull her hostility until a setting that might meet it appeared. She had the good sense to survive and protect others from herself until help was possible. And if deeper help did not come, episodic institutionalization was a "small enough price to pay" to go on.

As we have seen, even with therapy there was still a question as to how far Rena would let herself go. In her sessions, she worked toward greater tolerance of light–dark, head–womb and front–back experiences associated with fear–hate. However, she may have overestimated the power of excitement to genuinely cure. This might be a phase-appropriate excess that later development would correct. But we leave her at a point where excitement is equated with goodness in a somewhat naive way. Fairbairn has suggested ways the ego can split itself in using excitement defensively.[17] In Session E, Rena used excitement as a defense against separation and loss. She rationalized this by the fact that in her life depression often masked excitement.

Rena's situation was more complex than she wanted to admit. Her leaving her children provoked self-hate, which was overwhelmed by excitement with her new-found sexuality and assertion. Hidden hate went along with hidden mental control. If previously she had used hostility to dampen excitement, now she used excitement to blur hostility. In leaving her children, she enacted a drama that wounded her children and herself. To a certain extent, separation was employed in a hostile way. She would soon admit to feeling a certain malicious triumph at the pain she caused them and herself. For her,

---

17. Fairbairn, *An Object Relations Theory of the Personality*, pp. 111–117, 121–125, 170–179.

separation was a safer weapon than aggression with which to re-enact the secret pain of her childhood. She was now the parent who could inflict injury with impunity, yet also the child who could separate. Her children also played dual mother–child roles, the mother who lets go, the child who was hurt. It might well be that as Rena gradually became more at home with aggressive/assertive feelings, she would not have to stay away and her sense of excitement would be less easily threatened. Yet she was doubtless right that her leaving was a maturational step. Her joyful and hostile excitement was an affirmation of her vital self, her will to be.

Epistemology and Reversal

In this discussion, epistemological and ontological concerns are inter-woven. Both Schreber and Rena were forced to recreate their worlds, themselves, and their ability to know and relate to anything. Or, better, they were witness to and part of a process that broke self and world down and built them up. Sensations, thoughts, feelings, and images seemed to fall apart and come together in startling ways. Schreber and Rena were enthralled by breakdown. Ostensibly, each would have been happy never to have known such horror, but each also felt she or he had been let in on a secret, a vision of Truth. The experience of madness was precious. It sought to expose rottenness and find a surer footing. At the same time, it demanded that all the subject's real energies stay fixed in the task of reconstruction.

With Schreber, reconstruction took the form of a fixed vision, a delusional system that, in the long run, was unequal to life's tasks. For Rena, reconstruction remained a relatively open task associated with an ideology of personal growth. A major difference between Schreber's and Rena's paths was that Schreber's vision did not allow for falling apart as an ongoing condition of change. He and the world fell apart, died, and came together. His mission was to help human-kind participate in this rebirth. However, rebirth was taken as a final state, an achievement that, in principle, could and must be absolute.

In therapy, Rena learned that falling apart was a constant part of growth processes. The life of the self thrives on falling apart over and over again. Rena took falling apart as a necessary part of her path and not something to be transcended, bypassed, or overcome once and for all.

To be sure, Rena tended to organize herself around an idea of the primacy of excitement. But her ideology of excitement had built into it the notion that she would explode, die, fragment, and lose herself repeatedly, either as a defense against or a result of the valued state. For Rena going to pieces became one pole of growth. Even if the quality of her death–rebirth experiences remained skewed by an ideology of excitement, she would have made decisive gains in plasticity and firmness.

We have noted how phallic light and dark womb emerged as basic organizing reference points as Rena's self and world repeatedly broke down and reconstituted. Rena was broken down by and reborn through principles of light and darkness. Yet aspects of each were short-circuited. I wish to emphasize here Rena's possible avoidance of a particular form of darkness.

In session E, I called attention to her use of phallic separation to ward off depression associated with leaving her womb-home. For Rena, leaving home was associated with phallic light, excitement, and growth. To stay at home made her feel entombed and stagnant. She was looking for a frame of reference outside of home that might make home life bearable. However, it soon appeared that phallic excitement was used partly as a manic defense to deny depressive feelings associated with the separation that she needed in order to find herself. In order to fight the pull of the womb, she wished to convert everything into Light.

Of particular interest is the turn she gave the Demeter–Persephone scenario. She, the mother as child in the grip of developmental needs, initiated separation by her movement toward phallic light. In the classical myth, Persephone, the daughter, initiated separation (via a masculine element) by a journey through darkness. My patient tried to transcend depression by her new sense of adventure, whereas Demeter was plunged into depression by her daughter's new underworld life. Both versions move toward a deeper self-world order, each a corrective of the other. Yet my impression was that Rena fled toward and overused light and balked at undergoing a more thorough immersion in the womb journey. This is understandable, given her desire to escape a lifelong underlying depressive undertow associated with a controlling mother and husband. However, her wish to overcome her stultification raised the danger of rejecting the depressive phase of creativity and growth. Even falling apart became a manic, triumphant activity, part of an idealized version of progress rather than the burial and gestation it sooner or later must become allied with.[18]

One result of her growing one-sidedness was the melding of the light principle with personal and, especially, sexual excitement. Rena's tendency to fuse light with sexuality expressed and led to a better spirit–flesh or mind–body interweaving. However, it greatly expanded the meaning of sexuality at light's expense. Her lopsided exploitation of light had the paradoxical effect of reducing the full scope of the dimension light represents. In the end, only light associated with personal excitement strongly tied to sexuality was important to her. The light became a partial darkness, a movement at once releasing and restricting. She once more was stuck in the darkness she had tried to get out of, this time in a lighter way, with more pleasure and verve. Her contact with light allowed her to return to the underworld with new passion and with a greater ability to use the materials she was mired in.

Rena's precocious jump toward light grew out of a need to establish herself beyond the controlling mother–abused/abusive father couple. In general, the Demeter–Persephone mythos functions to aid evolution of the primal scene. In Rena's case, an internal couple modeled on her parents' relationship tied up and distorted her emotional life. Male and female elements were antagonistic and uncommunicative. Like a child caught between impossible parents, she tried

18. For an excellent account of the depressive feelings associated with burial imagery and the function of gestation, see Ehrenzweig, *The Hidden Order of Art*, pp. 212–227.

to right things. This was not possible on a realistic level. In a disintegrative and murderous spin, her psyche began bringing up images of a potentially deeper self-world order. Phallic light and dark womb provided materials with which to work out a better internal male–female relationship. Her attempts to do this were held together by the therapy relationship. Therapy gave her a setting that could allow her psyche to work things out.

Rena would periodically lose her I-feeling in surges of light or darkness. This could be pleasant and uplifting or terrifying. The light shattered her I into meaningless or menacing debris, but also acted as a medium of rebirth. Darkness was more often repaired to for comfort, but the latter also could be obliterating. She associated light with coming out into the open and darkness with remaining hidden. If she hid from the light, she felt stale and her I-feeling would die out. At the same time, her I could not sustain too much light. It was a matter of carving out areas in which personal feeling could be supported in the encounter with anonymity. One realizes how anonymous even I-feeling is at the same time one discovers how thoroughly anonymous and personal aspects of experience feed and challenge each other.

For Rena, the light felt both personal and impersonal. She discovered an I in the light and light in the I and a not-I in both. She was more vague about darkness. The latter remained the maternal home for better and worse, but she held back from turning it into a place of genuine search. She fulfilled more of her journey as Demeter (a child Demeter) than Persephone. Nevertheless, one ought not equate Rena's light with consciousness and darkness with the unconscious. Such an equation would be too easy. For the light, too, worked un- or semi-consciously, and the darkness had its style of consciousness. The surface of the earth on which Rena's Demeter walked was itself a kind of underground. Light intensified experiencing, but not necessarily clarity of consciousness. Neither Jahveh–Jesus nor Brahma–Vishnu–Shiva nor Zeus can be accused of transparent clarity. Opacity is at the very heart of their existence or, at least, is one pole of being. Light reveals obscurity and hiddenness as a permanent fact and principle, a condition of its own possibility. Light itself thrives on its own opacity.

The distinction Neumann made between "solar" and "phallic" masculinity is thus too simple, however useful.[19] He distinguished a higher principle of consciousness associated with light, head, and vision from a lower chthonic activity and attachment. He virtually equated "phallus" with "penis" and tied both to the realm of the mother and the instinctual unconscious. This tends to miss the differentiating role of phallus as a symbol that links spiritual and instinctual levels. The literal penis may be mother-addicted but the phallus, as active principle, cuts through the usual male–female stereotypes. Similarly, the work of solar light as a symbolic principle of growth may be as opaque to itself as the work of darkness. Solar consciousness, in Neumann's sense, was not constituted in Rena's case, yet dynamics of light were crucial.

Schwartz-Salant spoke of imaginal consciousness linked with body feelings as the medium of the Demeter–Persephone journey.[20] A vision and light touched by, immersed in, and somehow even a part of darkness was suggested as intrinsic to the feminine side of separation–individuation. Although Rena used phallic light to try to take her away from the darkness, it finally brought her deeper into it. She became Persephone in spite of herself. For even her defensive use of excitement took her closer to establishing healthier inner parents and her own inner mate, the phallic principle as the maturing Other deep within her psychic womb.

Schreber, unlike Rena, did not suffer an apparent loss of I-feeling. He fought against it. But hints of such a loss are seen in his belief system. He experienced a gap or caesura in the nature and course of things and believed he and the world died and returned transformed. His intense intellectual efforts warded off more immediate experiencing of the loss and return of self-feeling, but such waning–waxing achieved expression in his hallucinatory delusions. One can read the

19. Neumann, *The Origin and History of Consciousness*, pp. 92, 109.
20. Schwartz-Salant, *Narcissism and Character Transformation*, pp. 113–132.

twists and turns of his visionary thinking as barometric indicators of
the state of self: self-tightening and thrashing in face of threatened
crumbling, then expanding from a safe-enough sense of constriction.
The basic overall movement of Schreber's psychosis went from
angry self-defense (accusing stance, sense of persecution, dread of
and rage at pain, injury, annihilation), through successive phases of
self-constriction to a point of safety (intense concentration of self and
nothingness), to an expansive celebration of the spiritual body. Yet
even in nothingness, Schreber's sense of bi-polarity never completely
left him. His dramas always involved self and other, whether as
enemies, partners in death–rebirth, or lovers. The sign of relationship
varied (+, −, 0), but for Schreber, the sense of duality was constant.
Self and Other died out and returned together or not at all.

Schreber and world broke apart, vanished, and returned through
an array of personal and anonymous materials. Schreber's self-feeling
was supported by anonymous spiritual voluptuousness. Sensuous
beatitude vibrated from the heart of I-feeling, yet remained Other.
God remained stupid and incomprehending at the height of bliss.
The Other, if not menacing, was somehow blank, perhaps benignly
vampirish, a dumb brute or an animal capable of ecstasy. Even while
seemingly involved in free, mutual enhancement, Schreber's self and
other were mutely parasitic. Everything depended on performing
their erotic act correctly. If they faltered, the whole edifice of salvation would tumble. A great cosmic collapse was always imminent.
God and Schreber's lovemaking was intensely phobic. The anonymous capability of the body for pleasure was turned to good stead by
an act of grace, by luck, and could be lost as instantaneously as it
appeared. God Himself seemed to blunder on the happy use of His
equipment and resources. At any moment, Schreber and God might
lose the wavelength that worked best for them as partners and once
more be at the mercy of the capacities that could make or break them.

Both Schreber's and Rena's worlds of experience were subject to
reversal. Reversal characterized the overall course of Schreber's psychosis, as well as Rena's moment-to-moment oscillations. His hate
relationship to Dr. Flechsig and God gave way to erotic bliss, although currents of mutual mistrust and control remained. His

achievement of visionary bliss and realistic prudence gave way once more to mental disintegration and actual death. For years, he was able to achieve some type of integration by means of a messianic identification. His script partly paralleled the great reversals of religion. In the West, sin is met by God becoming man, suffering as man, dying and being resurrected. Reversal thrives in the oneness–twoness of God–man, mortality–immortality, death–resurrection, innocence–evil, sin–grace, and so on. The stage is set for reversal by the act of birth. The interaction of two sexes is a condition of our beings, and our mind forever swings back and forth between them. Our mind swings back and forth between different worlds of experience from infancy on, and psychosis is one vehicle for bringing home the gamble inherent in multidimensionality.

As we have seen, Rena and Schreber were concerned with working out relationships between top–bottom, front–back, activity–passivity, mind–body or spirit–flesh, male–female, personal being–anonymous functioning, might–weakness, and so on. Co-constitutive terms of the distinction–union structure collapsed into fusions, broke apart antagonistically, and underwent various dissociations and mixtures. Double and triple reversals were used defensively and/or as part of a larger reshuffling of experiential possibilities. Self and world dissolved and reformed in myriad ways.

In psychosis, it often seems that reversals speed up in an attempt to throw off or dissolve tenacious character rigidities. The subject is so thoroughly dominated by profound dissociations that nothing short of a catastrophic overturning of the whole edifice will seem to do. This often becomes part of a vicious circle, in which reversals and character rigidities alternate and compete. Nevertheless, a perspective large enough to situate one's stiffness and swings may emerge. The subject may catch on that growth requires barriers and malleability. In contrast, Schreber attempted to subvert a potentially open-ended breakthrough into a finality, a last word.

Whether one wills it or not, the work of reversal continues. The origin and momentum of our mental processes seem to depend on it. Either one works with this constitutive capacity or is dragged along by it, although even a cooperative attitude cannot outwit or outflank the difficulties. However, with luck, one may learn some tolerance for letting one's problems speak. But even those who tap into this speaking are far from immune to suicide and madness. One must also be able to bear to listen. And for this, there are no formulas. The whole psychotherapeutic enterprise is concerned with finding ways of hearing and working with the speaking that never stops.

Interventions and the Distinction–Union Structure

A basic principle that underlay my interventions with Rena (and would have with Schreber) is to "feel out" what is happening with the distinction–union structure at any moment. My assumption is that a sense of union and distinction pervades all mental action in one or another form and any psychic production can be situated in terms of it.[21]

For example, the amalgam of polarities in Rena's quasi-hallucinatory imagery could be viewed as a regression to a more "undifferentiated" phase of development or a failure to sustain spontaneous distinctions. In fact, both tendencies were at work. The blend or kaleidoscopic hodgepodge of light–dark, front–back, top–bottom, phallus–penis–womb–anus–vagina, and the like, seemed, at first, to be a veritable outpouring of confusion. Everything was mixed up with everything else. Boundaries were everywhere collapsing. Yet persistent themes surfaced and a self–other–world order based on elemental distinctions gradually emerged. This temporary dissolu-

---

21. Eigen, "On the Significance of the Face," pp. 427–441; idem, "Instinctual Fantasy and Ideal Images, pp. 119–137; idem, "Expression and Meaning," pp. 291–312; idem, "The Area of Faith in Winnicott, Lacan and Bion," pp. 413–433; idem, "Guntrip's Analysis with Winnicott," pp. 103–117; idem, "Reflections on Eating and Breathing as Models of Mental Functions," pp. 177–180; idem, "Creativity, Instinctual Fantasy and Ideal Images," pp. 317–339; idem, "A Note on the Structure of Freud's Theory of Creativity," pp. 41–46; idem, "Dual Union or Undifferentiation," pp. 415–420.

tion of distinctions was most useful while genuine distinctions were striving to be born and evolve.

On the one hand, my interventions stressed distinctions inherent in various swirls of imagery. At various points I might say, "You have light and darkness all mixed up" or "You have phallus and penis confused" or "Aren't you speaking of womb and anus as if they were the same?" or "Are vagina and anus no different at all?" Such remarks are often less important than their intention, which is to note and perhaps even install a barrier against the perverse re-working and collapse of valid distinctions. The message conveyed is that there *is* an ordering process at work, which at present is being ignored or stupefied. It is a call and perhaps a goad or challenge to psychic perception. I do not think the restructuring of hallucinatory messages is possible without a sense or atmosphere of challenge.

On the other hand, hallucinatory activity can be used as a defense against a deeper mindless moment. Rena's restless rotation of imagery kept her confused, but alive. For a long time, her entire waking existence was a kind of chronic insomnia, a nervous activity that mimicked consciousness, a kind of frantic mental control that kept her from losing herself. She could not relax. Her psychosis took the image-filled form it did precisely because she was so afraid of losing her mind. In a sense, hallucinatory agitation was a madness that defended against a more profound madness, one loss that warded off another. In fact, she never lived more intensely than when she was caught in a hallucinatory spin. It was something rather than nothing, a leap or fall into another level of existence. The very act of hallucinating made her stand out from life. Thus, interventions might emphasize the confusional, evasive, or differentiating aspects of hallucinatory activity.

The fear of and need for mindlessness might be expressed in such remarks as "You seemed to sink into nowhere for moments, then got out of it with a rich display of imagery" or "Where were you when you let yourself stop speaking? Perhaps you weren't anywhere at all." Here the aim is to begin building a tolerance for blankness and lack of distinctions. The moment's rest between surges of mental content might come to be valued as an opening in Being. In this regard, the therapist's silence may be a source of frustration, but also a model of courage in the face of chaos, noise, and subterfuge. One learns the value of waiting and identifying with the dark, blank horizon that encompasses and subtends all psychic figures.

Boundaries between polarities slide and harden. In Schreber's case, love and hate turned into one another, yet oppositions solidified. Schreber was in a battle for his masculinity and life against hostile powers. He was in a world governed by malevolent intentions. He contracted himself to an accusing stance in which he could apprehend and ward off encroachment. All his powers were bent on spotting the approach of the enemy so he would not be caught off guard. It seemed that he congealed to a constricted mode of vigilance that would go on forever. It appeared that hallucinatory activity was caught in an overly differentiating swing. Yet within this magnification of the distinction between self and other were basic mix-ups.

A therapist might repeatedly have said, "You have God and the devil mixed up." "You can't tell the difference between God and the devil." Such an intervention does not challenge hallucination with the facts of reality, which would be fruitless and even damaging. It elicits curiosity and interest by touching the depths of psychic confusion in their own terms. It begins to work toward a reordering of psychic processes from the bottom up, rather than impose an order from the top down. It does not inculcate a split between controlling and disordered aspects of the ego or self and drives, but rather seeks to generate a response in which all psychic levels participate in an integral way.

Similarly, the therapist might have hoped to capitalize on Schreber's sense that all has died and reformed. He might have said, "You are wrong in thinking that dying and reforming is only a thing of the past and future." "How are we dying out and returning now? And now? And now?" Schreber, at least, showed he had the capacity to die out and return. He would need help in sustaining and interacting with that capacity. He was not in any working dialogue with the capacities that led to the events he envisioned. But he was open enough to allow a certain unfolding of an elemental process, whereby war turned into a kind of heaven. Not every madman, paranoid or not, could permit such a reversal in so rich a way.

Schreber did not come to grips with the apprehension that he had nothing to do with his return from death. He kept on thinking it was up to him to keep himself in life by his erotic and mental exertions. He had lost control without grasping its implications. One might have said, "Where were you when you died?" "The main thing you disliked about dying was you had nothing to do with coming back." "You returned without knowing it. And that's something you can't stand to know." Such remarks appear rationalistic, but they give paradoxical credence to the power and futility of knowledge. They are clear, yet cryptic and koan-like enough to double bind the patient into thinking about what enabled him not to be there and return without his doing anything. I am reminded of the Zen story in which the village thief is punished by being harmlessly hung from a tree while everything he might wish for is brought to him in abundance. One designs remarks to interest the patient's dazzling mind in the hope it will explode into mindlessness—without loss of awareness.

The paradoxical result aimed at is seemingly impossible because the patient cannot rest. Cessation of mental activity is more a drop into oblivion or inertia than quietude. The background screen of psychic life is filled with "nameless dread," a kind of boundless horror. In Rena's and Schreber's cases, specific images/objects were used as targets to give a sense of coherence to what otherwise threatened to be an electrifying and shapeless sense of annihilation. It is as if undulating waves of terror–rage congealed into specific areas of relatively stable density. Rena's and Schreber's thinking about their psychic productions was tainted by the more formless horror and hate they crystallized out of.

In Rena's case, the problem was joined by the distinction-yet-interchangeability of the face–womb polarity. She seemed to be caught between two kinds of abortive containers. She needed the womb as a source of safety, yet felt anything but safe in it. It was a suffocating tomb and holder of fusional terrors. She needed the face for stimulation, but could not bear the light necessary to see it.

However, the face is not simply a stimulus, but rather a potential container of multiple desires. The womb is not simply placid or binding, but rather a potential place of adventure. Rena's task was to participate in creating a face–womb relationship capable of sustaining the diverse tensions, ambiguities, and shifts of tone and perspective inherent in multidimensionality.

Admittedly, words alone cannot do this. A crucial factor is the ability of the therapeutic situation to act as a double (multiple) and open-ended container (containerless container) in which the analyst comes to be used and related to as both face and womb. In the most difficult cases, a condition for this is the analyst's capacity to move back and forth between more personal and anonymous experiences, to function as both a prescient and a dark presence, to create an atmosphere that allows the patient to feel that in psychic life almost anything is possible, and at the same time that a sense of limits deepens and sharpens the search.

The analyst is at once a speaking, moving, seeing figure and a representative of the quiet and quasi-motionless background integral to the play of sight and sound. Ideally, he is at home in silence and the active word or gesture that silence needs in order to be fertile. What he says must be alive, yet ready for the attacks and admiration aliveness courts. I might say to Rena, "How can your face survive my womb?" "How can your womb survive my face?" "How can my face survive your womb?" "How can my womb survive your face?" "How can your face survive your mother's womb?" "Did your mother have a face?" "How did your face and womb survive it?" "How many faces?" "How many wombs?" And so on. Words count and so does the silence they create, cut through, and grow out of.

With a more blank, stupefied patient, such questions or remarks seem to fall on deaf ears. It is for good reason that autistic children were often misdiagnosed as deaf (a mistake that must be made less often today). It is as if hearing would precipitate the most ghastly pain. The therapist is caught in the bind of having to say, "I know what pain my speaking must cause you, but I see you are no more

comfortable with my silence." The patient cannot stand the therapist's presence or absence. The deafness is quite real, yet it permits a
kind of hearing as if on the other side of a wall, a protective barrier or
filter that makes a type of listening possible. One patient who gradually left the world of the deaf for the hearing remarked, "Your words
were drops of warm water falling on ice. Each drop made me scream.
Words are knives. I'm so tender. I felt you knew that somehow
though you continued to speak. I heard the listening in your words
at the same time they brushed me aside."

This person's speech, even in the early phases of therapy when it
was more chaotic and abrasive, spontaneously (or automatically)
made its way via disjunctive–conjunctive tendencies. Figures were
brought together and held apart (warmth–ice, tender–knives, listening–brush aside). This dual movement was reflected in the most
fusional and fragmented moments. My own speaking acknowledged
the double current of all speaking. My remarks expressed dualities.
Perhaps this is part of the broader background of the adage that
psychoanalytic interpretation is concerned with conflict.

Tendencies to link together and hold apart permeate our psychic
field with variable antagonisms and complementarities. Whatever
level or quality of self we touch, the distinction–union structure is
there. And whatever we touch we touch through this structure.
Therapeutic remarks are rooted in this foundation, whether willfully
or not. The therapist is often called upon to witness the massive
mutilation and impoverishment of our most basic feelings and capacities and participate in the (re)constitution of an injured soul from the
ground up. He is privileged and challenged to face the requirements
of a self that may seem beyond repair. The therapist's own sense of
distinction–union vis-à-vis the patient in his care will likely be a
crucial ingredient in the brew both partners drink or refuse.

The sense of self and distinction–union grow and die together.
The question in therapy is how and with what quality they do so, at
any moment and in the long run. The focus may be on the self's
relationship to anonymous capacities that constitute and permeate it
or to its intertwining with a personal–impersonal other. Patients are

radically threatened, baffled, and confused by how near and far they feel to themselves and others. This distance–closeness is not something that is "curable." It is an elemental given, our raw material, a condition of our beings. Therapy provides a new distance–closeness field in which these terms begin to redefine and spontaneously reorder themselves. It is one of the miracles of life that such fixed and inescapable terms can give rise to limitless mystery.

CHAPTER EIGHT

The Psychotic Self

PSYCHOSIS IS A FACT of human life, one that humankind is never far from experiencing on a personal or a grand scale. Today, madness is frequently used as an image to depict human destructiveness. We call the brinksmanship between nations armed with nuclear weapons mad. We feel that most outbreaks of violence by individuals and nations are somehow insane, even when they may be motivated by real injustices. We can point to some leaders who appear more obviously mad than others, but we can also see through some who wear a mask of sanity. Our daily newspapers are filled with references to events as "demonic," "evil," and "mad" when machinations of power and need grotesquely violate one's sense of limits. Our consciousness seems to have evolved to the point where we can sense and, at least implicitly, trace the thread of madness throughout our social, cultural, and political fabric.

Somewhat like our newspapers, although often more imaginatively and penetratingly, our nightly dreams broadcast the mad news of the day. They mirror our mad selves and search for antidotes. Often they seek to call attention to and deal with what horrifies us. Or they simply try to release the tension of difficult or impossible situations, chronic wounds, and characterological deficiencies. In many ways, dreams and reality converge and comment one on the other. In optimal instances, they take each other forward.

Here we are mainly concerned with images of madness. We can trace aspects of a mad self in dreams as we can radioactive elements in the body. Some poetic license must be granted. Even the locution *aspects of the self* is a dramatic substitute for more or less cohesively organized attitudes, dispositions, capacities, functions, processes, and structures. Yet something would be lost if we could not speak of a mad self or aspects of the self. Expressive language has its own rigor and claims. It must be judged as to whether or not our sense of psychic reality is enriched or taken forward.

Not all the patients in this chapter were diagnosably psychotic. One does not have to be technically psychotic to have some psychotic traits. The failure to test reality and uphold proper boundaries between self and other is more widespread than usually acknowledged. Clinical work with psychotic patients and psychotic elements of personality can alert us to what must be faced in the broader social–political arena.

The Corrupt Body Self

In previous chapters (Chapters 2, 3, 4, and 6) I recounted aspects of Carl's breakdown, his hallucinatory spin, and the reconstitution of his sense of self. Here I want to recount Carl's encounter with a particular dream figure as he was getting better. This dream figure mirrored an aspect of Carl's madness and paved the way for a more wholesome relationship with his body.

Carl dreamt that he saw a hideously fat man in a bar or restaurant. The man was eating maniacally. He threw his head back and closed his eyes in greedy self-absorption. Carl stared at this man in fascinated horror. He seemed infantile, yet grotesque, as if something had gone very wrong. The man had totally given in to his weakness, yet Carl felt he had great power. The man's skin glistened almost to the point of having an eerie glow.

Carl recalled seeing a cheap statue in Chinatown, "The Happy Buddha," a fat, little, greedy Buddha enjoying his self-indulgence. Carl had been taken aback; he had never thought of Buddha that way. He immediately realized the Buddha was a popular debasement of a deeper truth, much like a plaster of Paris Christ. "Most people simply can't tolerate the Buddha very long," he thought. "They need to make pigs of themselves." In the streets packed with restaurants and hidden vices for tourists and residents, a Buddha who acknowledges and gives in to physical desire naturally becomes a stock souvenir. "Look how gross I am," he seemed to be saying. "If it's OK for me, why not you?"

I did not have to say anything about Carl's use of *they* as a distancing technique. By the time this dream appeared, he was already in the habit of reversing in–out and easily applied what he said about others to himself (or vice versa). He spoke of his fear of letting himself go like the happy Buddha. Since his breakdown he severely castigated himself for sins of the flesh. Before his breakdown, he felt himself lucky when he found a sexual partner and greatly relished his experiences. Now the split between his mental and physical self was apparent and he felt tormenting guilt for "giving in." In a sense, he had gone from unself-conscious enjoyment to hell.

At the same time, he was aware that guilt must not have been absent earlier. Obtaining sexual partners had never been easy. He had oscillated between periods of sexual pleasure and extreme loneliness. He had understood this in terms of his fear of people. He felt he had always had to overcome tremendous inhibitions in order to reach out and persist to the point at which good sex became possible. However, it had never occurred to him to think that guilt was an important factor in his difficulty. As far as he had been concerned, some kind of fear stood in his way. If he could only get rid of fear, all would be fine. Now guilt seemed at least as important as fear. Guilt now sullied his successes, just as fear had inhibited them. He had to look back on his life and begin to read it in terms of guilt as well as fear, and found evidence of both.

I wish here to stay close to Carl's thoughts and feelings about the fat man in his dream. The more I can catch about his vision of the fat man, the more meaningful developmental considerations would be if we discussed them. My principal aim is to delineate the self-structure crystallized through Carl's fat man. As is usually the case with prepossessing dream images, Carl's thoughts ran in opposite directions. On the one hand, he felt that the fat man could not be all bad. Carl struggled to find something positive about him. After all, one could liken the fat man to a big baby. He expressed infantile oral wishes. He greedily affirmed himself. He exuded great power and force, a Buddha baby. If one could assimilate such energy, one might be stronger.

Yet Carl's strongest feeling was that there was something terribly wrong with this man. He had the power and force of a madman. All his power and force were bent on stuffing himself. He was totally blind to all other forms of existence. He reached for nothing except whatever food he could get his hands on. "Wasn't this just like a baby?" Carl reasoned. But babies do not have the expression this man did, at least not under normal circumstances. The word Carl found best to describe the expression he saw was *corrupt*.

Carl could rationalize the corruption he saw as a pure distillation of elemental greed. The fat man indulged in a tendency that marks human nature. It is the underside of Buddha's transcendence, Buddha's shadow, an aspect of the desire–desirelessness duality. But the sense of corruption Carl felt went beyond the oscillation of natural polar tendencies. The rhythm of needing, getting, and becoming satiated had been broken. The time element involved in lack and acquisition was short-circuited. It is not even clear that the fat man truly felt desire. He simply went on stuffing himself with a mad, blind leer. This was all he did or would ever do. His grimace was grotesque and locked in place. The aberrant infinity he seemed caught up in was not one of desire, but rather one in which desire would never again occur.

Carl recalled some other powerful figures in his dreams. In particular, he thought of a Mafia boss who intimidated him in a number of dreams over the years. In one dream, the Mafia boss was going to have thugs kill a flute player in the woods. In another, the boss threatened Carl with sodomy. In most of these dreams, Carl was afraid of being killed and always suffered the terror associated with helplessness. The Mafia boss seemed invulnerable. Nevertheless, the Mafia boss did not always win in the dreams. The flute player, for example, went on playing, and Carl was not always paralyzed.

Carl saw some connection between the fat man and the Mafia boss, that the fat man was the Mafia boss stripped naked. He mused how close Chinatown and Little Italy were to each other in Manhattan, as if this physical proximity represented some psychological truth. We spoke of the terrible father aspect of the Mafia boss and the father-baby duality inherent in the boss–fat man combination. These were clearly related to ways Carl had been cowed during childhood as well as the negative aspects of my personality. They represented his own identification with the real and imaginary tyrants of his life. But, above all, the underlying feeling that had to be faced was the sense of relentless and insurmountable corruption. There was no getting around the encounter with what Carl and I both came to call *the corrupt self*.

Carl's fat man dream gave him a potential advantage, a toe hold in a field of negative power. He came upon the fat man in a bar while walking down a street at night. He first saw the man through a window; then he entered the cafe. Although he was partly mesmerized by the sight, he did not entirely lose his freedom. He was not simply one with the fat man. Carl was able to see and move. If he was the fat man, he was also not him. It was as if the dream offered Carl the chance to see something important, something to take away with him and reflect upon during waking hours. It was letting him in on a secret. No matter that the secret could only be guessed about. What is important for therapy is that the fat man truly engaged and alarmed Carl. Meanings arose from the meeting and affective intensity was stimulated and structured. With help, Carl stayed open to the impact of the figure and let it speak. As a result, his sense of self underwent another shift.

The dream presented the fat man as a revelation. It was a good dream because it preserved a certain distance between Carl and a fascinating, if ghastly, sight of the gorger. Carl was not swallowed up by the fat man. He gazed intently, as if taking in what he saw so as to learn and grow. It is difficult to admit such wholesale despair and corruption in the human soul. One tends to blunt or look away from such degradation. We cannot bear to look long at the horrors of our condition, and we find it especially difficult to deal with the grotesque.

Carl imagined what it would be like to meet the fat man and the Mafia boss. There could be no real talking with either. Neither would be capable of dialogue. The otherness of others would slide off them. Both are utter materialists. The Mafia boss of Carl's dreams was only interested in material power, whether instinctual dominance through sodomy or annihilation of the cultural soul (the gentle but persistent flutist). The fat man knew only food in the most concrete way possible. They are body ego figures with different emphases. They are similar, inasmuch as food = people and people = food: emotional life is reduced to dominance and ingestion. The Mafia boss exercises his practical mentality on people. The fat man is more obviously encapsulated. He has limited his world to what can be put inside him in a quite literal way. The Mafia boss needs other living beings to exercise his nullifying functions. He operates in a larger landscape, the city streets, the countryside. The fat man stays in one spot and does one thing, yet how ultimately freeing it was to see him.

Carl likened his seeing the fat man to the times he felt clear and clean after vomiting. It was as if the dream had puked this figure up and all that it meant. "For so long I felt I was standing in one spot, doing one thing," Carl said. "Years went by that way. I acted like the Mafia boss but deep down I was addicted to such a small part of myself." Carl now saw the Mafia boss and the gorger in people around him without being paranoid about it. Previously, he had felt the need to fight wildly or hide when he sensed compulsive power drive or total greed in the air. Now people seemed more transparent in a positive way. He could increasingly see how potentially good souls became distorted. Perhaps there is a certain finality to corruption. But even psychopathic and perversely addictive characters suggest deeper messages.

For Carl, a new infinity opened in the heart of evil. After seeing the gorger and linking him with the Mafia boss, new body ego figures began to appear. He dreamt of good soldiers, dancers, and musicians. Sustaining his vision of the fat man released good body feelings. The fat man had left no room for the free play of feeling life. I fancied he was a kind of bad container who kept the dancers, soldiers, and musicians trapped inside him, a type of black hole that compressed and annihilated the psychic materials drawn into its force field. By means of the dream, his chronic activity was discovered and unmasked.

Carl began his contact with the fat man with fascinated horror, but as he continued he began to smile. The fat man was grotesquely corrupt, but he was also funny. Something about him tickled Carl and made him feel like laughing. In part, it was doubtless relief at not being swallowed up. Carl felt bigger and healthier upon being able to meet and work with figures like the fat man and the Mafia boss. Yet he also felt something irreducibly funny about the sight of the fat man, which escaped words. He could not say why, but seeing this fat man broadened his sense of humor or, better, made humor more possible. It was as if keeping the fat man a secret from himself had made him heavier and glummer, whereas facing this oddity made him lighter and, as his dreams showed, more able to dance.

I do not pretend to have exhausted the meaning of the fat man for Carl or myself. The fact that I am writing about him so many years after his appearance indicates that for me he is still an alive or suggestive presence. Such images must be taken on their own terms as "eternal states," as well as symbols of developmental syndromes. Carl's smile recognized this. At first I thought I saw the "happy Buddha" in his smile, a smile of corruption identifying with the figure born through him. But I felt something innocent, too, beyond the corrupt figure he confronted. His smile through the horror tacitly acknowledged that there was more to him than his sense of corruption, although certainly not less. It was a smile of enlightenment, a smile of reconciliation and transcendence.

The Corrupt Mental Self

Corrupt body self figures are often caught up in dramas revolving around a delusion of or a wish for omnipotence. Corruption of the mental self hinges more on a sense of omniscience.[1] Omniscience refers to limitless mental power, whereas omnipotence refers to limitless physical power. Colloquial speech distinguishes between the know-it-all and the bully, between brains and brawn. Many fables suggest that the self must face dual tendencies in extreme forms, as expressed by such figures as the Magus–Magician and stupid, fearsome monsters. The Old Testament God condenses omniscience and omnipotence in ways that at times make Him seem like a big baby. Omniscience and omnipotence can be seen, in part, as two aspects of infantile narcissism, one emphasizing mental, the other physical reality. In psychosis, the spread of either can be horrifying, but the work of omniscience is finally more dreadful.

It is difficult to overestimate the role omniscience plays in deadening one's capacity to experience. If one knows what is going to happen ahead of time, one does not have to experience it. The individual scarcely realizes he is inured in omniscience. In effect, he lives from omniscience without knowing it: He may feel ignorant and inferior, yet a certain obliviousness pervades his existence. The details he experiences, which might make a difference, are glossed over. Experience is not static but the omniscience-trapped individual may act as if it were. He knows what fate has allotted. Everything is evaluated in terms of his omniscient frame of reference.

Paradoxically, this sense of omniscience can heighten as well as

1. See also Eigen, "On Omniscience" (in press).

dull experience. For example, one who acts the magician may feel a thrill in mesmerizing others. In such a case, a magus-like character may exploit the ignorance and stupefaction of his audience and victims. He assumes the role of one who knows, a mental magician capable of bending wills or exercising mind over matter. One who is after mental–spiritual power often moves in a highly charged atmosphere in which ineffable forces are invoked.

Omniscience tends to combine with omnipotence in hallucinatory–delusional scenarios. Omnipotence is brutal in its demand for servility. It can distort body and soul, exact obedience, and lead to collapse. Yet omnipotence without guiding omniscience would be dumb. In subtle ways, a gnostic element lends omnipotence its greater force. To be sure, omniscience may be an empty pretension. But an omniscience-inflated subject fills himself with a sense of infinite privilege and foists his personality on others instead of suffering limits in the struggle to know. Exacting privilege through assertion of omniscience seems to be a peculiarly human mode of achieving power. It is a subtle form of madness that is widespread and it takes on arrestingly florid forms in overt psychosis.

Dramas revolving around omniscience play an important role as therapy unfolds. Patients often expect the therapist to possess more (or less) knowledge about the patient and therapy than the therapist actually does. A therapist may be revered for possessing godlike qualities or despised for not being godlike enough. In the latter instance, the patient may assume that the analyst ought to know more. A collusive situation can develop in which the therapist feels guilty at not being better, becomes angry at the patient's demands, affects superior knowledge, or plays dumb. The patient's (or therapist's) tacit wish for and adhesion to omniscience may go undetected, be catered to, or provoke retaliation.

Either the therapist or the patient can abuse his just claim to know more (or less) than the other about what is happening between them. Often enough, the therapy couple resists therapy because each partner fights the other's claim to know or not know more. Each seems to be a know-it-all or a know-nothing to the other. Omniscience opposes omniscience. In such instances, a power struggle

revolves around the issue of who is more omniscient. An omniscient
one invites others to join in the omniscience game. Neither analyst
nor patient can get out of this situation simply by pretending not to
know what he knows. We must enter and wrestle with the capacities
and tensions that constitute us. In this case, we must enter the field of
omniscience and try explore it.

An Omniscient Therapist, the Snake, and the Mouse

Dr. Omnis (as I shall call him) began supervision with me in the
wake of a broken marriage. His world fell apart and he tried to pull
himself together. During this period, a long-standing tendency to
give advice and play parent to his patients intensified. His ability to
tolerate their suffering diminished and he tried to find ways to
exhort, comfort, and help them over their hurdles as quickly as
possible. He acted as if he knew what they should do, and it was his
job to help them do it.

With some patients this seemed to work for a time, but other
patients became more troubled. He became panicky as they became
more disorganized and suicidal. He wisely reentered therapy and
supervision. He was aware that his need to cover up his patients'
wounds was related to his need to blunt his own pain. He hoped to
soothe himself by calming his patients. He tried to hide the realization that he was putting up a front and that his patients were paying
for his falsity.

At the point in his supervision relevant here, we focused on his
omniscience. He acted as if he knew best and expected his knowing
to have magical effects, as if he should be able to say something to
make his patient's problems vanish. He knew this was not possible,
but he could not stop himself. His need for omniscience buttressed
his own shaky self.

Dr. Omnis soon observed that a sense of "knowing better than"
pervaded much of his life. It had been an element in the making and

breaking of his marriage. He and his ex-wife had each been attracted to the other's air of mental superiority. However, this trait did not wear well. The chronic contempt implicit in this attitude made living together impossible. Similarly, knowing better than his superiors had led to self-destructive difficulties in various job settings. In social life, his all-knowing stance severely limited the kinds of people he could tolerate. His hidden omniscience sabotaged his whole life.

Dr. Omnis was able to experience more truly how badly he felt about giving advice when his own life was such a wreck. When he advised his patients, he felt a superior well-being, but he could sense how he subtly made his patients more miserable in order to gain a momentary sense of mastery. As his patients lived out a turmoil similar to his own, he could taste what it felt like to be above the storm. Their dependency allowed his omniscience freer play than it ever had had in ordinary life.

As time went on, he allowed himself to confess his own underlying despair as a person and as a therapist. He had always felt inferior-superior and becoming a therapist seemed to offer a way out. People looked up to him and wider social circles opened. But secretly, he remained cynical and lost. He tried to manipulate his defects by proxy through his patients, but real healing escaped him.

Although the problems Dr. Omnis had required psychotherapy, our supervision meetings were helpful. He gradually became better able to voice what it was like to be in a room with his patients without knowing what to do every moment. Not knowing required him to be more attentive to what he and his patients actually were undergoing from moment to moment. His dread of resourcelessness in face of his own and his patients' situations had contributed to his premature speaking from a position of "seeming to know."[2] The unconscious and conscious omniscience that permeated his life prevented experiential sequences from unfolding. Pretending to know in order to be on top of things kept him sealed off from himself. To

2. The "dread of resourceless surrender in the analytic situation" that Khan writes about applies to therapists as well as patients. Khan, "Dread of Resourceless Surrender in the Analytic Situation," pp. 225–230.

give up this safety and venture forth called for staying close to the genuine impact of his patients and making fuller use of what was evoked.

Dr. Omnis's struggle with his misuse of the sense of omniscience was reflected in his patients' dreams. A male patient dreamt that a playful seal could solve problems a wise old owl could not. A female patient dreamt that a blind woman now could see. Having to know everything had made this person blind, and correlatively, not having to know everything allowed her to see. In the dreams of other patients, such images as eyeglasses, books, or a camera were juxtaposed with images of bike riding, driving a car, walking, or dancing. That is, clearer images of mental and body self were more easily encompassed within a single dream or dream sequence. As Dr. Omnis got below his false front and tried to tolerate his own real experience within sessions, his patients could also begin to struggle with basic polar tensions.

I would like to focus here on one of the dreams of one of Dr. Omnis's patients (we will call her Ms. Ferva). It brings out some of the issues concerning omniscience with special clarity. Ms. Ferva sought help for states of panicky disintegration and depression, which she coped with by superficial social activity. She felt she was running around in circles going nowhere. In therapy, she became more disorganized, and Dr. Omnis feared he would have to hospitalize her. His regimen of support, advice, and pointing out her life patterns seemed to make matters worse. His intolerance of his own and her pain reinforced her desperate escapist maneuvers, which resulted in further fragmentation.

As his persona began to crack and his engagement with psychic reality deepened, his patient could also begin to face the full force of what she was caught in. She showed she was a very sensitive woman, most responsive to his states. The following dream exhibited and amplified the complexity of what he was going through, but it did so in a way that proved germane and authentic to her own sense of self.

Ms. Ferva dreamt that a mouse was trapped or somehow had trapped itself in such a way that it acted as a plug for the water in a pond. When the mouse would get stuck or stick itself in a certain hole, the pond filled with water. When the mouse got out, the water would disappear down the hole as if it were a drain. When the pond was filled, fearsome snakes swam in it. The snakes vanished when the pond was empty. The sequence of mouse getting stuck and the pond filling with water and snakes, followed by the mouse freeing itself and the water and snakes disappearing, occurred repeatedly. It was unclear whether the dream ended with the mouse victorious and free, or with the snakes still threatening.

Ms. Ferva and Dr. Omnis both felt, according to the latter, that the dream reflected Ms. Ferva's dilemma. She was torn apart. A good side fought a bad side. She must find a way of following her constructive, not her destructive, tendencies. Both felt good if the mouse won, bad when the snakes did. They saw the mouse as innocent and the snakes as evil. Dr. Omnis associated the snakes with destructive attacks upon needs and strivings. Ms. Ferva felt some attraction to the snakes' power, but consciously identified more with the mouse. She thought she may have been chased by snakes, perhaps near the dream's end, but this remained vague as she also recalled the mouse's sense of panic and triumph.

A dream like this can be worked with profitably in many ways (e.g., references to birth and sexuality are obvious and useful; similarly, one might tie the scene to early childhood relationships, the therapy relationship, or other aspects of the patient's link with reality). Since we were working with Dr. Omnis's omniscience, I suggested they tune into the mouse's fleeting sense of triumph. This led the therapy couple to an array of childhood stories in which the smaller, weaker, and smarter party turned the tables on the bigger, stronger, more stupid one. The physically tiny baby manipulates surrounding giants: mind over *mater*. The baby disarms the evil mother and seduces the good one. In truth, baby and mother disarm and seduce one another.

That both therapist and patient believed the dream expressed an inner drama was already a good prognostic sign. Yet they felt both justified and uneasy about the overly sure way they had structured the dream. Were the snakes only evil and the mouse only good? Such a stereotypical viewpoint must be taken as a signal that experiencing is short-circuited. The mouse's sense of triumph is too easy and smug. The hungry baby's victory over violent fears is precarious. In Western symbology, snakes *and* mice are viewed as tricky with regard to higher powers. In addition, in many myths, a snake may symbolize the dangers of the unconscious and, at times, a deeper wisdom.[3]

In accord with my experience of a certain naiveté and rigidity in Dr. Omnis's and, by proxy, Ms. Ferva's cognition of psychic reality, I suggested they explore positive aspects of the snake and negative aspects of the mouse, as well. In the dream, snakes are associated with water and so they suggest the more mysterious and uncontrollable unconscious processes. Yet the mouse repeatedly provokes their appearance by acting as a water plug, as if it is bent on mastering its fears. In effect, by siding with the mouse the therapy couple tried to master a deeper emotional reality prematurely, or even wish the unconscious away. The triumphant mouse made water and snakes appear or disappear, in effect placing life's dangers and unconscious forces in its power. The smaller, survival-oriented ego (mouse) wishes to preempt the place of the larger, mysterious self (snakes in water: many = intensity), to the point of doing away with the latter entirely. We may be terrified of the depths of our nature, of what is uncontrollable in life, of death, of the predator, and of creativity. The mouse's gambit is to find a way of making what is ubiquitous vanish.

In part, the terrifying snakes in water symbolize an omniscience far greater than the mouse's cleverness. It is the type of cognition that creates dreams (the "wisdom of the unconscious") in contrast with the more technical type that learns how to manipulate actual physical surfaces. Both forms of knowing are necessary, and, in optimal circumstances, feed each other. They are often in conflict and the subject is caught between them, now allying with one, now the other. The dream's indecisiveness mirrors an ambiguity inherent in oscillating polar tendencies.

Insofar as Dr. Omnis could open himself to the fuller play of

3. Eigen, "On Demonized Aspects of the Self," pp. 99–123; idem, "Comments on Snake Symbolism," pp. 73–79.

possibilities, Ms. Ferva could more readily experience what was snake- and mouse-like about herself along a number of dimensions. For example, she became a mouse to avoid her snake power, which nonetheless tormented her. Primal sources of creativity gave way to survival greed. The partial victory of her smaller ego endangered her psychological environment as a whole. In retaliation, or as part of a dissociative process, the snakes doubtless did become evil. In reality, both mouse and snakes likely possessed creative and destructive elements.

The relevance of Ms. Ferva's dream symbols for our broader cultural scene should be mentioned. With the immense and virtually instantaneously responsive military and economic powers in the hands of today's nations, political machinations are more snake than cat and mouse. Today a mouse (or groups of mice) may assume serpent powers and act for the psychosocial whole, only to be governed by misguided slivers of "omniscience." Wisdom as a cultural ideal seems an archaic relic at this point of time. The mouse swallows the snake and turns its poison into service of a calculus of minute advantages. The pose that we know more than we do at a moment when we are poised on the edge of catastrophe invites mayhem. It is wishful thinking, indeed, that a mouse can make snakes come and go as it pleases. Perhaps we need the experience of vanishing in order to discover anew the process of building ourselves and our world up from nothing. Indeed, we may need the challenge of beginning from a horrific shambles far worse than nothing, a place from which we may at last read objectively and incisively what we are capable of spoiling or undoing.

Omniscience, Invisibility, and Tausk's "Influencing Machine"

Our sense of knowing is an implicit part of all or much of our experience. It is so much part and parcel of experience that we often feel we know when, in fact, we do not. The sense of knowing often becomes a refuge and an anesthetic. In certain cases, it can be abstracted from specific contents: it becomes its own content. The philosopher may turn this mental gesture into a creative act and investigate the knowing of knowing. But in everyday life and psychopathology, empty knowing can substitute for the struggle to know. It is enough to recall the ancient distinction between opinion and knowledge to suggest how ubiquitous and presumptuous the sense of knowing can be.

At the same time, the sense of *unknowing* also pervades our experience. One can distinguish several sorts of unknowing in daily life, scientific discourse, mystical experience, and psychopathology. For example, there is the unknowing of simple ignorance. One does not know many things. However well educated one is, there always are gaps. One may know something about working with psychosis, but not be able to repair an airplane or cardiovascular block. From infancy on, our life is shot through with matrices of knowing and blank spots. Knowing and not knowing are so finely interwoven that together they constitute an essential characteristic of our capacity to experience. We may focus on what we know or do not know or various combinations. We may focus on our knowing–unknowing capacity. At certain moments, we may choose to emphasize the gaps, the blank spots, and unknowing may seem mysterious. The "way of unknowing" can become a method of approach to Divinity or a valued state for its own sake. One lives in and through unknowing and the unknowable as simple, everyday ignorance gives way to the numinous.

It is a paradoxical and essential characteristic of our beings that knowing and unknowing can be imbued with a sense of infinity. Almost any important area of experience can be infinitized. For example, in our dreams the sense of danger can become boundless, as can bliss. The sense of unknowing gives rise to a profound, yet elusive intimation of knowing, whereas knowing can mutely lose itself in a blank expanse. Through consciousness we have intimations of unconscious life. Through gaps and blanks we sense a deeper subject. Ambiguity pervades our double sense of knowing–unknowing. At moments we feel knowing and unknowing fuse in ineffable breathtaking suspense, a thrilling peace that passes, yet nourishes, understanding.

The sense of convergence of knowing and unknowing, together with a sense of infinity, is possible, in part, because experiencing as such is intangible and ineffable. We cannot locate a thought as we do the brain. However much we associate emotions and centers of consciousness with the body or read a soul in a face or a gesture, something invisible remains. This may be summarized in the adage that consciousness sees and hears but cannot be seen or heard, at least the way spatially localizable events can. The basic invisibility of experiencing contributes to a sense of boundlessness that tinges our existence.

Mystical experience and madness offer privileged areas for witnessing the convergence and breaking apart of the sense of knowing and unknowing. Both thrive on the invisibility of experiencing as such. Invisibility can assume contrary valences and function for good or ill. Evil uses invisibility as a mask. It exploits the invisible quality of mental life so as to move naked but unseen in stark daylight. The horrors of certain mass movements would be illustrative, but I will confine myself here to a paradigmatic use of the "influencing machine" delusion, since *influence* is so important a part of learning and menace. As we will see, the influencing machine delusion involves an overwhelming sense of impending evil fed by hidden omniscience that thrives on and malevolently exploits the invisibility of mental life.

In the influencing machine delusion, the psychotic patient feels that his mind is being taken over and influenced by a distant machine.[4] Tausk understood this as a projective expression of a mechanized body self. For Tausk, the machine is a symbolic petrification of the sexually alive body, an attempt to freeze or deanimate the threat of feeling, of life itself. According to the perspective developed

4. Tausk, "On the Origin of the Influencing Machine in Schizophrenia," pp. 519–556. Much of the material on omniscience, invisibility, and the influencing machine in this chapter is drawn from Eigen, "Comments on Snake Symbolism," pp. 73–79; idem, "On Demonized Aspects of the Self," pp. 106–116; idem, "On Omniscience" (in press).

330 THE PSYCHOTIC CORE

here, Tausk's analysis is one-sided in its emphasis on crucial body ego elements. The influencing machine delusion must also be illuminated by the role of mental ego, in particular, the sense of omniscience and the immateriality–invisibility of mental life as such.

From the perspective of omniscience, the permeability and penetrability of the subject by an alien mind is at stake. The "between" is petrified, dissolved, and/or demonized. Thought is taken as an invasive, alien power emanating from a foreign, controlling mind. The body is immobilized and a megalomanic, immaterial dimension of mental power holds sway. Space and physical boundaries become meaningless. Thoughts can instantaneously be everywhere and anywhere. The patient's greatest fears seem to focus not merely on a reduced and mechanized body (the latter is almost comforting), but also on the electrifyingly impalpable threat of invisible mental power as such. A devitalized or mechanized body self and a perverse mental self form parts of a dissociative system lived out in a ruthless proliferation of ways. In the example of the influencing machine, the body self is not strong enough or alive enough to withstand the onslaught of a demonized mind. Such a dissociative structure with its attendant dangers characterizes many phenomena today. It oscillates with "fusional" tendencies, which provide temporary relief but often intensify the predicament: the collapse and heightening of tensions between psychic and social structures viciously spiral.

In humans, the problem of boundaries is problematic in a far more momentous way than is territoriality in animals. The boundlessness involved in our invisible sense of self infinitely magnifies material stakes. Omniscience is rooted in an invisible sense of boundlessness and draws on the intangible to befuddle embodied souls. In omniscience, the structure and resistance of physical reality give way. The mind's immateriality seems to spread through physical existence, more radically than with delusive omnipotence, wherein the world retains a primacy of the physical. In omniscience, physicality collapses in face of mental power. This is not to say that omniscience is unconcerned with physical existence. On the contrary, it seeks to master and triumph over it, to wrest its secret. Its transcendence, however, easily becomes perverse, losing respect for competing powers. Omniscience manipulates omnipotence. Omnipotence becomes an arm of omniscience. Tyrant enslaves tyrant. The psyche is swallowed up by its own intangibility.

Our journey in the sense of the infinite is, ironically, limited not by realistic finitude (which is its raw material), but rather by our discovery of alternate infinities, infinite pretensions. If we are moderately honest, sooner or later we glimpse how thoroughly enmeshed we can be in a sense of omniscience gone wrong. Omniscience is not something that can simply be rooted out of our nature, any more than breathing can. We must learn how to breathe with it, how to follow its transpositions, and how to interact with it in saving ways. We should be as careful of omniscience as we are with any vital capacity that constitutes us, since our gropings may have unanticipated results.

Omniscience and Winnicott's Unintegration

Winnicott's major clinical concern throughout his writings is a hidden madness that spoils human lives. A major symptom of the madness Winnicott addresses is a nagging sense that one is not quite real, that there is something false or empty about one's life, that one is not truly living. Winnicott's work explores in depth the emphatic importance Federn placed on the link between madness and the sense of not being real ("depersonalization").[5]

In certain individuals, madness is obvious and the sense of unreality inescapable. In many others, it works silently; perhaps it is visible only in the gradual erosion of the quality of one's life and the deterioration of the capacity to generate vital and viable meaning. Winnicott describes the possibility of therapy exploring what seems healthy in a patient, but glossing over difficulties that seem intractable, but are central to the most basic sense of self. For example, in

5. Federn, "Some Variations in Ego Feeling," pp. 25–37; see also Chapter 4, pp. 143–147, this volume.

speaking of borderline cases, he cautions against the danger of being
taken in by neurotic defenses, when the core problem is psychotic.
He writes,

> In such cases the psychoanalyst may collude for years with the patient's
> need to be psychoneurotic (as opposed to mad) and to be treated as
> psychoneurotic. The analysis goes well, and everyone is pleased. . . .
> But, in fact, the patient knows that there has been no change in the
> underlying (psychotic) state and that the analyst and the patient have
> succeeded in colluding to bring about a failure.[6]

In order to work with the psychotic dimension, which is crucial to
reconstituting the self at the deepest levels, a setting that allows the
subject to play, to drop into formlessness, and to become unintegrated for periods of time is required. For Winnicott, "play," "formlessness," and "unintegration" are parts of a nexus of related experiences that reinforce and enrich each other. The atmosphere that
permits such phenomena to emerge is in important part evoked by
the quality of the therapist's percipience. Above all, what is necessary is that the subject tastes the sense of creativeness that is the very
essence of true self-feeling. Winnicott writes,

> It is in playing and only in playing that the individual child or adult is
> able to be creative and to use the whole personality, and it is only in being
> creative that the individual discovers the self.

> The person we are trying to help needs a new experiencing in a special-
> ized setting. The experience is one of a non-purposive state, as one might
> say a sort of ticking over of the unintegrated personality. I referred to this
> as formlessness in the case description.[7]

The individual who feels unreal to himself must be helped to learn
how to play. In order for playing to occur, Winnicott tries to create
an attitude and mood in which the individual can relax into a deeper

6. Winnicott, "The Use of an Object and Relating through Identifications," p. 712.
7. Winnicott, "Playing, Creative Activity and the Search for the Self," p. 54; *ibid.*,
p. 55.

intensity, psychically doodle, let happen what may. This does not mean that playing is simply nonpurposive. Psychoanalysis and other disciplines teach us only too well what pain the child seeks to assuage in play. Yet a nonpurposive moment is necessary before the form one needs to work on becomes clear. A child's play oscillates between building up and tearing down, vague or restless scanning, chance discoveries, passionate interest, brushing achievements aside, painful inability, happy and unhappy accidents, luck and determination. The child is intensely alive in real play and this is just what the patient plagued with a sense of unreality is unable to achieve.

Winnicott stresses the need for the analyst to be receptive. He must lend to the patient an alive and perceptive presence, an atmosphere implicitly rich with psychic nutrients. He, too, must be able to play, to allow spontaneous oscillations between form and formlessness. So often it is the analyst's attitude or mood that determines whether or not a drop into formlessness is possible. A crucial element in creating a facilitating atmosphere is that the analyst not make believe he is omniscient.

The danger of the therapist playing omniscient is virtually ubiquitous. In Lacan's apt locution, the analyst is beset with the temptation of assuming the role of "the one who is supposed to know."[8] Both patient and analyst would like the security of someone knowing. Much hard work, patience, and revisualization of self and other is necessary in order to begin to get used to not knowing the answers (or even the right questions and problems), yet remaining open. One suffers the realization that freedom grows out of the darkness of unknowing and the limits of what it is given one to see. The more we tolerate being grounded in darkness, the less profligate our relationship to light becomes. Our elusiveness to ourselves and one another keeps us from promiscuous omniscience.

Winnicott writes, "I think I interpret mainly to let the patient know the limits of my understanding."[9] He speaks so that the patient

8. Lacan, *Four Fundamental Concepts*, p. 230.
9. Winnicott, "The Use of an Object and Relating through Identifications," pp. 711–716.

will know that he is not omniscient, so that the patient experiences
that lack of omniscience is possible. This does not mean that Winnicott feigns stupidity. Playing dumb is the other side of omniscience.
Winnicott is not stupid. His best interpretations are inspired and
even, he tells us, seemingly mad. They preserve and further the link
between experiencing and knowing. The method of unknowing he
recommends works at or beyond the edge and limits of knowing and
is not simply the acquiescence of the will not to know.

In Winnicott's work, unknowing and unintegration go together.
What is crucial is that the analyst does not pretend to know the
patient more than he really does. This gives the patient and analyst
space. The patient, too, is relieved at not having to know more than
he does. This helps him let go of the myths he has spun around
himself and become unintegrated. For Winnicott, *disintegration*
means one would hold on to something if one could, but a process
one cannot control is spinning one out of existence. The ways one
has tried to hold oneself together have not worked, and the mess one
is takes over.

Unintegration, by contrast, is a "purer" state. The subject dips into
creative formlessness. He lives between the lines of his built-up
personality. He gets to where he was before defensive encapsulation
took over. It is implicit in Winnicott's vision that we sense our baby
soul as it was before it was marred, that intimations of a pristine
thread continue throughout our lifetime, that we never quite lose
contact with something that we sense is our most precious self.

Unintegration refers to the chaos of experiencing before it congeals into psychic formations that can be used defensively. It refers to
a time or dimension of experiencing before the ability to split off and
oppose aspects of the self to one another (particularly mind–body,
thinking–feeling). It remains a state between organizations one can
repair to, a kind of rest in which one forgets who one thinks one is, a
moment's absent-minded immersion in nothing in particular. It is a
letting go and clearing out. It is a relief to be rid of oneself and feel
the deeper order unintegrated "chaos" leads to. In it one senses a
groping toward an "original face."

This does not mean that one's original face is always "pretty" or that there is no friction. In unintegrated moments, one may experience a profound well-being one could have scarcely imagined possible. But all-consuming rages also rise and fall, as the emotional weather changes. Or one may be gripped by terror beyond words. In unintegration, one is not frozen into any one position. It refers to a time in infancy before one can adequately process or make sense out of much that one is experiencing. One cannot yet split oneself off from experiencing.

In a state of unintegration, one does not know or think one knows what will happen next. One is not closed off from oneself. To be sure, the infant shuts off, falling into a "stupor" or averting attention. But usually attention returns. The storm or irritant passes. The infant starts from scratch, all new. In extreme instances, it must deaden itself most of the time, but this is not normal. It is more usual for human beings to shut and split off from themselves in a more chronic way a bit later, when they develop the mental resources to do so.[10] From Winnicott we gain a sense of how much living goes on in an unintegrated state and how desolate and unreal we can feel without it.

Winnicott connects the aliveness of dreaming with unintegration and opposes both to the rote rehearsal of chronic fantasies. In his vision, unintegration leads to dreaming, which works over, enriches, and stimulates vital emotional experiences. Through unintegration, the personality gains a chance to reset or reform itself. In genuine rest and emptiness images arise that reflect the state of self and redirect the latter's movement. Insofar as a person is addicted to stale, compensatory fantasies, he tends to cut himself off from deeper and more spontaneous urges to reshuffle himself. For most of us, fantasying may be inevitable. Fantasies mark our wounds and hopes. But insofar as they cover the same ground and do not lead anywhere, they function as mirages, even if they finally come true.

10. Elkin, "On Selfhood and the Development of Ego Structures in Infancy," pp. 57–76; Eigen, "On the Significance of the Face," pp. 427–441; see also Chapter 4, this volume.

Not so the capacity to dream. Dreaming rubs our noses in the realities we hope to escape in fantasy. In dreams, an enemy may appear in a good light, a possibility denied him in our conscious daydreams. In this sense, our dreams are truly Christian, and without regard to persons. They force us to focus on what we would rather push aside. They teach us that the very fabric of the self includes what antagonizes us. Our dreams give the lie to our pretensions to be in control, no matter what. But they may also do more. For in dreaming one can glimpse an experiential world beyond conscious imagining and will do so in unexpectedly uplifting ways. Wish-fulfilling fantasies seem pale in comparison with the unanticipated ecstasy dreams can bring. To an extent, Winnicott's portrayal is reminiscent of the Hindu adage that conscious life is the past, dreaming the present, and the void of dreamless sleep the future. He has elaborated this ancient intuition in light of psychoanalytic concerns and contemporary living.

Unintegration, Madness, and Suicide

To speak of a zero point of personality or a moment of formlessness is metaphorical, but also more than metaphor. It touches on a sense of mystery that pervades existence. In negative theology, God is defined by what he is not, his lack of definition, the unknowable of unknowables. The polarity of order–disorder gives way. Concepts of chaos and nothingness converge asymptotically. A feeling permeates us that something goes on beyond what is graspable and that we are its results. The notion of causality, whether magical, theological, poetic, or scientific, has so far not exhausted this informing intuition.

Berdyaev[11] speaks of a "meontic freedom," a sense of ever being

11. Berdyaev, *Slavery and Freedom*, pp. 20–80, 232–266; Macquarrie, *Existentialism*, pp. 138–141.

undone and reborn, as a constituting and potentially saving dimension of our being. He depicts a kind of limitless darkness associated with a collapse of the usual categories, collective ties, and personal distortions. Images of womb, birth, sleep, and death are drawn from to depict the formless loss of self, but they are themselves too limiting. In Berdyaev's Christian view, he associates this loss of self with a complementary rebirth through an ultimately mysterious, if personal, Other. Winnicott, too, associates creative formlessness, unknowing, unintegration, and chaos with transubstantiation, communion, an "I but not I" feeling, the dimension "between," and a paradoxical generative sense of self and other that cannot be strictly localized.[12] A systematic investigation of the link between a drop into formlessness and rebirth through the Other is beyond the scope of the present work. However, the fact that major religious and psychological thinkers have made and emphasized this link is important.

Neither dissolution nor rebirth can be used as a criterion for illness or health. Whether in illness or in health, unintegration can be menacing as well as renewing. The psychotic self often lives close to the sense of rebirth. In manic moments, the self feels that all things are possible. In depression, the self feels nothing is possible. Both in health and madness one meets the variegated moods and attitudes that mark the field of human experience. Perhaps an element of health is the ability to work with the moods and visions that are our common lot and allow them to turn into something useful. To speak of reality-testing as the essential function that discriminates the sane from the mad is not enough. We are learning only too cruelly how enslaving, corrupting, impoverishing, and dangerous addiction to "reality" can be. The biblical warning that "thou shalt know them by their fruits" is perhaps as close as we can get to a sane test of who

---

12. Winnicott, "Transitional Objects and Transitional Phenomena," pp. 89–97. A rigorous comparison between Berdyaev's primordial freedom and Winnicott's transitional space is beyond the scope of this book, although such a study would be illuminating.

we are. Our "tests," like reality, remain elusive and suggestive, variable in quality and results. The biblical tradition itself is one of our greatest testaments to the fragility and potential of what reality can mean.

In the past several years, two of the seemingly sanest members of the psychological community jumped out of windows to their death. One had been the president of a prestigious professional organization. We will perhaps never know the details fully. Apparently both were enjoying a manic episode that showed signs of waning. I heard a friend of one of these men comment, "He was feeling so good, he did not want to come down again." Come down he did. Perhaps he hoped to fly. Perhaps he wanted to fly forever. Perhaps he made sure that he would finally come down to earth. Perhaps he dramatized what it was to be up, then down, in the fullest way he could. Perhaps he took control of the downward movement of the self in as sure a way as possible. We could spin many more fantasies. Whatever moved these men, they are not isolated instances. Today we often hear of the exemplary life of a suicide.

I knew one of these men moderately well. We would sometimes get together at professional meetings and exchange ideas. He presented himself as a very gentle, loving man, a prince of a man. One of our disagreements over the years centered on the place of hate in therapy. He emphasized love and tended to see hate as defensive, even unreal. The reality of love would dissolve it. He firmly believed that if the therapist were truly loving enough, the patient would not hate. For him, the patient's hate bore witness to a deficiency in the therapist. The therapist's own hate, too, was a defense against vulnerability and must be dissolved by contact with a deeper love. In contrast, my feeling was that the devil must be given his due. If hate is ultimately secondary, it is still real and has its place. It ought not to be short-circuited too easily or treated condescendingly.

My colleague's attitude toward hate seemed to be part of a larger stance. He was a good and sane man. I cannot recall ever seeing him indulge in a truly crazy moment. In public, he always "looked good." I don't think that he was guarded so much as he was in love with a persona that worked for him. I think he liked me for the "crazy things" I might say, but, ultimately, he presented himself as more centered and parental.

The masks of sanity people wear do not always work well for them. The addiction to elements of personality one considers sane can be destructive. Some people would rather die than risk madness. Ernest Hemingway, for example, lived out a macho image. He idealized a particular sort of physical courage. But he blew his brains out rather than face the kind of journey required of him by his impending psychosis. He lacked the courage and resources to face and make something of his madness. The Tao saying, "In the storm the tree breaks but the reed bends," may apply here. For Hemingway, madness was a humiliation he was not willing to undergo. His sense of dissolution was final, rather than a gateway. It marked the end of everything he knew himself to be, everything he valued and bet on. That it might also mark the end of a constricting one-sidedness would have seemed appallingly beside the point.

Mythic heroes often undergo wounds, dismemberment, and a tortured death as part of a larger transformation process. There is a danger of becoming overly masochistic through identification with this aspect of growth, which "male" aspects of the personality rightly fight. Hemingway would or could not give in to this kind of fragmentation. Nietzsche understood the effeminization attached to the dying god image and sought to rise above it. He sought to go through madness with a spiritual machoism, which is a mental ego foil and counterpart to Hemingway's circumscribed body ego orientation. In a peculiar sense, each possessed a brittle, paranoic ego not equal to its task nor able to make peace with failure. But each knew fire and gave off sparks in the process.

Sylvia Plath was caught between a creative breakthrough that made use of madness and an overly constricted, "good girl" persona. Her letters to her mother oscillated between expressions of hate and her need to be good. Her mother took Plath's hate to be an expression of madness and the good, loving girl to be her real self. Her therapist, too, seemed to side with her sane self against her madness, a distinction that proved to be artificial as her personal and creative journey continued. She did not seem to meet with a context capable of sustaining her need to love and hate, to spew out and hold back. Her creativity used both tendencies and acted as a partial vehicle to allow sanity and madness to interweave.

In *The Savage God*, Alvarez depicts Plath's suicide as a self-affirmation over and against what are felt to be unbearable inner and outer conditions.[13] He elaborates on Binswanger's famous viewpoint, which the latter developed in his write-up of the case of Ellen West.[14] After a long psychotic illness, Ellen West was treated at Binswanger's clinic. A short time after he told her parents she was hopeless, she killed herself. He saw her suicide as a final self-affirmation in a hopeless situation. She affirmed herself in the one dignified way left to her.

Binswanger's case is considered to be a classic of existential psychology. It has superb descriptions of various aspects of Ellen West's phenomenological world. A generation of existential psychotherapists used it as a model for phenomenological analysis. In the course of his work, he writes scornfully of Ellen West's previous "classical" psychoanalysis as dry and ineffective. Yet he seems to be oblivious to the fact that at least she lived through it. He does not link her suicide with his expression of hopelessness, except in a seemingly self-serving way. He seems to feel she was better off dead than alive in a living death and that his statement precipitated a genuine choice.

In commenting on this case, Carl Rogers simply said that Binswanger never heard her.[15] Perhaps no one did. Certainly the atmosphere presented in Binswanger's write-up is heavy and suffocating. Perhaps this is in accord with Ellen West's world. Yet Rogers' simple comment seems to the mark. Binswanger did not want Ellen West to be aggressive. An attitude of disgust permeates his comments on her misbehavior. He unself-consciously depicts his own punitive attitude toward her when she was not a "good girl." She had no room in Binswanger's clinic to be herself. He seemed totally unaware that he

13. Alvarez, *Savage God*, pp. 97–98.
14. Binswanger, "Case of Ellen West," pp. 237–364.
15. Rogers, "The Loneliness of Contemporary Man as Seen in 'The Case of Ellen West'," pp. 94–101.

evaluated her productions according to the way he wanted her to behave. Such naiveté and blindness in a position of power is chilling, all the more so when the one in charge is so brilliant, sensitive, and searching.

More recently, feminist critics have portrayed Sylvia Plath as a victim in a male-dominated society. The voice of the "bitch goddess" ("Out of the ash / I rise with my red hair / And I eat men like air") is taken as Plath's attempt to voice her deeper feelings in a male world, a voice of rageful longing, horror, and revenge so long smothered. The tendency of male critics to blame Plath's psychosis on her mother is also responded to. In her moving play, "Letters Home," Rose Leiman Goldemberg portrays the many nuances of Sylvia and Aurelia Plath's relationship to each other in a way that makes it difficult and beside the point to say that one or the other was to blame.[16]

If we must, we can easily enough construct a clinical history. There can scarcely be any doubt that Plath's mother pushed her and nourished her and that her father's death (as she was nearing puberty) wounded her. Also, one ought to note that her father was engaged in writing a book on bees during Sylvia's first two years, with her mother helping him. The household must have been torn between absorption in his task and the new baby. We might also speak about her double identification with her mother's energy and her father's ill health. After speaking of mother, we mention father, and vice versa. We have not even mentioned sibling or relatives (or, later, husband, social and cultural world, and so on). The deeper we go into history, the more ambiguous and spiraling causality becomes.

As is often the case, the debate over causality (who or what is to "blame") obscures significant structural realities and problems. Both father and mother images in Plath's poems are alternately menacing and inspiring. She uses the language of catastrophe and breakdown. Mirrors (the mind) oscillate between being stainless and shattered. I open "Ariel" at random and on the two pages, or 37 lines, before me I find more than a dozen references to murder, death, burning,

16. Goldemberg, *Letters Home*, pp. 105–176.

weapons, and the holocaust.[17] A soul is being torn and cut through. Even the darkness within is burning and shattering. The sense of horrific disintegration is intensified by its contrast with pristine wholeness, the cry of an ill-fated child (e.g., "It is a heart, / This holocaust I walk in, / O golden child the world will kill and eat").

But what is even more important in her poetry are the amalgams and fusions between sexes, properties of objects, body areas and functions, dimensions (up–down, inner–outer, materiality–immateriality), and, in general, the way the sense of devastation and wounded purity spreads through all polarities. Distinctions tend to be wedded and collapse in the oneness of horrific pain and, finally, a devastation beyond pain. Distinctions shoot like meteors and her poems shriek across a horizon of incandescent pain that fades almost as if it never was. We collapse into this darkness with her only to find it is cleanly lacerating as it and we slide away. Perhaps the final paradox is that as we slip into oblivion we feel her and our minds working at top speed.

We are at the crossroads of what is possible. The top speed whirl, collision, and melding of distinctions may be a prelude to a profound reshuffling that may yet produce an experience capable of redirecting and sustaining us. It may be a drop into an abyss in which all things are possible, the formless infinite, the pregnant void. At moments in Plath, it is close to that. She seems to sense she can dip into an oblivion that heightens her creativity. At the same time the void she glimpses and is gripped by is a black hole of infinite horror. The "airy nothingness" she names is nameless dread, laceration as such with no home or boundaries. It is an achievement of her poems that she gives formless horror the shape and feel of a knife moving as fast as light. One can feel the agony of darkness as light cuts it.

In Winnicott's terms, potential unintegration oscillates with and gives way to fragmentation and disintegration. In Bion's terms, the unconscious container is deformed and deforming, a misshapen internal horizon that warps whatever appears in it. For a time, the container may stretch to try to accommodate the thoughts and

17. Plath, "A Birthday Present," p. 44; idem, "Mary's Song," pp. 44–45.

feelings that threaten to mutilate it. It is in danger of fragmentation or thinning to such an extent that the result is total diffusion. Bion likened the possibility of thinning, rather than breaking, to surgical shock, wherein one bleeds to death within one's own dilated capillaries.[18] On the other hand, the breaking up of a container does not result in its disappearance so much as in a proliferation of fragments wherein each one of which can function as persecuting or engulfing.[19] The situation then is a rapid fire bombardment of fiendish or ameboid fragments of psychic life incessantly penetrating and swallowing each other, highly charged slivers of mind hurtling toward oblivion.

This situation is not unlike van Gogh's. Van Gogh experienced a heightened reality that threatened to flood him. At his best, the excitement of his perceptual–imaginative breakthrough was one with a searching, aesthetic realization. A spontaneous link between his hypercathexis of certain areas of experience and sensuous forms sustained him. In few painters has the "dialectic" between the radiance of the capacity to feel and the darkness of oblivion reached such a peak. As he grew closer to making his choice between madness and suicide, his work grew darker. Yet the darkness itself is the more ominous insofar as it glistens with light.

In his last works, it is hard to say whether darkness devoured light or vice versa. They fuse in a desperate, macabre way somewhere between madness and death. If his final paintings express, ward off, and fly in the face of madness, they are also death masks. The death that appears in them is an illuminated blackness. Death shines. It absorbs and becomes part of the madness. It is impossible to say whether death absorbs madness or madness absorbs death. These paintings are the face of death and what shines on this face is madness. Heightened and misshapen reality converges with a zero point. The death van Gogh depicts is itself infinitely mad, a warped oblivion. As one stares into the face of his death, one feels that beyond the

18. Bion, *Attention and Interpretation*, pp. 12–13.
19. Bion, *Elements of Psycho-Analysis*, pp. 40, 84.

344 THE PSYCHOTIC CORE

grave not death, but madness has the last word. But it is, finally, the painting we are staring at.

We cannot say with certainty what would have helped van Gogh. We do not know what combination of alcoholism, epilepsy, and madness brought him down. The usual clinical picture offered is of a hypersensitive soul who was rejected by his father and who consequently suffered profound self-attack seizures. There is no question that self-hatred was a crucial element of his nature. But so was a deep faith in himself and, above all, the power of creation. Something in him persisted tenaciously with minimal encouragement and acceptance. He *had* to paint—and he did. It is often pointed out that his self-attacks and self-doubts slowed him down. He painted best when he felt good, or at least during periods of remission. But his stubbornness was the other side of his attacks and doubts. A rigidity and fixedness persevered with the same blind force as his attacks. It was as if his self-hatred fueled as well as suffocated him. Perhaps he needed the challenge of doing something against great and impossible odds in order to do anything at all. He needed debility as a foil to radiance.

Over and over his attacks sought to cancel him out and he emerged with fresh vision. He lived the rebirth archetype in a deformed and quasi-aborted way. He needed to break himself down in order to begin freshly and nakedly. If he could have found the help he needed, his self-attack system might have achieved its cleansing function more wholesomely. But given his temperament, family, and social conditions, he made use of the tools he had available. In his case, a distorted self-hate had to assume the function of ripping his personality apart in order to keep tapping into the primordial ground of his being (see Chapter 5).

In the long run, Plath, van Gogh, and Hemingway could not find a way to work with the basic rhythm of falling apart–coming together. They struggled against it as if it were a foreign body. They felt it should not be this way and resisted. They were right in the sense that they knew something was wrong with them, something that was beyond their control. Something horrible gripped them and made them impotent. Plath began by feeling her madness was alien and removeable, but ended sensing it was the most real part of her, essential to her creativity. She lacked the resources and emotional frame of reference to absorb this growing realization. Van Gogh had an inkling that his vision and attacks had something in common, but fought to the end to maintain the distance between them. In doing so, he exacerbated his split against himself, a vicious spiral that gathered momentum.

It would have taken a subtle and profound adjustment of their beings to allow unintegration its way. Yet each tasted, courted, and thrived on it. Van Gogh was exhilarated by his emerging freedom as an artist, his growing ability to be himself. He spoke somewhat apologetically, but also defiantly about his rough and spotty canvases in which the bare canvas showed. His works, like Plath's later poems, had a life of their own and assumed a startling Otherness. Plath did not have a visible landscape in front of her and was perhaps more consciously aware of the abyss from which her poems emerged. Van Gogh was more tuned in to how art transformed rather than created reality. He was deeply involved in the ways art and reality fed and transcended each other. More and more, Plath could not keep her eye off the formless darkness from which words arose. Van Gogh was possessed more and more by how darkness took over primordial light. There was something unformed and brittle about each of them, yet also dogged and determined. But finally, each was unequal to his and her own sensitivity.

Plath and van Gogh demonstrate that an individual can simultaneously thrive on and be destroyed by unintegration. Jung, in his discourse, developed a threefold approach to understanding how an individual can be wiped out by fascination with creativity. He informally speaks of the dangers of the unconscious and, particularly, of the ego being overwhelmed by an archetype. However, he tends to emphasize that it is a constricted attitude and a weakness on the part of the ego that makes the unconscious so dangerous. At times, he lets himself go and grimly rhapsodizes about the dangerous powers of the unconscious depths and moralizes about the strengths and weaknesses of ego-consciousness. But what he seems to stress above all is a narrow, one-sided, and inflexible attitude of the ego (viz., its preoccupation with practical survival), which conditions it to be hostile toward psychic reality as a whole. In the end, the ego's hostility is mirrored by and met with hostility throughout the psyche.

I discussed this formulation earlier (Chapters 2, 5) and will not explore its problems now. What I wish to note here is the rightness of Jung's phenomenological emphasis on a certain inflexibility that permeates the personality in its drive toward madness. He emphasizes a narrow and superficial tyranny of the ego, which must be broken down. He is not wrong, but the resulting schism-flooding between ego and deep unconscious is misleading, since the rigidity he perceives runs through the entire psyche. It seems to stain and mold the self. It goes hand in hand with the individual's hypersensitivity, so much so that a link between hypersensitivity and rigidity seems almost a psychosomatic given.

The rigidity that marks psychosis is more than insulation for hypersensitivity. It seems as basic a fact as the sensitivity itself. As I have mentioned earlier, passionate determination went along with van Gogh's vulnerability. Obsessive and passionate interest is part of creative work in general.[20] Structural restraints and the elusive, fluid responses that work with and through them constitute two basic aspects of our nature. In good functioning, the tension between these aspects of experiencing is productive. In psychosis, it degenerates into warfare or worse. A macabre caricature of possibilities may occur. Polarities become extreme or reverse or both: what is hard becomes harder and what is fluid becomes chaotic, or what is hard becomes soft and what is soft rigidifies.

The interlocking of rigidity and fluidity, so important in the phenomenology of psychosis, is reflected in the basic concepts of psychoanalysis (see also Chapters 1 and 6). For Freud, libido is both rigid and fluid. Libido is fluid and electrical in its ability to change forms and to invest a wide range of objects, but its basic functions are the same, as fixed as respiration or the circulation of blood. It is too simple to equate rigidity with superego and fluidity with id, as is often done. Freud wrote of the id as a caldron of seething excitations, but also apologized for its monotonous, inflexible makeup and aim.

20. Köhler, "Obsessions of Normal People," pp. 398–412.

Indeed, he wrote of instances of extreme rigidity in terms of the "stickiness" and "inertia" of libido and id.

The conjunction of rigidity and fluidity that characterizes Freud's picture of libido and the unconscious is a characteristic of psychic life in general. For Jung, the archetypes functioned as fixed stars that constitute the overall architecture of one's life, yet a good deal of reversal and amalgamation is possible. Jung noted how instinct and spirit easily change into one another in labile personalities and, more generally, that the self evolves through reversals.

Ehrenzweig contrasted the fixed drives of the id with a fluid unconscious ego matrix that dissolves, scans, and reshuffles experiential possibilities. He charted phases the ego goes through in repeatedly dissolving and reconstituting itself, finding a typical rigidity in the work of psychotic artists in spite of its striking content.[21] According to Ehrenzweig, psychotic individuals are in extreme horror of giving themselves over to the ebb and flow of more and less differentiated modes of perception. They fight ego loss or more "undifferentiated" functioning. The ego is caught in the grip of a relentless rigidity and is bent on sealing itself off. It neither trusts itself nor the psyche as a whole.

Ehrenzweig thus felt that it was a mistake to intensify psychic rigidity further by simply or mainly trying to help the psychotic individual strengthen his defenses. What is necessary is the discovery of an entirely new way of relating to deeper modes of perception. The unconscious life of the ego or self needs nourishment and growth. By degrees, the individual has to be helped to let go and trust the rhythms of deeper processes. At the same time, one's work must facilitate the incessant reorganization of these deeper processes. More important than reinforcing superficial ego defenses is a kind of wholesale replenishing and redirection of psychic life, so that the subject can become more receptive to the mystery of experiencing. The unconscious ego matrix must come to act more as a fertile womb or a container capable of sustaining the play of opposites, particularly the plasticity and determination of psychic work.

What is the relationship between the unconscious working as a

21. Ehrenzweig, *Hidden Order of Art*, pp. 122–127, 194–195.

good container and creative unintegration? Is not unintegration, by definition, containerless? Or is unintegration possible only because one trusts the containing capacity? I raise these questions although I cannot answer them at this point. They touch issues that are crucial for understanding psychosis, mind, and self. Much work by such authors as Winnicott and Bion is concerned, in one form or another, with the paradoxical container–containerless duality.[22] In psychosis, unintegration is menacing. One is terrified of disintegrating forever. One sees and feels annihilation both as impending and ongoing. At the same time, containment and containerlessness also are menacing. In Green's locution, psychic space in psychosis tends to be too stuffed or empty rather than "ventilated."[23] In psychosis, even a "good" container may be felt to be a suffocating trap, although to be containerless is to remain unborn and faceless. Many schizophrenic individuals complain about looking too young and unwritten on, yet they cannot bear being pinned down, as if lack of definition is freedom. In such instances, both freedom and definition are experienced as catastrophic. One may kill oneself to throw off either freedom (fluidity) or definition (rigidity), particularly as the former dissolves and the latter entombs the self. At least in madness a miracle may still happen, although much futile anguish is premised on this hope.

The Human Face: A "Containerless Container"

Work at deep levels with many patients suggests that the sense of self and other spontaneously arises seamlessly. Self and other seem inherently to order one another. At certain moments, individuals may find themselves reporting experiences that may be summarized in the following way:

22. Winnicott, *Playing and Reality*, pp. 11, 112, 130, 141; Bion, *Learning from Experience*, pp. 91–98; idem, *Attention and Interpretation*, pp. 16, 79, 96, 106, 107, 122; Eigen, "The Area of Faith in Winnicott, Lacan and Bion," pp. 413–433.
23. Green, "The Analyst, Symbolization and Absence in the Analytic Setting," pp. 1–22.

I see you but not just you. I am experiencing a more real, perfect version of you, a glowing-light you, inexpressibly radiant and fluid. I can go in and through you yet feel more myself than ever. It is as if I entered and passed through a highly charged yet resistanceless medium and feel newly conscious and restored.[24]

In such experiences, the other retains his specific, everyday personality—his definition. At the same time, he is transformed into something more or other than himself, a carrier of a translucent sense of immateriality, ineffably fluid. Personal being is here felt to be distinct, yet to exist fully and mysteriously in a state of union, each pole made possible and fulfilled by the other. Insofar as one lives in this subject–subject psychical reality, expressive meanings, moods, intentions, and attitudes appear to be experienced with direct, immediate transparency. The feeling of wholeness may initially be rooted in the implicit awareness of self and other giving rise to one another, permeating yet transcending one another—a primary creative act repeated anew at every developmental juncture.

The human face is the physical center of self–other awareness. The centrality of the human face as symbolic of personality permeates the fabric of human experience. Face-to-face sexual intercourse and the infant staring raptly at the mother's face during feeding bear witness to how thoroughly we are molded by our perception of expression. Human expression is the heart of human perception. The appearance of a face is an indicator that another personality is present. When the child panics at the mother's absence, it is likely that an image of her face, not her breast, brings more comfort. It may be that for the infant the world often is a kind of fluid, kaleidoscopic mandala with the human face at its center.[25] The other is experienced not simply as limit, but also as a vehicle of rebirth, an infinite opening. The container–containerlessness distinction fades away.

24. Eigen, "On the Significance of the Face," p. 439. Also see Eigen, "Instinctual Fantasy and Ideal Images," pp. 119–137; idem, "Expression and Meaning," pp. 291–312; idem, "Creativity, Instinctual Fantasy and Ideal Images," pp. 316–339.
25. Eigen, "Expression and Meaning," p. 291; Elkin, "On the Origin of the Self," p. 67.

One of the great distortions of psychoanalytic theory has been its tendency to equate face with breast. Psychoanalysts have usually taken the face to be a symbol of the breast, rather than a crucial psychic reality in its own right. This resulted from a prejudice that placed greater emphasis on tactile (in the first place, oral) than on visual experience in the early formation of the self. An excellent example of how this prejudice has distorted the interpretation of clinical and experimental data is the work of Spitz, whose findings mark a turning point in understanding infantile experience.

Spitz found that the infant smiled at a face or face mask with eyes and nose represented by approximately two or three months of age.[26] The coherent and radiant smile in question required a visual experience and did not arise from touch alone. Nevertheless, in spite of his own data, which emphasized vision and a distance element, Spitz persisted in trying to understand his findings in terms of "oral perception," which he called the "hallmark of 'things',"[27] whatever these things may be. In keeping with his bias, he interpreted the infant's smile as a survival technique, a kind of oral coercion. That is, the smile was taken to be mainly an adaptive gesture that ensured the mother's attentive caretaking and, particularly, feeding. Spitz read into the infant's smile a more or less purely manipulative, controlling intent, allied with Freud's will to mastery.

It is unlikely that one can account for the emergence of the smiling response in question, in essence as Spitz has tried to do, in terms of a psychoanalytically informed biological signal theory, that is, in terms of the smile's functional value in eliciting empathic maternal responses to ensure the infant's survival. The novelty and felt significance of the smile, the surplus of its expressive coherence, marks a dimension of responsive cognition that goes beyond the range exhausted by animal signaling and consciousness. Spitz's attribution of an adaptive, seductive-controlling intent to the baby's early smile does not sufficiently acknowledge the implications of what is most significant about it: its essentially open and undefensive expression of

26. Spitz, *First Year of Life*, pp. 20, 84, 91, 100, 103.
27. Ibid., p. 92.

alive and vibrant delight. His need to couch his findings in a theory that accounts for them in terms of biological purpose (reworked in psychobiological, psychoanalytic terms) mitigated against his working out a fuller phenomenology of the smile.

The smiling response Spitz studied appears to reflect a time in which radical dissociations between thinking–feeling–action have not evolved. Soon enough the infant will smile when angry or frightened (doubtless by or around eight months). His smile may take a seductive turn, develop blank or dead spots, and even harden or freeze. But it seems to me that the earlier smiling response, coherent and whole, points to a non-paranoid element at the ego's foundation, which, in time, will undergo all manner of crises attached to awareness of injury and power inequalities.

I suspect Spitz's limitation grows out of one of the great strengths of psychoanalysis. Psychoanalysis has developed what may be the most systematic study of body symbolism in the history of ideas. Freud's dictum that the ego is "first and foremost a body ego" capsulizes this orientation.[28] It is not surprising that Spitz worked within the confines of a bias that has proved most fruitful. Nevertheless, a corrective is in order.

It now seems necessary to distinguish diverse sources of ego- or self-feeling without reducing one to the other. Support for the double (or multiple) rootedness of self-feeling is found in the recent acknowledgment of the importance of infantile gazing (and hearing) as well as infantile touching.[29] The simultaneous input of both distance and contact senses throws the infant into different worlds of experience, which must be coordinated. The long-standing theoretical controversies over whether vision or touch is the first or more powerful organizer have had such a stormy history because of the

28. Chapters 4 and 6 of this volume; Eigen, "Dual Union or Undifferentiation," pp. 422–424.
29. Zelner, "Organization of Vocalization and Gaze in Early Mother–Infant Interactive Regulation," pp. 18–22, 31–33; Eigen, "On the Significance of the Face," pp. 427–441; idem, "Reflections on Eating and Breathing as Models of Mental Functions," pp. 177–180; Elkin, "On Selfhood and Ego Structures in Infancy," pp. 57–76; Bion, *Elements of Psycho-Analysis*, pp. 95–96.

radical contribution of both. Bion's playful descriptions of the difficulties involved in achieving "common sense" draw on the kinds of
experiential worlds we pass through under the direction of different
sensory modalities. My own observations suggest that when not
tired, hungry, or otherwise uncomfortable, the infant's response is in
tune with a visually coordinated field. His sense of self tends to
collapse with the loss of visual support. Problems in achieving the
right balance of distance–closeness in any situation are partly rooted
in the shifting sense of self and other connected with vision and
touch.

The theoretical collapse of distinct sources of self-feeling often
leads to clinical confusion. A cogent example of this may be found in
Milner's account of her long therapy with a schizophrenic woman.[30]
At certain junctures, Milner's patient produced drawings and fantasies in which the sun and eye were located in the anus. Milner took
this to be a sign that a potentially positive state of undifferentiation
was occurring. Top and bottom elements fused in a loss of distinctions, which would be regenerative. Although this viewpoint is
helpful, I feel that it is too simple.

On the negative side, the sun and eye in anus represents a collapse
or perversion of spontaneous distinctions. I believe it to be a deterioration product linked to the threatened loss of self-feeling that is
normally fed and sustained by the tension between different experiential dimensions. The fecalized or spoiled self, a shit or garbage
self, tends to pull down and debase personality functions.[31] In terms
of the anus–sun/eye fusion, solar consciousness (associated with
vision, light, distance) is brought down and undone. The specifically
visual contribution to the sense of self collapses and is, so to speak,
sucked up by the asshole.

On the positive side, the sun/eye-in-anus is not simply a fecalization of consciousness, but also an attempt of consciousness to suffuse
the body, a potential movement toward embodied selfhood (Milner

30. Milner, *Hands of the Living God.*
31. Eigen, "Dual Union or Undifferentiation," p. 424; see also Chapter 5, this
volume.

said this). It is also an attempt to take a look inside the anus and see one's pathology. Rather than celebrate non-differentiation, such imagery can be used to dramatize elemental urges to see and to be. Mental and physical aspects of self-feeling in any situation must be brought out rather than conceptually reduced to non-differentiation.

I write this despite my feeling that Milner's account is one of the best in the clinical literature. Yet she herself complains that her patient's creativity tends to slacken and lose intensity as therapy goes on. This is a familiar complaint in work with psychological illness of creative people. I would like to suggest that, in Milner's case, such loss of creative intensity may be partly related to interpretations stressing undifferentiation as the subject's starting point, rather than maintaining the tensions and harmonies between distinct yet inter-locking dimensions.[32]

In psychosis, top–bottom distinctions tend to be exaggerated and collapse as a result of sealing and spoiling processes. This is particu-larly so with regard to experiences having the face as a center. Images of the face are often spoiled and debased in the course of therapy. In psychosis or in deep phases of therapeutic work, the genitals or the anus may be seen or felt to be inscribed upon the therapist's face and vice versa. At such moments, the analyst is quite literally seen as a "prick" or an "asshole." To an extent, such perceptions may be accurate. But they often express a bad self-image and a need to spoil not only any goodness, but also the reality and coherence of the other. The subject attempts to pull potentially healing distinctions down into an unredeemable swamp, or turns them into an array of weapons, phallicizing and fecalizing experience. I have written else-where[33] on the vicissitudes of the face as a center of psychic expe-rience, but I wish to bring out aspects of this phenomenon with one of my patients', Rena's, sessions, a session that took place roughly half a year after those reported in Chapter 7.

Rena was expressing her fear of my seeing her as distorted. It was an old fear that she was being twisted out of shape by her feelings,

32. Eigen, "Dual Union or Undifferentiation," p. 424.
33. See fn. 24, this chapter, p. 349.

that I would see everything that was wrong with her. In the past she often felt her head was elongated and feared that if I looked at her she would turn to stone. I wondered if something stony about me chilled her and noted that she reversed the Medusa image. For some time she had been speaking about thawing out. The week before she dreamt of a woman "with glass, penis eyes," one she and I created in a voodoo ritual. This woman was invulnerable, bewitching, and penetrating. Her body was stiff. In part, she represented an occult sense of omniscience fed by the gnostic element of therapy and pinpointed a crazy, megalomanic aspect of our personalities. Rena said in response to her, "I don't want to be excited or have feelings." She then said she was a wreck. A demon pounding inside her kept her awake at nights: "Something dark and relentless won't let me melt and flow." She remembered her mother coming after her with a ruler, but acknowledged that in addition to her mother's force, her own, originary mind was now demonized. The agitation her mother provoked or added to change the shape of her entire being.

This particular session progressed with a report of thawing out of phallic defenses. Her allergy was worse. "I used to be invulnerable. I never let physical things bother me. I was immune. Now I just can't bull through things. My armor is melting."

After some silence, she continued, "I'm afraid of smell. I dreamt I was in bed cuddling a little girl's breasts. I want to swamp her breasts by making her little girl genitals the devil."

> *ME:* You mean touching her breasts includes sex but is more, not primarily sexual. Breasts are feelings, intimacy.
> *R.:* I want to see her face and not be swamped. I feel a connection between face and breasts now. I don't want to bury her. Yes, I want to be intimate. I'm not ready for genitals. They bury everything. I feel such deep damage and fill it with sex. It used to make the hurt go away.
> I spent the weekend feeling the damage. I saw damage everywhere. I identify with people who sleep in doorways, homeless people. I know what they're feeling with their bent-over backs. They are curled up in self-loathing. In womb positions in doorways, curled toward their own odors. I feel in them the pain of my own damaged soul.
> I saw a woman urinating bent over with her head between her legs. Her ass faced the cars passing on the street. Her face was hidden by the

rags she wore. Her ass was her face smeared with shit. What must she feel toward herself? Such total degradation and collapse to this horror. All filth, smell. So isolated it's almost self-sufficiency. I mean that woman was not in the world. Yet her fingers were capable, dexterous, intelligent looking. Once I saw a bum sitting in a gutter with his pants down. His hat, scarf and beard hid his face. What I saw of his face was red roughness, snot, and filth. He wore a coat or long shirt. I saw his penis in the center of a totally scummy world, like a beautiful flower in the center of all the scum. This woman's hand—so purposeful, waiting 'til she finished was like that.

The fact that I couldn't see her face was very important in this picture. Her face was down there between her legs. There was garbage around her and dried blood. I picture her guts coming out. I stand in the blood and guts swinging a sword and screaming "I've a right to live." I go into my mother's womb and come out white and clean and uncomplicated. But the blood is strength and life. One has to be stained. I fight for my face. I don't think I can have one. It must be possible. The bum's penis, the rag lady's hand survive. They are my eternal hope. I'm on my knees supplicating. I never felt whole on my knees before, so different from murderous defiance. A spiritual part of me comes out of the blood vitality. What a relief to be on my knees, to be able to ask. A hope deeper than pain.

Rena has begun to work out the difference-connection between face–breast–ass–penis and shows signs of deepening the dialectic between self-assertion and surrender. The face emerges as a center, which must be fought and prayed for. It cannot be taken for granted, since it is always in danger of being swamped and spoiled by anal attacks and genital excitement. Rena's relationship to the personal is not yet secure enough to absorb and coordinate the rich diversity of body feelings that rush through her. Yet over and over the face is lost and returns. It is a matter of time and hard work before she will learn to trust in its spontaneous re-emergence, no matter what overtakes her.

In this session, the relationship between personal face and anonymous body functions is extremely complex. Rena is momentarily saved and uplifted by experiencing the intelligence of a quasi-anonymous hand or the surprising beauty of a penis in the midst of corruption. In the latter instance, it is as if the Freudian equation, penis = child, holds and Rena is brought to herself by the pathos of innocence aglow in horror, like the babe in the manger. In the former instance, the human hand, even about to wipe bottom, preserves a link with spirit. In the graves of the holocaust it was, above all, the victims' hands that said everything. The skeletal faces were too direct. The hands of the expert mime, whose face looks like death, say the unsayable. Yet without their inherent link with the personal face, the ultimate vehicle of intimacy with distance, hands would be blank. In Rena's experience, the anonymous and personal intertwined, fed and set each other off. In her case, hand and penis pointed to the face.

Some individuals with early disturbances are unable to create a rich and freeing image of a face. The latter remains distorted, blank, or missing. For example, one's own face is felt to be hideous or one cannot construct a viable image of the other's face in the latter's absence. In Oscar Wilde's *The Picture of Dorian Gray*, an individual suffered a split between an outside face, which looked normal, but was false, and an inside face, which was evil, but true. In time, one could not tell which was true or false, as both faces dropped into oblivion. In therapy, it is often a question of tuning into and eliciting silent growth processes from which a wholesome and coherent face can be constituted.

Such a face may first emerge in dreams and fleeting images that gradually take forward a new sense of self and other. In cases of severe personality deficits and spoiling processes, elements of health in dreams are easily overwhelmed by force of habit and inertia. New aspects of faces are misperceived and reduced to the lowest possible denominator. The individual must be helped to attend to subtle differences in the characters he produces. The same character who appears many times may, like a new character, say things never said before. Here the worker must not allow himself to be taken in by the negative undertow that seeks to drown the new, no matter how hopeless the appearances. With a firm grasp of principles, one can try to support a person in the midst of disturbances to allow a complex face to surface and evolve.

Of all body areas, the human face is most centrally expressive of human personality and exerts its prominence as an organizing principle in the field of meaning. It acts as a reference point by which all other body areas may acquire deeper personal significance. Other body areas also act as powerful experiential foci which co-refer to one another and often challenge the primacy of the face. For example, for a time lust may dissolve a face. However, body-oriented pressures and lines of association are usually situated within an experiential horizon in which the face has primacy.

As therapy unfolds, a patient's face may actually change. Of course, life alone can and should do this. But many people remain blocked or change for the worse if left to their own devices and the play of time. For example, without help Rena would likely have tied herself in tighter and tighter knots. Instead, as the above session suggests, she could discover herself in defiant and supplicating modes and let both sides of her nature develop. Her face grew in subtlety and richness of feeling, at once ironic and joyful. It deepened in the appreciation of finitude it conveyed and at the same time seemed touched by the infinite.

The human face is the containerless container *par excellence.* Through it we read and show the results of our labors. It flashes the sign of presence, however opaque, and demands a sign of knowing from the center of the unknown. It arises as a focal point in a vast, faceless surround and discovers anonymity to be its intimate partner. The centerlessness of facelessness oscillates with the face as a pointer toward a center—a dancing search through unending horizons.

Symbols of Madness: Bugs

Throughout this book, many symbols of madness are discussed in case examples. Some emphasize mental, others physical aspects of the self. Some emphasize sharpness of definition, others amorphous explosiveness and inertia. Symbols of madness take the form of demons and fiendish machines, but also the relative formlessness of water, electricity, and air. One of the great ironies or paradoxes of psychic life is that any tendency can function in multiple ways. The relentless spoiling processes of demons may be the underside of enlivening self-assertion. A dream of being a hero flying in the air may express a flight from painful realities, but also a panoramic vision that presages growth of consciousness. Dreams of overwhelming floods may portend suicide or psychosis, but also a wayward and desperate wish for rebirth. Earlier in this chapter, I spoke of different forms of madness symbolized by a mouse and snakes, a war between different psychic orientations. My emphasis was on the rigidity of the psychotic character, a relentlessness that persevered through fluid or hard elements, flooding or spoiling, dissolving or stuffing, laceration or fusion.

Of the various symbols of madness, few characterize its rigidity and relentlessness so well as bugs. It is no accident that *bugs* is a colloquial or slang term for madness. Often a psychotic individual complains of thoughts assailing him like swarms of bugs. In Jodorowski's movie *El Topo*, the hero's journey toward enlightenment requires him to assimilate madness. In one scene, his face is covered with stinging bees as he writhes on the ground in torment. A turning point in one person's illness was a dream in which a poisonous spider descended. In the midst of his terror, the dreamer suddenly realized he did not have to be a paralyzed watcher and that there was something histrionic about his state. For a moment he felt clear and able. Years of paranoia seemed to fall from him as he tasted what feeling free was like.

One usually points to one's head when referring to bugs as a state of being. However, bugs combine references to body as well as mental ego. Flying bugs, in particular, can refer to the head divorced from body. But the very sight of a bug's body evokes a sense of a highly narrow, rigid, perhaps even ossified range of body experiencing. The body of a bug is easily converted into a symbol of a dwarfed and gnomish body self. In science fiction movies, bugs are magnified into dangerous monsters, variously stupid or clever. What is often most shocking in such movies is how faceless the bug remains, despite the magnification of its eyes and mouth. It is as if the body has been reduced to its skeletal nature, with everything soft, warm, and personal shorn away.

In an important sense, this is an illusion. Bugs are soft as well as brittle. They are squooshy and crushable. Many children's first questions about death arise from playing with a bug that, finally, stops moving. A child may repeatedly crush bugs to study this experience. Bugs are early associated with the mystery of mortality as well as madness.

Psychoanalysts find that bugs may symbolize baby, nipple, penis, and feces. These four terms often transform into one another. Bugs are tiny and crawl or fly. Their association with nipple and penis, in part, refers to their activity. In severe pathology, the fecal element tends to spoil the others. A more complex integration of passivity and activity is required in anal experience, since the sense of in–out and, correlatively, self–other, is basically ambiguous (Chapter 5). Oral sucking and phallic penetration become absorbed by the anus and remolded by spoiling, obsessional, and perverse scenarios. The latter include tormenting self-doubt and omnipotent and addictive tendencies.

A psychotic patient recounted sitting in the sand and eating beetles as a child, some time between two and four years of age. He enjoyed thus upsetting his parents. However, he would also do it when alone. In retrospect, he felt the bugs expressed his lack of self-worth, "small and shitty." They became a vehicle of provocation and defiance, but deep down he could feel the ugliness of his being through and through. He would search for them in the sand. Digging for them was an essential part of the ritual. When he found one he would pick it up, examine and squeeze it, then place it in his mouth, chew, and swallow. Each part of the process was important. He would dwell on each step as if savoring it. Yet he recalled feeling thick, vague, and blurry. No matter how finely and precisely he followed the steps, he remained adrift and "buggy." He remembered the tan of the sand, the brown–black of the beetles, the green grass and blue sky. Colors were more important than objects. He did not know why he was sitting there eating beetles except he had to. He must be filthy and

worthless if he could put them in his mouth. He thought it was
funny. At the same time he had the sickening premonition that he
would never feel better.

In Jodorowski's movie the hero, El Topo, followed a wise old
woman's example in eating a disgusting bug. The bug was associated
with a mock birth. Something came in, something went out. The
hero, like the bug, had to be reborn through the hag. There was no
doubt that the hero had to assimilate his sense of worthlessness. He
had to come to terms with what was most repulsive in life—with
repulsiveness as such. The bug could stand for all physical corruption, birth and death, the horror of existence. Psychoanalysts might
see in it the phallic mother or a horror of castration and the whole
sado-masochistic circle. In the movie, it was something nameless.
Clearly, it was associated with overcoming a resistance, with some
kind of immolation or surrender. To be reborn through eating the
bug meant somehow going further than the bug. It was the end of a
painful avoidance and one more step toward meeting what must be
met. For my patient who ate bugs this meant, in part, meeting and
not being done in by the insistent self-hate that marred his existence.

Like many persons with similar feelings, my patient was deeply
taken by Kafka's portrayals of helpless self-loathing. In his late teens
he repeatedly read *The Metamorphosis*. However, unlike Kafka's
man-bug, my patient was called upon and given the support to
endure and go beyond "bugginess." The bug image acted as a
vehicle for contacting and working with profoundly arrested active
and passive tendencies. On the positive side, bugs are persistent.
They never seem to give up. They go on wriggling and struggling
to the end. Bees and ants are called busy and are viewed as incessantly productive. In this they seem to serve as models for the will to
live and try. By becoming a bug the madman affirms this tenacity.

Yet the underside of this tenacity is a kind of mute passivity. Bugs
appear to behave in more or less rigidly determined and stereotypical
ways. They cling to the way they have been programmed and
adhere to systems of movement that work for them. They do not
seem to need to go beyond themselves in any radical way. In human
terms, the very tenacity of their innate strivings paradoxically por-

trays an adhesive, clinging aspect of the self. El Topo's swallowing of the bug and rebirth through the hag emulates aspects of this "passivity," just as Kafka's bug-man succumbs to it. Our sense of the bug's helplessness in face of its own nature is reinforced by its tininess and vulnerability to the human thumb or foot. We easily read in it our own fragility and unyieldingness. Yet we keep looking for a way out of ourselves. El Topo's journey toward and through the center ultimately led him to burn away his inner skeleton altogether. He went up in smoke and became spaceless. It was his final solution to the bug within, his message of transcendence.

It would be worthwhile, but beyond our purpose, to pursue an exhaustive phenomenology of bugs as symbols of madness. We have sketched a wide range of possibilities. Bees are associated with honey and flowers, but they also sting. Flies gather on garbage and feces. Crawling bugs may be helpful and poisonous. Insect feeds on insect. We say, "He's crazy as a bedbug," and laugh at the implicit reference to getting one's behind bitten. "He has a bug up his ass" makes the association of madness and anality emphatic. We also say, "He has bees in his bonnet" and point to our buzzing, haywire brain. A kind of anonymity dominates these references. All of them are concerned with bare structures, functions, experiences, or states shorn of personality: ass-brain, active–passive, beautiful–ugly, alive–dead. They are reminiscent of the apparently sane and playful, if derogatory, army adage that all women are the same with their faces covered. Whether bugs are eating one's brain or burrowing up one's anus, what is missing is the face.

Perhaps the most dramatic images of madness involving bugs are precisely those wherein the face is swarmed on, stung, and bitten to the bare bone. It is as if insects will not be satisfied until they make us like themselves, skeletons exposed. Horror is most focused on what happens to the face. When my patient who ate bugs as a child was well on his way to overcoming his illness, he dreamt that he discovered his son in the rubble of a collapsed building. He cradled him with one arm, while actively waving the other in front of his boy's face to keep the gathering bugs from harming it. At the dream's end, the outcome was in doubt. But there was no let-up in his concentra-

tion. His efforts were unflagging. At an earlier period of his psychosis, he would not have stood a chance. He would not have been able
to separate the helper and the helped. The bugs would have attacked
and mutilated or destroyed him. Now he could use his relentlessness
to help a besieged aspect of himself. He could try to hold out until
help came or the swarming passed or the next, unforeseen transformation evolved. If necessary he would give his life to save his face,
his son's face—a commitment that represented an enormous growth
of integrity and love.

My patient's "solution" was very different from El Topo's. The
former's path involved the advent of the face as a psychic center. His
life had been premised on a deficit of all the face stands for, the
richness and promise of the personal dimension. El Topo's journey
culminated in the burning away of his face and all trace of himself, of
all trace of the personal. For El Topo, only absolute emptiness or
nothingness was the antidote for human vanity. The ego was overcome by absolute facelessness. What a contrast this seems to be to the
wish to see God's face and live. The two together encompass an
enduring polarity: the paths of emptiness and plenitude, infinite
openness and the fullness of the face. Both my patient and El Topo
came to live as honestly, as emptily–fully as possible. One wonders
how and where in their journey through everythingness–nothingness they may meet.

The Point of No Return

Many patients complain of an endless sense of aloneness. They do
not find a social milieu in which they can feel they really belong.
They feel that they do not fit in anywhere. The usual categories of
connection, such as family, race, nation, work, various subgroups,
and friends, do not work for them. They feel, in spite of knowledge
to the contrary, that this is unique to them. They are convinced they
have been singled out to be worse off than others. They lack a sense
of brother- or sisterhood.

In the course of therapeutic work, some of these patients will become well enough to seek a way out in relationships or work of one sort or another. For some, family may provide a sense of community. Others may find broader social or religious ties. But for an increasing number, nothing can truly palliate the nagging sense of being different and not quite connecting. In some basic sense, one is not understood and does not understand oneself. One has nowhere to go. One is on one's own. One feels this in the midst of familial, social, church, or vocational life. One feels something has gone irremediably wrong.

For such persons, the sense of connection is achieved by going deeper into aloneness. At some point, if one only goes far enough, one discovers oneself to be part of a community of alone people. The hallmark of the therapeutic session is the discovery of intimacy in the face of unflinching aloneness. The stigma and shame one feels for being alone transforms into an awareness that one's aloneness itself is part of a larger process, although we can only guess its meaning and outcome.

EPILOGUE

Hindu, Buddhist, and Christian ideals and methods of detachment, together with their late sibling, scientific objectivity, bear witness to the persistent wish and partial capacity to transcend immediate ties. Jesus' warning that he brings a sword, not simply peace, is part of and portends a profound individuation process in which ties of spirit take precedence over flesh and blood. The convert who leaves all behind and is reborn through Jesus paradoxically discovers a new community of living souls, the movement of the living God, and is wrapt in mystery.

In some analogous sense, we can say that the mad patient is reborn through the therapist. But here we meet with danger. Where only two are, madness remains. Twoness lends itself to fight–flight–fusion. Two seek a third for arbitration. We ultimately appeal to the one beyond for fairness—for justice and mercy. This appeal keeps us honest and able to move past premature closures. One of the psychological virtues of Trinitarian thinking is that it safeguards the division–unity structure of generativity. God is not a blank hodgepodge or collapsed morass, but, whatever else, a relational being in the depths of his own nature, a dynamic movement that supports our openness to revelation and response and requires us to live on the cutting edge of faith.

What comparable safeguards does psychoanalysis provide? There are, of course, rules of professional conduct and the larger professional community. Perhaps group therapy ensures the necessary otherness. Within psychoanalysis proper, there are the principles of theory and method and a steadfast appreciation of the depths of self-deception. There is, above all, the drive to come to grips with psychic reality in spite of all obstacles, perhaps, at times, a destructive need for Truth. Perhaps, too, there is a love as well as a mistrust of the imaginal, and an abiding love for psychic reality as such.

Whereas St. Paul knew that human nature was given to sin, Freud knew that it was immersed in madness. In an important sense, Freud's entire enterprise may be regarded as an extended meditation on our response to psychic pain. He made wounded desire the cornerstone of his depth phenomenology and charted ways the hurt, fearful, angry, demanding self worked its way out or became frozen in symptoms, life patterns, and character structure. He deepened the psychology of lying, linking up with and remolding the Christian image of the devil as the father of lies. In particular, he initiated the most detailed investigation in the history of Western thought into the ways pleasure is substituted for pain. In doing so, he went too far in reducing beatific experience to mere wishful thinking. But in the process he opened up crucial vistas into the subtle nuances of the ways we live or fail to live our lies. By demonstrating the kinship between unconscious lying and madness, he both expressed and helped restructure the sensibility of our culture.

We must discriminate between the boundless joy rooted in the depths of our nature and its systematic deployment for the sake of avoiding and falsifying painful realities. Today our inherent capacity for pleasure and good feelings is systematically exploited in the commercial and political arenas. To an extent, this was always so. But the current economic manipulation of incredibly effective public media, particularly television, can arouse and structure our wish to feel good to an extent scarcely conceivable in earlier ages.

The recent (1984) U.S. presidential election campaign amply demonstrated the power exerted by the illusion of good feelings vis-à-vis the claim of painful realities. One candidate focused on painful realities, the other dismissed him as a harbinger of gloom and doom. The implicit winning message seemed to be that accuracy of perception and thoughtfulness breeds pessimism. To think problems through is too troublesome. Better to enjoy the positive side of life and count our blessings rather than to take too close a look. Why make things out to be worse than they are when we are doing fairly well, at least better than before?

A good mother also reassures her troubled child. She tries to turn pain into pleasure with kind words and caresses. Everything hinges on attention to details. If she has managed to divine (often unconsciously) with some accuracy what is bothering the child, she may spontaneously respond in ways that increase his stature and capacity for experiencing. If that is not possible, his concerns may drown in the global good feeling she provides. The specific anxiety dissipates in her reassuring atmosphere and he gets over the hurdle. But nuances of his being are lost, and he learns to go on by increasing his ability to disregard himself. This may be a necessary and useful achievement, given the conditions in which he finds himself, and it ought not to be devalued. It helps one get through things. Nevertheless, such a tendency may become so habitual or second nature that one begins to lose or to fail to exercise the ability to be attentive to experiential details that count. The results of such a failure may eventually prove destructive, inasmuch as one's capacity to reach out and care for others and oneself is blunted.

Freud cautions us that the capacity to be out of contact is more ubiquitous than commonly imagined. The ability to be in touch richly and accurately with ourselves and others is a precious capacity and one not to be taken for granted. Freud may not have solved the problems his work raised, but his preoccupation with the inherent link between madness and the lie we live stands as a bulwark and warning against the dangers of a silently megalomanic self-righteousness. We have been warned about human vanity, hubris, and pride through the ages. The depth psychologies round out this warning with special urgency, inasmuch as life on earth, not just after death, is now in jeopardy in a most emphatic and literal way.

To be sure, the failure to achieve enough good feeling to support healthy mental functioning is as real a danger as the exploitation of good feeling in collective brainwashing maneuvers. To a certain extent, the "maternal" voice of the President or the TV announcer helps soothe the terrors that threaten to break through one's imperturbable good sense. Nevertheless, there is always a price to pay. The rash of recent youthful suicides, bombings of abortion clinics, violence against synagogues and private property of Jews and blacks, and the like are symptoms of an illness, a madness that threatens the social body. The attempted induction of mass scale "good feelings" and the potential for violence seem to go together. They are elements of a broader structure handed down through the ages, which we are only beginning to understand.

There is a mixture of cynicism and naiveté in madness that hideously mocks the innocence and sophistication of health. The joy that arises and persists in the developed personality takes account of and absorbs human suffering and is tempered by an ironic awareness of evil. It is instinctively cognizant of the play of reversal and, so, wary of absolute polarizations in daily life. It is no less pristine for being chastened. It is enriched through experience in ways that make a difference.

In madness, joy dulls crucial aspects of reality. It goes round in circles and ends in bitterness and blindness. Its partner is horror and catastrophe. Popular caricatures are right in portraying the smile of madness as an odd mixture of innocence and cynicism, a kind of malicious yet blank triumphant glee. Madness smiles at what it takes to be a foregone conclusion, the certainty that we are entombed by suffering, that we can never break out of what is worst about us, that we are hopeless beings. Yet the mad person often hopes against hope. He may have a vision he clings to. He may be moved by the spirit. Moments of joyful realization can catapault him out of his grim condition and animate a profound rebirth movement. Unfortunately, too much reality is usually sacrificed in the process. The gain in intensity does not always outweigh the loss in breadth. In the end, what is positive in psychotic vision must rise to the challenge of life. In the mature personality, irony and faith balance each other. Mystical vision and the requirements of situations meet.

Meeting may heighten rather than reduce tension. Martin Buber writes, "All real living is meeting."[1] Meeting is not free of difficulty and lack of fit. On the contrary, we are born and reborn through each other precisely because of our difficulties. We come through our own and each other's blocks. We get through to ourselves and each other over and over. We collide head on, we wait it out, we try out possibilities, we give up, we try again. Visionary hope will not settle for less than breaking through our cynicism and despair. At the same time, our cynicism tells us that distance is important. We cannot trifle with the gaps between and within us. We learn to live with and through unintegration, in the movement between face and faceless-ness, at the point where distinction-union co-create one another.

As we have seen throughout this book, madness may heighten a particular reality or drop a soul into oblivion. One may be caught up in manic flight and not be able to "turn off" one's excitement or so sink into vacuousness as to not "turn on" at all. One may disperse or rigidly compress oneself in order to find respite from pain. In such instances, madness mimics the natural alternation of inspiration and rest. In general, madness feeds on and exploits polarities in ways that reinforce an inflexible mixture of sensitivity and encapsulation. The madman may see God's face and live (just as psychotic individuals may be able to stare directly into the sun without blinking) and go on to do great things. More often, he fuses God's face and anus and mocks it. He is unable to allow the experiencing of different worlds or dimensions to offset one another correctively.

However, is extreme rigidity always a symptom of madness? Is not rigidity widespread in human affairs? If we live in a combustible-conservative universe, what right have we to call the persistence of either side of this doubleness in social and personal life insane? Is the universe itself mad?

Whether or not we live in a mad universe, we are beings who have become aware of insanity and have begun fine explorations of how madness works. We make light remarks about how we are all crazy and how insane human life is. Humor makes insight livable, but the

1. Buber. *I and Thou*, p. 11.

reality hinted at is grim and horrifically destructive, although in some ways it can also be humorous. Wherever madness comes from, it is with us. We must learn to live and work with it. We must find ways of letting it speak to us. We must listen to and digest its voices, visions, and enactments. We must learn to absorb and evolve with its impact.

It is hard to say, but we would not be who we are without madness, anymore than we would be who we are without death. We would be the poorer without its truths and contradictions. But we must fight to get to a place where the mutual correctiveness of seemingly exclusive viewpoints, worlds, experiential capacities, and strategies is possible. We must keep getting to places where mutual correctiveness can become a way of life. This means not only fidelity to one's own vision, but also fidelity to the impact of the vision of others. We live in a caldron of seething possibilities. It is doubtful that madness can be eliminated any more than death can. But we can seek an attitude large enough and open enough to encompass it. We can learn from it and treat it as a partner in evolution. We move with our mad–sane self through and past oblivion into worlds we can barely glimpse, worlds without end.

References

Abraham, K. (1973). *Selected Papers*. London: Hogarth Press.

Alvarez, A. (1972). *The Savage God*. New York: Random House.

American Psychiatric Association (1980). *Diagnostic and Statistical Manual of Mental Disorders*, 3rd ed. Washington, D.C.: American Psychiatric Association.

Arieti, S. (1979). Cognition in psychoanalysis. Symposium presented by the American Professional Seminar Center, Columbia University, New York.

Balint, M. (1959). *Thrills and Regressions*. New York: International Universities Press.

―――― (1968). *The Basic Fault*. London: Tavistock.

Barfield, O. (1964). *Poetic Diction: A Study of Meaning*. New York: McGraw-Hill.

Becker, E. (1973). *The Denial of Death*. New York: The Free Press.

Berdyaev, N. (1943). *Freedom and Slavery*. Trans. R. M. French. London: Geoffrey Bless, The Centenary Press.

Bettelheim, B. (1961). *Paul and Mary*. New York: Doubleday.

Bick, E. (1964). The experience of the skin in early object relations. *International Journal of Psycho-Analysis* 49:484–486.

Binswanger, L. (1958). The case of Ellen West. In *Existence: A New Dimension in Psychiatry and Psychology*, ed. R. May, E. Angel, and H. F. Ellenberger. New York: Basic Books.

Bion, W. R. (1962). *Learning from Experience*. New York: Jason Aronson, 1983.

―――― (1963). *Elements of Psycho-Analysis*. New York: Jason Aronson, 1983.

―――― (1965). *Transformations*. New York: Jason Aronson, 1983.

―――― (1967). *Second Thoughts*. New York: Jason Aronson, 1983.

371

—— (1970). *Attention and Interpretation.* New York: Jason Aronson, 1983.

Blake, W. (1804–08). Milton. In *Blake: Complete Writings,* ed. G. Keynes. London: Oxford University Press, 1976.

Bleuler, E. (1911). *Dementia Praecox or the Group of Schizophrenias.* Trans. J. Zinkin. New York: International Universities Press, 1959.

The Book of Margery Kempe (1436). In *Medieval English Prose and Verse,* eds. R. S. Loomis and R. Willard. Trans. Laura Hibbard Loomis. New York: Appleton-Century-Crofts, 1948.

Boring, E. G. (1970). *A History of Experimental Psychology.* Englewood Cliffs, N.J.: Prentice-Hall.

Breuer, J., and Freud, S. (1893–1895). Studies on hysteria. *Standard Edition* 2. London: Hogarth Press, 1973.

Brody, B. (1973). Freud's attitude toward the United States. *Review of Existential Psychology and Psychiatry* 12:93–103.

Buber, M. (1958). *I and Thou.* New York: Charles Scribner's Sons.

Campbell, J. (1951). *The Flight of the Wild Gander.* New York: Viking Press.

Carotenuto, A. (1982). *A Secret Symmetry: Sabina Spielrein Between Jung and Freud.* Trans. A. Pomerans, J. Shepley, and K. Winston. New York: Pantheon.

Chasseguet-Smirgel, J. (1974). Perversion, idealization and sublimation. *International Journal of Psycho-Analysis* 55:349–357.

—— (1984). *Creativity and Perversion.* New York: Norton.

Derrida, J. (1978). Freud and the scene of writing. In *Writing and Difference,* ed. Alan Bass. Chicago: University of Chicago Press.

Deutsch, S. (1983). *Early Parental Separation in Children at Risk for Schizophrenia.* Unpublished doctoral dissertation, Yeshiva University.

Ehrenzweig, A. (1971). *The Hidden Order of Art.* Berkeley: University of California Press.

Eigen, M. (1974). On pre-oedipal castration anxiety. *International Review of Psycho-Analysis* 1:489–498.

—— (1975). Psychopathy and individuation. *Psychotherapy: Theory, Research and Practice* 3:289–290.

—— (1977). On working with "unwanted" patients. *International Journal of Psycho-Analysis* 5:109–121.

—— (1979a). Ideal images, creativity and the Freudian drama. *Psychocultural Review* 3:287–298.

—— (1979b). Female sexual responsiveness and the therapist's feelings. *Psychoanalytic Review* 66:3–8.

—— (1980a). Expression and meaning. In *Expressive Therapy,* ed. A. Robbins. New York: Human Sciences.

—— (1980b). Instinctual fantasy and ideal images. *Contemporary Psychoanalysis* 16:119–137.

—— (1980c). On the significance of the face. *Psychoanalytic Review* 67:427–441.

—— (1981a). Breaking the frame: stopping the world. *Modern Psychoanalysis* 6:89–100.

—— (1981b). Comments on snake symbolism and mind–body relations. *American Journal of Psychoanalysis* 41:73–79.

—— (1981c). Guntrip's analysis with Winnicott. *Contemporary Psychoanalysis* 17:103–117.

—— (1981d). Maternal abandonment threats, mind–body relations and suicidal wishes. *Journal of the American Academy of Psychoanalysis* 9:561–582.

—— (1981e). Reflections on eating and breathing as models of mental functions. *American Journal of Psychoanalysis* 41:177–180.

—— (1981f). The area of faith in Winnicott, Lacan and Bion. *International Journal of Psycho-Analysis* 62:413–433.

—— (1982). Creativity, instinctual fantasy and ideal images. *Psychoanalytic Review* 69:317–339.

—— (1983). Dual union or undifferentiation? A critique of Marion Milner's sense of psychic creativeness. *International Review of Psycho-Analysis* 10:415–428.

—— (1984). On demonized aspects of the self. In *Evil: Self and Culture*, eds. M. C. Nelson and M. Eigen. New York: Human Sciences.

—— (1985). Toward Bion's starting point: between catastrophe and faith. *International Journal of Psycho-Analysis* 66:321–330.

—— (1986). Aspects of mindlessness-selflessness: a common madness. *The Psychotherapy Patient* 2:75–81. Also published as a Special issue entitled *Psychotherapy in the Selfless Patient*, ed. J. Travers, pp. 75–81. New York: Haworth Press.

—— (in press). On omniscience. In *The Facilitating Environment: Clinical Applications of Winnicott's Theories*, eds. M. G. Fromm and B. L. Smith. New York: International Universities Press.

Einstein, A. (1945). Letter to Jacques Hadamard. In J. Hadamard, *The Psychology of Invention in the Mathematical Field*. Princeton: Princeton University Press, 1945. Also in *The Creative Process*, ed. B. Ghiselin. Berkeley: University of California Press, 1952.

Eisenbud, J. (1984). On the death wish. In *Evil: Self and Culture*, eds. M. C. Nelson and M. Eigen. New York: Human Sciences.

Elkin, H. (1958). On the origin of the self. *Psychoanalytic Review* 45:57–76.

—— (1972). On selfhood and the development of ego structures in infancy. *Psychoanalytic Review* 59:389–416.

Fairbairn, W. R. D. (1954). *An Object–Relations Theory of the Personality.* New York: Basic Books.

Fechner, G. T. (1860). *Elemente der Psychophysik.* In E. G. Boring, *A History of Experimental Psychology,* pp. 284–295.

Federn, P. (1926). Some variations in ego feeling. *International Journal of Psycho-Analysis* 7:25–37.

―――― (1957). *Ego Psychology and the Psychoses.* London: Maresfield Reprints.

Fliess, R. (1956). *Erogeneity and Libido.* New York: International Universities Press.

―――― (1973). *Symbol, Dream and Psychosis.* New York: International Universities Press.

Fordham, M. (1978). *Jungian Psychotherapy.* New York: John Wiley & Son.

Freud, S. (1898). *The Origins of Psycho-Analysis: Letters to Wilhelm Fliess, Drafts and Notes: 1887–1902,* eds. M. Bonaparte, A. Freud, and E. Kris. New York: Basic Books, 1954.

―――― (1900). The interpretation of dreams. *Standard Edition* 4/5:1–361.

―――― (1905). Three essays on the theory of sexuality. *Standard Edition* 7:125–245.

―――― (1911). Psycho-analytic notes on an autobiographical account of a case of paranoia (dementia paranoides). *Standard Edition* 12:3–82.

―――― (1913). Totem and taboo. *Standard Edition* 13:1–162.

―――― (1914). On narcissism: an introduction. *Standard Edition* 14:73–102.

―――― (1915). Instincts and their vicissitudes. *Standard Edition* 14:117–140.

―――― (1916). A mythological parallel to a visual obsession. *Standard Edition* 14:337–338.

―――― (1917). A metapsychological supplement to the theory of dreams. *Standard Edition* 14:217–235.

―――― (1920). Beyond the pleasure principle. *Standard Edition* 18:1–64.

―――― (1921). Group psychology and the analysis of the ego. *Standard Edition* 18:65–143.

―――― (1925). Negation. *Standard Edition* 19:235–239.

―――― (1927). The future of an illusion. *Standard Edition* 21:5–56.

―――― (1930). Civilization and its discontents. *Standard Edition* 21:59–145.

―――― (1937). Constructions in analysis. *Standard Edition* 23:255–269.

―――― (1939). Moses, his people and monotheist religion. *Standard Edition* 23:54–137.

―――― (1940). An outline of psycho-analysis. *Standard Edition* 23:141–207.

―――― (1941a). Shorter writings. *Standard Edition* 23:297–300.

―――― (1941b). Findings, ideas, problems. *Standard Edition* 23:299–300.

Freud, S., and Jung, C. G. (1906–1914). *The Freud/Jung Letters.* Trans.

R. Manheim and R. F. C. Hull, ed. W. McGuire. Princeton: Princeton University Press, 1974.

Frosch, J. (1983). *The Psychotic Process*. New York: International Universities Press.

Goldemberg, R. L. (1980). Letters home. In *The Women's Project*, ed. J. Miles. New York: Performing Arts Journal Publications and The American Place Theatre.

Green, A. (1975). The analyst, symbolization and absence in the analytic setting (on changes in analytic practice and analytic experience). *International Journal of Psycho-Analysis* 56:1–22.

――― (1981). Negation and contradiction. In *Do I Dare Disturb the Universe? A Memorial to Wilfred R. Bion*, ed. J. S. Grotstein. Beverly Hills, CA: Caesura Press.

Green, H. (1964). *I Never Promised You a Rose Garden*. New York: Holt, Rinehart & Winston.

Greenacre, P. (1952). *Trauma, Growth and Personality*. New York: International Universities Press.

Greenson, R. R. (1967). *The Technique and Practice of Psychoanalysis*. New York: International Universities Press.

Grotstein, J. S. (1980). A proposed revision of the psychoanalytic concept of primitive mental states. Part I. *Contemporary Psychoanalysis* 16:479–546.

――― (1981). *Splitting and Projective Identification*. New York: Jason Aronson.

――― (1982). Newer perspectives in object relations theory. *Contemporary Psychoanalysis* 18:43–91.

Guntrip, H. (1969). *Schizoid Phenomena, Object-Relations and the Self*. New York: International Universities Press.

Gurwitsch, A. (1966). *Studies in Phenomenology and Psychology*. Evanston: Northwestern University Press.

Hartmann, H. (1953). Contribution to the metapsychology of schizophrenia. *The Psychoanalytic Study of the Child* 8:177–198.

Heidegger, M. (1957). *Identity and Difference*. New York: Harper & Row, 1969.

Henle, M. (1984). Freud's secret cognitive theories. *Annals of Theoretical Psychology* 1:111–134.

Husserl, E. (1929). *Cartesian Meditations*. Trans. D. Cairns. The Hague: Martinus Nishoff, 1970.

Jacobson, E. (1964). *The Self and Object World*. New York: International Universities Press.

Janet, P. (1898). *Un Cas de Possession et l'Exorcisme Moderne*. In *Neuroses et Idées Fixes*, vol. 1. Paris: Alcan.

Jung, C. G. (1907). The psychology of dementia praecox. *The Collected Works of C. G. Jung.* Bollingen Series, vol. 3. Princeton: Princeton University Press, 1960.

—— (1908). The content of the psychoses. *The Collected Works of C. G. Jung.* Bollingen Series, vol. 3. Princeton: Princeton University Press, 1960.

—— (1934). *Psychological Analysis of Nietzsche's Zarathustra, Part 1.* Unpublished notes on the seminar edited by M. Foote. Kristine Mann Library, C. G. Jung Institute, New York City.

—— (1945). On the nature of the psyche. *The Collected Works of C. G. Jung.* Bollingen Series, vol. 3. Princeton: Princeton University Press, 1960.

—— (1911–1952). Symbols of transformation. *The Collected Works of C. G. Jung.* Bollingen Series, vol. 5. Princeton: Princeton University Press, 1956.

—— (1943, 1945). Two essays on analytical psychology. *The Collected Works of C. G. Jung.* Bollingen Series, vol. 7. Princeton: Princeton University Press, 1966.

—— (1950). Aion: researches into the phenomenology of the self. *The Collected Works of C. G. Jung.* Bollingen Series, vol. 9. Princeton: Princeton University Press, 1959.

—— (1952). Answer to Job. *The Collected Works of C. G. Jung.* Bollingen Series, vol. 11. Princeton: Princeton University Press, 1958.

—— (1957). Recent thoughts on schizophrenia. *The Collected Works of C. G. Jung.* Bollingen Series, vol. 3. Princeton: Princeton University Press, 1960.

—— (1958). Schizophrenia. *The Collected Works of C. G. Jung.* Bollingen Series, vol. 3. Princeton: Princeton University Press, 1960.

—— (1961a). *Memories, Dreams and Reflections,* ed. A. Jaffe. New York: Random House.

—— (1961b). Approaching the unconscious. In *Man and His Symbols,* eds. C. G. Jung, M. L. von Franz, J. L. Henderson, J. Jacobi, and A. Jaffe. New York: Dell, 1964.

Kernberg, O. (1975). *Borderline Conditions and Pathological Narcissism.* New York: Jason Aronson.

Khan, M. Masud R. (1971). Dread of resourceless surrender in the analytic situation. *International Journal of Psycho-Analysis* 52:225–230.

—— (1974). *The Privacy of the Self.* London: Hogarth Press.

—— (1979). *Alienation in Perversions.* New York: International Universities Press.

Klein, M. (1946). Notes on some schizoid mechanisms. In *Developments in Psycho-Analysis.* eds. M. Klein, P. Heimann, S. Isaacs, and J. Riviere. London: Hogarth Press, 1952.

—— (1948). Some theoretical conclusions regarding the emotional life of the infant. In *Developments in Psycho-Analysis*. eds. M. Klein, P. Heimann, S. Isaacs, and J. Riviere. London: Hogarth Press, 1952.

——— (1957). *Envy and Gratitude*. London: Tavistock; New York: Basic Books.

Koffka, K. (1935). *Principles of Gestalt Psychology*. New York: Harcourt, Brace & World.

Köhler, W. (1971). The obsessions of normal people. In *The Selected Papers of Wolfgang Kohler*, ed. M. Henle. New York: Liveright.

Kohut, H. (1971). *The Analysis of the Self*. New York: International Universities Press.

——— (1977). *The Restoration of the Self*. New York: International Universities Press.

Kraepelin, E. (1896). *Psychiatric: Ein Lehrbuch für Studierende und Aerzte*. Leipzig: Barth.

——— (1906). *Clinical Psychiatry*, ed. T. Johnstone. New York: William Wood & Co.

——— (1919). *Dementia Praecox and Paraphrenia*. Trans. R. M. Barclay, ed. G. M. Robertson. Edinburgh: E. S. Livingstone.

Lacan, J. (1977). *Ecrits*. Trans. A. Sheridan. New York: Norton.

——— (1978). *The Four Fundamental Concepts of Psycho-Analysis*. Trans. A. Sheridan, ed. Jacques-Alain Miller. New York: Norton.

Laplanche, J., and Pontalis, J.-B. (1973). *The Language of Psycho-Analysis*. New York: Norton.

Lewin, B. (1973). *Selected Writings of Bertram D. Lewin*, ed. J. A. Arlow. New York: The Psychoanalytic Quarterly.

Lewontin, R. C. (1983). The Liberation of Biology. In *The New York Review of Books*, January 20, p. 37.

Loewald, H. (1980). *Papers on Psychoanalysis*. New Haven: Yale University Press.

Mahler, M. S. (1968). *On Human Symbiosis and the Vicissitudes of Individuation*. New York: International Universities Press.

Maquarrie, J. (1972). *Existentialism*. New York: Pelican Books, 1973.

Marcus, S. (1984). *Freud and the Culture of Psychoanalysis*. Boston: George Allen & Unwin.

Matte-Blanco, I. (1975). *The Unconscious as Infinite Sets*. London: Duckworth.

McCurdy, H. (1961). *The Personal World*. New York: Harcourt, Brace & World, pp. 222–230.

McGhie, A. (1969). *Pathology of Attention*. Middlesex, England: Penguin Books.

Meltzer, D. (1966). The relation of anal masturbation to projective identification. *International Journal of Psycho-Analysis* 47:335–342.

——— (1973). *Sexual States of Mind*. Perthshire, Scotland: Clunie Press.

———, Bremner, J., Hoxter, S., Weddell, D., and Wittenberg, I. (1975). *Explorations in Autism*. Perthshire, Scotland: Clunie Press.

Merleau-Ponty, M. (1962). *Phenomenology of Perception*. London: Routledge & Kegan Paul.

Miller, A. (1983). *For Your Own Good*. New York: Farrar, Straus & Giroux.

Milner, M. (1957). *On Not Being Able to Paint*. New York: International Universities Press.

——— (1969). *The Hands of the Living God*. New York: International Universities Press.

——— (1977). "Winnicott and Overlapping Circles." *L'Arc* 69:70–83.

Nelson, M. C., and Eigen, M., eds. (1984). *Evil: Self and Culture*. New York: Human Sciences.

Neumann, E. (1954). *The Origin and History of Consciousness*. New York: Pantheon.

——— (1956). *Amor and Psyche*. Trans. H. E. Butler. Bollingen Series. Princeton: Princeton University Press.

Perls, F. (1970). *Gestalt Therapy Now*. Palo Alto: Science and Behavior Books.

Perry, J. W. (1974). *The Far Side of Madness*. Englewood Cliffs, NJ: Prentice-Hall.

——— (1976). *The Roots of Renewal in Myth and Symbols*. San Francisco: Jossey-Bass.

Plath, S. (1965). *Ariel*. New York: Harper & Row.

Pontalis, J. B. (1981). *Frontiers in Psychoanalysis*. New York: International Universities Press.

Rank, O. (1968). *Art and Artist*. New York: Agathon Press.

Read, H. (1955). *Icon and Idea*. Cambridge: Harvard University Press.

Reich, W. (1949). *Character Analysis*. New York: Farrar, Straus & Cudahy.

Ricoeur, P. (1970). *Freud and Philosophy: An Essay on Interpretation*. New Haven: Yale University Press.

Rimbaud, A. (1871). Letters. In *Illuminations*, ed. L. Varèse. New York: New Directions, 1957.

Rogers, C. R. (1961). The loneliness of contemporary man as seen in "The Case of Ellen West," *Review of Existential Psychology and Psychiatry* 1:94–101.

Roustang, F. (1982). *Dire Mastery: Discipleship from Freud to Lacan*. Baltimore: The Johns Hopkins University Press.

——— (1983). *Psychoanalysis Never Lets Go*. Baltimore: The Johns Hopkins University Press.

Runes, D. D. (1968). *Dictionary of Philosophy*. Totowa: Littlefield, Adams & Co.

Rycroft, C. (1968). *Imagination and Reality.* New York: International Universities Press.

Sandner, D. F., and Beebe, J. (1982). Psychopathology and analysis. In *Jungian Analysis*, ed. M. Stein. LaSalle, Canada: Open Court.

Sartre, J. P. (1957). *The Transcendence of the Ego: An Existentialist Theory of Consciousness.* New York: Noonday Press.

Schatzman, M. (1974). *Soul Murder: Persecution in the Family.* New York: New American Library.

Schuré, E. (1961). *The Great Initiates.* Blauvelt, NY: Steinerbooks.

Schwartz-Salant, N. (1982). *Narcissism and Character Transformation: The Psychology of Narcissistic Character Disorders.* Toronto: Inner City Books.

Searles, H. F. (1975). The patient as therapist to his analyst. In *Tactics and Techniques in Psychoanalytic Psychotherapy, Volume II: Countertransference*, ed. P. Giovacchini. New York: Jason Aronson.

Shakow, D. (1977). *Schizophrenia: Selected Papers.* New York: International Universities Press.

Spitz, R. (1965). *The First Year of Life.* New York: International Universities Press.

Stern, D. (1977). *The First Relationship.* Boston: Harvard University Press.

Stirner, M. (1885). *The Ego and His Own: The Case of the Individual Against Authority.* New York: Dover Books, 1973.

Stolorow, R., and Atwood, G. (1979). *Faces in a Cloud: Subjectivity in Personality Theory.* New York: Jason Aronson.

Stone, M. (1980). *The Borderline Syndromes.* New York: McGraw-Hill.

Sulloway, F. J. (1979). *Freud, Biologist of the Mind.* New York: Basic Books.

Tausk, V. (1933). On the origin of the influencing machine in schizophrenia. *Psychoanalytic Quarterly* 2:519-556.

Thomas, D. (1939). *Collected Poems.* New York: New Directions.

Von Franz, M.-L. (1975). *Creation Myths.* New York: Spring Publications.

Weil, E. (1958). The origin and vicissitudes of the self-image. *Psychoanalysis* 6:3-19.

Winnicott, D. W. (1949). Mind and its relation to the psyche-soma. *British Journal of Medical Psychology* 27:201-209. Reprinted in *Collected Papers—Through Paediatrics to Psycho-Analysis.* New York: Basic Books, 1958.

—— (1952). Ego integration in child development. In *The Maturational Processes and the Facilitating Environment.* New York: International Universities Press, 1974.

—— (1953). Transitional objects and transitional phenomena. *International Journal of Psycho-Analysis* 34:89-97.

—— (1958). *Collected Papers—Through Paediatrics to Psycho-Analysis.* New York: Basic Books.

—— (1967). The location of cultural experience. *International Journal of Psycho-Analysis* 48:368–372.

—— (1969). The use of an object and relating through identifications. *International Journal of Psycho-Analysis* 50:711–716.

—— (1971). Playing, creative activity and the search for the self. In *Playing and Reality*, pp. 54–55. New York: Basic Books.

—— (1974). *The Maturational Processes and the Facilitating Environment.* New York: International Universities Press.

—— (1974). Fear of breakdown. *International Review of Psycho-Analysis* 1:103–107.

Zelner, S. (1982). The Organization of Vocalization and Gaze in Early Mother–Infant Interactive Regulation. Unpublished doctoral dissertation, Yeshiva University, New York.

Index

Abraham, K., 172
Abstinence, rule of, 135
Adler, A., 39
Alvarez, A., *The Savage God*, 340
Anal metaphor, 181–184
Analysis of the Self (Kohut), 82–83
Anonymity, the I and, 230–238
Archetypal self, 55, 61
Archetypes, origins of, 62–63
Arieti, S., 20
Artist, "vague stare" of, 126–127
Attention and Interpretation (Bion),
   135–136, 138, 223
Atwood, G., 21n
Autism, 111–112, 126, 310
   normal, 148

Balint, M., 157, 239–242
   The Basic Fault, 130–131
Barfield, O., 86
Berdyaev, N., 336–337
Bettelheim, B., 20
Bick, E., 165
Binswanger, L., 340
Bion, W.R., 21n, 85–86, 114–119,
   128–130, 203, 206, 343, 348,
   352

Attention and Interpretation, 135–
   136, 138, 223
"Big Bang" theory of, 114
Elements of Psycho-Analysis, 116
on hallucination, 65–70, 77–78
Learning from Experience, 223
on reversal, 243–244, 247, 249
sign psychology of, 133–134
on space, 223, 225
Transformations, 67–68, 97–98
Blake, W., 85–86, 140
   "Milton," 132
Blank psychosis, 105–109
Blanking out, 112–113, 120–124
Bleuler, E., 3
Body ego, development of, 143–
   144
Boring, E.G., *History of
   Experimental Psychology*, 11–
   13
Boundaries, 32–33, 139–168, 290–
   294
   hallucinations and mindlessness,
   166–168
   identification and, 163–166
Boundlessness, and everyday
   experience, 139–143

381